Activity Interests
and Occupational Choice

Activity Interests
and Occupational Choice

by
Frederic Kuder

SCIENCE RESEARCH ASSOCIATES, INC.
Chicago, Palo Alto, Toronto, Henley-on-Thames, Sydney, Paris, Stuttgart

A Subsidiary of IBM

Library of Congress Cataloging in Publication Data

Kuder, Frederic, 1903-
    Activity interests and occupational choice.

    Bibliography: p.
    Includes index.
    1. Vocational interests. 2. Vocational interests—Testing. I. Title.
HF5381.5K77   158.6   76-21765
ISBN 0-574-20010-X

Figures 3, 4, and 5 are reprinted from "A note on the comparability of occupational scores from different interest inventories" by Frederic Kuder in *Measurement and Guidance*, 1969, *2* (2). Used by permission of American Personnel and Guidance Association.

To Linn

who brightens the world for everyone around her

Preface

"This country has many industrial problems at the present time — problems of equipment, method, organization, and so on. But I do not think it will be denied that the overwhelmingly important one is the problem of incentives to effort. However well organized and equipped we may be, we cannot succeed industrially unless we find some kind of satisfaction in our work." (Balchin, 1947, p. 125)

Although these words were written in England a generation ago, they are generally applicable to many countries and strikingly so to the United States today. The publication of *Wheels* by Hailey (1971), *Where Have All the Robots Gone?* by Sheppard and Herrick (1972), and *Working* by Terkel (1974); the reissue of Charlie Chaplin's *Modern Times;* and the recent appearance of a rash of articles on the monotony and disagreeableness of certain kinds of work all serve to emphasize that worker discontent is a problem of enormous importance. That there is growing concern for the quality of working life has been noted by Bradburn (1974). Of course the problem has always been with us, but there was a tendency in former times to overlook the situation simply because so many workers had no alternative to staying on jobs they did not like. Today more people are in a position to pick and choose; thus the problem of dissatisfaction shows up in high turnover and in almost intolerable absenteeism. The probability has greatly increased that a worker will say to his or her employer some version of these words written by Balchin:

This is unreasonable, I have only one life to live. Why should I spend the best part of it in factories and mines? They may be air-conditioned, but I don't want to be in them. The work may be light, but I don't want to do it. . . . You can go and climb a tree. (p. 127)

Balchin later goes on to say:

I believe that the days when we could buy large parts of the lives of other human beings for a little money and nothing else are passing. We are reaching a stage where neither management nor society will be in a position to demand from any man work which is not enjoyable or satisfactory. This may well mean that society may have to do without some jobs that it has been able to get people to do in the past. If no member of society is willing to hew coal, then there are two possibilities — society must do without coal or some men must be slaves. In civilizations of the past, the answer has always been that some men were slaves. (p. 133)

It seems to me that we who enjoy our work, and would be horrified at the suggestion that we should spend our working lives doing something completely dull and pointless, have little right to complain if other men now demand that they enjoy their working lives too. I believe that in this demand we are facing the greatest development and the greatest crisis in Industry since the Industrial Revolution. (p. 134)

Can all jobs be made pleasant? Can all jobs that are unpleasant be abolished? It is difficult to imagine a Utopia in which no unpleasant work would be needed. If people are not to be slaves, then some must be bribed to do the unpleasant but necessary tasks, much as they are today, with the expectation of higher pay and more leisure hours for compensating enjoyment. There is every reason to believe that the price of getting unpleasant work done will continue to go up. It is even conceivable that in time the most menial jobs will receive the highest pay.

Abolishing unpleasant jobs, as proposed by Balchin, is fortunately not the only way of raising the general level of satisfaction in work. There are some kinds of work that are without question distasteful to everyone. But there is also some work that is disliked by many but not by all. Some people, for example, like monotonous work, incredible as this may seem to those who cannot stand routine, repetitive work. There are also people, though not many, who prefer to work under close supervision. Thus the prospect is good that differences of this kind can be made to serve as the foundation for having a certain amount of work generally regarded as distasteful done by the few who like it. Offering young people more effective help in finding work they will enjoy is a realistic way of alleviating the problem Balchin describes so eloquently.

The thing that strikes one working in the field of human interests is that people differ tremendously in what they enjoy doing. I have been surprised again and again by comments on certain questions in which the task is to indicate which of three activities a person would like most and would like least.

"Surely," people sometimes say, "no one would choose anything but *this* activity first." An actual check of the choices that have been recorded shows as often as not, however, that people in general distribute their first choices rather evenly among the activities named in the question.

Perhaps, then, it may not be necessary or even desirable to

abolish many jobs. After making a few of the least popular ones more attractive, perhaps we will be able to find people who can pursue all the different available vocations with true enjoyment. If this goal be unrealistic, let us still accept it as a goal.

By this time there is little doubt that a consideration of interests can make a substantial contribution to answering the challenge of locating people in the kind of work they will enjoy. Much of the data reported here have been collected through a simple inventory called the Occupational Interest Survey. The survey is not an impressive document. It looks like something a junior high school student might have thrown together on a rainy Sunday afternoon; this format is deliberate. The language is simple; the concepts are simple; the task is simple. Although the inventory is intended to help young people ultimately find suitable occupations, the questions are not about occupations. Each one consists of descriptions of three activities that almost anyone above the sixth-grade level can understand. The subject is asked to indicate which of the three activities he or she would ordinarily like least and which he or she would ordinarily like most.

In spite of the apparent simplicity of the inventory, it represents an amount of developmental work that is startling to me in retrospect. The surprise is somewhat reduced, however, by the realization of what could have been accomplished with the same effort if present-day computers had been available ten or twenty years earlier. Thousands of high school students, college students, and adults have recorded their preferences in more than two thousand experimental questions over a period beginning about forty years ago. During that time, six different interest inventories have been published. The experimental forms used in the research total between twenty-five and thirty, and more than 150,000 men and women and boys and girls participated in the development of the published inventories. It may be of interest that over the years some seventy million young people have filled out the published inventories.

The experimental items have been studied with respect to a number of variables such as age, sex, education, membership in a specific group, and relation to dissimulation, as well as to a number of test scores. No wonder a well-known professor used to tell his classes that psychological tests are like icebergs because so little of them is visible!

The development of methods to help young people find the work for which they are well suited is of such vital importance that it may come as some surprise that a project of the magnitude of the one reported in the following pages has been carried on without subsidies of any kind. That this is so is largely a matter of circumstances combined with a certain degree of impatience in my nature.

I became concerned with interests during the disastrous depression of the early thirties, and undertook some very modest research on my own as a graduate student. Later, when I wished to expand the project, there was no possibility that a junior member of the University of Chicago staff could obtain a grant to try out some new ideas. Under the circumstances, I decided to borrow on my life insurance. During the early years, the research and development work were carried on in my spare time.

After six years of research, the first inventory was distributed in 1939 by the University of Chicago bookstore. It was taken over a year later by Science Research Associates as SRA's first publication in the testing field. During World War II millions of members of the armed forces took Form B of the Preference Record, which was published in 1943; it was scored for nine areas of interest. When friends in the Adjutant General's Office of the Army asked me on what terms I would let them reproduce the Preference Record for use in the armed forces, I told them they were welcome to do so, but that I would like access to the records for a follow-up study. That was the agreement made. The opportunity for a significant study still exists and is awaiting the availability of funds.

The form that has had the greatest use during the past forty years is Form C, which was published in 1948 and is scored for ten areas of interest instead of the nine used for Form B. Summaries of the data obtained from occupational groups are reported in appendix E for forms B and C, as well as for the Kuder Preference Record—Personal, Form A.

The multitude of data from the thousands upon thousands of subjects who obligingly filled out experimental interest inventories for the writer over the past forty years has almost demanded a report in the form of a book. But there has always been something new and exciting just around the corner, something that called for attention in more commanding tones. And now, alas, there is no possibility of reporting everything in a single volume. What has emerged is neither a handbook nor a manual. It is, rather, a presentation of some data collected and some ideas developed over four decades of work on the problem of helping young people make satisfying career choices on the basis of a systematic survey of their interests. In these pages the reader will find the inevitable occasional discrepancy between current theory and early practice. It is heartening to observe, at the same time, that there has been substantial progress in both theory and practice.

To preclude any misunderstanding, it should be stated plainly at this point that interest inventories are fallible and do not furnish all the answers needed for every counseling situation. It is apparent that intensive research should be continued, just as it is apparent that we now know a great deal more about the role of interests in occupational choice than we knew fifty years ago. It is notable that reviewers do not advocate abandoning the use of interest inventories even in their present imperfect form. The justification for their use in guidance must be essentially the same as that for any psychological instrument: namely, that they contribute to doing a better job of counseling.

A Note on Statistical Significance

Perhaps a brief explanation is in order concerning the lack of reports of statistical significance in the following pages. Anyone who does research in the field of interests soon discovers that with the rather large numbers of cases ordinarily used, even small differences between groups are almost always highly significant and that those differences can be considered "real." The question that needs to be answered in most cases, then, is not whether a difference is stable but whether it is important. The degree of importance is a matter of opinion

The fact that there is a significant difference between two groups does not necessarily mean, for example, that the members of the groups can be easily sorted into the correct categories with few errors. It might merely reflect the fact that many cases were used and that a similar difference can be expected in other samples with the probability as defined.

The differences found between pairs of groups of engineers used in my studies are highly significant. These differences are small enough and the overlappings are large enough, however, to justify raising the question of whether it is worthwhile from a practical point of view to report scores for several kinds of engineers. This is one of the questions now under study. The answer will be based on a consideration of the relative importance of a number of factors, but it cannot be obtained neatly by applying tests of statistical significance.

Acknowledgments

If I seem to refer to Professor E. K. Strong, Jr., an inordinate number of times in the pages that follow, I hope the reader will forgive me for doing what to me is the inevitable. The firm foundation of scholarly research provided by Strong for further advance in interest measurement is so extensive that it is almost impossible to do anything in the field that does not have some background in Strong's work. It is only right that appropriate acknowledgment be made, even though doing so may at times seem repetitious.

The pleasant duty of acknowledging help of a more specific nature cannot possibly be done adequately. In particular, I am indebted to Dr. John A. Hornaday, Jr., Geraldine Ross Thomas, and Vivian H. Lyndon — all of whom have been associated with the project described in this book for many years. Their contributions, made with interest and enthusiasm, have far exceeded those called for by duty. I also want to thank Joan F. Hornaday, Mary Alice Walker, and Dr. William B. Walker for help along the way. Alice Fisher Thuman has contributed many helpful suggestions for improving the form of presentation in these pages. Dr. Alexis Epanchin and Dorothy Shuford have rendered invaluable help in preparing the extensive bibliography that is now appendix F.

In recent years, the following members or former members of the Science Research Associates staff have given valuable assistance and encouragement in ways too numerous to mention in detail: Esther E. Diamond, John J. O'Keefe, John W. Lombard, William V. Clemans, Burton W. Faldet, Norma L. Thiemann, Barbara H. Mann, William J. Figel, George Heigho, and Sally Boyd.

A great many other people have taken part in the long research reported in these pages, and I wish it were feasible to thank each one individually. To the many thousands of subjects who participated, often with enthusiasm, in the various research studies, I wish to express my appreciation. The willingness of people to contribute their time to an undertaking that they considered worthwhile has been a deeply satisfying aspect of the project.

Finally, to a versatile and tolerant wife who has repeatedly come to my rescue in an amazing number of ways — from punching item responses on IBM cards to breathing meaning into dull sentences — I wish to express more gratitude than can possibly be put into words.

F. K.

Durham, North Carolina
January, 1977

REFERENCES

Balchin, N. Satisfactions in work. *Occupational Psychology*, 1947, *27*, 125-134.

Bradburn, N. M. Is the quality of working life improving? *Studies in Personnel Psychology*, 1974, *6*, 19-34.

Chaplin, C. (Producer). *"Modern Times."* New York: United Artists, 1936. (Film)

Hailey, A. *Wheels.* Garden City: Doubleday, 1971.

Sheppard, H. L., and Herrick, N. Q. *Where have all the robots gone?* New York: Free Press, 1972.

Terkel, S. *Working.* New York: Pantheon, 1974.

Contents

I. The Role of Interests in the Choice of an
Occupation   1

II. Some Principles of Interest Measurement   7

III. A Rationale for Evaluating Interests   28

IV. Some Special Aspects of Interests   76
    A. Score Distances between Groups   76
    B. Sex Differences   126
    C. Some Characteristics of Best Impression
       Responses to Interest Inventory Items   133
    D. Interests and Satisfaction in Work   145
    E. Score Level   156
    F. Interests and Age   163
    G. Career Matching   163

V. The Problem of the Structure of
Occupational Interests   170

VI. A Few Remarks   208

Appendices

A. The Criterion Vector Method of Test
Construction   211

B. Intercorrelations of the Proportions of 217
Groups Marking Each of the 600 Item-Response
Positions in the Occupational Interest Survey   215

C. The Wherry-Wherry Hierarchical Rotation
Method   241

D. Factor Loadings, Factor Analysis VI   243

E. Interest Profiles of Occupational Groups from
    Forms B, C, and A of the Preference Record   259

F. Bibliography of Publications Pertaining to
    Kuder Interest Inventories   280

Index   323

LIFE IN DURHAM

A score of years ago Norris Eubanks was over at Amos and Andy making hot dogs at lightning speed.

But more than making them fast, he made them delicious.

Which is what really counted.

Because the fame of the little cafe spread until it was known from Maine to Florida.

And people who stopped over in the Washington Duke (Jack Tar) got to eating at Amos and Andy as part of their trip to Durham.

And, of course, Norris got famous too because he was always giving hot dog banquets to high schools and all.

Especially when his son Johnny was a high school football star.

It was nothing for Norris to throw a free meal for the squad — and anyone else that showed up.

Just winning a game was enough of a reason.

Then Johnny grew up and took his place in Amos and Andy next to his dad.

It took a while but soon Johnny could make 'em as good as his daddy.

And just as fast.

That suited Norris just fine because he must have made a million of them and was ready for Johnny to take over.

So Norris sort of retired to his place in the country.

Coming to town just when the mood struck him.

Of course, when he came by he always put on an apron and got behind the counter to make a few dogs.

It was sort of a red letter day for all the old customers.

To come in Amos and Andy and see Norris back there working.

The occasion always called for an extra dog or so.

But Norris just didn't come by often enough.

And then hardly at all.

So old friends got to asking, "Where's Norris?"

"Taking it easy," was always the answer.

Which was true, too.

But after a while it got so it wasn't fun any more to Norris.

That's why he was back in the cafe the other day.

Explaining to his friends, "Just say I'm back behind the counter again."

He won't say for how long.

Or even why.

But there is such a thing as liking your job.

And the people you come in contact with.

— SID

Reprinted with permission from the Durham (N.C.) *Morning Herald*, May 21, 1968.

1

The Role of Interests in the Choice of an Occupation

Is it any wonder that most young people are bewildered when confronted with the question of occupational aims? The more than thirty-five thousand entries in the *Dictionary of Occupational Titles* (1965) are enough to dismay anyone trying to make a systematic approach to the problem of choosing a life's work. True, a good many titles are synonyms, but the almost twenty-two thousand different occupations represented are enough to be discouraging!

Since it is impractical for an individual to explore all occupations, or even those that remain after obviously inappropriate ones are eliminated, how should he or she go about making a decision? In real life everyone uses a shorter method. Everyone *has* to use a shorter method. It hardly needs to be added that the particular approach used is often woefully inadequate and leads to tragic mistakes. Fortunately, the old attitude that everyone will automatically find an appropriate place in the working world by some act of Providence is not as prevalent as it used to be. The fact remains, however, that in many cases the decision might just as well have been made by the medieval practice of putting a baby in a room with a number of objects and letting his vocation be determined by the momentarily intriguing object which he happens to touch first.

The chance of a happy outcome will be greatly increased if commitment to a career comes after a series of carefully planned steps gradually narrow the possibilities to a relatively few promising occupations. It is true that every choice a person makes has the effect of limiting, to a greater or lesser degree, what that person can do from that time on. Certain choices are so important, however, that they call for as comprehensive a review of the situation as possible. Certain points in life, such as those that require the selection of courses, the selection of curriculum, or, indeed, the choice of a school or a college stand out for everyone. At these points it is important to take a fresh look at one's interests, abilities, and accomplishments in the light of existing circumstances.

1

The fact that stability of interests increases with age is now well established. Considering this, it is desirable to keep open a broad range of promising choices as long as possible and to keep to a minimum those avenues that are closed as the result of decisions made. In practice this means that although possibilities for the future should be given intensive study and exploration and that tentative plans should be made for the more promising, it is desirable not to make irrevocable decisions sooner than necessary. If this principle is followed, these important decisions can be made in the light of the widest experience and the most stable preferences.

Even so, one may well ask, "Why measure interests? Why not simply ask the individual what he or she wants to do?" The facts are that expressed interests in specific occupations appear to be the least stable of the interests of young people, and that measured interests can yield useful suggestions at an earlier age than would otherwise be the case.

Darley and Hagenah (1955) found, for example, that ". . . claimed interests have somewhat less permanence than measured interests; claimed interests emerge from different causal factors — factors more associated with prestige, family pressures, aspirational levels, transient considerations, and misconceptions of the world of work — than do measured interests." (p. 75)

Craven (1961) pointed out that ". . . measured interests usually tap only affective responses — likes and dislikes, and preferences. Expressed interests may have the same affective components, but they also represent conscious efforts to integrate pressures and needs, hopes and aspirations . . . ". (p. 11) These efforts might result in a false picture of the individual's interests and camouflage the disparity between his or her real interests and aspirations.

That stated preferences for occupations are often unrealistic, particularly among adolescents and young adults, has been noted by Nunnally (1959), among others. Young people, he maintained, are usually quite unaware of the specific activities entailed in different occupations; the individually stated preferences for occupations are often "prompted by glamorized stereotypes." (p. 316).

A child often expresses a preference for a particular occupation because someone admired is in that occupation, because schoolmates have mentioned it as their choice, because it has acquired a spectacular quality through prominence in the news, or simply because of the pressure from a concerned relative to say he or she has decided upon *something*. Changes in expressed choices are likely to be simply the reflection of one or more factors — changes in the child's knowledge about occupations, new acquaintance-ships that make him or her aware of additional occupations, or the replacement of one glamour occupation in the news — such as astronaut or nuclear physicist — by another. In addition, expressed interests in specific occupations are likely to change as the in-dividual is exposed to new experiences and acquires more knowl-edge.

The popular impression that children's interests have little stability appears to be based largely on the observation that children frequently change their minds about what they want to be when they grow up. The facts that there are not many occupa-tions with which children are really familiar, and that occupational titles take on different meanings for them over the years, are probably the best explanation for a large part of the changes that occur. Cronbach (1960) pointed out that a single direct question such as "Would you like to be a teacher?" does not yield adequate information for guidance, because the individual's answer may be based on ignorance or superficial understanding of a vocation.

The fact is that measured interests based on preferences for activities that are well understood by the counselee show a fair degree of stability even for junior high school students; and, as already noted, the degree of stability increases with age (Kuder, E Manual, 1964). White (1958) found that the chances are about even that a ninth-grader's top interest area will be the same when he or she is a senior, and the odds are more than four out of five that it will be among his or her top three. Similar results were found by Mallinson and Crumrine (1952) and by Tutton (1955).

Although interests of young people are subject to change, there is considerable stability for a fairly high proportion; this situation furnishes a basis for keeping open promising avenues for the future. Some avenues will be closed automatically at points of decision. It is important that the avenues eliminated be those that are least likely to be remembered with regret.

Emphatically, a survey of one's interests is only a beginning. As complete a picture as possible of pertinent information should be collected, and such a picture must include measures of aptitude and records of accomplishments and activities, to say nothing of an assessment of financial resources and the miscellaneous con-siderations peculiar to each individual.

Nevertheless, a survey of interests may well be the best way to begin. From the standpoint of sheer convenience and economy, interests are the logical starting point in the search for a suitable occupation. On the basis of a relatively short but systematic survey of interests, it is possible to narrow prospects down to a manageable number of particularly promising occupations. As noted by Gilbert (1963):

The identification of the individual's interests and values, which initially described a vocational area for which the person appears best suited, should be followed by the testing of objective aptitudes relevant to this area. This sequence is economical of time and effort and appears more likely to result in successful counseling and selection than the reverse sequence, especially in view of the diffuse and time-consuming nature of aptitude tests in their present stage of development. (pp. 355-356).

This recommendation is based on the assumption that interests should be an important consideration, and there is evidence to this effect. After reviewing the available evidence, Clark wrote, in 1961, "One cannot escape the obvious conclusion that when the problem is one of prediction of occupational choice or occupational classification, the use of interest measures should receive more considerations than the use of aptitude measures." (p. 112)

Thorndike, who later made a study with Hagen of ten thousand careers (1963), observed:

Evidence has been accumulating that, at least in college level groups, differences in interests may be fully as important as differences in abilities in determining curricular and occupational choices. Thus Berdie found interest test scores to be the most differentiating and aptitude test scores the least differentiating for curricular groups at the University of Minnesota. McCully found large differences by type of job in Kuder interest scores of veterans tested in the VA and followed up several years later — differences that I would estimate were fully as marked as those reported in the Kuder manual. Even in our data, the biographical items seemed to differentiate occupational groups about as well as did the tests. Better interest measures might have sharpened the differentiation still further. (p. 183)

Certain differences between the ideal counseling outcome and life as it exists must be recognized from the start. For one thing, it is not possible to arrange for everyone in our society to be in the line of work for which he or she is best suited. It is too much to hope that the needs of society and of the individuals in that society could ever mesh that well. In the real world some modification of the ideal situation is unavoidable. Although society is not incapable of showing some flexibility over a period of time, it is the individual members who must make the necessary accommodations required in planning for the future.

For another thing, it is not possible to present a person with the name of one particular occupation with the assurance that it is without doubt the one for which that individual is best suited.

Psychological measurement is not that precise. Any score has a degree of error in it, thus there is some uncertainty whether the occupation with the highest score represents the "best" occupation. The problem then becomes one of giving the counselee a list of several occupations on which the very best one for the person is likely to appear, even though it may not be first on the list.

In preparing this list, however, it should not be forgotten that if the inventory has been well designed, the occupation with the highest score is the one that has the highest *chance* of being best for the counselee (from the standpoint of interests). The occupation with the next highest score has the next highest chance of being best, and so on. In other words, in terms of giving appropriate time and attention to the consideration of specific occupations, the most useful form in which to present occupational scores is in order of magnitude. Just how far down the list it is worth going is a judgment that must be made in the specific situation and with a knowledge of the standard errors of the scores involved. In many cases special circumstances — including the limitation of the individual's resources and the current supply of workers in various occupations — may necessitate going farther down the list than would be the case in more favorable conditions.

We need to recognize that the greatest validity will come from the system that is based on the most comprehensive collection of available information that pertains to the individual. In this book we are concerned with the important area of interests. The general approach outlined here is applicable, however, to the whole field of those human characteristics that have any bearing on the choice of a career.

REFERENCES

Bureau of Employment Security, U.S. Department of Labor. *Dictionary of occupational titles.* Washington: U.S. Government Printing Office, 1965.

Clark, K. E. *Vocational interests of nonprofessional men.* Minneapolis: University of Minnesota Press, 1961.

Craven, E. C. *The use of interest inventories in counseling.* Chicago: Science Research Associates, 1961.

Cronbach. L. J. *Essentials of psychological testing.* New York: Harper & Row, 1960.

Darley, J. G., and Hagenah, T. *Vocational interest measurement.* Minneapolis: University of Minnesota Press, 1955.

Gilbert, J. Vocational archetypes: A proposal for clinical integration of interests and values in vocational counseling and section. *Psychological Reports*, 1963, *13*, 351-356.

Kuder, G. F. *General interest survey manual.* Chicago: Science Research Associates, 1964.

Mallinson, G. G., and Crumrine, W. M. An investigation of the stability of interests of high school students. *Journal of Educational Research*, 1952, *45*, 369-383.

Nunnally, J. C., Jr. *Tests and measurements.* New York: McGraw-Hill, 1959.

Thorndike, R. L. The prediction of vocational success. *Vocational Guidance Quarterly*, 1963, *11*, 179-187.

Tutton, M. E. Stability of adolescent vocational interests. *Vocational Guidance Quarterly*, 1955, *3*, 78-80.

White, R. M. The predictive relationship of selected variables to the vocational interest stability of high school students. Doctoral dissertation, University of Minnesota, 1958.

2

Some Principles of Interest Measurement

If we accept the premise that the purpose of an occupational interest inventory is to help young people discover the occupations they will find most satisfying, then it follows that two fundamental requirements must be met by such an inventory. One is that it must be valid with respect to the criterion of job satisfaction. The other is that it must be suitable for use with young people who may have quite limited backgrounds of training and experience.

Given these two requirements it is possible, with the aid of a few reasonable assumptions, to derive a number of principles appropriate to the development and use of an interest inventory. Some of the principles presented in the following pages may seem so obvious and well established that they are hardly worth mentioning. Still, they should be on the record. On the other hand, some of the principles suggested are at considerable variance with established practice and, indeed, with a number of things the writer has done during a learning period of forty years in this field. The principles are as follows:

1. The ability to differentiate well between occupational groups is one of the essential characteristics of an occupational interest inventory.

2. The questions in an occupational interest inventory should be well distributed throughout the domain of interests relevant to vocational choice.

3. The activities described in the questions must be clear and easily understood by the subjects, both by those who answer the inventory for their own guidance and by those who, as members of criterion groups, answer the inventory for the purpose of establishing occupational scoring systems.

4. The use of an interest inventory in occupational counseling rests on the assumption that the domain of interests in generally well-understood activities is essentially the same as the domain of interests in activities that are not generally well understood.

7

5. A form of item should be used that is known to be affected relatively little by changes in context.

6. The form of question should be as free as possible from the effects of response bias.

7. Occupational titles should not be used in the items in an interest inventory intended for use in occupational counseling.

8. The questions should not be unpleasant or threatening.

9. It is highly desirable that a means be available for checking on the confidence that can be placed in the answers to the inventory.

10. It is highly desirable to use the same inventory for both sexes.

11. The set of scores from an occupational interest inventory must have high reliability and stability, and these characteristics should be measured in terms of reliability and stability within the person.

12. The most useful form in which to report scores from an interest inventory is in order of magnitude.

The reasoning leading to these principles is discussed below under ten topical headings. As a rule there is one principle to a topic, but "The Criterion" calls for two principles, as does "Obtaining True Answers."

The Criterion

Because the purpose of occupational counseling in general and of occupational interest measurement in particular is to help the young person identify the career that will be most congenial, it might at first appear that degree of satisfaction should be set up as the criterion for developing a measure of suitability for each occupation. The resulting estimates of the absolute degree of job satisfaction that people could be expected to derive from various occupations would be designed to be comparable not only from one person to another in any occupational group, but also from one occupation to another for any one person.

If only the task were as simple as it sounds! The approach is impractical, however, for a number of reasons. One particular difficulty is serious enough to prevent a satisfactory solution. Even if one assumes that absolute and comparable estimates of the criteria can be obtained, there remains the seemingly insurmountable problem of obtaining a good representation of the *possible* range of satisfaction from people actually engaged in an occupation.

The fact is that people in any one occupation are a highly selected group who adequately represent only a small part of the continuum that extends from high satisfaction to extreme dissatisfaction. There are a number of occupations — such as those of physician and minister — in which almost no one dislikes the work, and for which the range of job satisfaction is especially restricted. We cannot assume for any occupational group, however, that those who say they dislike their work are close to the lower end of the continuum. After all, they are still engaged in the occupation. Those who can't stand it have left!

Yet good representation is the first essential for developing a dependable prediction system. It is questionable practice to apply a formula to those ranges that are poorly represented in the criterion. It is even more questionable to extrapolate beyond the limits of the sample studied.

These remarks are not meant to imply that studies using ratings of job satisfaction are not worthwhile in certain circumstances, even though they are limited in the degree of validity that they can possibly reveal.

In the search for a more feasible approach to the problem, we should keep in mind that it is not essential that absolute measures be used — or even that the measures be comparable from one person to another — in order that an inventory can be valid for use in counseling. After all, the reason for using an interest inventory in counseling is not to rank a number of people but to rank a multitude of occupations for one person. The absolute degree of satisfaction derived from occupations may vary greatly from person to person, but the variation that is relevant to the individual is the one that exists within the person. The criterion needed for standardizing an interest inventory or, indeed, a counseling program, is some index of the relative satisfaction that each participant in the study receives from many kinds of work.

Obtaining measures of the relative degree of satisfaction to be expected by the individual from a number of jobs may at first appear to be just as impractical as attempting to use absolute measures. It would be convenient, of course, if groups of people in each occupation could be identified as being, without doubt, in the very best occupation for them. In that case, the problem of the criterion would be solved, and the task would be reduced to developing a system designed to classify each of the people in his or her own occupation. The ideal sample for this purpose would consist of a number of immortals who had had experience in all possible occupations and had finally settled upon the occupation that each of them liked best.

Fortunately, there is a more realistic solution to the problem. The approach described below rests on the plausible assumption that our present system of getting people into occupations, inefficient as it may sometimes be, is considerably more successful than random selection would be. Of course, it cannot be assumed that all workers in a given occupation are in the very best occupation for them, or even that those who say they like their work are in the occupation they would find most satisfying. As noted by Clark (1961), there no doubt are some people who would derive little or no satisfaction from any job, and there are others who might really enjoy as many as fifty occupations. The fact that a person reports pleasure in his or her work is no guarantee that the person could not find substantially greater satisfaction in a number of other kinds of work, nor can it be assumed that a person who dislikes the work would like any other work better.

It seems reasonable to assume that those members of an occupation who have stayed in that occupation long enough to give it a real trial, and who report they like their work, are better satisfied *on the average* than they would be if they were all in any other one occupation. For example, if a large sample of carpenters were converted into barbers after suitable training, there probably would be a loss in the general level of job satisfaction. In other words, the carpenters would be less satisfied as barbers, on the average, than they had been as carpenters. This assumption does not preclude the possibility that some of the carpenters might be better satisfied as barbers.

If the general assumption stated is true, trends observed for differences between occupational groups should give an indication of the direction of the larger differences to be expected from hypothetical "pure" groups — that is, groups composed entirely of people in the occupation they would have found most congenial if they had been able to try out all possible occupations. Since there is some error in the system of fitting people to jobs, a difference, for example, in the responses of carpenters and barbers to a specific item would not be as pronounced as the corresponding difference between pure groups. The differences, however, would be in the same direction. Scales based on a composite of items also would produce differences in the same direction.

A scale that is successful in differentiating between actual groups of carpenters and barbers therefore should reflect, with some degree of error, the extent to which a person resembles a hypothetical ideal group of carpenters more than that person resembles a hypothetical ideal group of barbers, or vice versa. The

10

extent to which the two real groups can be differentiated is an indication of how well this purpose is accomplished. Other things being equal, the less the overlapping between two groups, the better the scale will be for that particular comparison, and the greater will be the confidence with which young people can be told they probably will like one occupation more than another.

Thus the problem of establishing validity for counseling purposes becomes one of classification, and the following principle can be stated:

Principle 1   The ability to differentiate well between occupational groups is one of the essential characteristics of an occupational interest inventory.

In applying this principle, it seems desirable to restrict the occupational groups used to those persons who *like* their work from among those who have been in an occupation long enough to have a good basis for judgment. No doubt the system would work in any case, but sharper differentiation can be expected if some mistakes are eliminated at the outset.

Principle 1 means that one of the fundamental questions in judging a vocational interest inventory is how well it differentiates among the specific occupational groups for which it is scored. This question makes sense in terms of the counseling situation. After all, the process of deciding upon a vocation consists of making a series of choices in which one specific occupation is compared with another specific occupation. It is also true that the more scales there are available for this purpose, the greater will be the usefulness of the instrument.

The task of determining how well an inventory differentiates among occupational groups breaks down to one of finding out how well the two groups in each possible pairing of occupational groups are differentiated from each other. For each pair of groups, this differentiation can be expressed as the percentage of cases classified correctly. A summary figure can then be obtained for all of the pairings of the occupations for which the inventory is scored.

In evaluating such data, it must be kept in mind that not all of those in an occupation are in the very best occupation for them. In any pair of occupational groups there probably are some people who really would enjoy the other occupation in the pair more than they enjoy their own. This means that ordinarily it is too much to expect perfect differentiation between any two groups. The differentiation can never be any higher than the imperfections of the criterion allow; but in any case, the higher it turns out to be, the better the instrument is for counseling purposes. Within any pair of groups, the upper limit must surely depend on how similar the two occupations are, and the evidence so far collected appears to bear out this generalization.

Two quite different approaches to the problem of differentiating among occupational groups have been used over the years. When Moore (1921), for example, studied sales engineers and design engineers, his problem was the relatively simple one of differentiating between two groups. Other early investigators such as Ream (1924) and Freyd (1924) studied two groups, and Cowdery (1926) used three.

When it came to dealing with many occupations, however, the task of developing a scale for each possible pair must have appeared to be preposterously impractical. Fortunately, Strong proposed the ingenious idea of using a general reference group as a basis for developing occupational scales. It was not that such scales could be expected to differentiate as well between occupations in each pair as would a series of scales made specifically for each pair. At that time, however, the use of a general reference group must have appeared to be the only practical way of dealing with the problem.

While it apparently was solving one problem, the use of a general reference group raised another troublesome one: What should the composition of such a group be? It might be supposed that a sample of the general population would be most logical, but Strong (1943) soon discovered that scales based on a reference group of this kind did not give good differentiation among professional groups. His studies indicate that there is no single reference group that is satisfactory for the whole range of occupations. He has demonstrated that a scale developed for a certain occupation with respect to one reference group may have little correlation with another scale developed for that same occupation with respect to another reference group.

Another disadvantage in the use of a general reference group is that sharpness of differentiation between specific occupations is sacrificed. The items that differentiate best between an occupational group and a general reference group are not likely to be the same as those that differentiate best between that same occupation and another specific occupation. Indeed, each comparison of one occupation with another will produce its own set of items or its own set of weights, depending on the technique used.

After wrestling with this problem over a period of several years, the writer finally developed a rationale (1963) that is essentially a return to the early idea of differentiating between two occupations at a time. The advantages of the rationale are that (1) it is possible to apply it to any number of occupations, and (2) it markedly improves the accuracy of classification over that achieved by the general reference group approach. The rationale of the system and the results of a comparative study, using cross-validation groups, have been presented in the literature (Kuder, 1963, 1968) and also are discussed in chapter 3.

Briefly, the new system produced 32 percent fewer errors than the general reference group system. It is just as logical, of course, to make the comparison in the other direction. In that case, the general reference group system was found to produce 47 percent more errors than the new system.

Good differentiation among occupational groups does not occur by accident. It is not enough for an investigator to assemble a collection of questions that he or she considers appropriate to the problem. If an effective instrument is to be developed, a series of studies involving the administration and analysis of a succession of experimental forms, with each study based on the experience and information previously gained, is essential. There was a time when it appeared that the number of interest factors pertinent to vocational choice might be as few as four or five (Thurstone, 1931). Now it appears the number may well be several times that many. Obviously, the best possible differentiation between two groups cannot be obtained if pertinent factors are not even represented in the inventory. The next principle can be stated as follows:

Principle 2   The questions in an occupational interest inventory should be well distributed throughout the domain of interests relevant to vocational choice.

Ideally, the questions should be evenly distributed throughout factorial space, and they should have equal communalities. When these conditions exist, the centroid of the items that meet a certain standard of validity will necessarily coincide with the criterion. This situation is illustrated in figure 1 for a two-space example. Let us suppose the items are evenly distributed with respect to the two factors and that all item communalities are the same. Economical coverage of the whole two-factor space can be facilitated by entering each possible answer twice — once when it is scored positively and once when it is scored negatively. In the diagram, therefore, circles that are exactly opposite each other could represent the same response scored in opposite ways.

Let vector C represent the criterion, and suppose that all responses that correlate with the criterion in excess of a certain

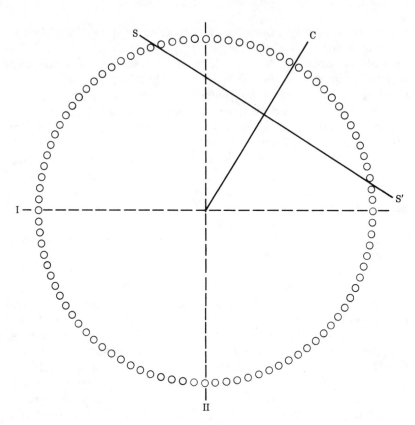

Figure 1. Application of a standard (*s-s'*) in selecting items
to be scored for a test (reprinted with permission from
Educational and Psychological Measurement).

standard, designated by line *s-s'*, are scored. Since line *s-s'* cuts
off equal arcs on either side of vector C and since the items are
evenly distributed in these arcs, it follows that the resulting score
will coincide with vector C or at least will be very close to it. This
line of reasoning holds true for any level at which the standard of
validity may be set. It also holds true for any weighting system
that assigns weights that are a function of validity. Of course, the
general principle illustrated here for two factors is applicable to
any number of factors.

It must be recognized from the outset that there are bound to
be differences between the ideal model and the results of efforts
to achieve it. In order to make the task even possible, approxima-
tion procedures must be used. For one thing, the intensive sort of
coverage shown in figure 1 cannot be attained in a relatively short
inventory. The fact that it is much easier to construct reliable

items in some areas than in others is another of the complications involved. Still another is that it is more difficult to force coverage of some areas of factorial space with some forms of items than with other forms.

The development process inevitably requires a succession of laborious steps aimed at getting better approximations of the model. In actual practice, a shortage or even absence of items with certain required characteristics will be revealed as soon as the first item analysis is made. This will be true even if a large number of items are used in the first place and every effort is made to make the original coverage comprehensive. In this situation new items must be written and possibly old items revised, and the resulting collection must be administered to a variety of new groups. These groups must be given the items already selected as well as older items that identify the frame of reference being used. After the next analysis, another set of experimental items must be administered in the effort to fill in the gaps. This process can be continued as long as necessary to achieve the standards desired or until funds and the investigator are exhausted.

Nevertheless, as noted by Wright (1967), it often is possible to capitalize on the characteristics of a theoretical model even if the model is not achieved precisely. To draw on personal experience, the Kuder-Richardson formulas for estimating test reliability have turned out to be useful even though the assumptions on which they are based are seldom strictly fulfilled.

Vocabulary Level

From the standpoint of both validity and stability, the questions in the inventory must be well understood by the subjects. An answer can be valid only by chance if the counselee does not understand the question. The answer scarcely can have stability, either, if it is likely to change over a period of time because of improvement in the counselee's comprehension of the question content. Furthermore, not only will some of the users of the inventory have very limited backgrounds, but many of the members of the groups on whom the inventory should be standardized are likely to be similarly limited. The following principle allows for both situations:

Principle 3 The activities described in the questions must be clear and easily understood by the subjects — both those who answer the inventory for their own guidance and those who, as members of criterion groups, answer the inventory for the purpose of establishing occupational scoring systems.

On the Comparability of Two Domains of Interests

It has been noted that the validity of a vocational interest inventory rests on its ability to differentiate between specific occupational groups. It should be added immediately that ability to differentiate between groups is not the only essential requirement. In fact, it is possible to obtain excellent differentiation between occupational groups with questions it would be absurd to ask young people.

Probably it would be possible to differentiate almost perfectly between computer programmers and podiatrists by asking the straightforward question, "Would you rather be a computer programmer than a podiatrist?" Or two separate questions, "Would you like to be a podiatrist?" and "Would you like to be a computer programmer?" could be asked. Except for those who answered both questions in the same way, differentiation would probably be close to perfect. It cannot be denied, however, that a limited number of computer programmers might actually prefer to be podiatrists, and vice versa.

But what counselor would put such questions to a young person in search of an occupation? No counselor needs to be reminded that the conversation must be kept within the understanding of the counselee. Words that the counselee does not understand fully are equally inappropriate in an interest inventory, as suggested in principle 3.

Two quite different domains of interests in activities can be identified. One is the domain of interests in activities that are as a rule well understood by people in general, including young people. The other is the domain of interests in activities that are understood best by people who have had experience in specific occupations. Almost everyone understands the former type of activities and relatively few fully understand the latter. No one is familiar with more than a small proportion of the activities of the latter type; this would make it extremely difficult and complicated to work out a factor analysis in the second domain.

On the surface, it might appear that it would be impossible to obtain an adequate picture of the interests of people in a specific occupation without resorting to questions about activities that are specific to the occupation and generally unfamiliar to people not in the occupation. There is really no reason to suppose, however, that the dimensions of interests in little-known activities are essentially different from the dimensions of interests in well-known activities. If the factorial dimensions are essentially the same, then it should be possible to generalize from the domain of the familiar to the domain of the unknown. If the inventory is cast in terms of activities that are generally well understood, it should be possible to give counselees estimates of the extent to which their interests correspond to the interests characteristic of people in a wide range of occupations. These include occupations about which they know nothing or even have erroneous ideas. After all, vocational counselors have been operating for years on the basis of assumptions similar to this one. The principle involved is as follows:

Principle 4   The use of an interest inventory in occupational counseling rests on the assumption that the domain of interests in generally well-understood activities is essentially the same as the domain of interests in activities that are not generally well understood.

Context and Item Form

The process of developing and improving an inventory calls for the elimination of the least useful items in experimental forms and the addition of new ones that are believed likely to meet certain specifications. The process continues until a combination of items is finally achieved that accomplishes the objectives established. This procedure is not possible without changing the context of individual items.

In the cognitive realm, such rearrangement may have little effect on the answers given. In the case of interest items, however, it should not be taken for granted that the nature of the surrounding items can have no effect on the answers. A person's judgment concerning the attractiveness of a specific activity might well be different if the activity is contained in a list of unpleasant activities one time and in a context of very pleasant activities another time. It also appears likely that some forms of items may be less susceptible than others to this effect.

In view of these considerations, there should be some assurance that the sort of item used will continue to measure the same thing even when the nature of the surrounding items is changed considerably. It was this line of reasoning that led the writer (Kuder, 1939) to study the effect of changes in context on the stability of forced-choice questions before committing himself to the use of this type of item in the development of his interest inventories. The appropriate principle can be stated as follows:

Principle 5   A form of item should be used that is known to be affected relatively little by changes in context.

The use of a form of item known to be stable does not eliminate the need for making validation studies of the inventory in its final form. It does, however, increase the likelihood that the general level of validity of a set of items will be maintained after changes in context; its use therefore greatly facilitiates the developmental process.

Response Bias

The next principle concerns response bias, namely, the effect that the form of a question may have on the answer given, quite apart from what the content of the question may be. It is now well established that check lists of questions cast in true-false, agree-disagree, or like-dislike form are particularly susceptible to such an effect, as revealed by the early studies of Mathews (1929), Lorge (1937), and others. Cronbach (1946, 1950) published two excellent summary articles on this subject and the evidence has since continued to mount. For example, Jackson and Messick (1962) found that from one-half to three-fourths of the variance of a number of scales based on items of this type was "interpretable in terms of . . . acquiescence and desirability." (pp. 151-152) Dolliver's more recent study (1968) is another of a long series by many different investigators. These establish that items calling for the kinds of responses mentioned are subject to substantial response bias.

The validity of a counseling instrument must be regarded as an individual matter; that is, validity is specific to the individual and can vary from one person to another. If a person agrees with or says he or she likes everything presented, it is apparent that the failure to express any discrimination has defeated the purpose of the inventory and that it can have no validity for the individual. This is an extreme case of a tendency that varies from one person to another; the effect on the upper limit of validity attainable would not be so drastic for people with more typical response patterns. Even so, the differential effect of substantial response bias on the average validity attainable can be only downward. As observed by Jackson and Messick, ". . . one rapidly approaches an upper limit on the amount of information elicited by items which permit massive response-style effects like generalized acquiescence and desirability bias." (p. 154) The following principle is therefore advanced as desirable:

Principle 6 The form of question should be as free as possible from the effects of response bias.

On the Use of Occupational Titles in Interest Inventories

The next principle bears indirectly on the question of face validity and the possibility that in the case of interest inventories face validity may actually be false validity. The fact that a form is classified as an occupational interest inventory does not mean it must include occupational titles in the items. Indeed, there is something incongruous about asking young people if they would like to engage in various occupations when the purpose of the procedure is to give *them* such information. If a counselee already knows enough about occupations to judge how well he or she would like them, it is pertinent to ask whether the information from an interest inventory would contribute to better counseling. If, on the other hand, people do not know enough about the occupations listed to make intelligent judgments about them, the scores obtained would be even less useful. In fact, scores based on answers made in ignorance could be actually misleading.

As noted in the preceding chapter, children often express a liking for an occupation for reasons that have nothing to do with the nature of the work. The fact is that most young people do not know enough about occupations to make intelligent judgments on the spur of the moment; and as they acquire more information, their preferences are likely to change. Nor is imperfect knowledge about occupations confined to the very young. Morris and Murphy (1959) found substantial evidence of misunderstandings and misconceptions by the general public as to what an individual actually does in any given occupation.

Another reason for avoiding occupational titles is found in a theory advanced by Bordin (1943) to the effect that a person answers an interest inventory in terms of his conception of an occupation with which he identifies himself. As a generalization, Bordin's idea is difficult to accept, since it does not appear likely that every young person in search of an occupation already identifies with an occupation, either consciously or unconsciously. As a statement of an influence that might operate to a greater or lesser extent in some cases, Bordin's idea appears more plausible.

If young persons have decided, for reasons that may or may not be pertinent, that they want to be physicians, then conceivably they might tend to mark answers they think physicians would mark. If the specific question regarding being a physician were one of the items, they would certainly mark that they would like to be one. To use their expressed preference for the occupation of physician to raise their Physician score is reasonable only if they know enough about a physician's work to make a sound judgment.

In his book *Vocational Interests of Men and Women* (1943, p. 624), Strong presents the hypothetical case of a young man "who actually ought to go into public accounting" but who marks that he is indifferent to the item, Certified Public Accountant, "because he had never heard of the occupation." In situations of this kind Strong raises the question of whether items should be weighted "as the statistics indicate in order to secure maximum differentiation of occupational groups or shall weights be reduced in order, on the one hand, to make it more difficult for someone to fudge the results or, on the other hand, to not penalize an honest person who doesn't happen to know the meaning of the items?"

Strong puts his finger here on two big drawbacks of the use of occupational titles in interest inventories: (1) Answers to such items are particularly susceptible to faking, either consciously or unconsciously, and (2) young people may not be familiar with certain occupations, including those that may be suitable for the particular individuals. In fact, the less a person knows about occupations, the more he or she is likely to need help in finding an appropriate one; answers to questions about specific occupations the individual does not know well are not likely to provide that help. These considerations suggest that it is better to avoid this type of item altogether, as stated in the following principle:

Principle 7   Occupational titles should not be used in the items in an interest inventory intended for use in occupational counseling.

There was a time when the writer thought it permissible to use some of the more common occupational titles in items. Continued consideration of the problem has led, however, to the conclusion that in the absence of evidence from young and unsophisticated subjects concerning the validity of specific items of this nature, it is more prudent to avoid the use of occupational titles entirely. It is quite possible that long-term follow-up studies of items answered by college upperclassmen and graduate students would show some degree of validity for items composed of the better-known occupational titles. The prospect of obtaining valid results would appear to be considerably less for students at the high school level. In any case, whatever the group, the average validity obtained cannot be taken as a true indication of validity for the less well-informed young people in the group.

The use of occupational titles is a tricky business that carries the risk of reducing validity in the counseling situation. An occupational title is not an ordinary word or phrase. It can encompass a whole world of impressions and experiences for some persons and carry almost no meaning for others. Occupational titles give the appearance of validity, and actually can be valid for those people who have a comprehensive knowledge of the terms. It does not follow that these titles are valid for those young people who are most in need of good advice.

Obtaining True Answers

Implicit in the use of interest scores in counseling is the assumption that the counselee has been completely cooperative and candid and has understood the directions and questions. The next two principles deal with different aspects of this assumption. Principle 8 is concerned with keeping the process of answering the inventory as free of tension as possible and with minimizing those influences that might lead to invalid answers. Principle 9, on the other hand, is concerned with discovering, after the fact, whether anything has actually happened in answering the questions that might affect the usefulness of the scores in counseling. These principles are as follows:

Principle 8 The questions should not be unpleasant or threatening.

Principle 9 It is highly desirable that a means be available for checking on the confidence that can be placed in the answers to the inventory.

There is, of course, no way of compelling a person to answer questions carefully and sincerely and with understanding. Fortunately, however, it is possible to build into an inventory devices that will identify most of the cases in which the answers are not true indications of a person's interests.

The earliest study of faking was made by Strong in 1927, although it was not reported in the literature until the publication of Strong's book in 1943. A later study by Steinmetz (1932) was actually the first to appear in the literature. Both studies demonstrated that Strong Vocational Interest Blank responses can be faked easily and scores shifted in the desired direction. Subsequent studies by other investigators have corroborated this finding and extended the conclusion to inventories in general.

There is room for differences of opinion as to whether one kind of item is more resistant to faking than another, but there actually is no experimental evidence that any one inventory is superior to others in this respect. It seems likely that the possibility of faking is related more to the content of the questions than to their form. Questions that obviously are related to occupations presumably would be more transparent than those that are not.

Although subjects *can* fake answers in the desired direction, it does not follow that they will choose to do so. When they are taking an inventory for purposes of personal guidance, there is little reason to doubt that they will answer the questions carefully and sincerely. Even so, it would sometimes be helpful to the counselor to know whether there was a probability that some special circumstance — such as pressure to finish too quickly for reasonable consideration of the questions, a distracting situation, some influence that motivates the subject to conceal or distort real preferences, lack of understanding, or just plain carelessness — was operating to prevent the scores from reflecting a true picture of a counselee's interests.

Should the Same Inventory Be Used for Both Sexes?

As time goes on, women are entering more and more occupations previously considered the exclusive domain of men. In view of this accelerating trend, it becomes increasingly desirable that the same interest inventory be usable for both men and women.

This means that young women often must be counseled about the possibility of entering an occupation for which a scale for women workers has not been developed because of the lack of women in the field. The situation immediately stimulates the question of using masculine scores for such occupations. A study by Hornaday and Kuder (1961) and a more recent study by the writer (1966) have indicated the feasibility of such an approach. If women's inventories are to be scored for masculine scales, however, the questions answered must be the same as those used in collecting data from male occupational groups. As a consequence the following principle can be stated:

Principle 10   It is highly desirable to use the same inventory for both sexes.

It is logical that feminine scores could be used in a similar manner in the guidance of young men. This question deserves further exploration.

Reliability and Stability

The fact is sometimes overlooked that an inventory intended to discriminate within the person has its own special requirements. They are not necessarily the same as those for a measure intended to discriminate among people. A single test that differentiates well among people is useless in itself for differentiating within the person, and scores that are comparable within the person are not necessarily comparable from person to person. One important area in which the difference is particularly apparent is that of reliability and stability; these can be thought of as short-term and long-term consistency. High correlations obtained for scales administered at one time and then at another to a heterogeneous group of people do not give adequate information on this point; they may well be misleading. The important information needed, as applied to counseling, is the reliability and stability of the set of scores for each subject.

An appropriate measure of this consistency might well be a correlation computed between two sets of scores from the same subject. The correlation will vary from person to person, of course, and will no doubt depend somewhat on the length of the interval between testings. In our present state of knowledge, there is no way of knowing in advance what the correlation will be for a specific counselee. It is possible, however, to get a general idea of the consistency of sets of scores by studying a distribution of the correlations obtained from a representative group of subjects.

The stability of the answers to an item undoubtedly is influenced by quite a number of characteristics of both the items offered and the subjects tested. Some of these influences have already been touched upon. For example, subjects with extremely limited education and experience cannot be expected to show the same consistency in their responses to questions about a complicated activity as subjects whose backgrounds have familiarized them with the activity involved. If an inventory is to be generally useful, it must be composed of items that are stable for the vast majority of the subjects for whom it is intended. The general principle toward which this discussion has been leading is as follows:

Principle 11   The set of scores from an occupational interest inventory must have high reliability and stability, and these characteristics should be measured in terms of reliability and stability within the person.

It is important to bear in mind that reliability within groups is not synonymous with reliability within the person. Reliability within the person is largely a reflection of the extent to which different factors are being measured. In the extreme case in which a single factor is being measured by several scores, the reliability of measurement within the person is bound to zero, except for chance variation. This will be the case even though the measures used may have high reliability within the group.

On the other hand, if a variety of unrelated characteristics are represented in a set of scores, the likelihood is good that the scores of an individual will cover a wide range. A favorable condition for achieving good reliability and differentiation thus will have been established. The best indication of how well this purpose has been accomplished is through a direct measure of the reliability of individual sets of scores. Reliabilities within the person cannot be inferred with confidence from test reliabilities within groups unless a great deal of supplementary information is obtained.

Principle 11 does not mean that differentiation among people has suddenly become of no importance. After all, principle 1 calls for differentiating members of one occupational group from members of other occupational groups as an essential step in establishing validity. It is apparent that in order to differentiate among groups, the items in an inventory must sample the dimensions in which occupational groups differ from each other. In addition, the way to settle on a suitable frame of reference for this purpose is to study the many ways in which people differ. But once an inventory has been developed in accordance with the rationale outlined, the appropriate measures of reliability and stability needed for evaluating the system in practice are those concerning individual sets of scores.

Under certain circumstances the average standard error of a score may be theoretically the same regardless of whether correlations are computed for groups or for individuals. In such a case, it would be possible to estimate the average correlations of individuals from a knowledge of the standard errors obtained from group studies. The direct computation of reliability and stability for individuals avoids a resort to assumptions, however, and also furnishes information concerning the variation in these qualities from one person to another.

A corollary of principle 11 is that the items of an interest inventory should be unaffected by age. This objective may appear almost hopeless of accomplishment. In practice it may have to be modified to apply to groups of items in the same general area rather than to single items, or its application may be in trying to keep the relation of age to item response to a minimum. Nevertheless, the ideal model should be kept in mind.

Perhaps an alternative approach to the age problem is to develop corrections for differences in age. The practical obstacles to such a solution are greater than might at first appear, but the approach remains a possibility.

The Question of Reporting Scores for Families of Occupations

For many years it was common practice to present interest scores for specific occupations grouped in families of similar occupations, and the writer accepted this practice as reasonable without giving it particular thought. In time, however, it became necessary to face the question of how scores from the Occupational Interest Survey should be presented. An intensive study of the problem led to the decision to present scores in order of magnitude rather than by occupational families.

The main objection to listing scores by job families is that doing so has the effect of allowing information known about average relationships in groups to influence individual decisions more than does specific information known about the individual. It is true that a knowledge of average group relationships can be useful in counseling, but inferences based on data from groups of people should not be allowed to outweigh conflicting data known about the individual. Yet there is a marked tendency for people to think that if they obtain high scores on most of the occupations listed in a family they should consider all occupations in that family regardless of the specific scores.

It may be true that all occupations in a family are about equally attractive to most people, but there are important individual exceptions to the rule. Not all professors of psychology would enjoy being practicing clinical psychologists, and not all mathematicians would enjoy being statisticians. In the counseling situation, large differences in scores should not be ignored for the individual simply because the corresponding differences are small on the average for people in general. The listing of occupations in families on the report of scores makes it easy for the subject to ignore evidence concerning important ways in which he or she differs from the group. In this way the arrangement defeats to some extent the purpose of providing information about individual differences. The principle involved is as follows:

Principle 12   The most useful form in which to report scores from an interest inventory is in order of magnitude.

REFERENCES

Bordin, E. S. A theory of vocational interests as dynamic phenomena. *Educational and Psychological Measurement*, 1943, *3*, 49- 65.

Clark, K. E. *Vocational interests of nonprofessional men.* Minneapolis: University of Minnesota Press, 1961.

Cowdery, K. M. Measurement of professional attitudes. Differences between lawyers, physicians, and engineers. *Journal of Personnel Research*, 1926, *5*, 131- 141.

Cronbach, L. J. Response sets and test validity. *Educational and Psychological Measurement*, 1946, *6*, 475-494.

Cronbach, L. J. Further evidence on response sets and test design. *Educational and Psychological Measurement*, 1950, *10*, 3-31.

Dolliver, R. H. Likes, dislikes, and SVIB scoring. *Measurement and Evaluation in Guidance*, 1968, *1*, 73-80.

Freyd, M. The personalities of the socially and mechanically inclined. *Psychological Monographs*, 1924, *33* (Whole No. 151), 101 pp.

Hornaday, J. A., and Kuder, G. F. A study of male occupational interest scales applied to women. *Educational and Psychological Measurement*, 1961, *21*, 859-864.

Jackson, D. N., and Messick, S. Response styles and assessment of psychopathology. In *Measurement in personality and cognition*, edited by S. Messick and J. Ross. New York: Wiley, 1962.

Kuder, G. F. The stability of preference items. *Journal of Social Psychology*, 1939, *19*, 41-50.

Kuder, G. F. A comparative study of some methods of developing occupational keys. *Educational and Psychological Measurement*, 1957, *17*, 105-114.

Kuder, G. F. A rationale for evaluating interests. *Educational and Psychological Measurement*, 1963, *23*, 3-12.

Kuder, G. F. *Occupational Interest Survey general manual.* Chicago: Science Research Associates, 1966, 1968, 1970, 1971, 1974.

Lorge, I. Gen-like: Halo or reality? *Psychological Bulletin*, 1937, *34*, 545-546.

Mathews, C. O. The effect of the order of printed responses on an interest questionnaire. *Journal of Educational Psychology*, 1929, *20*, 128-134.

Moore, B. V. Personnel selection of graduate engineers. *Psychological Monographs*, 1921, *30* (Whole No. 138), 85 pp.

Morris, R. G., and Murphy, R. J. The situs dimension in occupational structure. *American Sociological Review*, 1959, *24*, 231-239.

Ream, M. J. *Ability to sell: its relation to certain aspects of personality and experience.* Baltimore: William & Wilkins, 1924.

Steinmetz, H. L. Measuring ability to fake occupational interest. *Journal of Applied Psychology*, 1932, *16*, 123-30.

Strong, E. K., Jr. *Vocational interests of men and women.* Stanford, California: Stanford University Press, 1943.

Thurstone, L. L. A multiple factor study of vocational interests. *Personnel Journal*, 1931, *10*, 202-206.

Wright, B. D. Sample-free test calibration and person measurement. Invitational conference on testing problems, Educational Testing Service, 1967.

3

A Rationale for Evaluating Interests

The principle that the validity of an occupational interest inventory rests on its power to discriminate between occupational groups is the starting point for the rationale that follows. We must recognize at the outset that validity in this sense is not an absolute amount that is the same for all possible pairs of occupations. It can hardly be expected that people in two quite similar occupations could be classified correctly in their own occupations with as much success as people in quite dissimilar occupations could be so classified. Validity for any inventory is therefore likely to be reflected in a fairly wide variation in the degree to which distributions overlap, with the exact overlapping for each comparison of occupations depending on how similar the people in those occupations are in terms of what they like to do.

A circumstance that influences the upper limit of possible differentiation is the fact that the criterion is fallible. Not everyone is in the occupation that is best for him or her. In some comparisons of occupational groups a few people therefore may "belong" in the other occupation of the pair in the sense that they actually would have preferred it had they been able to try out both occupations. This means that their answers have to some extent contaminated the scoring system to which those answers counted.

Measurement of the degree of discrimination achieved between two groups can be expressed by various means. One way is simply by noting the proportion of cases correctly classified when the dividing line between the two distributions is placed at a point designed to keep classification errors at a minimum. Sometimes the degree of discrimination is expressed in terms of overlapping, that is, by the sum of the proportions of the two distributions that are in the overlapping area. Overlapping is usually about twice the proportion of errors; this ratio is exact under certain specific conditions. Sometimes degree of discrimination has been expressed in terms of point biserial correlation, and there is a direct relation between it and the other measures. For all of these indices, the areas of the two distributions ordinarily are treated as though they were

28

equal. Some investigators have used biserial correlation, but such usage is inappropriate.

Little information has become available over the years on how well interest inventories discriminate between two specific occupations. Strong recognized this aspect of validity, but simply stated that data of this sort were not available for his scales — and no wonder! Until the advent of electronic computers it would have been impractical to collect the evidence for all the possible combinations within as many as fifty or sixty occupations. Even today the task is not inconsiderable. As far as the Occupational Interest Survey is concerned, we have had to be content for the present with studying samples. In the course of time we expect to study more.

Strong also recognized implicitly the need for discriminating between occupational groups when he rejected, after trying it out, a general reference group representative of the general population. He found that the occupational scales developed with such a reference group did not discriminate well among professional groups. Thus the scores were of relatively little help to college students who were already fairly sure that they were headed for a profession. The trouble was simply that all the occupational scales tended to be heavily weighted with items that discriminated well between the general population and the people in the professions.

The rationale that follows rests on an article by Findley (1956) entitled "A Rationale for Evaluation of Item Discrimination Statistics." From Findley's discussion, it follows that the differences in the proportions of two groups marking responses to items furnish an index of the degree of effective discrimination achieved by those items.

In spite of a general trend toward very simple weights, let us explore the application of Findley's system to the scoring of interest inventories. As will become evident later, there are some special advantages to using this approach that more than compensate for the lack of simplicity of weights. Findley's idea can be expressed in formula form for determining the weight for a single response as follows:

$$W = p_A - p_B$$

Here p_A represents the proportion of group A marking the response and p_B represents the proportion of group B marking the response.

If these weights are determined for all responses in the inventory, then the difference score D for any subject becomes the sum of the weights assigned to all of the subject's responses. Thus,

$$D = \Sigma(p_A - p_B), \tag{1}$$

the summation being over the responses of the subject.

If group B happens to be a heterogeneous general reference group of the kind used by Strong, scores obtained can be expected to be highly correlated with SVIB scores, since Strong's weights are roughly proportional to differences in the percentages of two groups that mark a response.

In practice, the formula in equation (1) involves a great deal of time and labor. For each differentiation we want to make we must obtain the differences between proportions for every response in an inventory. The score for a subject is the sum of the differences corresponding to the responses marked by each subject. If we want to discriminate between one occupational group and a number of other specific occupational groups, we must develop a separate set of weights for each comparison to be made. When quite a few occupations are to be compared with each other, this becomes an enormous job.

Now let us see how a simple manipulation of equation (1) into a slightly different form can increase substantially the validity of our evaluation of a person's responses to an interest inventory.

Consider this equation:

$$D = \Sigma p_A - \Sigma p_B, \tag{2}$$

the summation being over the responses of the subject. Equation (2) is a little different from equation (1), but it is algebraically equivalent. In terms of the operations called for and the possibilities opened up, however, the differences are tremendous.

In order to get the difference score in this case we must get two sums. One is the sum of the proportions of the members of group A who marked each of the responses marked by our subject. The second is a corresponding sum obtained by using proportions of group B who marked the responses indicated by our subject. At first this may seem like a roundabout way to obtain a score. Instead of one sum, we have to get two and also have to make a subtraction.

But see what happens when we want to obtain scores for a

series of occupations. All we need do is obtain sums for each of the occupations and for the general reference group. The differences from the general reference group represent our scores; it has not been necessary to develop "scales" by going through the laborious procedure of finding the differences in proportions for hundreds of responses for each of the occupations involved. Furthermore, we are likely to notice sooner or later that getting the differences between the proportion sums of the reference group and of the occupational group is a superfluous operation. We can compare these proportion sums directly, so that in effect we have a tailor-made scale for differentiating between the two occupations that we are comparing in each case.

These proportion sums have an interesting property. A person's proportion sum for the occupation of architect represents the average score that the 333 architects in the criterion group would obtain if they all were scored with a key consisting of the subject's answers. Similarly the subject's proportion sum for the occupation of journalist represents the average score that the 400 journalists in our sample would obtain if the subject's answers were used as a key for scoring the journalists. We can then say that the architects obtained a higher or a lower score than the journalists obtained on the subject's key, depending on the relative size of the proportion sums.

The Problem of Variations in Homogeneity

On the face of it, the system so far described appears to be the answer we are seeking. Indeed, it would be eminently satisfactory if all groups were equally homogeneous, for then the best cutting point between the two distributions of score differences in a comparison would ordinarily fall at zero for groups of equal size.

When we are comparing the scores of two such groups (A and B) on a particular measure in order to differentiate between them, the best differentiation is obtained when the cut is made at the point of intersection of the two distributions. If group A has the higher mean, we will make the fewest errors if we guess that everyone with scores above the point of intersection belongs to group A and everyone with scores below that point belongs to group B. The farther a score is from the point of intersection, the greater is the confidence with which a classification can be made. When the standard deviations of the two groups are equal and the numbers of cases are the same, the point of intersection of two normal distributions is exactly halfway between the two means.

When the two occupations used as the basis for the scores have about the same degree of homogeneity, there is therefore little problem. The zero point is halfway between the means and usually is close to the point of intersection of the two distributions. For the purpose of classification, it is unnecessary to compute differences; it simply is necessary to see by inspection which proportion score is larger. If cutting points were always at zero, then, a comparison of proportion scores would be adequate for guidance purposes.

Differences in homogeneity raise a special problem. A case in which the best cutting point does *not* fall at zero is illustrated in the upper portion of figure 2 for groups of clinical psychologists and journalists. The interests of clinical psychologists are known to be somewhat more homogeneous than those of journalists. The differentiation is excellent when the cutting point on the difference scale (Clinical Psychologist Proportion Score minus Journalist Proportion Score) is set at about 18. That is, the fewest errors of classification are made when all subjects with scores above 18 are classified as clinical psychologists. In this early study, proportion scores were carried to three places and decimal points were omitted. How a modification — to be described later — of the proportion scores can shift the position of the best cutting point on the scale of differences to close to zero is illustrated in the lower part of figure 2.

It is important for the best cutting point to be close to zero for all comparisons, since it obviously is impractical to find and use different cutting points for the multitude of comparisons to be made. For example, the 79 scores reported for masculine occupations on the Occupational Interest Survey can serve as the basis for 3081 difference scales, each designed for the specific purpose of differentiating between the two occupations involved.

Plainly it is impractical to compute all these differences and to evaluate each of them in relation to a cutting point established for each scale. If, on the other hand, the best cutting point in each case is approximately zero, differences do not have to be computed in order to tell the counselee which occupational groups are closest to the counselee's occupational interests. This information can be obtained simply by scanning the scores for the high one.

When homogeneities are not equal, there is a tendency for a disproportionate number of the less homogeneous group to obtain

Differences in Proportion Scores (Clinical Psychologist Score Minus Journalist Score)

100 Clinical Psychologists

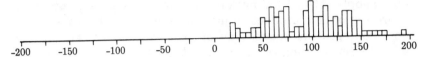

100 Journalists

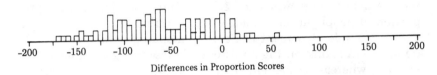

Differences in Proportion Scores

Differences in Lambda Scores (Clinical Psychologist Score Minus Journalist Score)

100 Clinical Psychologists

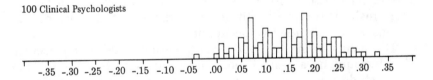

100 Journalists

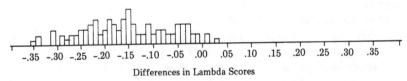

Differences in Lambda Scores

Figure 2. Distributions of differences in proportion scores
and in Lambda scores.

scores which would classify them with the more homogeneous
group. This sort of situation is illustrated in the upper part of
figure 2. The fact is that groups differ considerably in homogeneity, as Strong has pointed out, and these differences have
often proved troublesome in connection with other inventories
as well as with the OIS. For example, in his 1955 book Strong
discussed the difficulties arising from differences in the homo-

geneities of psychiatrists and internists, and surmised that "this sort of situation is present in Kreidt's difficulty in differentiating clinical psychologists from other psychologists." (p. 162)

Differences in homogeneity may also account for the fact that more people get high ratings on the Strong scales for president of a corporation and production manager than get high scores for the more homogeneous occupations of social worker and carpenter. In order to get a rating of A, a subject must get a score at least as high as half a standard deviation below the mean of the occupational groups used as the criterion. When there is very little overlapping, a very small number of the general reference group achieve high ratings; when there is much overlapping, a larger proportion of people in general achieve high ratings.

For example, 4 percent of Strong's men-in-general group would obtain an A rating on the minister scale (assuming a normal distribution), whereas 18 percent of them would obtain an A rating on the president of a corporation scale. Seventy-two percent of Strong's men-in-general group would get A or B ratings on the scale for realtor as compared with 25 percent who would get these ratings on the scale for carpenter. There is no reason to believe there really is this great a difference in the extent to which men in general would like the two occupations.

The achievement of good discrimination between an occupational group and a general reference group is in itself a reflection of a high degree of homogeneity in the occupational group. On the other hand, when a group is so heterogeneous (with respect to the items used) that it closely resembles the general reference group, this lack of uniformity will be reflected by a lack of good discrimination in whatever scale is developed.

When we face the problem of differentiating between two specific occupational groups, we are dealing with essentially the same situation except that, generally speaking, neither occupational group is likely to be as heterogeneous as is a general base group. Nevertheless there are variations in homogeneity from one occupational group to another. The degree of homogeneity is directly related to the range within which it is possible to obtain scores and to the extent to which it is possible to differentiate between occupational groups.

In his review of the Minnesota Vocational Interest Inventory (1966), Campbell notes an instance in which the mean occupational score of an occupational group on its own scale is actually exceeded by the mean score of another group on the same scale. It is conceivable that this apparent incongruity is a function of differences in homogeneity.

A Measure of Homogeneity

The homogeneity of a group is defined here as the extent to which the answers of its members are in agreement. The more homogeneous a group, the larger will be the proportion marking the most popular choice in each group of three responses, and the larger will be the sum of the squared proportions. Perfect homogeneity, where the same choice is marked by 100 percent of a group throughout the inventory, is theoretically possible but never found in practice. For purposes of illustration, let us consider a somewhat more realistic, although still highly unlikely, case. Let us suppose that for every one of the 100 triads there is one choice in the Most column marked by 80 percent of the group, and one choice in the Least column marked by 80 percent. Each of the remaining two choices in each column is presumed to be marked by 10 percent of the group, as in the following triad.

	M		L
(1)	.80	(4)	.10
(2)	.10	(5)	.80
(3)	.10	(6)	.10

The sum of these proportions squared is 1.32; the total for 100 triads in which the same situation existed would be 132. If 70 percent mark the same choices throughout the inventory with other choices split evenly between the two alternatives, the sum of the squared proportions for 100 triads would be 107. If 60 percent mark the same choices with other choices split evenly, the corresponding sum of squares would be 88. If the members of a large group answer at random, the expected index of homogeneity is $66\frac{2}{3}$. In practice, the extent to which even the most homogeneous of groups mark the same responses will usually vary considerably.

In general, the results from actual groups reported in table 1 seem to make sense in terms of what is known about occupations. Department store salesmen are the least homogeneous of all the occupational groups, and female pediatricians are the most homogeneous. It is interesting that the groups of women tend to be more homogeneous than the groups of men. The homogeneity of groups of social workers and psychologists is relatively high for both sexes, and that of florists tends to be relatively low.

TABLE 1

HOMOGENEITIES Σp^2 AND HIGHEST POSSIBLE
PROPORTION SCORES (HPPS) OF 217 GROUPS

1. MALE OCCUPATIONAL GROUPS

	Group	Code	N	Σp^2	HPPS
001	Accountant (AAA Members)	AC AAA	200	91.876	111.900
002	Accountant	AC	200	94.038	114.030
003	Accountant CPA	AC CPA	335	96.703	117.600
004	Accountant, Industrial	AC IND	285	95.900	116.544
005	Architect	ARCH	333	94.309	114.889
006	Auto Mechanic	AUTO M	200	95.541	118.705
007	Baker	BAKER	150	87.838	108.026
008	Banker	BANKER	320	94.514	115.659
009	Barber	BARBER	250	87.530	108.556
010	Bookkeeper	BKKPR	165	92.671	114.680
011	Bookstore Manager	BKSMGR	200	89.482	109.500
012	Bricklayer	BRKLYR	162	89.118	110.738
013	Building Contractor	BDG CN	200	93.338	115.785
014	Buyer	BUYER	200	93.192	114.350
015	Carpenter	CRPNTR	200	94.748	117.255
016	Chamber of Commerce Executive	CC EX	200	95.034	116.668
017	Chemist	CHEMST	200	98.515	119.525
018	Clothier, Retail	CLTH R	250	93.424	114.171
019	Computer Programmer	COMPRG	200	93.279	114.140
020	Counselor, High School	COUNHS	200	94.953	115.745
021	County Agricultural Agent	COAGAG	500	97.234	118.636
022	Dentist	DNTIST	333	93.245	115.033
023	Department Store Salesman	DPTSTS	200	87.107	107.215
024	Director, Funeral	DRCTFN	200	93.581	114.975
025	Editor, Newspaper	EDNWSP	200	96.677	118.395
026	Electrician	ELECTR	250	95.339	117.732
027	Engineer, Civil	ENGCVL	400	95.217	115.053
028	Engineer, Electrical	ENGELE	250	95.200	115.580
029	Engineer, Heating & Air Conditioning	ENGHAC	200	95.586	115.555
030	Engineer, Industrial	ENGIND	333	97.307	118.615
031	Engineer, Mechanical	ENGMCH	200	96.490	116.560
032	Engineer, Mining and Metallurgical	ENG MM	250	94.930	115.528
033	Farmer	FARMER	150	97.675	119.873
034	Florist	FLORST	200	90.875	111.695
035	Forester	FORSTR	250	96.817	118.040
036	Insurance Agent	INS AG	200	93.569	114.825
037	Interior Decorator	INTDEC	190	94.330	115.304
038	Journalist	JOURN	400	95.758	116.940
039	Lawyer	LAWYER	250	95.812	117.192

TABLE 1 (Continued)

1. MALE OCCUPATIONAL GROUPS

	Group	Code	N	Σp^2	HPPS
040	Librarian	LIBRAR	200	93.254	114.775
041	Machinist	MCHNST	200	94.998	117.365
042	Mathematician	MATHM	200	95.518	116.700
043	Mathematics Teacher, High School	MATHHS	200	93.981	114.910
044	Meteorologist	METEOR	150	96.190	117.878
045	Minister	MINIST	300	94.172	116.291
046	Motel Manager	MTLMGR	200	91.740	113.340
047	Nurseryman	NRSRYM	200	92.706	113.010
048	Optometrist	OPTMST	300	95.076	115.880
049	Osteopath	OSTPTH	200	95.746	116.415
050	Painter, House	PNTR H	200	88.845	110.880
051	Pediatrician	PEDTRN	333	96.399	117.117
052	Personnel Manager	PERS M	200	95.823	117.055
053	Pharmaceuticals Salesman	PHAR S	400	95.301	116.617
054	Pharmacist	PHARM	200	92.383	113.335
055	Photographer	PHOTOG	200	90.457	111.870
056	Physical Therapist	PHYTHR	300	95.048	115.581
057	Physician	PHYSN	200	94.634	115.815
058	Plumber	PLUMBR	200	93.466	116.310
059	Plumbing Contractor	PLMBCN	200	95.747	118.090
060	Podiatrist	PODRST	200	91.988	113.410
061	Policeman	POLICE	200	94.574	116.300
062	Postal Clerk	POSTCL	200	91.974	113.185
063	Printer	PRNTER	200	91.356	112.965
064	Psychiatrist	PSYTST	200	97.687	119.489
065	Psychologist, Clinical	PSYCCL	400	98.902	120.577
066	Psychologist, Counseling	PSYCCN	250	96.823	118.348
067	Psychologist, Industrial	PSYCIN	200	96.591	117.880
068	Psychology, Professor of	PSYPRF	300	96.847	118.320
069	Radio Station Manager	RADSTA	250	94.428	115.492
070	Real Estate Agent	REALES	200	91.874	112.220
071	Sales Engineer, Heating & Air Conditioning	SLSENG	200	96.735	117.645
072	Science Teacher, High School	SCITHS	250	95.637	116.188
073	School Superintendent	SCHSUP	200	95.122	116.665
074	Social Case Worker	SOCCWK	400	96.668	118.555
075	Social Worker, Group	SOCWKG	333	97.741	120.178
076	Social Worker, Medical	SOCWKM	175	97.856	118.818
077	Social Worker, Psychiatric	SOCPSY	333	97.407	119.523
078	Social Worker, Research	SOCRES	100	99.230	121.550
079	Social Worker, School	SOCSCH	163	98.802	121.193
080	Statistician	STATCN	200	95.949	116.875
081	Supervisor-Foreman, Industrial	SUPVFM	200	92.479	114.200

TABLE 1 (Continued)

1. MALE OCCUPATIONAL GROUPS

	Group	Code	N	Σp^2	HPPS
082	Travel Agent	TRVLAG	200	91.358	112.395
083	Truck Driver	TRKDRV	185	94.807	118.106
084	Television Repairman	TV REP	250	91.392	113.312
085	University Pastor	U PSTR	164	98.371	121.957
086	Veterinarian	VETRN	300	96.618	118.636
087	Welder	WELDER	157	91.835	113.708
088	X-Ray Technician	X RAY	200	92.909	113.965
089	YMCA Secretary	YMCASC	250	95.543	117.433

2. FEMALE OCCUPATIONAL GROUPS

	Group	Code	N	Σp^2	HPPS
090	Accountant	FACNT	250	94.127	114.548
091	Bank Clerk	FBNKCL	200	96.228	117.645
092	Beautician	FBEAUT	200	93.109	114.600
093	Bookkeeper	FBKKPR	250	95.684	116.808
094	Bookstore Manager	FBKMGR	163	93.206	113.789
095	Cataloger, Library	FCTLIB	110	99.410	120.962
096	Computer Programmer	FCMPRG	175	94.291	115.069
097	Counselor, High School	FCHSHS	250	98.558	119.316
098	Dean of Women	F DEAN	250	97.375	117.940
099	Dental Assistant	FDNTAS	250	95.306	116.304
100	Department Store Saleswoman	FDPTSW	200	95.295	116.785
101	Dietitian, Administrative	FDTNAD	200	92.752	112.985
102	Dietitian, College Dormitory	FDTCDM	100	95.853	116.690
103	Dietitian, Commercial	FDTCOM	80	93.877	114.569
104	Dietitian, Hospital	FDTHOS	200	94.168	113.365
105	Dietitian, Public School	FDTSCH	188	94.993	115.791
106	Dietitian, Therapeutic	FDTTHR	100	94.979	116.040
107	Florist	FFLRST	250	91.817	111.492
108	Home Demonstration Agent	FHMDEM	250	96.741	117.224
109	Home Economics Teacher, College	FHOMEC	200	98.589	118.535
110	Interior Decorator	FINTDC	143	97.908	118.973
111	Key Punch Operator	FKYPCH	200	89.035	109.060
112	Lawyer	FLAWYR	250	95.104	116.436
113	Librarian	FLIBR	250	97.131	118.356
114	Math Teacher, High School	FMATHS	200	98.018	118.215
115	Motel Manager	FMTLMR	250	91.530	112.096
116	Nurse	FNURSE	200	95.576	115.880
117	Nutritionist	FNUTRN	200	97.579	117.715
118	Nutrition Instructor to Nurses	FNUTIN	100	96.720	116.680
119	Occupational Therapist	FOCCTH	250	97.973	118.704
120	Office Clerk	FOFCLK	200	95.627	116.830
121	Pediatrician	FPEDRN	69	101.963	122.486
122	Physical Therapist	FPHYTH	300	95.750	115.771

TABLE 1 (Continued)

2. FEMALE OCCUPATIONAL GROUPS

	Group	Code	N	Σp^2	HPPS
123	Primary School Teacher	FPRSCT	200	96.365	116.985
124	Psychologist	FPSY	200	97.793	118.480
125	Psychologist, Clinical	FPSYCL	150	100.292	121.897
126	Psychologist, Counseling	FPSYCN	90	98.271	119.197
127	Religious Education, Director	FRELED	150	101.215	122.690
128	Science Teacher, High School	FSCTHS	100	98.362	118.670
129	Secretary	FSECY	200	94.174	114.705
130	Social Case Worker	FSOCCW	500	99.695	120.104
131	Social Worker, Group	FSOCGR	333	98.597	118.929
132	Social Worker, Medical	FSOCMD	400	100.222	120.498
133	Social Worker, Psychiatric	FSOCPS	400	101.098	121.697
134	Social Worker, School	FSOCSC	300	100.679	120.211
135	Stenographer	FSTENO	200	95.478	116.370
136	X-Ray Technician	FX RAY	200	94.163	115.195

3. MALE COLLEGE MAJOR GROUPS

137	Agriculture	MAG	200	93.258	114.835
138	Animal Husbandry	MANLHS	120	94.518	116.365
139	Architecture	MARCH	165	94.635	116.618
140	Art & Art Education	MARTED	200	94.502	115.785
141	Biological Sciences	MBIOSC	250	94.078	115.856
142	Business, Accounting & Finance	MBUSAC	250	94.824	116.132
143	Business, General	MBSGEN	200	91.821	113.590
144	Business and Marketing	MBSMRK	200	94.510	116.345
145	Business Management	MBSMGT	250	93.296	115.112
146	Economics	MECON	175	92.827	115.060
147	Elementary Education	MELED	162	90.040	111.214
148	Engineering, Chemical	MENGCH	175	95.830	117.448
149	Engineering, Civil	MENGCL	200	95.116	116.480
150	Engineering, Electrical	MENGEL	400	95.020	115.775
151	Engineering, Mechanical	MENGMH	300	94.709	116.363
152	English	MENGL	170	93.464	116.415
153	Foreign Languages	MFRNLG	200	88.962	110.695
154	Forestry	MFORST	150	94.505	114.869
155	History	MHIST	190	92.541	114.268
156	Law (Graduate)	MLAW	200	96.402	119.030
157	Mathematics	MMATH	200	92.814	113.870
158	Music & Music Education	MMUSIC	300	91.729	112.620
159	Physical Education	MPHYED	250	90.840	111.940
160	Physical Sciences	MPHYSC	333	94.377	115.751
161	Political Science & Government	MPOLYS	180	95.601	117.638

TABLE 1 (Continued)

3. MALE COLLEGE MAJOR GROUPS

	Group	Code	N	Σp^2	HPPS
162	Premed, Pharm & Dentistry	MPREMD	250	95.686	117.160
163	Psychology	MPSY	185	95.846	117.499
164	Catholic Teaching Brother	MCATHB	290	87.099	107.730
165	Sociology	MSOC	200	91.746	113.930
166	US Air Force Cadet	MAFCAD	300	95.952	118.146
167	US West Point Cadet	MWPCAD	400	92.604	115.412

4. FEMALE COLLEGE MAJOR GROUPS

	Group	Code	N	Σp^2	HPPS
168	Art & Art Education	GARTED	150	97.313	117.579
169	Biological Sciences	GBIOSC	300	95.878	116.262
170	Business, General	GBUSGN	285	92.122	113.116
171	Drama	GDRMA	136	96.725	118.639
172	Elementary Education	GELED	400	95.352	115.773
173	English	GENGL	333	95.945	117.376
174	Foreign Languages	GFRNLG	400	93.604	114.505
175	Health Professions	GHELTH	250	96.164	116.812
176	History	GHISTO	250	94.189	115.080
177	Home Economics Education	GHMEC	250	92.622	112.400
178	Mathematics	GMATH	285	92.685	112.931
179	Music & Music Education	GMUSIC	285	94.898	114.867
180	Nursing	GNURSE	250	95.789	115.656
181	Physical Education	GPHYED	300	92.885	113.650
182	Political Science	GPOLYS	250	97.582	119.576
183	Psychology	GPSYCH	300	96.005	117.272
184	Catholic Teaching Sister	GCATHS	367	94.619	116.049
185	Social Sciences, General	GSOCSC	200	95.419	116.205
186	Sociology	GSOC	300	96.550	117.836

5. GROUPS USED FOR THE EXPERIMENTAL SCALES

	Group	Code	N	Σp^2	HPPS
187	Fathers	FATHRS	250	88.351	108.788
188	Sons	SONS	250	86.658	107.040
189	Mothers	MTHRS	333	92.480	113.181
190	Daughters	DGHTRS	333	89.897	110.880
191	Base Group, Male	MALES	1000	89.450	110.604
192	Base Group, Female	FEMALE	400	90.733	110.236

6. DISSATISFIED OCCUPATIONAL GROUPS OF MEN

	Group	Code	N	Σp^2	HPPS
193	Accountant	DACNT	120	91.601	112.177
194	Auto Mechanic	DAUTOM	50	91.983	112.100
195	Barber	DBRBER	100	88.716	109.700

TABLE 1 (Continued)

6. DISSATISFIED OCCUPATIONAL GROUPS OF MEN

	Group	Code	N	Σp^2	HPPS
196	Bricklayer	DBRKLR	79	89.680	110.896
197	Carpenter	DCRPNT	50	96.674	118.540
198	Clothier, Retail	DCLTHR	79	92.800	113.228
199	Electrician	DELEC	50	93.418	114.640
200	Machinist	DMACH	100	92.422	114.100
201	Painter, House	DPNTER	120	89.962	111.054
202	Pharmacist	DPHARM	67	93.450	113.912
203	Plumber	DPLUMB	50	91.755	112.700
204	Postal Clerk	DPSTCL	132	89.909	110.196
205	Social Worker	DSOCWK	100	91.975	113.900

7. DISSATISFIED OCCUPATIONAL GROUPS OF WOMEN

	Group	Code	N	Σp^2	HPPS
206	Dietitian	XDT	150	92.810	112.466
207	Office Clerk	XOFCLK	90	93.303	113.303
208	Secretary	XSECY	100	93.073	113.230
209	Social Worker	XSOCWK	100	96.617	116.969

8. DISSATISFIED COLLEGE MAJOR GROUPS OF MEN

	Group	Code	N	Σp^2	HPPS
210	Business Management	DBSMNT	150	90.709	112.243
211	Engineering	D ENG	150	90.086	111.489
212	Social Sciences	DSOCSC	150	89.077	111.140

9. DISSATISFIED COLLEGE MAJOR GROUPS OF WOMEN

	Group	Code	N	Σp^2	HPPS
213	Elementary Education	XELED	100	94.973	114.190
214	English	XENGL	100	91.379	113.200
215	Foreign Languages	XFRNLG	115	93.426	114.303
216	Social Sciences	XSOCSC	120	92.107	113.436
217	Sociology	XSOC	115	94.551	115.751

Clemans's Lambda Coefficient

It is fortunate that a means for dealing with the problem of variations in homogeneity exists in the form of the lambda coefficient of correlation devised by Dr. William V. Clemans (1958). This coefficient is similar in concept to biserial *r*, except that it involves no assumptions concerning the shapes of the distributions of the variables. The lambda coefficient is appropriate for expressing the correlation between a subject's responses and those of the members of a defined group without imposing the requirement of a normal distribution. The upper limit of lambda is 1.00 for all groups, regardless of the degree of homogeneity. The lambda coefficient turns out to be a very simple function of the proportion sum, and we are using lambdas as "scores" for the Occupational Interest Survey.

The derivation of the lambda coefficient has been presented by Clemans in the article "An Index of Item-Criterion Relationship." When applied to proportion scores from the OIS, the specific transformation formula is as follows:

$$\lambda = \frac{\Sigma p - 66\frac{2}{3}}{HPPS - 66\frac{2}{3}},$$

in which Σp is the proportion score of the subject for the occupation involved and HPPS is the highest possible proportion score obtainable for that occupation. Thus, in the transformation of proportion scores to lambda coefficients, the highest possible proportion score for an occupation receives a lambda value of 1.00 and a proportion score of 66.67 receives a lambda value of zero. The regression line between these two points is straight. The figure of 66.67, which is equated to a lambda of .00, represents the average score that would be obtained by people's marking responses at random.

Application of the transmutation formula automatically produces lambda scores that have a mean and standard deviation differing from the mean and standard deviation of the proportion scores of the group. The shape of the distribution is the same, however, for both the lambda and proportion scores.

In interpreting the highest lambda coefficients (which from now on will ordinarily be referred to as OIS scores) received by a counselee, we can say something like this: "Although allowances must be made for the fact that all psychological measurements are subject to some error, the scoring of your inventory indicates that your pattern of interests is most highly related to the interests of architects, with interior decorators and foresters next in order."

Another system that appears logical as a correction for degree of homogeneity is that of transforming proportion scores to standard scores. This idea has been tried out, but has not worked as well as the lambda transformation in producing optimal cutting points close to zero on difference scales.

Comparing Two OIS Scores

The use of two OIS scores in combination is illustrated in figures 3, 4, and 5 for groups of architects and journalists. Figure 3 is a scatterdiagram of the scores of architects on the Architect and Journalist keys. Each dot on the chart represents an architect whose Architect score can be read by referring to the scale along the vertical axis and whose Journalist score can be read by referring to the scale along the horizontal axis. It can be noted that almost all of the architects receive a higher score for their own

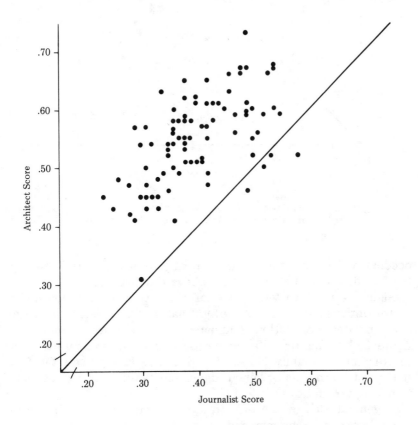

Figure 3. Scatter-diagram of the Architect and Journalist scores of a cross-validation group of 90 architects.

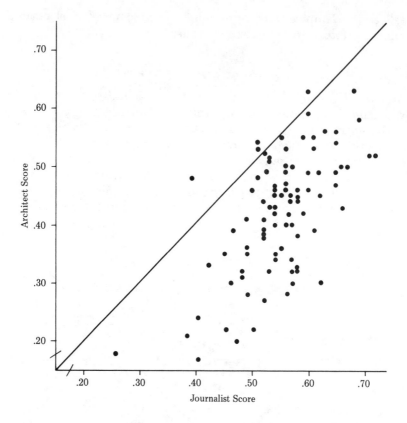

Figure 4. Scatter-diagram of the Architect and Journalist
scores of a cross-validation group of 90 journalists.

occupation than for the occupation of journalism, as reflected by
the fact that almost all entries are above the diagonal.

Figure 4 is a scatterdiagram of the Architect and Journalist
scores obtained from a group of journalists. The existence of a decided positive correlation is apparent in this figure as well as in
figure 3, but this time the entries occur in a different portion of
the diagram — mainly below the diagonal. This reflects the fact
that most journalists obtained higher scores for their own occupation than for that of architect.

A general idea of the effectiveness of the scores in differentiating between architects and journalists could be obtained by
superimposing one of the diagrams on the other. A simpler and
clearer picture of the differentiation can be achieved, however, by
the use of the difference scores obtained by the two groups when

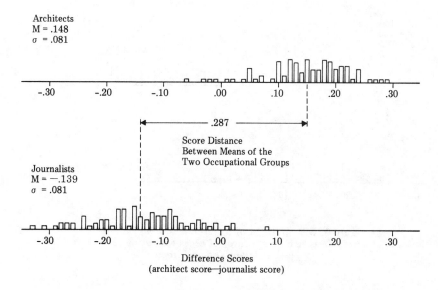

Figure 5. Distributions of difference scores (Architect score minus Journalist score) of cross-validation groups of architects and journalists.

the Journalist score for each person is subtracted from the person's Architect score. As anticipated, most of the difference scores for architects are positive and most of the difference scores for journalists are negative, as shown in figure 5.

Considering Scores in Relation to Each Other

Note particularly that although there are subjects who received relatively low scores for both occupations, they are almost always classified correctly when their own scores are considered in relation to each other. It is apparent that the position of a single score with reference to a group of subjects is not pertinent to the problem of classification.

Figure 5 also reveals that in this comparison of scores 86 of the architects and 86 of the journalists are classified correctly; thus of the 180 subjects involved, 95.6 percent are classified in their own occupations. Distributions of the difference scores for various pairs of occupational scores from samples of the corresponding occupational groups are shown in figures 6 through 9. Generally speaking, the differentiation that could be achieved by cutting the distribution at the very best point for these particular samples is only slightly, if any, better than that produced by the zero cutting

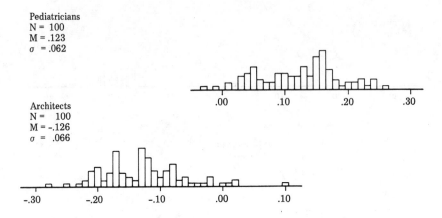

Figure 6. Distributions of difference scores (Pediatrician score minus Architect score) of cross-validation groups of pediatricians and architects.

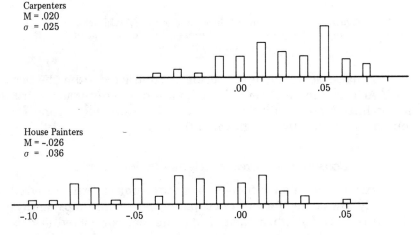

Figure 7. Distributions of difference scores (Carpenter score minus House Painter score) for cross-validation groups of carpenters and house painters.

point. In addition there is no assurance that this slight superiority would be maintained by that particular cutting point in other samples.

A consideration of the occupational scores reported for the OIS is complicated by the fact that these quantities are not scores in the conventional sense of the word. They are really terms in equations for difference scores, which are in turn the basis for differentiating between groups. There are thousands of difference scales,

46

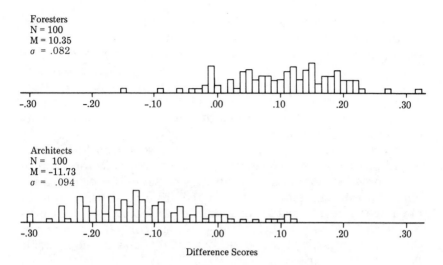

Figure 8. Distributions of difference scores (Forester score minus Architect score) of cross-validation groups of foresters and architects.

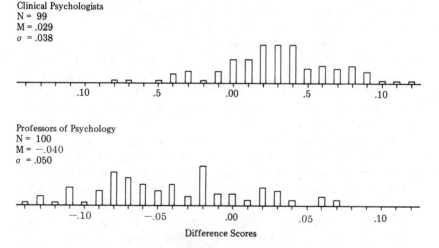

Figure 9. Distributions of difference scores (Clinical Psychologist score minus Professor of Psychology score) of cross-validation groups of 99 clinical psychologists and 100 professors of psychology.

and dealing with difference scores would be so cumbersome as to be impractical. The relatively few OIS scores are used as a faster way of reaching conclusions that would otherwise be obtained from a laborious consideration of a multitude of difference scores.

It may help in understanding this situation to consider the nature of scores from the well-known Strong Vocational Interest Blank, Scores from the SVIB are essentially *difference* scores, because scoring weights are assigned to each response in terms of how well that response differentiates an occupational group from a general reference group. Clemans (1968, p. 53) has pointed out that this procedure has the effect of factoring out "that great core of interests that people have in common."

On the other hand, single occupational scores on the OIS are *not* difference scores. The great core of interests is factored out of OIS scores in another way. A difference score is obtained when one of a subject's scores is subtracted from one of the subject's other scores, as illustrated for groups of architects and journalists in figures 3, 4, and 5. Difference scores are comparable from person to person in the same sense that SVIB scores are comparable from person to person.

Occupational Interest Survey scores for a single occupation are not comparable, however, from one person to another. When one score is taken in isolation or in relation to the scores of other people, it must be regarded as almost meaningless. True, if the score is large enough, it can be accepted as not having been obtained by chance. To use its absolute value as an indication of the presence or absence of interest in a specific occupation, however, would be a mistake. Nothing can be inferred with respect to the relative contribution of special and general factors to a single score until that score has been considered in relation to other scores from the same person. For an excellent discussion of this point, see Zytowski (1973, pp. 116–135).

The various scores on the OIS can lead to an amazing number of difference scales; indeed, the number of scales may at first appear to be forbiddingly large. For example, the 79 male occupational scores reported to counselees can serve as the basis for 3081 difference scales, each designed for the specific purpose of differentiating between the two occupations involved. Fortunately, the use of lambda scores makes the computation of all these differences unnecessary. Since counselee's are interested in knowing which occupational interests are most like their own, the information they require can be elicited from their scores simply by scanning them for the highest ones.

As noted previously, the best cutting point is not necessarily exactly zero for all OIS difference scales, although ordinarily the discrepancy is quite small. The evidence collected so far indicates that only rarely would the error amount to as much as .02, and that the average error is well below .01. The effect is to add a small amount of error variance to difference scores. This situation has been allowed for in the determination of the recommended range of scores within which occupations should be accorded particularly serious consideration by the counselee.

It may be that in time the accuracy with which the cutting point is determined will be improved somewhat by new techniques. On the other hand, there does not appear to be much room for improvement over the lambda transformation. In any case, the existence of some degree of error is a fact that must be taken into consideration in the interpretation of scores and the price that must be paid for a usable system. It is patently impractical to set up precise cutting points for all possible difference scales.

Olejnik and Porter (1975) explored alternative procedures concerning which they reported at the 1974 meetings of the National Council on Measurement in Education. They came to the following conclusion:

Considering that the discriminant analysis procedures are more difficult to calculate and have no greater accuracy than the lambda procedure, and since the latter had greater consistency than the chi-square technique, the lambda procedure seems preferable. Furthermore, the lambda coefficient is also preferable to the chi-square procedure since lambda weights are not a function of the occupations being compared while the chi-square weights for an occupation depend on the other occupations in the set being compared. (p. 45)

Degree of Differentiation Attained

At this point it would be desirable to present a report of the degree of differentiation attained within each possible pairing of the 162 occupations and college majors for which scores from the Occupational Interest Survey are reported. The number involved is 13,041! Even if the pairing is done only within each of the four major classifications, the number of comparisons is 4169.

It has not been possible to undertake a job of this magnitude. A study has been made, however, of a sample of 100 cases in each of 37 male occupational groups. These particular groups were used because the responses for them had been punched on cards according to a common uniform system, a computer program existed for obtaining scores, and it was financially feasible to conduct the study. This limited study still involves a substantial number of comparisons as reflected in the length of table 2, which reports the overlapping actually obtained within each of the 666 possible pairs of samples. In the computations, half of the tied scores (difference scores of zero), were classified as errors. Since tied scores involved only 2 percent of the cases, they did not have much of an effect on the outcome.

Table 2 also presents the theoretical minimum overlapping that could be expected if the cutting point on the difference scale for the occupations involved were placed exactly halfway between the two means. For the samples, this point is likely to differ somewhat from the zero used in actual practice. Computation of the theoretical overlapping has required obtaining the means and standard deviations of the two occupational groups on the difference scores between the corresponding occupational scales, and applying Tilton's formula and table for obtaining percentage of overlapping (1937). In a few instances, the obtained overlapping is less than the theoretical minimum overlapping. These discrepancies must be attributed to fortuitous distributions of cases in the samples that do not conform to the normal distributions assumed in computing the theoretical minimum overlapping. For the convenience of the reader, each 'overlapping appears twice — once for each of the occupations compared.

Since overlapping is defined by Tilton (pp. 657–65) as "the percentage of scores made by one group which could be matched with scores in the other group," it can be seen that overlapping corresponds to the sum of the proportions of errors of classification *in both distributions.* The theoretical minimum proportion of errors is thus half the estimated overlapping. It can be noted that Tilton's system assumes normal distributions and equal standard deviations, assumptions that are met only approximately in practice.

The averages of the two columns for all comparisons are 17.6 percent and 15.6 percent respectively. It does not appear that the loss in differentiation is excessive in view of the advantage that the zero cutting point provides. The comparison is a severe one, since the estimate of the minimum overlapping is based on the exact parameters of the sample used. The cutting point indicated for the sample could not be expected to produce quite as good differentiation in other samples, and the actual loss is probably less than 2 percent.

TABLE 2

OVERLAPPING ACTUALLY OBTAINED (A COLUMN)
VS. MINIMUM THEORETICAL OVERLAPPING (B COLUMN)
WITHIN ALL POSSIBLE PAIRINGS OF SAMPLES OF
37 OCCUPATIONAL GROUPS

No	Code	Group 3 AC CPA		Group 5 ARCH		Group 6 AUTO M	
		A	B	A	B	A	B
3	AC CPA			8	9	9.5	4
5	ARCH	8	9			12	7
6	AUTO M	9.5	4	12	7		
8	BANKER	23	22	13.5	12	20.5	16
12	BRKLYR	10	7	12.5	8	60	52
13	BDG CN	17	15	24.5	20	47	41
15	CRPNTR	8.5	4	13	8	76	69
17	CHEMST	11	11	11	8	11.5	7
18	CLTH R	13	14	15	14	17.5	16
19	COMPRG	28	27	13	12	14	11
26	ELECTR	10	5	11.5	6	70	61
28	ENGELE	30	28	27.5	25	16.5	12
31	ENGMCH	17	21	25	23	22.5	18
33	FARMER	12	8	8.5	4	18.5	16
35	FORSTR	19	15	21	16	17	16
37	INTDEC	4	3	25.5	23	4	2
38	JOURN	4	3	6.5	6	3	2
39	LAWYER	11.5	12	19.5	16	10	5
41	MCHNST	10.5	6	10.5	8	77.5	63
42	MATHM	17.5	17	11.5	15	7	3
48	OPTMST	14	18	16	13	17.5	15
51	PEDTRN	4.5	5	6	6	7.5	5
52	PERS M	24	18	18	17	10	7
54	PHARM	15	10	14.5	12	15.5	15
57	PHYSN	9.5	6	15.5	10	6.5	7
58	PLUMBR	11	6	11.5	10	58	50
61	POLICE	11	7	6	5	33.5	30
62	POSTCL	17.5	11	12.5	10	38.5	33
63	PRNTER	10	6	17.5	11	16	10
64	PSYTST	5.5	6	13	11	6.5	5
65	PSYCCL	8.5	7	9.5	10	5	3
66	PSYCCN	6.5	8	12.5	11	5.5	3
67	PSYCIN	13	11	11	13	6	3
68	PSYPRF	10	8	7.5	7	5	2
71	SLSENG	21.5	19	17.5	15	19	13
73	SCHSUP	8.5	7	11	8	10	10
74	SOCCWK	10.5	11	14.5	11	6	5
Mean		12.9	11.0	14.0	11.7	21.7	17.7

TABLE 2 (Continued)

No.	Code	Group 8 BANKER		Group 12 BRKLYR		Group 13 BDG CN	
		A	B	A	B	A	B
3	AC CPA	23	22	10	7	17	15
5	ARCH	13.5	12	12.5	8	24.5	20
6	AUTO M	20.5	16	60	52	47	41
8	BANKER			20	15	24.5	25
12	BRKLYR	20	15			40.5	38
13	BDG CN	24.5	25	40.5	38		
15	CRPNTR	24	18	60	54	53.5	50
17	CHEMST	13	12	6	7	14.5	14
18	CLTH R	35.5	36	21.5	17	28	28
19	COMPRG	21	18	15.5	11	24.5	20
26	ELECTR	23.5	19	38.5	41	45	42
28	ENGELE	34.5	33	13.5	13	31.5	28
31	ENGMCH	25.5	24	17.5	16	33.5	34
33	FARMER	19	16	6.5	7	15	12
35	FORSTR	28	24	9.5	14	28.5	27
37	INT DEC	8	4	6.5	4	10	7
38	JOURN	4.5	5	5	2	12	7
39	LAWYER	17	17	12	8	18	18
41	MCHNST	22	18	39	36	31	30
42	MATHM	15	10	7.5	5	12.5	10
48	OPTMST	22.5	19	19	17	26	23
51	PEDTRN	6	6	8	8	11.5	9
52	PERS M	19	22	8.5	9	16.5	20
54	PHARM	19.5	15	14.5	14	22	18
57	PHYSN	9.5	8	9	9	11.5	10
58	PLUMBR	23.5	22	54	51	52	48
61	POLICE	8.5	8	29.5	28	19.5	18
62	POSTCL	26	20	33.5	40	28	21
63	PRNTER	13	8	8.5	8	13	10
64	PSYTST	7	6	10	7	12.5	9
65	PSYCCL	7	6	9	5	9.5	9
66	PSYCCN	7	7	7	4	8.5	9
67	PSYCIN	11.5	9	8	4	14	12
68	PSYPRF	3.5	5	5	3	7.5	7
71	SLSENG	26	27	14.5	12	35.5	31
73	SCHSUP	18	13	16.5	13	22	19
74	SOCCWK	8	9	6.5	9	12	11
Mean		17.4	15.4	18.4	16.6	23.1	20.8

TABLE 2 (Continued)

No.	Code	Group 15 CRPNTR		Group 17 CHEMST		Group 18 CLTH R	
		A	B	A	B	A	B
3	AC CPA	8.5	4	11	11	13	14
5	ARCH	13	8	11	8	15	14
6	AUTO M	76	69	11.5	7	17.5	16
8	BANKER	24	18	13	12	35.5	36
12	BRKLYR	60	54	6	7	21.5	17
13	BDG CN	53.5	50	14.5	14	28	28
15	CRPNTR			8.5	7	20	16
17	CHEMST	8.5	7			12	10
18	CLTH R	20	16	12	10		
19	COMPRG	14.5	10	20	20	14	11
26	ELECTR	59	60	9.5	7	23	18
28	ENGELE	18	13	58.5	56	28	28
31	ENGMCH	24.5	19	38.5	42	17	17
33	FARMER	17	15	15	13	20.5	17
35	FORSTR	18	15	28	29	19.5	20
37	INTDEC	4.5	3	3	3	11.5	10
38	JOURN	0	2	9	6	5.5	5
39	LAWYER	8	6	19	18	19.5	15
41	MCHNST	46	49	11	10	16.5	14
42	MATHM	7	4	42.5	41	10	9
48	OPTMST	17	16	24.5	26	24	19
51	PEDTRN	10	7	19.5	14	8	5
52	PERS M	11	8	19.5	16	20.5	20
54	PHARM	18.5	13	24.5	25	21	20
57	PHYSN	13	9	25.5	23	11	11
58	PLUMBR	57	53	10.5	9	26	24
61	POLICE	30	25	5.5	5	13.5	10
62	POSTCL	41	33	13.5	14	26	24
63	PRNTER	12.5	11	7	10	17.5	20
64	PSYTST	9	6	18	17	10	7
65	PSYCCL	5.5	4	18	18	8.5	6
66	PSYCCN	6	3	21	18	14.5	8
67	PSYCIN	4.5	4	23	20	15	11
68	PSYPRF	4	3	25	24	9	6
71	SLSENG	17.5	13	18	19	28	23
73	SCHSUP	11.5	13	16.5	16	18	14
74	SOCCWK	8	8	10.5	9	18	11
Mean		21.0	18.1	17.8	16.8	17.7	15.4

TABLE 2 (Continued)

No.	Code	Group 19 COMPRG		Group 26 ELECTR		Group 28 ENGELE	
		A	B	A	B	A	B
3	AC CPA	28	27	10	5	30	28
5	ARCH	13	12	11.5	6	27.5	25
6	AUTO M	14	11	70	61	16.5	12
8	BANKER	21	18	23.5	19	34.5	33
12	BRKLYR	15.5	11	38.5	41	13.5	13
13	BDG CN	24.5	20	45	42	31.5	28
15	CRPNTR	14.5	10	59	60	18	13
17	CHEMST	20	20	9.5	7	58.5	56
18	CLTH R	14	11	23	18	28	28
19	COMPRG			16	12	51	47
26	ELECTR	16	12			15	15
28	ENGELE	51	47	15	15		
31	ENGMCH	40	42	26.5	20	95.5	94
33	FARMER	13.5	12	18	15	16	16
35	FORSTR	36	29	16.5	16	34.5	35
37	INTDEC	4	4	5	2	10.5	8
38	JOURN	7.5	5	1	2	6	6
39	LAWYER	19	16	10.5	6	29	28
41	MCHNST	18.5	15	39	36	24	18
42	MATHM	46.5	45	7	4	39	36
48	OPTMST	21.5	23	18.5	16	46.5	45
51	PEDTRN	16.5	10	6.5	5	23.5	18
52	PERS M	18	18	9	9	40.5	38
54	PHARM	19.5	17	17	15	25	23
57	PHYSN	13.5	11	9.5	7	18	16
58	PLUMBR	14.5	12	56.5	58	20	15
61	POLICE	14	10	24.5	24	10.5	9
62	POSTCL	19	18	37.5	30	18.5	16
63	PRNTER	10	10	11.5	8	10.5	12
64	PSYTST	18.5	13	8.5	5	23.5	19
65	PSYCCL	13	13	5.5	4	23.5	20
66	PSYCCN	19.5	15	4.5	3	24	24
67	PSYCIN	23	23	5	4	31	32
68	PSYPRF	19	15	3	2	27.5	24
71	SLSENG	19.5	18	22.5	16	51	53
73	SCHSUP	15	11	12.5	12	33	34
74	SOCCWK	16	12	7	6	21.5	18
Mean		19.6	17.1	19.5	17.0	28.5	26.5

TABLE 2 (Continued)

No.	Code	Group 31 ENGMCH		Group 33 FARMER		Group 35 FORSTR	
		A	B	A	B	A	B
3	AC CPA	17	21	12	8	19	15
5	ARCH	25	23	8.5	4	21	16
6	AUTO M	22.5	18	18.5	16	17	16
8	BANKER	25.5	24	19	16	28	24
12	BRKLYR	17.5	16	6.5	7	9.5	14
13	BDG CN	33.5	34	15	12	28.5	27
15	CRPNTR	24.5	19	17	15	18	15
17	CHEMST	38.5	42	15	13	28	29
18	CLTH R	17	17	20.5	17	19.5	20
19	COMPRG	40	42	13.5	12	36	29
26	ELECTR	26.5	20	18	15	16.5	16
28	ENGELE	95.5	94	16	16	34.5	35
31	ENGMCH			17	15	42	41
33	FARMER	17	15			28.5	24
35	FORSTR	42	41	28.5	24		
37	INTDEC	11	7	3.5	1	5.5	4
38	JOURN	6	5	5	3	6	6
39	LAWYER	21.5	20	15.5	14	25.5	20
41	MCHNST	27	25	12	11	14	14
42	MATHM	22	29	7	5	19	18
48	OPTMST	31	30	14	13	24	23
51	PEDTRN	15.5	14	10.5	7	20.5	17
52	PERS M	30	31	18	13	30	22
54	PHARM	19.5	18	14.5	11	17.5	15
57	PHYSN	11.5	15	11.5	8	18.5	15
58	PLUMBR	24	20	22	18	17	18
61	POLICE	10.5	8	9.5	9	5.5	9
62	POSTCL	22	18	11.5	7	15	14
63	PRNTER	14	14	3.5	3	4	6
64	PSYTST	19.5	15	10.5	5	17.5	13
65	PSYCCL	23	17	9.5	5	18	14
66	PSYCCN	18.5	18	10	5	19	15
67	PSYCIN	23.5	26	12	7	19	16
68	PSYPRF	21.5	19	8.5	5	19.5	15
71	SLSENG	39.5	44	19.5	15	27	26
73	SCHSUP	22	21	19	19	28.5	25
74	SOCCWK	18	13	7	7	16	14
Mean		24.8	23.7	13.3	10.6	20.3	18.3

TABLE 2 (Continued)

No.	Code	Group 37 INTDEC A	B	Group 38 JOURN A	B	Group 39 LAWYER A	B
3	AC CPA	4	3	4	3	11.5	12
5	ARCH	25.5	23	6.5	6	19.5	16
6	AUTO M	4	2	3	2	10	5
8	BANKER	8	4	4.5	5	17	17
12	BRKLYR	6.5	4	5	2	12	8
13	BDG CN	10	7	12	7	18	18
15	CRPNTR	4.5	3	0	2	8	6
17	CHEMST	3	3	9	6	19	18
18	CLTH R	11.5	10	5.5	5	19.5	15
19	COMPRG	4	4	7.5	5	19	16
26	ELECTR	5	2	1	2	10.5	6
28	ENGELE	10.5	8	6	6	29	28
31	ENGMCH	11	7	6	5	21.5	20
33	FARMER	3.5	1	5	3	15.5	14
35	FORSTR	5.5	4	6	6	25.5	20
37	INTDEC			2.5	3	8	6
38	JOURN	2.5	3			25	21
39	LAWYER	8	6	25	21		
41	MCHNST	5	2	2	2	11	6
42	MATHM	7	3	11	7	25.5	26
48	OPTMST	11	5	10	7	20	17
51	PEDTRN	2.5	3	6.5	5	12	10
52	PERS M	10.5	8	13.5	12	26	22
54	PHARM	10.5	6	4	4	16	13
57	PHYSN	8	4	6.5	5	17.5	14
58	PLUMBR	4.5	4	5	4	12	10
61	POLICE	7	2	3.5	3	10	6
62	POSTCL	4	4	6	5	14.5	14
63	PRNTER	12	7	18	16	17.5	15
64	PSYTST	7	5	10	8	19.5	14
65	PSYCCL	6	6	4.5	7	18.5	12
66	PSYCCN	4.5	5	6.5	8	13.5	11
67	PSYCIN	13	6	8	9	12	12
68	PSYPRF	4	3	11.5	9	21	18
71	SLSENG	10	7	3	3	11	11
73	SCHSUP	5	2	6	7	25.5	22
74	SOCCWK	6.5	4	8	8	17.5	13
Mean		7.4	5.0	7.0	6.1	16.9	14.2

TABLE 2 (Continued)

No.	Code	Group 41 MCHNST		Group 42 MATHM		Group 48 OPTMST	
		A	B	A	B	A	B
3	AC CPA	10.5	6	17.5	17	14	18
5	ARCH	10.5	8	11.5	15	16	13
6	AUTO M	77.5	63	7	3	17.5	15
8	BANKER	22	18	15	10	22.5	19
12	BRKLYR	39	36	7.5	5	19	17
13	BDG CN	31	30	12.5	10	26	23
15	CRPNTR	46	49	7	4	17	16
17	CHEMST	11	10	42.5	41	24.5	26
18	CLTH R	16.5	14	10	9	24	19
19	COMPRG	18.5	15	46.5	45	21.5	23
26	ELECTR	39	36	7	4	18.5	16
28	ENGELE	24	18	39	36	46.5	45
31	ENGMCH	27	25	22	29	31	30
33	FARMER	12	11	7	5	14	13
35	FORSTR	14	14	19	18	24	23
37	INTDEC	5	2	7	3	11	5
38	JOURN	2	2	11	7	10	7
39	LAWYER	11	6	25.5	26	20	17
41	MCHNST			9.5	6	20	17
42	MATHM	9.5	6			22.5	25
48	OPTMST	20	17	22.5	25		
51	PEDTRN	5.5	6	22.5	19	30	33
52	PERS M	10	9	16	17	18.5	18
54	PHARM	16	13	17.5	12	45	39
57	PHYSN	7.5	9	21	15	41.5	37
58	PLUMBR	34.5	32	10	6	19	17
61	POLICE	23.5	24	4	3	16	13
62	POSTCL	35	32	13	11	30.5	29
63	PRNTER	14	13	8	8	17.5	16
64	PSYTST	5.5	5	32.5	28	29	27
65	PSYCCL	5.5	4	27	25	28.5	22
66	PSYCCN	5.5	4	27	25	26	20
67	PSYCIN	7.5	4	22.5	23	19.5	16
68	PSYPRF	4	3	35	34	17.5	16
71	SLSENC	17.5	16	11	11	17	18
73	SCHSUP	12.5	12	17.5	12	19	18
74	SOCCWK	7	6	20.5	19	21.5	19
Mean		18.3	16.1	18.1	16.3	22.7	20.7

TABLE 2 (Continued)

No.	Code	Group 51 PEDTRN		Group 52 PERS M		Group 54 PHARM	
		A	B	A	B	A	B
3	AC CPA	4.5	5	24	18	15	10
5	ARCH	6	6	18	17	14.5	12
6	AUTO M	7.5	5	10	7	15.5	15
8	BANKER	6	6	19	22	19.5	15
12	BRKLYR	8	8	8.5	9	14.5	14
13	BDG CN	11.5	9	16.5	20	22	18
15	CRPNTR	10	7	11	8	18.5	13
17	CHEMST	19.5	14	19.5	16	24.5	25
18	CLTH R	8	5	20.5	20	21	20
19	COMPRG	16.5	10	18	19	19.5	17
26	ELECTR	6.5	5	9	9	17	15
28	ENGELE	23.5	18	40.5	38	25	23
31	ENGMCH	15.5	14	30	31	19.5	18
33	FARMER	10.5	7	18	13	14.5	11
35	FORSTR	20.5	17	30	22	17.5	15
37	INTDEC	2.5	3	10.5	8	10.5	6
38	JOURN	6.5	5	13.5	12	4	4
39	LAWYER	12	10	26	22	16	13
41	MCHNST	5.5	6	10	9	16	13
42	MATHM	22.5	19	16	17	17.5	12
48	OPTMST	30	33	18.5	18	45	39
51	PEDTRN			7	9	26.5	26
52	PERS M	7	9			19	16
54	PHARM	26.5	26	19	16		
57	PHYSN	66.5	71	13.5	17	27	29
58	PLUMBR	8.5	8	11.5	11	17	17
61	POLICE	6	6	14.5	10	8	8
62	POSTCL	14	15	18	13	24.5	22
63	PRNTER	9.5	8	15.5	16	16	11
64	PSYTST	36.5	37	16	16	19	20
65	PSYCCL	25.5	22	21	23	22.5	17
66	PSYCCN	14	12	25.5	27	14.5	13
67	PSYCIN	10.5	7	32.5	29	17.5	13
68	PSYPRF	11	12	19	20	13	14
71	SLSENG	7	4	24	22	19	16
73	SCHSUP	13	11	34.5	31	16	14
74	SOCCWK	13.5	11	35	33	11	12
Mean		14.5	13.1	19.3	18.0	18.3	16.0

TABLE 2 (Continued)

No.	Code	Group 57 PHYSN		Group 58 PLUMBR		Group 61 POLICE	
		A	B	A	B	A	B
3	AC CPA	9.5	6	11	6	11	7
5	ARCH	15.5	10	11.5	10	6	5
6	AUTO M	6.5	7	58	50	33.5	30
8	BANKER	9.5	8	23.5	22	8.5	8
12	BRKLYR	9	9	54	51	29.5	28
13	BDG CN	11.5	10	52	48	19.5	18
15	CRPNTR	13	9	57	53	30	25
17	CHEMST	25.5	23	10.5	9	5.5	5
18	CLTH R	11	11	26	24	13.5	10
19	COMPRG	13.5	11	14.5	12	14	10
26	ELECTR	9.5	7	56.5	58	24.5	24
28	ENGELE	18	16	20	15	10.5	9
31	ENGMCH	11.5	15	24	20	10.5	8
33	FARMER	11.5	8	22	18	9.5	9
35	FORSTR	18.5	15	17	18	5.5	9
37	INTDEC	8	4	4.5	4	7	2
38	JOURN	6.5	5	5	4	3.5	3
39	LAWYER	17.5	14	12	10	10	6
41	MCHNST	7.5	9	34.5	32	23.5	24
42	MATHM	21	15	10	6	4	3
48	OPTMST	41.5	37	19	17	16	13
51	PEDTRN	66.5	71	8.5	8	6	6
52	PERS M	13.5	17	11.5	11	14.5	10
54	PHARM	27	29	17	17	8	8
57	PHYSN			11	10	6.5	5
58	PLUMBR	11	10			29	27
61	POLICE	6.5	5	29	27		
62	POSTCL	15	16	39.5	37	30	27
63	PRNTER	9.5	7	16	13	6.5	6
64	PSYTST	34	38	7	6	7.5	6
65	PSYCCL	24	21	7	5	8	5
66	PSYCCN	20.5	14	6	4	8.5	5
67	PSYCIN	15	10	4.5	4	8.5	6
68	PSYPRF	18	14	5	3	4	2
71	SLSENG	10	6	19	17	11	5
73	SCHSUP	23.5	20	15	16	7	8
74	SOCCWK	17	15	6	9	6.5	9
Mean		16.8	15.1	20.7	18.7	12.7	10.9

TABLE 2 (Continued)

No.	Code	Group 62 POSTCL		Group 63 PRNTER		Group 64 PSYTST	
		A	B	A	B	A	B
3	AC CPA	17.5	11	10	6	5.5	6
5	ARCH	12.5	10	17.5	11	13	11
6	AUTO M	38.5	33	16	10	6.5	5
8	BANKER	26	20	13	8	7	6
12	BRKLYR	33.5	40	8.5	8	10	7
13	BDG CN	28	21	13	10	12.5	9
15	CRPNTR	41	33	12.5	11	9	6
17	CHEMST	13.5	14	7	10	18	17
18	CLTH R	26	24	17.5	20	10	7
19	COMPRG	19	18	10	10	18.5	13
26	ELECTR	37.5	30	11.5	8	8.5	5
28	ENGELE	18.5	16	10.5	12	23.5	19
31	ENGMCH	22	18	14	14	19.5	15
33	FARMER	11.5	7	3.5	3	10.5	5
35	FORSTR	15	14	4	6	17.5	13
37	INTDEC	4	4	12	7	7	5
38	JOURN	6	5	18	16	10	8
39	LAWYER	14.5	14	17.5	15	19.5	14
41	MCHNST	35	32	14	13	5.5	5
42	MATHM	13	11	8	8	32.5	28
48	OPTMST	30.5	29	17.5	16	29	27
51	PEDTRN	14	15	9.5	8	36.5	37
52	PERS M	18	13	15.5	16	16	16
54	PHARM	24.5	22	16	11	19	20
57	PHYSN	15	16	9.5	7	34	38
58	PLUMBR	39.5	37	16	13	7	6
61	POLICE	30	27	6.5	6	7.5	6
62	POSTCL			14	11	13	12
63	PRNTER	14	11			11.5	9
64	PSYTST	13	12	11.5	9		
65	PSYCCL	9.5	8	9.5	9	44.5	44
66	PSYCCN	9	6	15.5	10	20	21
67	PSYCIN	10	6	15.5	9	15	14
68	PSYPRF	5	5	9	8	31	31
71	SLSENG	15.5	13	14	13	8	5
73	SCHSUP	21.5	20	16.5	11	11.5	12
74	SOCCWK	15	13	11.5	9	23	24
Mean		19.9	17.4	12.4	10.3	16.4	14.6

TABLE 2 (Continued)

No.	Code	Group 65 PSYCCL		Group 66 PSYCCN		Group 67 PSYCIN	
		A	B	A	B	A	B
3	AC CPA	8.5	7	6.5	8	13	11
5	ARCH	9.5	10	12.5	11	11	13
6	AUTO M	5	3	5.5	3	6	3
8	BANKER	7	6	7	7	11.5	9
12	BRKLYR	9	5	7	4	8	4
13	BDG CN	9.5	9	8.5	9	14	12
15	CRPNTR	5.5	4	6	3	4.5	4
17	CHEMST	18	18	21	18	23	20
18	CLTH R	8.5	6	14.5	8	15	11
19	COMPRG	13	13	19.5	15	23	23
26	ELECTR	5.5	4	4.5	3	5	4
28	ENGELE	23.5	20	24	24	31	32
31	ENGMCH	23	17	18.5	18	23.5	26
33	FARMER	9.5	5	10	5	12	7
35	FORSTR	18	14	19	15	19	16
37	INTDEC	6	6	4.5	5	13	6
38	JOURN	4.5	7	6.5	8	8	9
39	LAWYER	18.5	12	13.5	11	12	12
41	MCHNST	5.5	4	5.5	4	7.5	4
42	MATHM	27	25	27	25	22.5	23
48	OPTMST	28.5	22	26	20	19.5	16
51	PEDTRN	25.5	22	14	12	10.5	7
52	PERS M	21	23	25.5	27	32.5	29
54	PHARM	22.5	17	14.5	13	17.5	13
57	PHYSN	24	21	20.5	14	15	10
58	PLUMBR	7	5	6	4	4.5	4
61	POLICE	8	5	8.5	5	8.5	6
62	POSTCL	9.5	8	9	6	10	6
63	PRNTER	9.5	9	15.5	10	15.5	9
64	PSYTST	44.5	44	20	21	15	14
65	PSYCCL			66	63	40.5	34
66	PSYCCN	66	63			50.5	47
67	PSYCIN	40.5	34	50.5	47		
68	PSYPRF	55	59	65.5	64	37.5	41
71	SLSENG	9.5	7	16	10	17	16
73	SCHSUP	18	15	20	19	25	19
74	SOCCWK	36	36	31.5	25	23.5	20
Mean		18.3	16.3	18.1	15.7	17.4	15.0

TABLE 2 (Continued)

No.	Code	Group 68 PSYPRF		Group 71 SLSENG		Group 73 SCHSUP	
		A	B	A	B	A	B
3	AC CPA	10	8	21.5	19	8.5	7
5	ARCH	7.5	7	17.5	15	11	8
6	AUTO M	5	2	19	13	10	10
8	BANKER	3.5	5	26	27	18	13
12	BRKLYR	5	3	14.5	12	16.5	13
13	BDG CN	7.5	7	35.5	31	22	19
15	CRPNTR	4	3	17.5	13	11.5	13
17	CHEMST	25	24	18	19	16.5	16
18	CLTH R	9	6	28	23	18	14
19	COMPRG	19	15	19.5	18	15	11
26	ELECTR	3	2	22.5	16	12.5	12
28	ENGELE	27.5	24	51	53	33	34
31	ENGMCH	21.5	19	39.5	44	22	21
33	FARMER	8.5	5	19.5	15	19	19
35	FORSTR	19.5	15	27	26	28.5	25
37	INTDEC	4	3	10	7	5	2
38	JOURN	11.5	9	3	3	6	7
39	LAWYER	21	18	11	11	25.5	22
41	MCHNST	4	3	17.5	16	12.5	12
42	MATHM	35	34	11	11	17.5	12
48	OPTMST	17.5	16	17	18	19	18
51	PEDTRN	11	12	7	4	13	10
52	PERS M	19	20	24	22	34.5	31
54	PHARM	13	14	19	16	16	14
57	PHYSN	18	14	10	6	23.5	20
58	PLUMBR	5	3	19	17	15	16
61	POLICE	4	2	11	5	7	8
62	POSTCL	5	5	15.5	13	21.5	20
63	PRNTER	9	8	14	13	16.5	11
64	PSYTST	31	31	8	5	11.5	12
65	PSYCCL	55	59	9.5	7	18	15
66	PSYCCN	65.5	64	16	10	20	19
67	PSYCIN	37.5	41	17	16	25	19
68	PSYPRF			7.5	8	20.5	18
71	SLSENG	7.5	8			14.5	12
73	SCHSUP	20.5	18	14.5	12		
74	SOCCWK	32	28	10	7	24.5	20
Mean		16.7	15.4	18.0	15.8	17.5	15.4

TABLE 2 (Continued)

		Group 74 SOCCWK					
No.	Code	A	B	No.	Code	A	B
3	AC CPA	10.5	11	42	MATHM	20.5	19
5	ARCH	14.5	11	48	OPTMST	21.5	19
6	AUTO M	6	5	51	PEDTRN	13.5	11
8	BANKER	8	9	52	PERS M	35	33
12	BRKLYR	6.5	9	54	PHARM	11	12
13	BDG CN	12	11	57	PHYSN	17	15
15	CRPNTR	8	8	58	PLUMBR	6	9
17	CHEMST	10.5	9	61	POLICE	6.5	9
18	CLTH R	18	11	62	POSTCL	15	13
19	COMPRG	16	12	63	PRNTER	11.5	9
26	ELECTR	7	6	64	PSYTST	23	24
28	ENGELE	21.5	18	65	PSYCCL	36	36
31	ENGMCH	18	13	66	PSYCCN	31.5	25
33	FARMER	7	7	67	PSYCIN	23.5	20
35	FORSTR	16	14	68	PSYPRF	32	28
37	INTDEC	6.5	4	71	SLSENG	10	7
38	JOURN	8	8	73	SCHSUP	24.5	20
39	LAWYER	17.5	13	74	SOCCWK		
41	MCHNST	7	6				
				Mean		15.5	13.7

Degree of Differentiation
Attained by Different Systems

Next, let us see how the system described in this chapter works in practice as compared with the working of a system based on a general reference group. Six cross validation groups that had filled out the Occupational Interest Survey were studied. There were 90 cases each of journalists, architects, foresters, professors of psychology, pediatricians, and automobile mechanics. We first applied Preference Board Form D scales, which had been developed with the use of a general reference group. The scores were converted into standard scores based on the means and standard deviations of the original criterion groups in accordance with Strong's procedure. Then for each pair of occupations the number of errors of classification was obtained.

In comparing journalists with architects, it was found, for example, that five journalists obtained higher scores for Architect than for their own occupation. Nine architects obtained higher scores on the Journalist key than on the Architect key. Of the 180 journalists and architects involved, fourteen therefore were classified in the wrong occupation on the basis of scales developed with the use of a general reference group. Then the OIS scores were compared for the same two occupations. It was found that four journalists obtained higher scores as architects than as journalists, and four architects obtained higher scores as journalists. There thus were eight errors of classification.

This procedure was carried through for all the fifteen pairings that can be made when six groups are involved. On the general reference group scales, the subjects obtained a higher score in the occupation not their own in 209 of the comparisons. This was 47 percent greater than the 142 errors obtained when OIS scores were used.

Details for all the pairings are presented in table 3. In only three of the fifteen comparisons reported in table 3 are the lambda errors of classification greater than the general reference group errors. These differences are very small, namely, 1, 1, and 3. (Although the 15 comparisons reported above the diagonal are identical to those below the diagonal, the duplicate figures are reported for ease of reference.)

These results justify the optimism generated by the logic of the situation. The fundamental validity of an interest inventory can be improved substantially by eliminating the use of a general reference group. It seems likely that use of a general reference group would produce better differentiation only by accident, that is, because of chance variations in samples.

An article by Lefkowitz (1970) should be noted at this time, not because it is pertinent to the question of using a general reference group in developing occupational scales, but because the title appears to be pertinent. Failure to mention it here might be inter-

TABLE 3

COMPARISON OF ERRORS OF CLASSIFICATION (EC), CORRECT CLASSIFICATIONS (CC), AND TIES FOR SIX OCCUPATIONAL GROUPS, OBTAINED FROM TWO SCORING SYSTEMS

(N = 90 in each of six cross-validation groups)

Occupational Group	System	Architect			Automobile Mechanic			Forester			Journalist			Pediatrician			Psychology Professor		
		EC	CC	Ties	EC	CC	Ties	EC	CC	Ties	EC	CC	Ties	EC	CC	Ties	EC	CC	Ties
Architect	Gen. Ref.	--	--	--	15	164	1	24	152	4	14	164	2	13	162	5	11	164	5
	OIS Scales	--	--	--	13	166	1	25	153	2	8	172	0	10	170	0	7	171	2
Automobile Mechanic	Gen. Ref.	15	164	1	--	--	--	19	159	2	3	177	0	11	168	1	3	177	0
	OIS Scales	13	166	1	--	--	--	12	162	6	2	178	0	6	173	1	4	176	0
Forester	Gen. Ref.	24	152	4	19	159	2	--	--	--	10	169	1	18	162	0	14	165	1
	OIS Scales	25	153	2	12	162	6	--	--	--	5	174	1	15	162	3	17	163	0
Journalist	Gen. Ref.	14	164	2	3	177	0	10	169	1	--	--	--	12	166	2	14	163	3
	OIS Scales	8	172	0	2	178	0	5	174	1	--	--	--	3	175	2	8	168	4
Pediatrician	Gen. Ref.	13	162	5	11	168	1	18	162	0	12	166	2	--	--	--	28	145	7
	OIS Scales	10	170	0	6	173	1	15	162	3	3	175	2	--	--	--	7	170	3
Psychology Professor	Gen. Ref.	11	164	5	3	177	0	14	165	1	14	163	3	28	145	7	--	--	--
	OIS Scales	7	171	2	4	176	0	17	163	0	8	168	4	7	170	3	--	--	--

NOTE: The column entries represent, respectively, the number of errors of classification, correct classifications, and ties found when the 90 members of each of two occupations being compared were classified into one of the two occupations, first on scales developed with the use of a general reference group, and then on the basis of OIS scales. (Reprinted from Occupational Interest Survey General Manual, Kuder DD, c 1975, 1968, 1966 G. Frederic Kuder.

preted to mean that an actual comparison of the two systems was being ignored. Despite the title — "Comparison of the Strong Vocational Interest Blank and the Kuder Occupational Interest Survey Scoring Procedures" — the article turns out to be a comparison of a Lefkowitz system and the Kuder system applied to SVIB items.

The distinguishing feature of the Strong scoring procedure is the use of a representative reference group of men in general or women in general as the basis for developing occupational scales. Lefkowitz's reference group, on the other hand, consisted only of men in a narrow range of occupations, all within the field of engineering. It cannot be considered to be equivalent to a Strong general reference group as used in the development of scales for the SVIB.

Theoretically, the Lefkowitz system of using a job family as a reference group falls somewhere between the Strong and Kuder procedures in its capacity for distinguishing between groups. It can be expected to differentiate better than the Strong procedure and less well than the Kuder procedure, except for those rare exceptions that might occur by chance or through inequities or errors in applying the systems. Which procedure it would resemble more in specific applications would depend on how restricted the Lefkowitz reference groups were made.

Lefkowitz interpreted his results to mean that his procedure is somewhat superior to the Kuder procedure. Before any generalization is justified, however, the study should be extended to other job families and should certainly include answers to the Occupational Interest Survey. There are also some aspects of the Lefkowitz study as noted by Zytowski (1973, p. 14) that indicate a replication is in order.

In any case, the Lefkowitz system is not likely to become practical in the foreseeable future, since a formidable program of research and development would have to be undertaken in order to make it operational. The program would require the construction of specialty scales for the occupations within each of many job families, with a different reference group for each job family. Then it would be necessary to develop a sound system for interpreting the differently based scores to counselees.

Since Lefkowitz decided to try out his own system on answers to the Strong Vocational Interest Blank, it would have been most appropriate to make his comparison with the Strong procedure for which he had the data readily at hand. It is pertinent to note that the Kuder scoring procedure was developed for use with the type of inventory described in chapter 2, and that the principles listed in that chapter are an integral part of the system.

It is appropriate to mention that Zytowski (1972) has studied the relative accuracy of the entire Strong and Kuder systems — that is, the Strong scoring procedure applied to the SVIB versus the Kuder scoring procedure applied to the KOIS — using the same subjects. He found the Kuder system significantly superior to the Strong system (at the 0.01 level) "in terms of comparing each inventory's ability to rank Ss' [subjects'] own occupations high." (p. 249)

Zytowski has more recently (1976) completed the most comprehensive follow-up study of specific occupational interest scores yet made. His subjects were among those used in early studies or in the actual development of the Kuder Occupational Interest Survey. He found that at the time of the follow-up (fifteen to nineteen years later), "Fifty-one percent were employed in an occupation that would have been suggested to them had their inventory been interpreted to them." The comparable figure obtained by Strong (1955) in his follow-up study was forty-five percent.

Although the interval between testings was similar for the two studies and both involved relatively large numbers of subjects (663 for Strong, 882 for Zytowski), certain differences should be noted. All of Strong's subjects, but only a few of Zytowski's subjects, received reports of their scores following the initial testing. Strong's college men were almost evenly divided between undergraduate and graduate school. Most of Zytowski's subjects, on the other hand, were in high school, and the rest were undergraduates in college. It therefore is not surprising that a broader range of occupations is represented in the Zytowski study. It seems likely that fewer of Zytowski's subjects had decided on an occupation at the time of taking the first test.

Perhaps the greatest contribution of the method described in this chapter will be in discriminating similar occupations from each other. The general reference group approach has not been very successful in differentiating within broad groups of similar occupations. This does not mean that a certain inventory cannot be used to differentiate occupations within these broad groups. It merely reflects the fact that responses with large differences between the reference group and the broad groups are not identical with those that are best for differentiating among the specific occupations in the broad group.

Some attempts have been made to meet this situation by using averages of these broad groups as the reference group. Sometimes the averages for the broad group, with the exception of the one occupation for which a key is being developed, have been used. If the reasoning involved is carried to its logical conclusion, the problem becomes one of differentiating among a number of specific occupations, which is exactly what OIS scores are designed to do with much less effort.

The success of the system described above depends in large measure upon the adequacy with which the domain of relevant interests is represented as called for in principle 2. In the discussion of that principle and the accompanying model, it was noted that in order to make the task even possible, approximations must be employed. In the case of the OIS, even these required several years to carry out.

It was assumed at the outset that use of the forced choice form of item would tend to spread out the items in factorial space around each centroid. For example, when an artistic activity is compared with a literary activity, the item achieves a different position in space than when an artistic activity is compared with a computational activity. Both responses, however, fall into an artistic cluster.

It was decided that since all the fifteen areas in the author's previous interest inventories had been found to be related to vocational choice, they should be represented in the new inventory. It also was decided to include two other variables that seemed to have some promise on the basis of evidence accumulated over a period of several years. These areas had to do with the preferences for working independently and for acting impulsively. It also was stipulated that the centroids of the clusters of items representing each of the seventeen areas should be kept as nearly independent as possible.

For the purpose of keeping correlations among the centroids of the clusters as low as possible, a modification of the criterion vector method of test construction (Kuder, 1954; see also appendix A) was used. As originally formulated, this method involves building up a test or scale by selecting items so that the scores for the composite of items will have as nearly as possible the same order of correlations with tests in an experimental battery as does the criterion. In this case, of course, the desirable correlation of the composite of items in one area with the composites in other areas is zero. The extent to which this objective of low intercorrelations was accomplished is reflected in table 4, which reports the intercorrelations obtained when the responses chosen to represent each factor were scored.

Comparison of the Degree of Discrimination Achieved
with Criterion and Cross-Validation Groups

The percentage of correct classifications obtained in the study of six cross-validation groups reported in table 3 turned out to be 94.7. In order to find out how close this was to the differentiation obtained in the original criterion groups used in establishing the scoring system, samples of criterion groups corresponding to those in the cross-validation study were included in the study reported in table 3. A compilation of the results from these six samples of criterion groups reveals that in the 3000 comparisons involved, 95.3 percent of the classifications were correct.

In computing the above percentages, tied scores were classified as correct. If tied scores are classified as incorrect, the percentages of correct classifications are 93.8 for the cross-validation study and 94.4 for the criterion group study. In each case, the difference between the cross-validation and criterion estimates is less than 1 percent.

Strong concluded long ago that cross-validation studies are not greatly superior to studies based on criterion groups in checking the degree of discrimination achieved if the scoring system is based on samples of sufficient size to begin with — that is, if the number of cases is in the range he used. The results reported above appear to confirm his position.

Intercorrelations

Since the scales that were derived for the purpose of discriminating between occupational groups are the difference scales, it is logical that intercorrelations should be computed among the difference scales for the purpose of making a factor analysis or even for developing a picture of the interrelations of the scales being used. On the face of it the task is so great that it seems ridiculous even to consider it.

At the least, this operation would involve 2926 variables for the male occupational groups for which scores are reported; 666 for the female occupational groups; 406 for the male college majors groups; and 171 for the female college major groups. The number of intercorrelations involved would be 4,279,275 for the male occupational groups alone!

Since the difference scores are a function of occupational scores, intercorrelations among one set are a function of the intercorrelations among the other. It is possible to work out a pro-

TABLE 4
INTERCORRELATIONS OF SCORES FOR 17 AREAS REPRESENTED IN THE OIS
(N = 250 men from the Form D norm group)

Scale	0. Outdoor	1. Mechanical	2. Computational	3. Scientific	4. Persuasive	5. Artistic	6. Literary	7. Musical	8. Social Service	9. Clerical	10. Preference for being active in groups	11. Preference for familiar and stable situations	12. Preference for working with ideas	13. Preference for avoiding conflict	14. Preference for directing or influencing others	15. Preference for working independently	16. Preference for acting spontaneously
0. Outdoor		-.12	-.12	-.04	-.01	-.05	.07	-.12	-.10	.08	-.28	-.32	-.15	-.02	-.15	.10	-.11
1. Mechanical	-.12		-.22	-.20	-.09	-.19	-.18	.01	-.14	-.08	-.08	-.02	-.20	-.13	-.18	.17	-.05
2. Computational	-.12	-.22		-.08	-.07	-.14	-.10	-.04	-.15	.33	-.01	.02	-.02	-.08	.03	-.08	-.02
3. Scientific	-.04	-.20	-.08		-.06	.05	.11	-.05	.03	-.29	.04	-.08	.38	-.03	.12	-.05	.06
4. Persuasive	-.01	-.09	-.07	-.06		.02	-.03	-.09	.16	-.32	.28	-.02	-.10	.03	.14	-.08	.03
5. Artistic	-.05	-.19	-.14	.05	.02		.01	-.13	.03	-.21	.03	-.14	.13	.08	-.01	-.08	.15
6. Literary	.07	-.18	-.10	.11	-.03	.01		-.16	-.14	-.10	-.13	-.06	.17	.15	-.06	-.07	.10
7. Musical	-.12	.01	-.04	-.05	-.09	-.13	-.16		-.04	-.05	-.01	-.01	.05	-.03	-.13	-.07	.12
8. Social Service	-.10	-.14	-.15	.03	.16	.03	-.14	-.04		-.23	.18	.22	.16	-.01	.10	-.13	.00

Area	0	1	2	3	4	5	6	7	8	9	10	11	12	13	14	15	16
9. Clerical	.08	-.08	.33	-.29	-.32	-.21	-.10	-.05	-.23		-.37	.17	-.21	.07	-.36	.12	-.26
10. Preference for being active in groups	-.28	-.08	-.01	.04	.28	.03	-.13	-.01	.18	-.37		-.19	.10	-.06	.33	-.30	.06
11. Preference for familiar and stable situations	.32	-.02	.02	-.08	-.02	-.14	-.06	-.01	.22	.17	-.19		-.01	.12	-.19	-.12	-.13
12. Preference for working with ideas	-.15	-.20	-.02	.38	.13	.17	.05	.16	-.21	.10	-.01			.20	.02	-.27	.10
13. Preference for avoiding conflict	-.02	-.13	-.08	-.03	.03	.08	.15	-.03	-.01	.07	-.06	.12	.20		-.15	-.07	-.13
14. Preference for directing or influencing others	-.15	-.18	.03	.12	.14	-.01	-.06	-.13	.10	-.36	.33	-.19	.02	-.15		-.19	.16
15. Preference for working independently	.10	.17	-.08	-.05	-.08	-.07	-.07	-.13	.12	-.30	-.12	-.07	-.19				-.08
16. Preference for acting spontaneously in a carefree manner	-.11	-.05	-.02	.06	.03	.15	.10	.12	.00	-.26	.06	-.13	.10	-.13	.16	-.08	

NOTE: Areas 0 through 9 include items representative of scales 0 through 9 of the Kuder Preference Record, Form C; areas 10 through 14 include items representative of scales A, B, C, D, and E of the Kuder Preference Record, Personal; and areas 15 and 16 are areas that overlap relatively little with the others and have been found to have some relation to occupational choice. (Reprinted from Occupational Interest Survey, General Manual, Kuder DD, © 1975, 1968, 1966 G. Frederic Kuder.)

gram for the intercorrelations of difference scores starting with the raw occupational scores, and to obtain average intercorrelations for subsets of scores. This task is a formidable and expensive one and has not been done.

Although intercorrelations have not been obtained for difference scores, some hypotheses can be formed concerning them.

1. They probably would have a much wider range than correlations among occupational scores.
2. The intercorrelations of a set of difference scales that involve subtracting one specific occupational score from all other occupational scores in turn would be positive.

The *raw* Occupational Interest Survey scores, on the other hand, must be evaluated and interpreted in terms of the difference scores that can be derived from them. The intercorrelations among occupational scores tend to be misleadingly high because of the common variance. One is likely to look at them and decide that a large number of them measure so nearly the same thing that surely some of them are unnecessary. This conclusion may well be true in certain cases. It is possible, however, for difference scores to discriminate fairly well between two groups in spite of a substantial correlation between the two corresponding occupational scores. The exact point of demarcation has yet to be determined. In the meantime, the philosophy being followed is that it is better to run the risk that the information being supplied may be redundant than to run the risk of its being inadequate.

Lambdas and Centours

It can be noted that lambda scores have much in common with the centour scores used by Rulon, Tiedeman, Tatsuoka, and Langmuir (1967) in their classification system. The fundamental concepts involved are strikingly similar. Both approaches are based on the idea that a person can be located in space relative to a number of independent variables and relative to the centers of various defined groups located in the same space. Both models call for a consideration of all possible comparisons. When a person's lambda scores on a number of occupations are compared, they furnish a basis for estimating in which group the person "belongs," and centour scores can be used in the same way. Both kinds of scores are intended for purposes of classification and assignment; in no way do they reflect relative standing within groups. The highest lambda or centour indicates the group in which the individual should be classified, other things being equal. All things considered, a high relation between lambda scores and centour scores is likely within the same domain for each individual.

A centour score is an indication of how close a score is to the central tendency of the group in a very special sense. Thus a centour score of 90 means that the subject's position in hyperspace is on a contour line that separates the 10 percent of the subjects closest to the center from the others. The points on the contour are not necessarily or even usually equidistant from the center of the cluster. In the two-dimensional case, the cluster of points formed by a group might be oval in shape. People at different places on the 90 percent contour therefore could be at quite different distances from the center of gravity. The center of the cluster of scores representing the group would be represented by a centour score of 100.

The reference axes for centours are independent variables. The test space that can be covered is a square for two dimensions, a cube for three dimensions, and so on, assuming for practical purposes that there is a finite limit to the theoretically infinite extent of a normal distribution. The individual subject is located at a point in space.

A lambda score, on the other hand, is a measure of similarity expressed in terms of correlation. A score of 1.00 represents the highest possible correspondence between the answers of an individual and the average answers of a specified group. A person can be represented as a vector in space, with that person's nearness to vectors representing occupational groups and to general reference vectors expressed in terms of correlations. The test space involved is a circle for two dimensions, a sphere for three dimensions, and so on. In the idealized theoretical form, both systems presumably would work equally well. For the practical situation a number of considerations would enter into the decision to use one or the other. Although the centour approach is easily applied to two or three variables, it becomes extremely cumbersome for the larger number of variables typical of the usual guidance or placement situation. Modifications introduced to overcome this difficulty reduce the precision of classification.

It hardly seems possible that scores obtained by such divergent methods could have anything in common. In obtaining centour scores, an individual's responses are first scored for a number of independent scales. The scores are then converted into centour scores by means of formulas or tables. Lambda scores, on the other hand, are based on the weighted scoring of items, the weights being the proportions of the specific group who marked each response. These totals are then adjusted for differences in homogeneity from group to group so that the upper limit for each score is 1.00. The centour method might well lead, however, to a different philosophy of item selection than that employed for the Occupational Interest Survey. The OIS was constructed with the idea of having items well distributed in space. The theoretically desirable distribution for the two-space situation is shown in figure 1 (see p. 14).

Since centour scores are based on test scores and high reliability is a necessary characteristic of scores, items with high correlations with each factor would naturally be chosen for inclusion in each scale. Items also would be selected that were nearly pure measures (negative or positive) of the factors, with the expectation that items would be in tight clusters about the test vectors.

In the latter case, items would not only be clustered closer together in the space represented in figure 1, but those in each cluster would probably appear to the subject to be similar. There might well be a greater impression of repetitiousness, at least in the case of interest inventories.

Nevertheless, for each subject there should be a fairly high relation (though probably not linear) between centour scores and lambda scores for instruments covering the same domain, whether it be the domain of interests or the whole field of human characteristics. Which system will lead to better discrimination for the same amount of effort remains to be seen. The two models are set up for the same purpose and presumably would accomplish it equally well if the requirements were fully met. In neither case, however, is it practical to satisfy the theoretical requirements fully. The unanswered question is whether the modifications forced by practical considerations cause less loss in the effectiveness of one system than in the other.

REFERENCES

Campbell, D. P. The Minnesota Vocational Interest Inventory. *Personnel and Guidance Journal*, 1966, *44*, 854-858.

Clemans, W. V. An index of item-criterion relationship. *Educational and Psychological Measurement*, 1958, *18*, 167-172.

Clemans, W. V. Interest measurement and the concept of ipsativity. *Measurement and Evaluation in Guidance*, 1968, *1*, 50-55.

Findley, W. G. A rationale for evaluation of item discrimination statistics. *Educational and Psychological Measurement*, 1956, *16*, 175-180.

Kuder, G. F. Expected developments in interest and personality inventories. *Educational and Psychological Measurement*, 1954, *14*, 265-271.

Lefkowitz, D. M. Comparison of the Strong Vocational Interest Blank and the Kuder Occupational Interest Survey scoring procedures. *Journal of Consulting Psychology*, 1970, *17*, 357-363.

Olejnik, S., and Porter, A. C. An empirical investigation comparing the effectiveness of four scoring strategies on the Kuder Occupational Interest Survey, Form DD. *Educational and Psychological Measurement*, 1975, *35*, 37-46.

Rulon, P. J., Tiedeman, D. V., Tatsuoka, M. M., and Langmuir, C. R. *Multivariate statistics for personnel classification.* New York: Wiley, 1967.

Strong, E. K., Jr. *Vocational interests 18 years after college.* Minneapolis: University of Minnesota Press, 1955.

Tilton, J. W. The measurement of overlapping. *Journal of Educational Psychology*, 1937, *28*, 656-662.

Zytowski, D. G. A concurrent test of accuracy-of-classification for the Strong Vocational Interest and Kuder Occupational Interest Survey. *Journal of Vocational Behavior*, 1972, *2*, 245-250.

Zytowski, D. G., ed. *Contemporary approached to interest measurement.* Minneapolis: University of Minnesota Press, 1973, pp. 14, 116-135.

Zytowski, D. G. Predictive validity of the Kuder Occupational Interest Survey: A 12- to 19-year follow-up. *Journal of Counseling Psychology*, 1976, *23*, 221-233.

4

Some Special Aspects of Interests

Score Distances Between Groups

An occupational group can be thought of as a cluster of individuals located in multidimensional space according to its members' interests, with the compactness of the cluster depending on the homogeneity of the interests of the group. A specific group will be closer to some groups than to others, needless to say, and a considerable intermingling of the members of the clusters that are close together can be expected.

The difference score between any two occupational groups (as illustrated for journalists and architects in fig. 5, p. 45) can be thought of as representing the distance between the centers of the two groups in space. The distances on the 23,436 scales involved in the comparisons within the 217 groups listed in table 1 have been computed, although limitations of space prevent reporting all of them here. A number of the distances have been illustrated in chapter 3.

As a further example, the score distances of architects from other occupational groups and college major groups are listed in table 5. As might be expected, the interests of architects are closest to those of college men majoring in architecture, the score distance being .114. Nor is it surprising that the interests of architects are close to those of photographers, interior decorators, engineers, and art majors also. Of all the groups listed, the interests of department store saleswomen are least like those of architects, the score distance being .567. Among the male groups, the interests of truck drivers and carpenters are least like those of architects. This finding concerning carpenters comes as a mild surprise. It appears that although architects may be very much interested in what carpenters produce, they have little in common with carpenters as far as enjoyment of specific activities is concerned.

On the other hand, carpenters are even more distant from research workers in the field of social welfare than they are from architects; the distance is .645, as shown in table 6. This is the greatest distance of carpenters from other groups of employed men. It is also the greatest separation found between any two male occupational groups. The group with which carpenters really have the fewest interests in common, however, is that of college women majoring in drama; the score distance is .841. It would be hard to find two groups more disparate than these two. There is one pairing in the entire study, however, that shows the even greater score distance of .884. This is the one between machinists and college women majoring in drama.

Other wide disparities can be noted. The greatest distance between groups of employed women is the one of .517 between department store saleswomen and clinical psychologists. Among groups of college men, the greatest distance is .585 between majors in agriculture and art; among groups of college women, it is .469 between majors in drama and students preparing to be Catholic teaching sisters.

These figures illustrate the fact that there is considerable variation in the extent to which people in one group resemble people in other groups. Some groups have much in common with others and some seem to stand almost alone. In table 7 male occupational groups are listed in order of their closeness to other male occupational groups as measured by median score distance, and in table 8 female occupational groups are listed in order of their nearness to other female occupational groups. Inspection of these tables reveals two cases of striking agreement in the rankings of certain occupations common to both lists. Motel managers are first on the male list and are tied for second place on the female list. Interior decorators are last on both lists. A starting point for speculation and research is furnished by the striking difference between the largest distances reported in the two tables. The distances are .432 and .292 for men and women, respectively.

The fact that men and women motel managers are high on their respective lists does not mean their interests are particularly close, though it does mean that each group is highly typical of its own sex. The two groups are actually much closer to other men and other women, respectively, than they are to each other, as revealed in tables 9 and 10, which list in order the score distances of these groups from other groups in the study. The score distance between the two groups of motel managers is .320.

A quite different situation exists with respect to men and women interior decorators. The interests of these two groups are much closer to each other than they are to those of any other groups, male or female, as revealed in tables 11 and 12.

TABLE 5

MEAN SCORE DISTANCE OF MALE ARCHITECTS (NO. 5)
FROM OTHER GROUPS

Employed Men			College Men			Employed Women			College Women		
55	PHOTOG	.133	139	MARCH	.114	110	FINTDC	.200	168	GARTED	.296
37	INTDEC	.140	140	MARTED	.205	96	FCMPRG	.223	178	GMATH	.327
27	ENGCVL	.165	147	MELED	.243	112	FLAWYR	.271	176	GHISTO	.328
29	ENGHAC	.176	153	MFRNLG	.246	119	FOCCTH	.286	183	GPSYCH	.344
32	ENG MM	.179	158	MMUSIC	.261	124	FPSY	.298	182	GPOLYS	.352
11	BKSMGR	.184	151	MENGMH	.272	94	FBKMGR	.309	174	GFRNLG	.359
31	ENGMCH	.190	149	MENGCL	.275	122	FPHYTH	.311	170	GBUSGN	.368
82	TRVLAG	.197	165	MSOC	.280	125	FPSYCL	.313	181	GPHYED	.377
80	STATCN	.201	157	MMATH	.282	90	FACNT	.315	177	GHMEC	.380
19	COMPRG	.201	150	MENGEL	.283	98	F DEAN	.329	169	GBIOSC	.385
47	NRSRYM	.208	160	MPHYSC	.292	126	FPSYCN	.338	179	GMUSIC	.401
39	LAWYER	.212	156	MLAW	.292	101	FDTNAD	.342	173	GENGL	.402
17	CHEMST	.215	154	MFORST	.295	121	FPEDRN	.345	185	GSOCSC	.404
34	FLORST	.215	155	MHIST	.300	131	FSOCGR	.346	172	GELED	.411
28	ENGELE	.218	146	MECON	.305	107	FFLRST	.356	186	GSOC	.413
42	MATHM	.219	148	MENGCH	.307	104	FDTHOS	.361	175	GHELTH	.421
71	SLSENG	.225	145	MBSMGT	.309	103	FDTCOM	.364	171	GDRMA	.428
48	OPTMST	.227	166	MAFCAD	.310	133	FSOCPS	.370	180	GNURSE	.493
44	METEOR	.229	143	MBSGEN	.314	105	FDTSCH	.374	184	GCATHS	.558
22	DNTIST	.230	163	MPSY	.317	117	FNUTRN	.375			
74	SOCCWK	.282									
3	AC CPA	.285									
54	PHARM	.287									
56	PHYTHR	.287									
20	COUNHS	.287									
78	SOCRES	.296									
59	PLMBCN	.297									
88	X RAY	.297									
43	MATHHS	.299									
8	BANKER	.304									
85	U PSTR	.306									
38	JOURN	.306									
76	SOCWKM	.307									
4	AC IND	.309									
75	SOCWKG	.309									
60	PODRST	.309									
45	MINIST	.310									
36	INS AG	.310									
73	SCHSUP	.310									
89	YMCASC	.315									

No.	Code	Value
30	ENGIND	.234
70	REALES	.235
2	AC	.235
64	PSYTST	.238
51	PEDTRN	.242
69	RADSTA	.243
40	LIBRAR	.245
13	BDG CN	.250
14	BUYER	.254
52	PERS M	.256
16	CC EX	.256
35	FORSTR	.257
18	CLTH R	.257
1	AC AAA	.259
68	PSYPRF	.262
63	PRNTER	.263
46	MTLMGR	.263
67	PSYCIN	.266
23	DPTSTS	.266
65	PSYCCL	.271
84	TV REP	.274
66	PSYCCN	.274
7	BAKER	.277
77	SOCPSY	.280

No.	Code	Value
72	SCITHS	.319
57	PHYSN	.320
24	DRCTFN	.320
25	EDNWSP	.322
79	SOCSCH	.329
49	OSTPTH	.330
81	SUPVFM	.334
9	BARBER	.343
50	PNTR H	.343
12	BRKLYR	.345
86	VETRN	.354
10	BKKPR	.361
62	POSTCL	.369
26	ELECTR	.371
21	COAGAG	.372
58	PLUMBR	.377
61	POLICE	.384
53	PHAR S	.385
87	WELDER	.402
41	MCHNST	.404
33	FARMER	.407
6	AUTO M	.419
15	CRPNTR	.422
83	TRKDRV	.482

No.	Code	Value
152	MENGL	.322
167	MWPCAD	.329
144	MBSMRK	.329
141	MBIOSC	.333
161	MPOLYS	.338
159	MPHYED	.349
164	MCATHB	.359
142	MBUSAC	.364
162	MPREMD	.367
137	MAG	.382
138	MANLHS	.395

No.	Code	Value
130	FSOCCW	.379
108	FHMDEM	.383
113	FLIBR	.384
115	FMTLMR	.386
102	FDTCDM	.386
132	FSOCMD	.399
128	FSCTHS	.404
134	FSOCSC	.406
97	FCHSHS	.407
109	FHOMEC	.407
136	FX RAY	.409
114	FMATHS	.413
95	FCTLIB	.420
118	FNUTIN	.423
129	FSECY	.424
106	FDYTHR	.424
111	FKYPCH	.431
123	FPRSCT	.440
127	FRELED	.443
92	FBEAUT	.462
99	FDNTAS	.466
116	FNURSE	.474
135	FSTENO	.477
93	FBKKPR	.489
120	FOFCLK	.514
91	FBNKCL	.523
100	FDPTSW	.567

TABLE 6
MEAN SCORE DISTANCE OF MALE CARPENTERS (NO. 15) FROM OTHER GROUPS

Employed Men						College Men			Employed Women			College Women		
6	AUTO M	.039	73	SCHSUP	.340	137	MAG	.291	92	FBEAUT	.388	181	GPHYED	.505
26	ELECTR	.040	49	OSTPTH	.341	154	MFORST	.310	115	FMTLMR	.416	178	GMATH	.550
58	PLUMBR	.043	71	SLSENG	.343	149	MENGCL	.311	93	FBKKPR	.420	170	GBUSGN	.588
41	MCHNST	.044	18	CLTH R	.343	138	MANLHS	.315	136	FX RAY	.435	184	GCATHS	.591
87	WELDER	.047	30	ENGIND	.346	151	MENGMH	.338	100	FDPTSW	.438	175	GHELTH	.598
50	PNTR H	.049	55	PHOTOG	.349	159	MPHYED	.344	120	FOFCLK	.439	180	GNURSE	.610
12	BRKLYR	.056	57	PHYSN	.355	150	MENGEL	.382	107	FFLRST	.447	177	GHMEC	.612
83	TRKDRV	.085	2	AC	.371	147	MELED	.402	91	FBNKCL	.455	169	GBIOSC	.652
81	SUPVFM	.088	82	TRVLAG	.372	164	MCATHB	.416	111	FKYPCH	.480	172	GELED	.679
13	BDG CN	.092	72	SCITHS	.377	143	MBSGEN	.424	108	FHMDEM	.482	176	GHISTO	.687
59	PLMBCN	.105	48	OPTMST	.380	145	MBSMGT	.427	122	FPHYTH	.483	185	GSOCSC	.690
62	POSTCL	.109	89	YMCASC	.413	148	MENGCH	.447	135	FSTENO	.487	186	GSOC	.692
9	BARBER	.137	19	COMPRG	.414	142	MBUSAC	.451	102	FDTCDM	.489	174	GFLRNG	.704
84	TV REP	.151	69	RADSTA	.416	157	MMATH	.459	114	FMATHS	.490	183	GPSYCH	.724
46	MTLMGR	.160	5	ARCH	.422	160	MPHYSC	.490	116	FNURSE	.493	179	GMUSIC	.728
61	POLICE	.167	52	PERS M	.428	144	MBSMRK	.490	99	FDNTAS	.495	168	GARTED	.752
10	BKKPR	.169	42	MATHM	.430	166	MAFCAD	.494	105	FDTSCH	.502	182	GPOLYS	.754
33	FARMER	.193	16	CC EX	.435	167	MWPCAD	.499	129	FSECY	.504	173	GENGL	.821
7	BAKER	.195	20	COUNHS	.438	146	MECON	.500	90	FACNT	.507	171	GDRMA	.841
14	BUYER	.205	4	AC IND	.441	162	MPREMD	.528	106	FDTTHR	.528			

24	DRCTFN	.211	51	PEDTRN	.446	165	MSOC	.533	119	FOCCTH	.435
8	BANKER	.213	39	LAWYER	.449	139	MARCH	.536	123	FPRSCT	.535
35	FORSTR	.225	17	CHEMST	.456	141	MBIOSC	.557	103	FDTCOM	.537
88	X RAY	.231	53	PHAR S	.463	153	MFRNLG	.576	96	FCMPRG	.543
34	FLORST	.242	60	PODRST	.469	156	MLAW	.592	101	FDTNAD	.544
63	PRNTER	.246	25	EDNWSP	.475	158	MMUSIC	.605	104	FDTHOS	.551
23	DPTSTS	.248	3	AC CPA	.493	155	MHIST	.618	94	FBKMGR	.568
27	ENGCVL	.252	76	SOCWKM	.497	163	MPSY	.636	128	FSCTHS	.580
36	INS AG	.261	38	JOURN	.498	140	MARTED	.664	109	FHOMEC	.603
21	COAGAG	.272	45	MINIST	.498	161	MPOLYS	.668	118	FNUTIN	.623
29	ENGHAC	.276	74	SOCCWK	.514	152	MENGL	.732	113	FLIBR	.626
22	DNTIST	.277	80	STATCN	.516				117	FNUTRN	.628
28	ENGELE	.279	40	LIBRAR	.532				95	FCTLIB	.629
47	NRSRYM	.284	77	SOCPSY	.543				97	FCHSHS	.630
70	REALES	.286	68	PSYPRF	.547				112	FLAWYR	.639
31	ENGMCH	.291	64	PSYTST	.547				131	FSOCGR	.640
43	MATHHS	.292	67	PSYCIN	.553				98	F DEAN	.642
86	VETRN	.293	66	PSYCCN	.566				134	FSOCSC	.655
54	PHARM	.296	75	SOCWKG	.568				130	FSOCCW	.677
32	ENG MM	.298	37	INTDEC	.580				110	FINTDC	.680
44	METEOR	.300	79	SOCSCH	.602				132	FSOCMD	.680
11	BKSMGR	.319	85	U PSTR	.606				126	FPSYCN	.682
56	PHYTHR	.337	65	PSYCCL	.623				121	FPEDRN	.684
1	AC AAA	.339	78	SOCRES	.645				127	FRELED	.694
									124	FPSY	.696
									133	FSOCPS	.718
									125	FPSYCL	.734

TABLE 7

MEDIAN SCORE DISTANCE OF EACH OF 89 MALE
OCCUPATIONAL GROUPS FROM THE OTHER
88 GROUPS IN ORDER OF NEARNESS TO THE
OTHER GROUPS

46	MTLMGR	.153	9	BARBER	.226	68	PSYPRF	.266
14	BUYER	.162	10	BKKPR	.226	57	PHYSN	.269
84	TV REP	.171	20	COUNHS	.226	58	PLUMBR	.272
32	ENG MM	.180	88	X RAY	.226	66	PSYCCN	.276
27	ENGCVL	.182	1	AC AAA	.227	89	YMCASC	.276
48	OPTMST	.186	63	PRNTER	.228	42	MATHM	.280
7	BAKER	.188	18	CLTH R	.233	5	ARCH	.281
24	DRCTFN	.190	30	ENGIND	.234	3	AC CPA	.282
8	BANKER	.191	69	RADSTA	.234	74	SOCCWK	.290
54	PHARM	.192	67	PSYCIN	.237	53	PHAR S	.294
29	ENGHAC	.195	23	DPTSTS	.238	64	PSYTST	.294
13	BDG CN	.196	71	SLSENG	.238	50	PNTR H	.296
59	PLMBCN	.196	55	PHOTOG	.240	87	WELDER	.296
44	METEOR	.202	56	PHYTHR	.240	41	MCHNST	.297
22	DNTIST	.204	62	POSTCL	.242	76	SOCWKM	.307
31	ENGMCH	.204	16	CCEX	.246	6	AUTO M	.308
36	INS AG	.204	86	VETRN	.248	65	PSYCCL	.319
47	NRSRYM	.205	17	CHEMST	.256	77	SOCPSY	.320
28	ENGELE	.208	21	COAGAG	.256	40	LIBRAR	.324
35	FORSTR	.208	72	SCITHS	.257	38	JOURN	.334
34	FLORST	.210	33	FARMER	.258	75	SOCWKG	.335
70	REALES	.210	51	PEDTRN	.258	25	EDNWSP	.336
52	PERS M	.214	4	AC IND	.260	83	TRKDRV	.336
73	SCHSUP	.214	61	POLICE	.261	15	CRPNTR	.340
82	TRYLAG	.214	80	STATCN	.263	45	MINIST	.342
11	BKSMGR	.215	19	COMPRG	.264	78	SOCRES	.342
43	MATHHS	.215	26	ELECTR	.264	85	U PSTR	.356
81	SUPVFM	.218	60	PODRST	.264	79	SOCSCH	.358
2	AC	.222	49	OSTPTH	.265	37	INTDEC	.432
39	LAWYER	.223	12	BRKLYR	.266			

TABLE 8

MEDIAN SCORE DISTANCE OF EACH OF 47 FEMALE
OCCUPATIONAL GROUPS FROM THE OTHER
46 GROUPS IN ORDER OF NEARNESS TO THE
OTHER GROUPS

97	FCNSHS	.158	103	FDTCOM	.194	127	FRELED	.220
115	FMTLMR	.162	108	FHMDEM	.194	133	FSOCPS	.220
104	FDTHOS	.162	136	F XRAY	.196	111	FKYPCH	.228
106	FDTTHR	.171	130	FSOCCW	.198	93	FBKKPR	.229
98	F DEAN	.172	94	FBKMER	.200	95	FCTLIB	.230
129	FSECY	.175	102	FDTCDM	.203	120	FOFCLK	.232
123	FPRSCT	.176	116	FNURSE	.203	124	FPSYC	.232
101	FDTNAD	.178	99	FDNTAS	.204	92	FBEAUT	.236
118	FNUTIN	.182	90	FACNT	.205	119	FOCTHR	.238
132	FSOCMD	.186	121	FPEDRN	.206	91	FBNKCL	.244
107	FFLRST	.187	113	FLIBR	.208	125	FPSYCL	.250
117	FNUTRN	.188	109	FHOMEC	.209	96	FCMPRG	.272
122	FPHYTH	.188	112	FLAWYR	.212	128	FSCTHS	.272
134	FSOCSC	.188	126	FPSYCN	.212	100	FDPTSW	.288
131	FSOCGR	.192	135	FSTENO	.214	110	FINTDC	.292
105	FDTSCH	.193	114	FMATHS	.216			

TABLE 9

MEAN SCORE DISTANCE OF MALE MOTEL MANAGERS (NO. 46)
FROM OTHER GROUPS

Employed Men						College Men			Employed Women			College Women		
14	BUYER	.049	50	PNTR H	.154	137	MAG	.178	90	FACNT	.310	170	GBUSGN	.375
59	PLMBCN	.053	22	DNTIST	.154	143	MBSGEN	.178	115	FMTLMR	.320	178	GMATH	.416
36	INS AG	.054	83	TRKDRV	.160	145	MBSMGT	.190	105	FDTSCH	.345	181	GPHYED	.425
8	BANKER	.056	15	CRPNTR	.160	149	MENGCL	.195	103	FDTCOM	.348	177	GHMEC	.471
70	REALES	.062	55	PHOTOG	.166	151	MENGMH	.205	107	FFLRST	.355	175	GHELTH	.505
13	BDG CN	.067	52	PERS M	.169	154	MFORST	.210	102	FDTCDM	.359	185	GSOCSC	.507
34	FLORST	.071	43	MATHHS	.169	142	MBUSAC	.211	101	FDTNAD	.362	176	GHISTO	.508
84	TV REP	.076	88	X RAY	.174	144	MBSMRK	.217	93	FBKKPR	.365	169	GBIOSC	.526
7	BAKER	.083	86	VETRN	.175	138	MANLHS	.218	114	FMATHS	.369	182	GPOLYS	.527
18	CLTH R	.085	4	AC IND	.182	159	MPHYED	.226	92	FBEAUT	.375	172	GELED	.528
9	BARBER	.085	48	OPTMST	.186	146	MECON	.234	136	FX RAY	.380	186	GSOC	.529
81	SUPVFM	.086	53	PHAR S	.202	150	MENGEL	.240	96	FCMPRG	.381	180	GNURSE	.531
24	DRCTFN	.088	39	LAWYER	.208	148	MENGCH	.241	112	FLAWYR	.385	183	GPSYCH	.535
47	NRSRYM	.090	3	AC CPA	.211	147	MELED	.261	108	FHMDEM	.388	174	GFRNLG	.552
27	ENGCVL	.105	89	YMCASC	.216	157	MMATH	.278	129	FSECY	.390	184	GCATHS	.566
58	PLUMBR	.108	20	COUNHS	.217	167	MWPCAD	.306	91	FBNKCL	.393	179	GMUSIC	.589
26	ELECTR	.108	56	PHYTHR	.233	166	MAFCAD	.308	122	FPHYTH	.395	173	GENGL	.628
82	TRVLAG	.109	49	OSTPTH	.233	156	MLAW	.327	104	FDTHOS	.396	171	GDRMA	.657
10	BKKPR	.110	72	SCITHS	.240	160	MPHYSC	.334	111	FKYPCH	.402	168	GARTED	.669
23	DPTSTS	.113	57	PHYSN	.244	164	MCATHB	.334	100	FDPTSW	.402			

No.	Code	Value
29	ENGHAC	.113
71	SLSENG	.116
33	FARMER	.117
32	ENG MM	.118
35	FORSTR	.120
62	POSTCL	.122
54	PHARM	.124
12	BRKLYR	.128
28	ENGELE	.130
1	AC AAA	.130
69	RADSTA	.134
87	WELDER	.139
31	ENGMCH	.139
61	POLICE	.140
21	COAGAG	.140
11	BKSMGR	.142
16	CC EX	.143
30	ENGIND	.143
6	AUTO M	.144
41	MCHNST	.145
2	AC	.146
73	SCHSUP	.147
44	METEOR	.148
63	PRNTER	.152

No.	Code	Value
19	COMPRG	.257
17	CHEMST	.261
67	PSYCIN	.262
5	ARCH	.263
60	PODRST	.265
80	STATCN	.289
42	MATHM	.291
25	EDNWSP	.292
51	PEDTRN	.296
38	JOURN	.304
66	PSYCCN	.315
74	SOCCWK	.320
68	PSYPRF	.322
76	SOCWKM	.324
45	MINIST	.354
40	LIBRAR	.356
64	PSYTST	.357
77	SOCPSY	.359
75	SOCWKG	.378
65	PSYCCL	.390
79	SOCSCH	.401
37	INTDEC	.405
85	U PSTR	.406
78	SOCRES	.424

No.	Code	Value
165	MSOC	.334
162	MPREMD	.341
155	MHIST	.377
163	MPSY	.390
141	MBIOSC	.390
161	MPOLYS	.392
139	MARCH	.412
153	MFRNLG	.419
158	MMUSIC	.448
152	MARTED	.562
140	MARTED	.562

No.	Code	Value
94	FBKMGR	.410
106	FDTTHR	.410
99	FDNTAS	.414
135	FSTENO	.418
120	FOFCLK	.424
98	F DEAN	.429
97	FCNSHS	.433
128	FSCTHS	.439
117	FNUTRN	.440
109	FHOMEC	.444
116	FNURSE	.452
118	FNUTIN	.455
126	FPSYCN	.464
124	FPSY	.474
119	FOCCTH	.475
123	FPRSCT	.478
131	FSOCGR	.485
110	FINTDC	.495
113	FLIBR	.496
134	FSOCSC	.504
132	FSOCMD	.509
95	FCTLIB	.513
130	FSOCCW	.513
125	FPSYCL	.522
121	FPEDRN	.534
133	FSOCPS	.534
127	FRELED	.547

TABLE 10
MEAN SCORE DISTANCE OF FEMALE MOTEL MANAGERS (NO. 115) FROM OTHER GROUPS

Employed Men						College Men			Employed Women			College Women		
9	BARBER	.254	83	TRKDRV	.391	164	MCATHB	.324	129	FSECY	.044	170	GBUSGN	.172
23	DPTSTS	.257	60	PODRST	.391	147	MELED	.357	135	FSTENO	.052	177	GHMEC	.189
24	DRCTFN	.267	87	WELDER	.396	153	MFRNLG	.372	107	FFLRST	.052	172	GELED	.204
11	BKSMGR	.273	58	PLUMBR	.398	158	MMUSIC	.423	92	FBEAUT	.053	180	GNURSE	.235
10	BKKPR	.286	13	BDG CN	.401	165	MSOC	.431	120	FOFCLK	.055	178	GMATH	.238
62	POSTCL	.288	16	CC EX	.401	159	MPHYED	.432	91	FBNKCL	.056	181	GPHYED	.242
37	INTDEC	.292	26	ELECTR	.402	155	MHIST	.473	93	FBKKPR	.057	185	GSOCSC	.243
34	FLORST	.292	64	PSYTST	.408	145	MBSMGT	.493	123	FPRSCT	.096	174	GFRNLG	.251
7	BAKER	.307	59	PLMBCN	.409	143	MBSGEN	.498	99	FDNTAS	.099	186	GSOC	.275
14	BUYER	.308	75	SOCWKG	.416	152	MENGL	.500	100	FDPTSW	.102	179	GMUSIC	.277
8	BANKER	.315	69	RADSTA	.416	142	MBUSAC	.501	111	FKYPCH	.111	175	GHELTH	.289
46	MTLMGR	.320	15	CRPNTR	.416	162	MPREMD	.506	90	FACNT	.127	176	GHISTO	.295
82	TRVLAG	.321	42	MATHM	.419	157	MMATH	.506	108	FHMDEM	.136	184	GCATHS	.304
18	CLTH R	.324	41	MCHNST	.419	137	MAG	.513	106	FDTTHR	.137	173	GENGL	.338
88	X RAY	.324	6	AUTO M	.423	146	MECON	.520	94	FBKMGR	.138	183	GPSYCH	.344
45	MINIST	.325	52	PERS M	.426	140	MARTED	.526	105	FDTSCH	.138	169	GBIOSC	.360
40	LIBRAR	.328	61	POLICE	.426	144	MBSMRK	.529	103	FDTCOM	.140	182	GPOLYS	.389
22	DNTIST	.329	32	ENG MM	.429	138	MANLHS	.539	116	FNURSE	.140	171	GDRMA	.404
81	SUPVFM	.331	33	FARMER	.440	141	MBIOSC	.543	102	FDTCDM	.146	168	GARTED	.424
54	PHARM	.333	27	ENGCVL	.443	163	MPSY	.543	114	FMATHS	.146			

50	PNTR H	.335
47	NRSRYM	.339
70	REALES	.342
20	COUNHS	.344
2	AC	.350
74	SOCCWK	.351
76	SOCWKM	.352
12	BRKLYR	.354
63	PRNTER	.356
84	TV REP	.360
48	OPTMST	.363
55	PHOTOG	.365
36	INS AG	.367
89	YMCASC	.368
73	SCHSUP	.370
51	PEDTRN	.370
39	LAWYER	.373
43	MATHHS	.377
57	PHYSN	.381
1	AC AAA	.384
77	SOCPSY	.385
5	ARCH	.386
49	OSTPTH	.386
79	SOCSCH	.389
56	PHYTHR	.389

72	SCITHS	.443
44	METEOR	.445
29	ENGHAC	.450
80	STATCN	.452
21	COAGAG	.453
66	PSYCCN	.453
28	ENGELE	.453
86	VETRN	.454
85	U PSTR	.460
25	EDNWSP	.477
35	FORSTR	.480
17	CHEMST	.482
3	AC CPA	.484
71	SLSENG	.489
53	PHAR S	.490
4	AC IND	.491
31	ENGMCH	.493
19	COMPRG	.493
65	PSYCCL	.495
78	SOCRES	.495
68	PSYPRF	.496
38	JOURN	.497
67	PSYCIN	.511
30	ENGIND	.512

154	MFORST	.544
156	MLAW	.549
149	MENGCL	.551
139	MARCH	.552
150	MENGEL	.556
160	MPHYSC	.561
161	MPOLYS	.564
148	MENGCH	.566
151	MENGMH	.568
167	MWPCAD	.603
166	MAFCAD	.608

136	FX RAY	.147
104	FDTHOS	.155
97	FCNSHS	.156
101	FDTNAD	.167
113	FLIBR	.172
95	FCTLIB	.192
132	FSOCMD	.193
134	FSOCSC	.194
118	FNUTIN	.201
98	F DEAN	.209
122	FPHYTH	.213
117	FNUTRN	.216
130	FSOCCW	.220
112	FLAWYR	.228
109	FHOMEC	.242
119	FOCCTH	.242
131	FSOCGR	.244
127	FRELED	.251
133	FSOCPS	.256
110	FINTDC	.262
126	FPSYCN	.264
121	FPEDRN	.293
96	FCMPRG	.293
124	FPSY	.315
128	FSCTHS	.316
125	FPSYCL	.325

TABLE 11

MEAN SCORE DISTANCE OF MALE INTERIOR DECORATORS (NO. 37)
FROM OTHER GROUPS

Employed Men			Employed Men			College Men			Employed Women			College Women		
5	ARCH	.140	56	PHYTHR	.434	140	MARTED	.193	110	FINTDC	.069	168	GARTED	.205
55	PHOTOG	.226	36	INS AG	.435	139	MARCH	.236	107	FFLRST	.218	171	GDRMA	.256
82	TRVLAG	.271	17	CHEMST	.437	153	MFRNLG	.280	94	FBKMGR	.233	174	GFRNLG	.265
11	BKSMGR	.281	31	ENGMCH	.437	158	MMUSIC	.306	119	FOCCTH	.266	177	GHMEC	.272
34	FLORST	.282	54	PHARM	.440	147	MELED	.347	112	FLAWYR	.271	176	GHISTO	.273
40	LIBRAR	.299	9	BARBER	.441	152	MENGL	.354	115	FMTLMR	.292	170	GBUSGN	.290
23	DPTSTS	.304	1	AC AAA	.441	165	MSOC	.369	98	F DEAN	.294	179	GMUSIC	.301
47	NRSRYM	.321	78	SOCRES	.443	155	MHIST	.381	133	FSOCPS	.301	173	GENGL	.302
69	RADSTA	.341	13	BDG CN	.443	164	MCATHB	.418	103	FDTCOM	.304	172	GELED	.310
70	REALES	.342	38	JOURN	.445	156	MLAW	.426	125	FPSYCL	.305	185	GSOCSC	.313
77	SOCPSY	.344	68	PSYPRF	.447	144	MBSMRK	.426	131	FSOCGR	.312	182	GPOLYS	.314
18	CLTH R	.345	84	TV REP	.450	163	MPSY	.435	113	FLIBR	.313	183	GPSYCH	.316
16	CC EX	.355	88	X RAY	.451	161	MPOLYS	.441	108	FHMDEM	.313	186	GSOC	.324
39	LAWYER	.356	25	EDNWSP	.453	145	MBSMGT	.450	130	FSOCCW	.316	181	GPHYED	.344
74	SOCCWK	.357	3	AC CPA	.454	143	MBSGEN	.458	96	FCMPRG	.318	178	GMATH	.371
45	MINIST	.358	28	ENGELE	.458	146	MECON	.461	101	FDTNAD	.322	169	GBIOSC	.408
64	PSYTST	.358	30	ENGIND	.458	159	MPHYED	.473	126	FPSYCN	.322	175	GHELTH	.417
52	PERS M	.380	50	PNTR H	.460	166	MAFCAD	.478	124	FPSY	.325	180	GNURSE	.437
22	DNTIST	.384	53	PHAR S	.463	167	MWPCAD	.485	132	FSOCMD	.325	184	GCATHS	.540
76	SOCWKM	.385	8	BANKER	.467	141	MBIOSC	.497	123	FPRSCT	.328			

51	PEDTRN	.385	44	METEOR	.469	154	MFORST	.504	134	FSOCSC	.329
79	SOCSCH	.389	73	SCHSUP	.480	151	MENGMH	.507	104	FDTHOS	.335
75	SOCWKG	.393	35	FORSTR	.486	157	MMATH	.519	122	FPHYTH	.335
48	OPTMST	.394	12	BRKLYR	.486	160	MPHYSC	.522	90	FACNT	.347
20	COUNHS	.395	59	PLMBCN	.486	149	MENGCL	.526	97	FCNSHS	.349
60	PODRST	.396	49	OSTPTH	.492	162	MPREMD	.529	129	FSECY	.350
14	BUYER	.398	57	PHYSN	.497	150	MENGEL	.531	105	FDTSCH	.350
65	PSYCCL	.398	4	AC IND	.503	142	MBUSAC	.539	102	FDTCDM	.355
7	BAKER	.398	81	SUPVFM	.512	148	MENGCH	.539	117	FNUTRN	.357
63	PRNTER	.399	72	SCITHS	.513	138	MANLHS	.562	121	FPEDRN	.357
66	PSYCCN	.400	43	MATHHS	.517	137	MAG	.569	92	FBEAUT	.362
71	SLSENG	.401	62	POSTCL	.530				95	FCTLIB	.363
85	U PSTR	.401	10	BKKPR	.533				111	FKYPCH	.372
29	ENGHAC	.401	61	POLICE	.544				127	FRELED	.376
80	STATCN	.404	58	PLUMBR	.547				118	FNUTIN	.382
46	MTLMGR	.405	86	VETRN	.549				135	FSTENO	.387
89	YMCASC	.407	21	COAGAG	.552				106	FDTTHR	.388
32	ENG MM	.409	26	ELECTR	.557				99	FDNTAS	.395
27	ENGCVL	.413	87	WELDER	.568				136	FX RAY	.409
2	AC	.415	15	CRPNTR	.580				116	FNURSE	.412
67	PSYCIN	.416	6	AUTO M	.589				109	FHOMEC	.425
42	MATHM	.420	33	FARMER	.595				120	FOFCLK	.429
24	DRCTFN	.429	41	MCHNST	.600				114	FMATHS	.441
19	COMPRG	.431	83	TRKDRV	.610				100	FDPTSW	.443
									93	FBKKPR	.444
									91	FBNKCL	.445
									128	FSCTHS	.477

TABLE 12
MEAN SCORE DISTANCE OF FEMALE INTERIOR DECORATORS (NO. 110) FROM OTHER GROUPS

Employed Men						College Men			Employed Women			College Women		
37	INTDEC	.069	46	MTLMGR	.495	140	MARTED	.257	94	FBKMGR	.166	168	GARTED	.200
5	ARCH	.200	1	AC AAA	.497	153	MFRNLG	.309	107	FFLRST	.195	174	GFRNLG	.221
40	LIBRAR	.304	27	ENGCVL	.500	139	MARCH	.324	112	FLAWYR	.209	176	GHISTO	.227
11	BKSMGR	.317	71	SLSENG	.503	158	MMUSIC	.367	98	F DEAN	.232	177	GHMEC	.240
55	PHOTOG	.326	25	EDNWSP	.505	152	MENGL	.369	113	FLIBR	.238	173	GENGL	.246
82	TRVLAG	.347	54	PHARM	.505	155	MHIST	.411	133	FSOCPS	.243	170	GBUSGN	.264
34	FLORST	.374	73	SCHSUP	.509	147	MELED	.415	132	FSOCMD	.256	172	GELED	.268
39	LAWYER	.375	3	AC CPA	.516	165	MSOC	.416	130	FSOCCW	.256	182	GPOLYS	.271
45	MINIST	.379	24	DRCTFN	.518	156	MLAW	.470	125	FPSYCL	.260	185	GSOCSC	.273
47	NRSRYM	.387	9	BARBER	.521	161	MPOLYS	.479	126	FPSYCN	.262	171	GDRMA	.277
77	SOCPSY	.392	36	INS AG	.522	164	MCATHB	.484	115	FMTLMR	.262	179	GMUSIC	.289
23	DPTSTS	.394	44	METEOR	.534	163	MPSY	.503	103	FDTCOM	.264	183	GPSYCH	.291
64	PSYTST	.400	31	ENGMCH	.535	144	MBSMRK	.521	131	FSOCGR	.264	186	GSOC	.299
74	SOCCWK	.400	13	BDG CN	.535	146	MECON	.523	119	FOCCTH	.267	178	GMATH	.334
70	REALES	.407	56	PHYTHR	.536	145	MBSMGT	.543	134	FSOCSC	.268	181	GPHYED	.380
18	CLTH R	.408	28	ENGELE	.541	143	MBSGEN	.545	123	FPRSCT	.269	169	GBIOSC	.399
79	SOCSCH	.416	8	BANKER	.541	141	MBIOSC	.566	124	FPSY	.269	175	GHELTH	.419
80	STATCN	.423	84	TV REP	.549	157	MMATH	.569	108	FHMDEM	.276	180	GNURSE	.438
69	RADSTA	.425	30	ENGIND	.551	159	MPHYED	.580	97	FCHSHS	.281	184	GCATHS	.552
85	U PSTR	.427	88	X RAY	.554	167	MWPCAD	.583	95	FCTLIB	.281			

No.	Code	Value
16	CC EX	.430
75	SOCWKG	.431
76	SOCWKM	.432
51	PEDTRN	.433
66	PSYCCN	.438
20	COUNHS	.441
65	PSYCCL	.441
42	MATHM	.443
52	PERS M	.457
78	SOCRES	.459
2	AC	.459
48	OPTMST	.460
22	DNTIST	.465
89	YMCASC	.470
67	PSYCIN	.472
68	PSYPRF	.474
7	BAKER	.475
60	PODRST	.477
14	BUYER	.479
63	PRNTER	.480
32	ENG MM	.484
17	CHEMST	.486
19	COMPRG	.492
38	JOURN	.493
29	ENGHAC	.494

No.	Code	Value
57	PHYSN	.557
50	PNTR H	.560
43	MATHHS	.564
72	SCITHS	.571
49	OSTPTH	.573
53	PHAR S	.576
4	AC IND	.577
35	FORSTR	.585
10	BKKPR	.589
12	BRKLYR	.600
59	PLMBCN	.601
81	SUPVFM	.603
62	POSTCL	.610
21	COAGAG	.619
86	VETRN	.633
58	PLUMBR	.651
33	FARMER	.666
26	ELECTR	.667
87	WELDER	.675
61	POLICE	.678
15	CRPNTR	.680
6	AUTO M	.700
41	MCHNST	.705
83	TRKDRV	.711

No.	Code	Value
166	MAFCAD	.588
160	MPHYSC	.589
162	MPREMD	.597
142	MBUSAC	.605
151	MENGMH	.614
154	MFORST	.617
148	MENGCH	.619
150	MENGEL	.628
149	MENGCL	.634
138	MANLHS	.653
137	MAG	.661

No.	Code	Value
101	FDTNAD	.284
96	FCMPRG	.287
90	FACNT	.287
104	FDTHOS	.296
117	FNUTRN	.298
129	FSECY	.301
105	FDTSCH	.307
121	FPEDRN	.307
102	FDTCDM	.314
127	FRELED	.328
118	FNUTIN	.331
122	FPHYTH	.332
92	FBEAUT	.335
135	FSTENO	.350
106	FDTTHR	.351
111	FKYPCH	.363
109	FHOMEC	.366
114	FMATHS	.375
99	FDNTAS	.384
120	FOFCLK	.391
116	FNURSE	.405
93	FBKKPR	.406
136	FX RAY	.408
91	FBNKCL	.410
100	FDPTSW	.413
128	FSCTHS	.449

TABLE 13

MEAN SCORE DISTANCE OF MALE COUNTY AGRICULTURAL AGENTS (NO. 21) FROM OTHER GROUPS

Employed Men						College Men			Employed Women			College Women		
33	FARMER	.080	23	DPTSTS	.257	137	MAG	.120	105	FDTSCH	.376	181	GPHYED	.480
35	FORSTR.	.123	63	PRNTER	.257	138	MANLHS	.158	128	FSCTHS	.376	178	GMATH	.485
73	SCHSUP	.132	52	PERS M	.258	154	MFORST	.218	101	FDTNAD	.379	170	GBUSGN	.498
47	NRSRYM	.133	83	TRKDRV	.259	149	MENGCL	.293	108	FHMDEM	.390	169	GBIOSC	.500
46	MTLMGR	.140	69	RADSTA	.260	159	MPHYED	.308	102	FDTCDM	.393	177	GHMEC	.525
86	VETRN	.158	48	OPTMST	.262	147	MELED	.312	103	FDTCOM	.401	175	GHELTH	.525
44	METEOR	.160	57	PHYSN	.263	151	MENGMH	.316	104	FDTHOS	.410	180	GNURSE	.561
8	BANKER	.168	6	AUTO M	.263	143	MBSGEN	.319	117	FNUTRN	.411	176	GHISTO	.567
34	FLORST	.170	87	WELDER	.266	148	MENGCH	.322	90	FACNT	.411	185	GSOCSC	.580
36	INS AG	.173	12	BRKLYR	.267	145	MBSMGT	.332	109	FHOMEC	.411	184	GCATHS	.586
13	BDG CN	.181	15	CRPNTR	.272	150	MENGEL	.337	122	FPHYTH	.421	172	GELED	.595
32	ENG MM	.185	41	MCHNST	.278	146	MECON	.348	114	FMATHS	.425	186	GSOC	.596
59	PLMBCN	.185	17	CHEMST	.282	142	MBUSAC	.355	136	FX RAY	.437	183	GPSYCH	.598
27	ENGCVL	.188	49	OSTPTH	.282	160	MPHYSC	.367	106	FDTTHR	.439	182	GPOLYS	.602
70	REALES	.195	53	PHAR S	.283	157	MMATH	.368	112	FLAWYR	.441	174	GFRNLG	.605
14	BUYER	.200	50	PNTR H	.284	144	MBSMRK	.376	118	FNUTIN	.445	179	GMUSIC	.670
24	DRCTFN	.200	61	POLICE	.286	141	MBIOSC	.379	96	FCMPRG	.446	173	GENGL	.673
84	TV REP	.208	56	PHYTHR	.293	164	MCATHB	.381	115	FMTLMR	.453	171	GDRMA	.755
43	MATHHS	.208	51	PEDTRN	.307	162	MPREMD	.388	98	F DEAN	.453	168	GARTED	.772
72	SCITHS	.212	55	PHOTOG	.308	167	MWPCAD	.401	97	FCNSHS	.463			

No.	Scale	Value	No.	Scale	Value	No.	Scale	Value	No.	Scale	Value
7	BAKER	.214	4	AC IND	.308	156	MLAW	.403	107	FFLRST	.470
81	SUPVFM	.215	68	PSYPRF	.320	166	MAFCAD	.404	93	FBKKPR	.481
29	ENGHAC	.217	67	PSYCIN	.326	165	MSOC	.405	124	FPSY	.484
54	PHARM	.219	80	STATCN	.335	155	MHIST	.430	126	FPSYCN	.489
9	BARBER	.220	42	MATHM	.335	161	MPOLYS	.466	129	FSECY	.490
28	ENGELE	.224	19	COMPRG	.335	163	MPSY	.470	131	FSOCGR	.492
16	CC EX	.227	60	PODRST	.337	153	MFRNLG	.471	94	FBKMGR	.493
58	PLUMBR	.228	25	EDNWSP	.340	139	MARCH	.539	116	FNURSE	.498
22	DNTIST	.231	3	AC CPA	.345	158	MMUSIC	.552	99	FDNTAS	.498
82	TRVLAG	.234	66	PSYCCN	.347	152	MENGL	.565	92	FBEAUT	.506
1	AC AAA	.236	38	JOURN	.353	140	MARTED	.677	111	FKYPCH	.509
31	ENGMCH	.237	76	SOCWKM	.360				100	FDPTSW	.519
11	BKSMGR	.238	45	MINIST	.362				135	FSTENO	.526
26	ELECTR	.238	74	SOCCWK	.362				121	FPEDRN	.528
89	YMCASC	.240	5	ARCH	.372				91	FBNKCL	.534
30	ENGIND	.243	40	LIBRAR	.392				120	FOFCLK	.535
10	BKKPR	.245	64	PSYTST	.397				134	FSOCSC	.537
18	CLTH R	.247	77	SOCPSY	.408				113	FLIBR	.539
20	COUNHS	.247	75	SOCWKG	.416				119	FOCCTH	.542
88	X RAY	.249	85	U PSTR	.425				95	FCTLIB	.543
62	POSTCL	.249	65	PSYCCL	.426				130	FSOCCW	.544
39	LAWYER	.250	79	SOCSCH	.433				127	FRELED	.546
2	AC	.255	78	SOCRES	.457				123	FPRSCT	.546
71	SLSENG	.256	37	INTDEC	.552				132	FSOCMD	.547
									125	FPSYCL	.547
									133	FSOCPS	.571
									110	FINTDC	.619

TABLE 14

MEAN SCORE DISTANCE OF MALE AUTO MECHANICS (NO. 6)
FROM OTHER GROUPS

Employed Men						College Men			Employed Women			College Women		
26	ELECTR	.030	56	PHYTHR	.308	137	MAG	.263	92	FBEAUT	.391	181	GPHYED	.501
87	WELDER	.032	1	AC AAA	.314	154	MFORST	.273	136	FX RAY	.407	178	GMATH	.538
41	MCHNST	.032	30	ENGIND	.316	149	MENGCL	.281	115	FMTLMR	.423	175	GHELTH	.577
15	CRPNTR	.039	57	PHYSN	.319	138	MANLHS	.281	93	FBKKPR	.428	184	GCATHS	.582
58	PLUMBR	.040	55	PHOTOG	.321	151	MENGMH	.293	100	FDPTSW	.446	170	GBUSGN	.592
12	BRKLYR	.060	18	CLTH R	.326	159	MPHYED	.325	120	FOFCLK	.448	180	GNURSE	.596
73	PNTR H	.064	73	SCHSUP	.338	150	MENGEL	.330	107	FFLRST	.457	169	GBIOSC	.618
50	SUPVFM	.076	48	OPTMST	.338	148	MENGCH	.396	91	FBNKCL	.457	177	GHMEC	.623
81	TRKDRV	.078	72	SCITHS	.340	164	MCATHB	.398	122	FPHYTH	.468	172	GELED	.688
83	PLMBCN	.086	2	AC	.344	147	MELED	.399	99	FDNTAS	.471	176	GHISTO	.694
59	POSTCL	.099	82	TRVLAG	.354	143	MBSGEN	.401	111	FKYPCH	.472	185	GSOCSC	.696
62	BDG CN	.101	19	COMPRG	.373	145	MBSMGT	.407	135	FSTENO	.487	186	GSOC	.700
13	TV TEP	.112	69	RADSTA	.382	157	MMATH	.415	116	FNURSE	.489	174	GFRNLG	.704
84	BARBER	.125	42	MATHM	.398	142	MBUSAC	.426	114	FMATHS	.490	183	GPSYCH	.705
9	POLICE	.143	17	CHEMST	.406	160	MPHYSC	.428	102	FDTCDM	.499	179	GMUSIC	.710
61	MTLMGR	.144	51	PEDTRN	.416	166	MAFCAD	.457	105	FDTSCH	.499	168	GARTED	.758
46	BKKPR	.152	5	ARCH	.419	144	MBSMRK	.464	90	FACNT	.504	182	GPOLYS	.764
10	BAKER	.183	52	PERS M	.420	162	MPREMD	.476	129	FSECY	.506	173	GENGL	.824
7	FARMER	.184	4	AC IND	.423	146	MECON	.476	96	FCMPRG	.507	171	GDRMA	.843
33	BUYER	.187	16	CC EX	.425	167	MWPCAD	.479	108	FHMDEM	.513			

24	DRCTFN	.191	89	YMCASC	.427	141	MBIOSC	.503	106	FDTTHR	.525
88	X RAY	.192	53	PHAR S	.427	165	MSOC	.520	119	FOCCTH	.534
35	FORSTR	.199	60	PODRST	.433	139	MARCH	.530	103	FDTCOM	.536
8	BANKER	.200	20	COUNHS	.439	153	MFRNLG	.558	104	FDTHOS	.544
63	PRNTER	.213	39	LAWYER	.442	158	MMUSIC	.564	101	FDTNAD	.547
27	ENGCVL	.223	25	FDNWSP	.452	156	MLAW	.586	128	FSCTHS	.548
34	FLORST	.227	3	AC CPA	.473	163	MPSY	.590	123	FPRSCT	.553
28	ENGELE	.227	38	JOURN	.476	155	MHIST	.606	94	FBKMGR	.561
22	DNTIST	.231	80	STATCN	.490	161	MPOLYS	.658	109	FHOMEC	.597
29	ENGHAC	.236	76	SOCWKM	.501	140	MARTED	.661	118	FNUTIN	.622
23	DPTSTS	.237	45	MINIST	.510	152	MENGL	.712	117	FNUTRN	.624
36	INS AG	.245	68	PSYPRF	.514				113	FLIBR	.631
31	ENGMCH	.245	74	SOCCWK	.521				95	FCTLIB	.631
54	PHARM	.248	40	LIBRAR	.524				97	FCNSHS	.643
86	VETRN	.251	67	PSYCIN	.524				112	FLAWYR	.646
32	ENG MM	.260	64	PSYTST	.527				98	F DEAN	.657
21	COAGAG	.263	77	SOCPSY	.543				121	FPEDRN	.664
47	NRSRYM	.268	66	PSYCCN	.546				131	FSOCGR	.668
43	MATHHS	.269	75	SOCWKG	.586				126	FPSYCN	.677
44	METEOR	.271	37	INTDEC	.589				134	FSOCSC	.678
70	REALES	.276	65	PSYCCL	.601				124	FPSY	.682
11	BKSMGR	.299	85	U PSTR	.612				130	FSOCCW	.690
49	OSTPTH	.301	79	SOCSCH	.613				132	FSOCMD	.694
71	SLSENG	.307	78	SOCRES	.638				110	FINTDC	.700
									127	FRELED	.706
									125	FPSYCL	.723
									133	FSOCPS	.729

TABLE 15
MEAN SCORE DISTANCE OF MALE BUSINESS AND MARKETING MAJORS (NO. 144)
FROM OTHER GROUPS

Employed Men						College Men			Employed Women			College Women		
3	AC CPA	.134	44	METEOR	.323	143	MBSGEN	.039	112	FLAWYR	.420	170	GBUSGN	.312
4	AC IND	.135	61	POLICE	.323	145	MBSMGT	.049	96	FCMPRG	.445	182	GPOLYS	.397
82	TRVLAG	.147	89	YMCASC	.325	146	MECON	.077	103	FDTCOM	.450	176	GHISTO	.450
69	RADSTA	.147	5	ARCH	.329	142	MBUSAC	.100	101	FDTNAD	.458	178	GMATH	.452
18	CLTH R	.147	63	PRNTER	.331	167	MWPCAD	.151	90	FACNT	.469	181	GPHYED	.454
71	SLSENG	.160	56	PHYTHR	.335	156	MLAW	.162	105	FDTSCH	.504	183	GPSYCH	.458
16	CC EX	.160	81	SUPVFM	.345	166	MAFCAD	.171	98	F DEAN	.510	177	GHMEC	.461
55	PHOTOG	.172	74	SOCCWK	.346	148	MENGCH	.174	124	FPSY	.518	185	GSOCSC	.463
53	PHAR S	.178	77	SOCPSY	.350	151	MENGMH	.184	126	FPSYCN	.520	186	GSOC	.484
14	BUYER	.182	43	MATHHS	.357	159	MPHYED	.198	110	FINTDC	.521	174	GFRNLG	.509
36	INS AG	.183	10	BKKPR	.359	161	MPOLYS	.207	104	FDTHOS	.526	172	GELED	.510
70	REALES	.184	68	PSYPRF	.363	149	MENGCL	.215	115	FMTLMR	.529	171	GDRMA	.518
52	PERS M	.188	65	PSYCCL	.366	163	MPSY	.219	111	FKYPCH	.530	173	GENGL	.528
67	PSYCIN	.190	75	SOCWKG	.367	147	MELED	.225	97	FCNSHS	.538	169	GBIOSC	.542
30	ENGIND	.200	38	JOURN	.369	165	MSOC	.227	94	FBKMGR	.539	175	GHELTH	.556
46	MTLMGR	.217	76	SOCWKM	.370	157	MMATH	.235	125	FPSYCL	.542	168	GARTED	.605
47	NRSRYM	.219	17	CHEMST	.375	150	MENGEL	.238	107	FFLRST	.543	179	GMUSIC	.608
34	FLORST	.228	21	COAGAG	.376	137	MAG	.250	102	FDTCDM	.545	180	GNURSE	.628
2	AC	.232	12	BRKLYR	.377	155	MHIST	.253	122	FPHYTH	.552	184	GCATHS	.758
7	BAKER	.233	86	VETRN	.378	138	MANLHS	.274	129	FSECY	.561			

1	AC AAA	.242	72	SCITHS	.388	154	MFORST	.281	118	FNUTIN	.564
29	ENGHAC	.245	25	EDNWSP	.389	162	MPREMD	.283	117	FNUTRN	.564
31	ENGMCH	.249	64	PSYTST	.392	139	MARCH	.296	133	FSOCPS	.565
48	OPTMST	.250	88	X RAY	.397	160	MPHYSC	.319	131	FSOCGR	.568
84	TV REP	.253	62	POSTCL	.398	153	MFRNLG	.341	106	FDTTHR	.570
32	ENG MM	.254	78	SOCRES	.401	141	MBIOSC	.345	108	FHMDEM	.586
27	ENGCVL	.257	33	FARMER	.405	152	MENGL	.375	130	FSOCCW	.595
23	DPTSTS	.261	26	ELECTR	.405	158	MMUSIC	.415	132	FSOCMD	.597
8	BANKER	.267	85	U PSTR	.406	164	MCATHB	.428	109	FHOMEC	.604
20	COUNHS	.272	79	SOCSCH	.412	140	MARTED	.444	114	FMATHS	.607
19	COMPRG	.278	40	LIBRAR	.419				93	FBKKPR	.611
11	BKSMGR	.280	49	OSTPTH	.419				119	FOCCTH	.612
54	PHARM	.281	42	MATHM	.422				136	FX RAY	.615
28	ENGELE	.291	37	INTDEC	.426				134	FSOCSC	.616
9	BARBER	.293	87	WELDER	.427				128	FSCTHS	.617
60	PODRST	.297	57	PHYSN	.429				91	FBNKCL	.623
59	PLMBCN	.297	58	PLUMBR	.431				99	FDNTAS	.624
24	DRCTFN	.303	50	PNTR H	.432				92	FBEAUT	.627
35	FORSTR	.304	51	PEDTRN	.439				135	FSTENO	.628
66	PSYCCN	.305	41	MCHNST	.450				113	FLIBR	.641
73	SCHSUP	.309	83	TRKDRV	.457				100	FDPTSW	.659
39	LAWYER	.309	6	AUTO M	.464				121	FPEDRN	.663
13	BDG CN	.321	45	MINIST	.481				116	FNURSE	.664
22	DNTIST	.321	15	CRPNTR	.490				127	FRELED	.666
80	STATCN	.322							123	FPRSCT	.671
									120	FOFCLK	.686
									95	FCTLIB	.699

TABLE 16
MEAN SCORE DISTANCE OF MALE CLINICAL PSYCHOLOGISTS (NO. 66) FROM OTHER GROUPS

Employed Men						College Men			Employed Women			College Women		
65	PSYCCL	.039	53	PHAR S	.277	165	MSOC	.118	124	FPSY	.146	183	GPSYCH	.238
68	PSYPRF	.058	2	AC	.277	163	MPSY	.124	126	FPSYCN	.164	185	GSOCSC	.287
67	PSYCIN	.060	3	AC CPA	.278	147	MELED	.159	125	FPSYCL	.169	186	GSOC	.293
20	COUNHS	.068	28	ENGELE	.281	156	MLAW	.190	98	F DEAN	.225	182	GPOLYS	.314
74	SOCCWK	.082	88	X RAY	.283	162	MPREMD	.196	112	FLAWYR	.238	176	GHISTO	.320
77	SOCPSY	.087	38	JOURN	.283	155	MHIST	.209	131	FSOCGR	.242	169	GBIOSC	.338
78	SOCRES	.089	70	REALES	.287	141	MBIOSC	.213	133	FSOCPS	.245	173	GENGL	.355
79	SOCSCH	.090	4	AC IND	.289	161	MPOLYS	.217	130	FSOCCW	.253	181	GPHYED	.355
64	PSYTST	.092	86	VETRN	.299	153	MFRNLG	.221	97	FCHSHS	.255	174	GFRNLG	.356
76	SOCWKM	.096	1	AC AAA	.299	146	MECON	.229	132	FSOCMD	.279	175	GHELTH	.357
75	SOCWKG	.105	71	SLSENG	.299	157	MMATH	.251	134	FSOCSC	.286	178	GMATH	.360
52	PERS M	.134	14	BUYER	.302	160	MPHYSC	.255	101	FDTNAD	.288	172	GELED	.365
85	U PSTR	.144	18	CLTH R	.303	159	MPHYED	.257	121	FPEDRN	.297	177	GHMEC	.373
48	OPTMST	.158	24	DRCTFN	.313	152	MENGL	.257	96	FCMPRG	.298	170	GBUSGN	.390
80	STATCN	.171	84	TV REP	.314	145	MBSMGT	.259	122	FPHYTH	.300	180	GNURSE	.397
51	PEDTRN	.176	25	EDNWSP	.315	148	MENGCH	.276	117	FNUTRN	.308	171	GDRMA	.427
60	PODRST	.177	46	MTLMGR	.315	166	MAFCAD	.281	128	FSCTHS	.313	179	GMUSIC	.448
45	MINIST	.186	7	BAKER	.322	143	MBSGEN	.288	104	FDTHOS	.318	168	GARTED	.510
89	YMCASC	.190	36	INS AG	.329	167	MWPCAD	.300	109	FHOMEC	.324	184	GCATHS	.511
56	PHYTHR	.192	47	NRSRYM	.331	150	MENGEL	.300	118	FNUTIN	.335			

98

73	SCHSUP	.196	23	DPTSTS	.331	144	MBSMRK	.305	127	FRELED	.337
39	LAWYER	.197	63	PRNTER	.343	164	MCATHB	.314	103	FDTCOM	.347
72	SCITHS	.201	9	BARBER	.345	151	MENGMH	.322	119	FOCCTH	.349
17	CHEMST	.203	34	FLORST	.345	158	MMUSIC	.327	105	FDTSCH	.364
22	DNTIST	.209	21	COAGAG	.347	142	MBUSAC	.332	106	FDTTHR	.367
57	PHYSN	.229	35	FORSTR	.348	149	MENGCL	.350	94	FBKMGR	.371
16	CC EX	.230	8	BANKER	.362	154	MFORST	.351	90	FACNT	.371
44	METEOR	.232	37	INTDEC	.400	139	MARCH	.353	136	FX RAY	.385
49	OSTPTH	.232	81	SUPVFM	.404	137	MAG	.382	102	FDTCDM	.404
42	MATHM	.236	61	POLICE	.405	138	MANLHS	.399	113	FLIBR	.411
32	ENG MM	.237	13	BDG CN	.406	140	MARTED	.431	108	FHMDEM	.418
40	LIBRAR	.239	59	PLMBCN	.408				111	FKYPCH	.429
11	BKSMGR	.239	33	FARMER	.433				110	FINTDC	.438
19	COMPRG	.243	10	BKKPR	.444				114	FMATHS	.440
43	MATHHS	.243	62	POSTCL	.463				116	FNURSE	.445
55	PHOTOG	.247	12	BRKLYR	.468				99	FDNTAS	.451
69	RADSTA	.247	50	PNTR H	.486				115	FMTLMR	.453
54	PHARM	.251	26	ELECTR	.492				95	FCTLIB	.459
30	ENGIND	.252	87	WELDER	.503				129	FSECY	.470
82	TRVLAG	.254	58	PLUMBR	.518				107	FFLRST	.475
31	ENGMCH	.260	41	MCHNST	.530				123	FPRSCT	.491
5	ARCH	.274	6	AUTO M	.546				92	FBEAUT	.554
29	ENGHAC	.276	83	TRKDRV	.547				93	FBKKPR	.557
27	ENGCVL	.276	15	CRPNTR	.566				135	FSTENO	.560
									91	FBNKCL	.599
									120	FOFCLK	.609
									100	FDPTSW	.639

TABLE 17

MEAN SCORE DISTANCE OF MALE CHEMISTS (NO. 17)

FROM OTHER GROUPS

Employed Men						College Men			Employed Women			College Women		
42	MATHM	.072	4	AC IND	.257	160	MPHYSC	.097	96	FCMPRG	.182	169	GBIOSC	.310
32	ENG MM	.075	46	MTLMGR	.261	157	MMATH	.150	128	FSCTHS	.220	178	GMATH	.324
44	METEOR	.077	7	BAKER	.261	150	MENGEL	.152	124	FPSY	.272	175	GHELTH	.382
19	COMPRG	.087	82	TRVLAG	.262	148	MENGCH	.158	122	FPHYTR	.299	183	GPSYCH	.402
80	STATCN	.095	34	FLORST	.274	141	MBIOSC	.164	109	FHOMEC	.302	176	GHISTO	.434
72	SCITHS	.095	70	REALES	.278	162	MPREMD	.193	121	FPEDRN	.306	181	GPHYED	.445
68	PSYPRF	.104	21	COAGAG	.282	154	MFORST	.208	112	FLAWYR	.318	182	GPOLYS	.457
28	ENGELE	.120	69	RADSTA	.284	151	MENGMH	.209	101	FDTNAD	.337	174	GFRNLG	.465
48	OPTMST	.121	74	SOCCWK	.284	149	MENGCL	.218	90	FACNT	.344	185	GSOCSC	.489
51	PEDTRN	.122	8	BANKER	.286	147	MELED	.239	125	FPSYCL	.347	177	GHMEC	.493
31	ENGMCH	.122	63	PRNTER	.286	163	MPSY	.251	104	FDTHOS	.348	170	GBUSGN	.495
27	ENGCVL	.125	77	SOCPSY	.287	137	MAG	.267	105	FDTSCH	.349	180	GNURSE	.497
29	ENGHAC	.131	13	BDG CN	.288	153	MFRNLG	.275	126	FPSYCN	.350	172	GELED	.513
43	MATHHS	.135	76	SOCWKM	.290	146	MECON	.282	117	FNUTRN	.361	179	GMUSIC	.517
22	DNTIST	.137	85	UPSTR	.303	165	MSOC	.283	136	FX RAY	.363	173	GENGL	.523
64	PSYTST	.163	24	DRCTFN	.304	166	MAFCAD	.283	114	FMATHS	.367	186	GSOC	.526
57	PHYSN	.168	38	JOURN	.308	156	MLAW	.285	103	FDTCOM	.370	184	GCATHS	.545
39	LAWYER	.168	18	CLTH R	.311	155	MHIST	.298	106	FDTTHR	.370	168	GARTED	.578
54	PHARM	.173	59	PLMBCN	.311	138	MANLHS	.303	94	FBKMGR	.379	171	GDRMA	.625
2	AC	.183	33	FARMER	.312	167	MWPCAD	.314	118	FNUTIN	.380			

86	VETRN	.185
35	FORSTR	.186
11	BKSMGR	.187
30	ENGIND	.187
67	PSYCIN	.189
49	OSTPTH	.190
56	PHYTHR	.199
66	PSYCCN	.203
88	X RAY	.203
1	AC AAA	.204
84	TV REP	.207
65	PSYCCL	.208
47	NRSRYM	.211
73	SCHSUP	.215
5	ARCH	.215
20	COUNHS	.226
71	SLSENG	.229
40	LIBRAR	.235
55	PHOTOG	.236
78	SOCRES	.237
60	PODRST	.246
14	BUYER	.253
52	PERS M	.255
3	AC CPA	.255

16	CC EX	.314
81	SUPVFM	.315
25	EDNWSP	.318
79	SOCSCH	.319
36	INS AG	.320
45	MINIST	.321
10	BKKPR	.323
75	SOCWKG	.330
62	POSTCL	.330
9	BARBER	.340
89	YMCASC	.348
53	PHAR S	.353
23	DPTSTS	.356
26	ELECTR	.360
61	POLICE	.381
12	BRKLYR	.381
87	WELDER	.384
58	PLUMBR	.387
41	MCHNST	.388
6	AUTO M	.406
50	PNTR H	.414
37	INTDEC	.437
15	CRPNTR	.456
83	TRKDRV	.486

142	MBUSAC	.316
143	MBSGEN	.321
145	MBSMGT	.321
159	MPHYED	.322
158	MMUSIC	.324
164	MCATHB	.329
161	MPOLYS	.331
139	MARCH	.340
144	MBSMRK	.375
152	MENGL	.385
140	MARTED	.481

102	FDTCDM	.380
98	F DEAN	.380
119	FOCCTH	.413
131	FSOCGR	.432
97	FCNSHS	.433
113	FLIBR	.437
95	FCTLIB	.440
133	FSOCPS	.444
130	FSOCCW	.448
132	FSOCMD	.454
99	FDNTAS	.477
134	FSOCSC	.479
115	FMTLMR	.482
108	FHMDEM	.484
110	FINTDC	.486
111	FKYPCH	.488
129	FSECY	.496
107	FFLRST	.501
116	FNURSE	.504
127	FRELED	.521
93	FBKKPR	.526
123	FPRSCT	.528
135	FSTENO	.559
92	FBEAUT	.560
120	FOFCLK	.580
91	FBNKCL	.589
100	FDPTSW	.649

TABLE 18

MEAN SCORE DISTANCE OF MALE MATHEMATICIANS (NO. 42)

FROM OTHER GROUPS

Employed Men					College Men			Employed Women			College Women		
80 STATCN .064	38 JOURN .284	160 MPHYSC .139	96 FCMPRG .132	178 GMATH .263
17 CHEMST .072	77 SOCPSY .286	157 MMATH .146	128 FSCTHS .241	169 GBIOSC .329
19 COMPRG .075	63 PRNTER .286	150 MENGEL .191	124 FPSY .243	176 GHISTO .373
44 METEOR .119	82 TRVLAG .287	148 MENGCH .228	112 FLAWYR .269	183 GPSYCH .378
43 MATHHS .123	46 MTLMGR .291	141 MBIOSC .234	90 FACNT .277	175 GHELTH .387
68 PSYPRF .128	25 EDNWSP .293	153 MFRNLG .236	114 FMATHS .282	174 GFRNLG .403
32 ENG MM .131	45 MINIST .295	149 MENGCL .239	122 FPHYTH .286	182 GPOLYS .412
27 ENGCVL .151	8 BANKER .295	147 MELED .250	121 FPEDRN .291	181 GPHYED .433
11 BKSMGR .156	76 SOCWKM .297	151 MENGMH .253	109 FHOMEC .298	170 GBUSGN .443
51 PEDTRN .157	85 U PSTR .298	154 MFORST .268	94 FBKMGR .302	185 GSOCSC .451
2 AC .161	13 BDG CN .300	162 MPREMD .276	126 FPSYCN .316	179 GMUSIC .451
72 SCITHS .162	7 BAKER .302	155 MHIST .280	125 FPSYCL .318	172 GELED .462
39 LAWYER .165	71 SLSENG .305	158 MMUSIC .282	105 FDTSCH .339	173 GENGL .463
48 OPTMST .167	62 POSTCL .305	165 MSOC .287	95 FCTLIB .339	177 GHMEC .469
28 ENGELE .169	79 SOCSCH .310	156 MLAW .292	101 FDTNAD .343	186 GSOC .489
40 LIBRAR .174	70 REALES .314	146 MECON .302	113 FLIBR .345	180 GNURSE .493
31 ENGMCH .176	34 FLORST .316	163 MPSY .303	117 FNUTRN .348	184 GCATHS .501
64 PSYTST .181	52 PERS M .318	142 MBUSAC .313	98 F DEAN .348	168 GARTED .533
29 ENGHAC .186	75 SOCWKG .323	164 MCATHB .314	104 FDTHOS .350	171 GDRMA .581
1 AC AAA .197	81 SUPVFM .328	137 MAG .316	106 FDTTHR .360	

22	DNTIST	.200	60	PODRST	.330	161	MPOLYS	.330	136	FX RAY	.365
78	SOCRES	.210	69	RADSTA	.333	139	MARCH	.333	102	FDTCDM	.365
5	ARCH	.219	21	COAGAG	.335	166	MAFCAD	.341	118	FNUTIN	.374
57	PHYSN	.224	33	FARMER	.341	152	MENGL	.344	103	FDTCOM	.375
35	FORSTR	.229	18	CLTH R	.343	143	MBSGEN	.351	131	FSOCGR	.385
65	PSYCCL	.231	59	PLMBCN	.349	167	MWPCAD	.355	130	FSOCCW	.391
66	PSYCCN	.236	9	BARBER	.353	138	MANLHS	.355	119	FOCCTH	.392
84	TV REP	.242	24	DRCTFN	.357	145	MBSMGT	.358	133	FSOCPS	.393
73	SCHSUP	.246	26	ELECTR	.359	159	MPHYED	.367	97	FCHSHS	.395
67	PSYCIN	.247	16	CC EX	.363	144	MBSMRK	.422	132	FSOCMD	.403
56	PHYTHR	.248	36	INS AG	.364	140	MARTED	.453	115	FMTLMR	.419
54	PHARM	.248	12	BRKLYR	.372				134	FSOCSC	.420
47	NRSRYM	.252	41	MCHNST	.376				129	FSECY	.425
30	ENGIND	.256	23	DPTSTS	.378				123	FPRSCT	.437
88	X RAY	.259	89	YMCASC	.383				111	FKYPCH	.440
20	COUNHS	.260	58	PLUMBR	.384				93	FBKKPR	.441
3	AC CPA	.262	87	WELDER	.387				110	FINTDC	.443
49	OSTPTH	.265	61	POLICE	.396				108	FHMDEM	.454
86	VETRN	.265	6	AUTO M	.398				107	FFLRST	.456
14	BUYER	.273	50	PNTR H	.406				127	FRELED	.473
74	SOCCWK	.276	37	INTDEC	.420				99	FDNTAS	.479
10	BKKPR	.277	15	CRPNTR	.430				116	FNURSE	.480
4	AC IND	.277	53	PHAR S	.478				135	FSTENO	.481
55	PHOTOG	.277	83	TRKDRV	.480				120	FOFCLK	.488
									91	FBNKCL	.502
									92	FBEAUT	.512
									100	FDPTSW	.592

TABLE 19

MEAN SCORE DISTANCE OF MALE ENGLISH MAJORS (NO. 152)
FROM OTHER GROUPS

Employed Men				College Men		Employed Women		College Women	
40 LIBRAR .197	18 CLTH R .456		153 MFRNLG .079		125 FPSYCL .248		173 GENGL .138	
38 JOURN .218	72 SCITHS .458		155 MHIST .124		112 FLAWYR .251		176 GHISTO .205	
77 SOCPSY .224	27 ENGCVL .459		165 MSOC .165		133 FSOCPS .273		174 GFRNLG .217	
65 PSYCCL .229	47 NRSRYM .460		161 MPOLYS .169		124 FPSY .276		183 GPSYCH .218	
78 SOCRES .232	4 AC IND .461		163 MPSY .197		94 FBKMGR .295		182 GPOLYS .223	
85 U PSTR .244	1 AC AAA .463		156 MLAW .207		126 FPSYCN .299		185 GSOCSC .266	
64 PSYTST .251	54 PHARM .475		158 MMUSIC .245		130 FSOCCW .305		171 GDRMA .286	
66 PSYCCN .257	35 FORSTR .480		147 MELED .247		98 F DEAN .310		186 GSOC .294	
25 EDNWSP .264	31 ENGMCH .480		140 MARTED .274		132 FSOCMD .325		172 GELED .340	
74 SOCCWK .265	53 PHAR S .483		141 MBIOSC .300		113 FLIBR .327		168 GARTED .350	
79 SOCSCH .268	49 OSTPTH .484		146 MECON .304		131 FSOCGR .336		179 GMUSIC .355	
11 BKSMGR .276	14 BUYER .495		139 MARCH .305		96 FCMPRG .354		169 GBIOSC .358	
68 PSYPRF .278	29 ENGHAC .496		164 MCATHB .318		134 FSOCSC .357		170 GBUSGN .371	
39 LAWYER .285	7 BAKER .498		157 MMATH .329		121 FPEDRN .368		181 GPHYED .394	
75 SOCWKG .285	43 MATHHS .499		160 MPHYSC .331		110 FINTDC .369		177 GHMEC .402	
76 SOCWKM .286	34 FLORST .501		162 MPREMD .351		97 FCNSHS .382		178 GMATH .406	
80 STATCN .292	28 ENGELE .508		166 MAFCAD .356		95 FCTLIB .383		175 GHELTH .434	
45 MINIST .301	88 X RAY .509		167 MWPCAD .360		122 FPHYTH .390		180 GNURSE .445	
67 PSYCIN .313	84 TV REP .514		159 MPHYED .366		127 FRELED .393		184 GCATHS .550	
5 ARCH .322	86 VETRN .519		144 MBSMRK .375		111 FKYPCH .417			

#		Value	#		Value
51	PEDTRN	.329	46	MTLMGR	.522
20	COUNHS	.333	9	BARBER	.522
19	COMPRG	.337	30	ENGIND	.524
55	PHOTOG	.343	71	SLSENG	.529
42	MATHM	.344	36	INS AG	.537
37	INTDEC	.354	8	BANKER	.559
69	RADSTA	.367	61	POLICE	.563
82	TRVLAG	.367	21	COAGAG	.565
52	PERsM	.368	24	DRCTFN	.569
48	OPTMST	.375	10	BKKPR	.576
17	CHEMST	.385	13	BDG CN	.596
60	PODRST	.390	62	POSTCL	.601
16	CC EX	.392	12	BRKLYR	.612
3	AC CPA	.395	81	SUPVFM	.616
56	PHYTHR	.413	50	PNTR H	.628
2	AC	.415	59	PLMBCN	.639
22	DNTIST	.434	33	FARMER	.644
23	DPTSTS	.434	87	WELDER	.679
73	SCHSUP	.440	26	ELECTR	.682
89	YMCASC	.440	58	PLUMBR	.698
44	METEOR	.441	83	TRKDRV	.702
32	ENG MM	.441	41	MCHNST	.709
57	PHYSN	.447	6	AUTO M	.712
63	PRNTER	.451	15	CRPNTR	.732
70	REALES	.455			

#		Value	#		Value
145	MBSMGT	.390	101	FDTNAD	.430
143	MBSGEN	.393	117	FNUTRN	.434
154	MFORST	.417	104	FDTHOS	.439
142	MBUSAC	.423	103	FDTCOM	.442
148	MENGCH	.431	119	FOCCTH	.449
150	MENGEL	.465	90	FACNT	.452
151	MENGMH	.475	118	FNUTIN	.457
149	MENGCL	.491	129	FSECY	.461
138	MANLHS	.506	128	FSCTHS	.463
137	MAG	.523	123	FPRSCT	.476
			109	FHOMEC	.482
			106	FDTTHR	.498
			115	FMTLMR	.500
			136	FX RAY	.500
			107	FFLRST	.505
			116	FNURSE	.510
			105	FDTSCH	.520
			102	FDTCDM	.530
			108	FHMDEM	.536
			135	FSTENO	.539
			99	FDNTAS	.555
			114	FMATHS	.571
			92	FBEAUT	.594
			120	FOFCLK	.608
			93	FBKKPR	.615
			91	FBNKCL	.624
			100	EDPTSW	.672

TABLE 20

MEAN SCORE DISTANCE OF MALE PHYSICIANS (NO. 57)
FROM OTHER GROUPS

Employed Men					College Men		Employed Women		College Women	
49	OSTPTH	.045	79	SOCSCH	.270	162 MPREMD .155	122 FPHYTH .194	175 GHELTH .277
22	DNTIST	.068	13	BDG CN	.273	141 MBIOSC .169	136 FX RAY .211	169 GBIOSC .281
51	PEDTRN	.068	55	PHOTOG	.273	160 MPHYSC .221	128 FSCTHS .235	180 GNURSE .307
88	X RAY	.087	1	AC AAA	.275	147 MELED .222	121 FPEDRN .249	181 GPHYED .329
56	PHYTHR	.092	8	BANKER	.275	159 MPHYED .235	104 FDTHOS .288	178 GMATH .348
86	VETRN	.103	63	PRNTER	.276	164 MCATHB .248	106 FDTTHR .288	183 GPSYCH .383
54	PHARM	.112	52	PERS M	.277	157 MMATH .261	109 FHOMEC .296	184 GCATHS .387
48	OPTMST	.123	33	FARMER	.278	154 MFORST .262	96 FCMPRG .296	185 GSOCSC .415
72	SCITHS	.139	59	PLMBCN	.278	150 MENGEL .270	116 FNURSE .296	186 GSOC .431
64	PSYTST	.147	47	NRSRYM	.278	148 MENGCH .278	124 FPSY .300	176 GHISTO .432
60	PODRST	.156	61	POLICE	.278	165 MSOC .283	101 FDTNAD .310	177 GHMEC .433
17	CHEMST	.168	67	PSYCIN	.283	137 MAG .283	99 FDNTAS .313	174 GFRNLG .441
44	METEOR	.169	78	SOCRES	.285	163 MPSY .285	118 FNUTIN .323	172 GELED .445
24	DRCTFN	.187	34	FLORST	.286	138 MANLHS .292	117 FNUTRN .325	182 GPOLYS .474
43	MATHHS	.187	10	BKKPR	.288	149 MENGCL .294	119 FOCCTH .326	170 GBUSN .478
73	SCHSUP	.192	26	ELECTR	.288	151 MENGMH .313	105 FDTSCH .329	179 GMUSIC .496
32	ENG MM	.193	23	DPTSTS	.291	153 MFRNLG .318	125 FPSYCL .340	173 GENGL .533
28	ENGELE	.205	12	BRKLYR	.292	166 MAFCAD .320	126 FPSYCN .340	168 GARTED .606
68	PSYPRF	.206	70	REALES	.296	156 MLAW .350	90 FACNT .350	171 GDRMA .625
20	COUNHS	.211	75	SOCWKG	.296	155 MHIST .353	112 FLAWYR .353	

84	TV REP	.212	53	PHAR S	.296	167	MWPCAD	.359	98	F DEAN	.357
76	SOCWKM	.220	87	WELDER	.297	146	MECON	.363	102	FDTCDM	.358
27	ENGCVL	.222	50	PNTR H	.297	145	MBSMGT	.370	114	FMATHS	.363
42	MATHM	.224	89	YMCASC	.300	143	MBSGEN	.372	103	FDTCOM	.363
35	FORSTR	.226	30	ENGIND	.301	142	MBUSAC	.385	132	FSOCMD	.365
9	BARBER	.227	82	TRVLAG	.302	158	MMUSIC	.387	111	FKYPCH	.367
66	PSYCCN	.229	36	INS AG	.305	161	MPOLYS	.412	97	FCNSHS	.377
65	PSYCCL	.232	85	U PSTR	.308	144	MBSMRK	.429	130	FSOCCW	.378
77	SOCPSY	.235	58	PLUMBR	.310	139	MARCH	.445	131	FSOCGR	.379
29	ENGHAC	.236	18	CLTH R	.315	152	MENGL	.447	115	FMTLMR	.381
31	ENGMCH	.237	69	RADSTA	.317	140	MARTED	.550	94	FBKMGR	.393
74	SOCCWK	.239	41	MCHNST	.319				133	FSOCPS	.395
39	LAWYER	.241	6	AUTO M	.319				134	FSOCSC	.397
46	MTLMGR	.244	5	ARCH	.320				129	FSECY	.410
11	BKSMGR	.249	71	SLSENG	.322				108	FHMDEM	.418
19	COMPRG	.249	40	LIBRAR	.340				92	FBEAUT	.427
7	BAKER	.252	16	CC EX	.346				93	FBKKPR	.432
62	POSTCL	.258	4	AC IND	.347				107	FFLRST	.432
81	SUPVFM	.259	38	JOURN	.349				127	FRELED	.435
80	STATCN	.260	83	TRKDRV	.350				123	FPRSCT	.440
14	BUYER	.262	15	CRPNTR	.355				113	FLIBR	.445
2	AC	.263	25	ENDWSP	.356				95	FCTLIB	.450
21	COAGAG	.263	3	AC CPA	.362				135	FSTENO	.455
45	MINIST	.268	37	INTDEC	.497				120	FOFCLK	.462
									91	FBNKCL	.471
									100	FDPTSW	.521
									110	FINTDC	.557

107

TABLE 21
MEAN SCORE DISTANCE OF FEMALE PUBLIC SCHOOL DIETITIANS (NO. 105) FROM OTHER GROUPS

Employed Men						College Men			Employed Women			College Women		
20	COUNHS	.272	62	POSTCL	.363	147	MELED	.300	101	FDTNAD	.040	177	GHMEC	.149
48	OPTMST	.285	66	PSYCCN	.364	164	MCATHB	.323	102	FDTCDM	.042	178	GMATH	.189
24	DRCTFN	.286	81	SUPVFM	.365	153	MFRNLG	.362	104	FDTHOS	.047	170	GBUSGN	.216
47	NRSRYM	.289	70	REALES	.366	165	MSOC	.385	103	FDTCOM	.053	172	GELED	.217
51	PEDTRN	.290	85	U PSTR	.369	162	MPREMD	.398	106	FDTTHR	.064	175	GHELTH	.229
74	SOCCWK	.296	84	TV REP	.371	137	MAG	.402	118	FNUTIN	.069	180	GNURSE	.242
22	DNTIST	.297	5	ARCH	.374	157	MMATH	.408	109	FHOMEC	.077	185	GSOCSC	.255
7	BAKER	.298	21	COAGAG	.376	158	MMUSIC	.410	117	FNUTRN	.085	181	GPHYED	.258
76	SOCWKM	.298	16	CC EX	.376	159	MPHYED	.415	108	FHMDEM	.108	174	GFRNLG	.264
45	MINIST	.299	55	PHOTOG	.379	141	MBIOSC	.415	90	FACNT	.136	169	GBIOSC	.270
43	MATHHS	.301	68	PSYPRF	.382	155	MHIST	.423	97	FCNSHS	.138	176	GHISTO	.280
34	FLORST	.302	36	INS AG	.382	145	MBSMGT	.426	115	FMTLMR	.138	186	GSOC	.288
11	BKSMGR	.306	29	ENGHAC	.382	146	MECON	.434	114	FMATHS	.145	179	GMUSIC	.298
73	SCHSUP	.307	86	VETRN	.383	160	MPHYSC	.437	98	F DEAN	.160	183	GPSYCH	.314
54	PHARM	.312	27	ENGCVL	.386	148	MENGCH	.439	107	FFLRST	.161	184	GCATHS	.328
72	SCITHS	.312	28	ENGELE	.393	142	MBUSAC	.440	129	FSECY	.165	182	GPOLYS	.340
82	TRVLAG	.313	19	COMPRG	.393	138	MANLHS	.442	99	FDNTAS	.168	173	GENGL	.366
2	AC	.313	78	SOCRES	.396	150	MENGEL	.445	93	FBKKPR	.169	171	GDRMA	.455
14	BUYER	.314	33	FARMER	.402	143	MBSGEN	.449	136	FX RAY	.177	168	GARTED	.475
88	X RAY	.315	4	AC IND	.404	156	MLAW	.464	122	FPHYTH	.178			

#	Code	Value	#	Code	Value	#	Code	Value	#	Code	Value
89	YMCASC	.316	30	ENGIND	.406	163	MPSY	.465	123	FPRSCT	.182
40	LIBRAR	.317	3	AC CPA	.406	149	MENGCL	.465	132	FSOCMD	.189
60	PODRST	.318	65	PSYCCL	.407	154	MFORST	.470	131	FSOCGR	.191
79	SOCSCH	.319	67	PSYCIN	.407	151	MEMGMH	.479	134	FSOCSC	.195
64	PSYTST	.323	63	PRNTER	.413	161	MPOLYS	.481	91	FBNKCL	.196
9	BARBER	.327	31	ENGMCH	.416	167	MWPCAD	.496	126	FPSYCN	.202
39	LAWYER	.328	13	BDG CN	.423	144	MBSMRK	.504	116	FNURSE	.202
57	PHYSN	.329	12	BRKLYR	.424	166	MAFCAD	.512	135	FSTENO	.202
8	BANKER	.329	35	FORSTR	.426	152	MENGL	.520	92	FBEAUT	.203
56	PHYTHR	.330	71	SLSENG	.429	139	MARCH	.524	112	FLAWYR	.203
75	SOCWKG	.331	69	RADSTA	.430	140	MARTED	.565	94	FBKMGR	.208
49	OSTPTH	.335	53	PHAR S	.432				120	FOFCLK	.209
32	ENG MM	.338	50	PNTR H	.433				130	FSOCCW	.209
42	MATHM	.339	59	PLMBCN	.436				128	FSCTHS	.213
77	SOCPSY	.342	26	ELECTR	.459				96	FCMPRG	.215
80	STATCN	.345	87	WELDER	.462				121	FPEDRN	.215
46	MTLMGR	.345	58	PLUMBR	.464				113	FLIBR	.222
23	DPTSTS	.346	83	TRKDRV	.483				111	FKYPCH	.223
44	METEOR	.349	41	MCHNST	.486				133	FSOCPS	.232
17	CHEMST	.349	61	POLICE	.489				95	FCTLIB	.234
10	BKKPR	.350	6	AUTO M	.499				124	FPSY	.236
18	CLTH R	.350	15	CRPNTR	.502				127	FRELED	.238
37	INTDEC	.350	25	EDNWSP	.520				100	FDPTSW	.241
1	AC AAA	.351	38	JOURN	.535				119	FOCCTH	.247
52	PERS M	.362							125	FPSYCL	.273
									110	FINTDC	.307

TABLE 22

MEAN SCORE DISTANCE OF FEMALE PHYSICAL EDUCATION MAJORS (NO. 181)
FROM OTHER GROUPS

Employed Men						College Men			Employed Women			College Women		
56	PHYTHR	.220	68	PSYPRF	.420	147	MELED	.179	122	FPHYTH	.126	175	GHELTH	.094
76	SOCWKM	.254	63	PRNTER	.424	159	MPHYED	.208	119	FOCCTH	.170	180	GNURSE	.118
77	SOCPSY	.256	46	MTLMGR	.425	164	MCATHB	.213	116	FNURSE	.174	177	GHMEC	.122
74	SOCCWK	.265	81	SUPVFM	.425	153	MFRNLG	.234	136	FX RAY	.193	172	GELED	.127
75	SOCWKG	.274	73	SCHSUP	.425	165	MSOC	.250	104	FDTHOS	.196	186	GSOC	.135
22	DNTIST	.276	19	COMPRG	.426	162	MPREMD	.294	111	FKYPCH	.203	174	GFRNLG	.152
79	SOCSCH	.278	67	PSYCIN	.427	141	MBIOSC	.297	99	FDNTAS	.210	185	GSOCSC	.156
51	PEDTRN	.279	44	METEOR	.429	158	MMUSIC	.302	106	FDTTHR	.210	169	GBIOSC	.162
64	PSYTST	.287	61	POLICE	.430	163	MPSY	.329	101	FDTNAD	.230	178	GMATH	.172
60	PODRST	.294	42	MATHM	.433	166	MAFCAD	.355	131	FSOCGR	.237	183	GPSYCH	.173
20	COUNHS	.296	39	LAWYER	.436	140	MARTED	.357	115	FMTLMR	.242	179	GMUSIC	.207
48	OPTMST	.298	29	ENGHAC	.437	139	MARCH	.368	133	FSOCPS	.243	170	GBUSGN	.208
88	X RAY	.301	32	ENG MM	.441	167	MWPCAD	.379	130	FSOCCW	.244	176	GHISTO	.211
45	MINIST	.301	17	CHEMST	.445	155	MHIST	.380	134	FSOCSC	.245	171	GDRMA	.236
49	OSTPTH	.306	36	INS AG	.446	157	MMATH	.393	103	FDTCOM	.246	173	GENGL	.255
24	DRCTFN	.317	8	BANKER	.448	152	MENGL	.394	127	FRELED	.246	184	GCATHS	.264
85	U PSTR	.325	2	AC	.449	145	MBSMGT	.401	98	F DEAN	.248	182	GPOLYS	.276
23	DPTSTS	.325	35	FORSTR	.449	160	MPHYSC	.401	132	FSOCMD	.248	168	GARTED	.280
55	PHOTOG	.327	31	ENGMCH	.453	154	MFORST	.404	118	FNUTIN	.250			
89	YMCASC	.328	27	ENGCVL	.456	156	MLAW	.406	107	FFLRST	.251			

No.	Code	Value
57	PHYSN	.329
9	BARBER	.330
37	INTDEC	.344
54	PHARM	.347
72	SCITHS	.349
66	PSYCCN	.355
65	PSYCCL	.357
34	FLORST	.373
11	BKSMGR	.376
5	ARCH	.377
7	BAKER	.378
82	TRVLAG	.381
86	VETRN	.381
40	LIBRAR	.383
53	PHAR S	.394
14	BUYER	.395
52	PERS M	.397
50	PNTR H	.402
12	BRKLYR	.403
43	MATHHS	.403
47	NRSRYM	.407
78	SOCRES	.413
18	CLTH R	.415
84	TV REP	.415
62	POSTCL	.420

No.	Code	Value
87	WELDER	.459
69	RADSTA	.459
16	CC EX	.460
80	STATCN	.461
70	REALES	.468
71	SLSENG	.469
10	BKKPR	.472
26	ELECTR	.473
59	PLMBCN	.475
28	ENGELE	.476
21	COAGAG	.480
13	BDG CN	.482
3	AC CPA	.483
4	AC IND	.490
83	TRKDRV	.495
41	MCHNST	.499
58	PLUMBR	.500
6	AUTO M	.501
30	ENGIND	.501
15	CRPNTR	.505
1	AC AAA	.506
33	FARMER	.517
38	JOURN	.523
25	EDNWSP	.537

No.	Code	Value
138	MANLHS	.406
137	MAG	.413
149	MENGCL	.426
150	MENGEL	.428
151	MENGMH	.431
148	MENGCH	.435
143	MBSGEN	.442
146	MECON	.443
161	MPOLYS	.445
144	MBSMRK	.454
142	MBUSAC	.472

No.	Code	Value
123	FPRSCT	.256
105	FDTSCH	.258
97	FCNSHS	.260
108	FHMDEM	.261
121	FPEDRN	.264
125	FPSYCL	.269
129	FSECY	.271
102	FDTCDM	.271
92	FBEAUT	.282
126	FPSYCN	.282
96	FCMPRG	.284
135	FSTENO	.286
117	FNUTRN	.287
124	FPSY	.301
128	FSCTHS	.316
91	FBNKCL	.316
94	FBKMGR	.324
93	FBKKPR	.326
113	FLIBR	.327
120	FOFCLK	.328
109	FHOMEC	.328
112	FLAWYR	.342
114	FMATHS	.350
90	FACNT	.350
100	FDPTSW	.372
110	FINTDC	.380
95	FCTLIB	.386

TABLE 23

MEAN SCORE DISTANCE OF MALE PSYCHIATRIC SOCIAL WORKERS (NO. 77)
FROM OTHER GROUPS

Employed Men						College Men			Employed Women			College Women		
74	SOCCWK	.026	3	AC CPA	.322	165	MSOC	.094	133	FSOPS	.131	185	GSOCSC	.178
76	SOCWKM	.035	24	DRCTFN	.326	147	MELED	.128	125	FPSYCL	.139	183	GPSYCH	.181
79	SOCSCH	.035	2	AC	.326	153	MFRNLG	.154	130	FSOCCW	.145	186	GSOC	.187
75	SOCWKG	.050	43	MATHHS	.329	163	MPSY	.161	124	FPSY	.159	176	GHISTO	.217
65	PSYCCL	.072	86	VETRN	.330	155	MHIST	.170	131	FSOCGR	.159	182	GPOLYS	.224
64	PSYTST	.075	14	BUYER	.333	156	MLAW	.190	126	FPSYCN	.165	174	GFRNLG	.248
66	PSYCCN	.087	18	CLTH R	.337	161	MPOLYS	.206	132	FSOCMD	.167	181	GPHYED	.256
78	SOCRES	.099	70	REALES	.338	162	MPREMD	.216	134	FSOCSC	.177	172	GELED	.259
20	COUNHS	.113	25	EDNWSP	.341	159	MPHYED	.221	98	F DEAN	.191	173	GENGL	.266
85	U PSTR	.123	7	BAKER	.342	152	MENGL	.224	112	FLAWYR	.210	180	GNURSE	.283
45	MINIST	.162	37	INTDEC	.344	141	MBIOSC	.234	122	FPHYTH	.218	175	GHELTH	.288
56	PHYTHR	.166	4	AC IND	.346	164	MCATHB	.263	97	FCNSHS	.234	177	GHMEC	.291
51	PEDTRN	.167	31	ENGMCH	.349	158	MMUSIC	.272	121	FPEDRN	.246	169	GBIOSC	.305
68	PSYPRF	.168	27	ENGCVL	.349	146	MECON	.272	101	FDTNAD	.258	171	GDRMA	.332
67	PSYCIN	.171	29	ENGHAC	.357	166	MAFCAD	.291	104	FDTHOS	.263	179	GMUSIC	.334
60	PODRST	.177	46	MTLMGR	.359	167	MWPCAD	.301	127	FRELED	.271	178	GMATH	.340
52	PERS M	.180	30	ENGIND	.365	145	MBSMGT	.303	119	FOCCTH	.274	170	GBUSGN	.352
48	OPTMST	.186	84	TV REP	.365	157	MMATH	.319	117	FNUTRN	.276	168	GARTED	.429
89	YMCASC	.211	47	NRSRYM	.366	160	MPHYSC	.323	118	FNUTIN	.291	184	GCATHS	.433
39	LAWYER	.217	36	INS AG	.375	143	MBSGEN	.329	106	FDTTHR	.310			

112

22	DNTIST	.226	28	ENGELE	.379	139	MARCH	.339	96	FCMPRG	.313
40	LIBRAR	.232	34	FLORST	.380	144	MBSMRK	.350	103	FDTCOM	.317
57	PHYSN	.235	71	SLSENG	.381	148	MENGCH	.361	94	FBKMGR	.330
49	OSTPTH	.238	1	AC AAA	.382	140	MARTED	.379	109	FHOMEC	.332
80	STATCN	.253	63	PRNTER	.392	150	MENGEL	.384	116	FNURSE	.334
11	BKSMGR	.260	35	FORSTR	.393	142	MBUSAC	.386	136	FX RAY	.337
73	SCHSUP	.261	61	POLICE	.395	154	MFORST	.387	105	FDTSCH	.342
55	PHOTOG	.271	8	BANKER	.397	151	MENGMH	.391	113	FLIBR	.349
82	TRVLAG	.273	21	COAGAG	.408	149	MENGCL	.401	128	FSCTHS	.352
72	SCITHS	.279	81	SUPVFM	.422	137	MAG	.417	111	FKYPCH	.355
5	ARcH	.280	13	BDG CN	.440	138	MANLHS	.423	102	FDTCDM	.371
42	MATHM	.286	12	BRKLYR	.443				108	FHMDEM	.375
17	CHEMST	.287	50	PNTR H	.445				90	FACNT	.381
54	PHARM	.290	62	POSTCL	.446				115	FMTLMR	.385
88	X RAY	.295	59	PLMBCN	.457				110	FINTDC	.392
16	CC EX	.296	33	FARMER	.468				99	FDNTAS	.392
23	DPTSTS	.304	10	BKKPR	.471				123	FPRSCT	.392
53	PHAR S	.307	87	WELDER	.488				107	FFLRST	.411
44	METEOR	.308	26	ELECTR	.498				129	FSECY	.411
19	COMPRG	.308	58	PLUMBR	.522				95	FCTLIB	.412
69	RADSTA	.309	83	TRKDRV	.525				114	FMATHS	.447
38	JOURN	.311	41	MCHNST	.530				92	FBEAUT	.462
9	BARBER	.317	15	CRPNTR	.543				135	FSTENO	.475
32	ENG MM	.319	6	AUTO M	.543				93	FBKKPR	.507
									120	FOFCLK	.529
									91	FBNKCL	.531
									100	FDPTSW	.551

TABLE 24

MEAN SCORE DISTANCE OF MALE MINISTERS (NO. 45)
FROM OTHER GROUPS

Employed Men						College Men			Employed Women			College Women		
85	U PSTR	.073	70	REALES	.346	164	MCATHB	.195	127	FRELED	.130	185	GSOCSC	.244
74	SOCCWK	.123	7	BAKER	.350	147	MELED	.196	98	F DEAN	.130	176	GHISTO	.250
79	SOCSCH	.124	46	MTLMGR	.354	165	MSOC	.211	131	FSOCGR	.143	186	GSOC	.266
76	SOCWKM	.137	34	FLORST	.356	153	MFRNLG	.213	134	FSOCSC	.183	184	GCATHS	.273
75	SOCWKG	.137	63	PRNTER	.357	155	MHIST	.238	97	FCNSHS	.183	174	GFRNLG	.281
89	YMCASC	.147	37	INTDEC	.358	152	MENGL	.301	130	FSOCCW	.186	172	GELED	.286
20	COUNHS	.153	25	ENDWSP	.358	161	MPOLYS	.302	126	FPSYCN	.188	180	GNURSE	.286
77	SOCPSY	.162	14	BUYER	.359	158	MMUSIC	.311	132	FSOCMD	.199	183	GPSYCH	.300
66	PSYCCN	.186	21	COAGAG	.362	163	MPSY	.317	112	FLAWYR	.206	181	GPHYED	.301
64	PSYTST	.188	18	CLTH R	.363	156	MLAW	.321	133	FSOCPS	.224	182	GPOLYS	.306
78	SOCRES	.193	2	AC	.363	159	MPHYED	.337	122	FPHYTH	.225	173	GENGL	.307
40	LIBRAR	.207	27	ENGCVL	.367	141	MBIOSC	.337	125	FPSYCL	.227	177	GHMEC	.310
39	LAWYER	.210	86	VETRN	.368	162	MPREMD	.339	124	FPSY	.229	179	GMUSIC	.323
51	PEDTRN	.210	47	NRSRYM	.369	146	MECON	.381	104	FDTHOS	.232	175	GHELTH	.330
73	SCHSUP	.225	53	PHAR S	.370	157	MMATH	.393	101	FDTNAD	.233	169	GBIOSC	.347
52	PERS M	.226	36	INS AG	.377	160	MPHYSC	.396	117	FNUTRN	.233	178	GMATH	.350
65	PSYCCL	.233	19	COMPRG	.378	145	MBSMGT	.419	118	FNUTIN	.239	170	GBUSGN	.396
68	PSYPRF	.241	31	ENGMCH	.380	139	MARCH	.428	109	FHOMEC	.245	171	GDRMA	.404
56	PHYTHR	.242	1	AC AAA	.382	166	MAFCAD	.434	121	FPEDRN	.253	168	GARTED	.453
11	BKSMGR	.244	84	TV REP	.384	154	MFORST	.436	119	FOCCTH	.253			

60	PODRST	.263
57	PHYSN	.268
22	DNTIST	.269
48	OPTMST	.274
49	OSTPTH	.283
24	DRCTFN	.285
72	SCITHS	.286
80	STATCN	.292
23	DPTSTS	.292
16	CC EX	.293
67	PSYCIN	.294
42	MATHM	.295
88	X RAY	.296
82	TRVLAG	.301
43	MATHHS	.307
5	ARCH	.310
17	CHEMST	.321
54	PHARM	.329
9	BARBER	.336
38	JOURN	.336
55	PHOTOG	.337
69	RADSTA	.339
44	METEOR	.339
32	ENG MM	.339

8	BANKER	.384
29	ENGHAC	.385
28	ENGELE	.397
30	ENGIND	.400
81	SUPVFM	.406
62	POSTCL	.408
35	FORSTR	.408
33	FARMER	.413
3	AC CPA	.418
13	BDG CN	.420
50	PNTR H	.426
71	SLSENG	.426
4	AC IND	.435
10	BKKPR	.437
12	BRKLYR	.439
61	POLICE	.444
59	PLMBCN	.450
83	TRKDRV	.468
26	ELECTR	.477
87	WELDER	.481
58	PLUMBR	.487
41	MCHNST	.494
15	CRPNTR	.498
6	AUTO M	.510

167	MWPCAD	.436
137	MAG	.447
143	MBSGEN	.449
140	MARTED	.456
150	MENGEL	.460
148	MENGCH	.461
138	MANLHS	.467
144	MBSMRK	.481
149	MENGCL	.482
142	MBUSAC	.484
151	MENGMH	.488

94	FBKMGR	.260
113	FLIBR	.272
106	FDTTHR	.272
128	FSCTHS	.276
108	FHMDEM	.278
136	FX RAY	.287
103	FDTCOM	.298
95	FCTLIB	.298
105	FDTSCH	.299
116	FNURSE	.300
102	FDTCDM	.315
123	FPRSCT	.319
90	FACNT	.322
115	FMTLMR	.325
107	FFLRST	.335
114	FMATHS	.340
111	FKYPCH	.345
96	FCMPRG	.346
99	FDNTAS	.347
129	FSECY	.362
110	FINTDC	.379
92	FBEAUT	.401
135	FSTENO	.423
93	FBKKPR	.426
100	FDPTSW	.440
120	FOFCLK	.446
91	FBNKCL	.467

TABLE 25

MEAN SCORE DISTANCE OF MALE ART AND ART EDUCATION MAJORS (NO. 140)
FROM OTHER GROUPS

Employed Men						College Men			Employed Women			College Women		
37	INTDEC	.193	88	X RAY	.525	139	MARCH	.108	110	FINTDC	.257	168	GARTED	.099
5	ARCH	.205	50	PNTR H	.528	153	MFRNLG	.218	119	FOCCTH	.314	171	GDRMA	.262
55	PHOTOG	.256	28	ENGELE	.530	158	MMUSIC	.265	96	FCMPRG	.355	183	GPSYCH	.272
77	SOCPSY	.379	44	METEOR	.533	152	MENGL	.274	125	FPSYCL	.364	174	GFRNLG	.282
64	PSYTST	.380	18	CLTH R	.535	165	MSOC	.297	124	FPSY	.404	176	GHISTO	.307
40	LIBRAR	.392	72	SCITHS	.535	147	MELED	.321	94	FBKMGR	.405	173	GENGL	.310
65	PSYCCL	.393	16	CC EX	.538	163	MPSY	.342	133	FSOCPS	.412	182	GPOLYS	.340
19	COMPRG	.395	70	REALES	.539	155	MHIST	.386	122	FPHYTH	.413	186	GSOC	.351
11	BKSMGR	.402	35	FORSTR	.540	166	MAFCAD	.395	131	FSOCGR	.439	181	GPHYED	.357
66	PSYCCN	.431	54	PHARM	.540	141	MBIOSC	.405	126	FPSYCN	.445	179	GMUSIC	.367
74	SOCCWK	.432	49	OSTPTH	.544	156	MLAW	.409	112	FLAWYR	.448	177	GHMEC	.373
85	U PSTR	.435	89	YMCASC	.545	160	MPHYSC	.424	130	FSOCCW	.448	169	GBIOSC	.375
75	SOCWKG	.439	30	ENGIND	.547	161	MPOLYS	.425	98	F DEAN	.458	185	GSOCSC	.383
51	PEDTRN	.439	57	PHYSN	.550	167	MWPCAD	.429	121	FPEDRN	.458	178	GMATH	.395
78	SOCRES	.442	13	BDG CN	.551	164	MCATHB	.436	107	FFLRST	.465	172	GELED	.399
68	PSYPRF	.448	9	BARBER	.554	159	MPHYED	.440	113	FLIBR	.480	170	GBUSGN	.411
79	SOCSCH	.450	2	AC	.556	144	MBSMRK	.444	132	FSOCMD	.484	175	GHELTH	.424
80	STATCN	.451	14	BUYER	.557	157	MMATH	.447	111	FKYPCH	.485	180	GNURSE	.503
63	PRNTER	.453	3	AC CPA	.561	151	MENGMH	.457	134	FSOCSC	.487	184	GCATHS	.608
42	MATHM	.453	46	MTLMGR	.562	154	MFORST	.459	127	FRELED	.504			

No.	Code	Value		No.	Code	Value		No.	Code	Value		No.	Code	Value
22	DNTIST	.453		12	BRKLYR	.572		145	MBSMGT	.471		104	FDTHOS	.505
82	TRVLAG	.453		1	AC AAA	.584		146	MECON	.477		101	FDTNAD	.505
45	MINIST	.456		53	PHAR S	.585		150	MENGEL	.480		103	FDTCOM	.512
76	SOCWKM	.456		43.	MATHHS	.594		162	MPREMD	.481		108	FHMDEM	.526
56	PHYTHR	.458		24	DRCTFN	.595		143	MGSGEN	.484		115	FMTLMR	.526
67	PSYCIN	.463		4	AC IND	.596		149	MENGCL	.494		123	FPRSCT	.532
48	OPTMST	.471		59	PLMBCN	.604		148	MENGCH	.504		136	FX RAY	.538
69	RADSTA	.472		86	VETRN	.609		138	MANLHS	.547		117	FNUTRN	.542
34	FLORST	.473		61	POLICE	.611		142	MBUSAC	.565		95	FCTLIB	.547
23	DPTSTS	.474		73	SCHSUP	.617		137	MAG	.585		97	FCNSHS	.548
17	CHEMST	.481		36	INS AG	.623						116	FNURSE	.552
38	JOURN	.481		81	SUPVFM	.624						129	FSECY	.553
47	NRSRYM	.484		87	WELDER	.628						128	FSCTHS	.558
31	ENGMCH	.485		26	ELECTR	.630						90	FACNT	.562
60	PODRST	.488		8	BANKER	.647						118	FNUTIN	.563
20	COUNHS	.492		62	POSTCL	.648						105	FDTSCH	.565
29	ENGHAC	.493		58	PLUMBR	.654						106	FDTTHR	.569
27	ENGCVL	.499		6	AUTO M	.661						102	FDTCDM	.572
32	ENG MM	.504		41	MCHNST	.662						92	FBEAUT	.575
39	LAWYER	.510		10	BKKPR	.663						99	FDNTAS	.583
52	PERS M	.515		15	CRPNTR	.664						109	FHOMEC	.595
84	TV REP	.520		21	COAGAG	.677						135	FSTENO	.598
71	SLSENG	.520		83	TRKDRV	.720						114	FMATHS	.647
25	EDNWSP	.522		33	FARMER	.733						120	FOFCLK	.649
7	BAKER	.523										93	FBKKPR	.677
												91	FBNKCL	.682
												100	FDPTSW	.712

TABLE 26

MEAN SCORE DISTANCE OF MALE MECHANICAL ENGINEERING MAJORS (NO. 151)
FROM OTHER GROUPS

Employed Men					Employed Men				College Men				Employed Women				College Women		
31	ENGMCH	.071		24	DRCTFN	.271		150	MENGEL	.036		96	FCMPRG	.317		178	GMATH	.367
29	ENGHAC	.088		5	ARCH	.272		149	MENGCL	.044		122	FPHYTH	.459		181	GPHYED	.431
30	ENGIND	.099		63	PRNTER	.276		148	MENGCH	.057		101	FDTNAD	.472		170	GBUSGN	.443
27	ENGCVL	.107		87	WELDER	.276		157	MMATH	.110		90	FACNT	.474		169	GBIOSC	.444
28	ENGELE	.107		18	CLTH R	.276		145	MBSMGT	.120		128	FSCTHS	.477		175	GHELTH	.467
32	ENG MM	.116		10	BKKPR	.279		143	MBSGEN	.132		105	FDTSCH	.479		183	GPSYCH	.485
19	COMPRG	.119		11	BKSMGR	.284		154	MFORST	.135		103	FDTCOM	.495		177	GHMEC	.516
71	SLSENG	.123		58	PLUMBR	.284		160	MPHYSC	.136		124	FPSY	.508		182	GPOLYS	.545
84	TV REP	.154		69	RADSTA	.285		166	MAFCAD	.139		102	FDTCDM	.509		176	GHISTO	.548
4	AC IND	.162		68	PSYPRF	.287		142	MBUSAC	.149		136	FX RAY	.511		174	GFRNLG	.572
35	FORSTR	.163		9	BARBER	.287		167	MWPCAD	.154		119	FOCCTH	.516		185	GSOCSC	.577
44	METEOR	.164		6	AUTO M	.293		137	MAG	.157		104	FDTHOS	.517		186	GSOC	.579
14	BUYER	.178		49	OSTPTH	.294		146	MECON	.166		112	FLAWYR	.525		172	GELED	.581
59	PLMBCN	.182		20	COUNHS	.296		144	MBSMRK	.184		114	FMATHS	.526		180	GNURSE	.598
48	OPTMST	.183		16	CC EX	.300		159	MPHYED	.195		106	FDTTHR	.538		168	GARTED	.616
3	AC CPA	.192		62	POSTCL	.300		138	MANLHS	.198		109	FHOMEC	.547		179	GMUSIC	.617
43	MATHHS	.196		73	SCHSUP	.301		147	MELED	.212		111	FKYPCH	.547		171	GDRMA	.645
1	AC AAA	.196		53	PHAR S	.303		162	MPREMD	.214		125	FPSYCL	.552		173	GENGL	.646
55	PHOTOG	.196		57	PHYSN	.313		141	MBIOSC	.231		126	FPSYCN	.555		184	GCATHS	.678
2	AC	.204		60	PODRST	.314		139	MARCH	.232		98	F DEAN	.566				

No.	Scale	r	No.	Scale	r	No.	Scale	r	No.	Scale	r
46	MTLMGR	.205	21	COAGAG	.316	163	MPSY	.244	115	FMTLMR	.568
13	BDG CN	.206	33	FARMER	.318	156	MLAW	.270	108	FHMDEM	.574
72	SCITHS	.209	66	PSYCCN	.322	165	MSOC	.286	118	FNUTIN	.576
17	CHEMST	.209	50	PNTR H	.324	161	MPOLYS	.359	117	FNUTRN	.586
22	DNTIST	.215	51	PEDTRN	.327	153	MFRNLG	.364	107	FFLRST	.589
67	PSYCIN	.224	23	DPTSTS	.331	155	MHIST	.371	93	FBKKPR	.591
7	BAKER	.230	15	CRPNTR	.338	158	MMUSIC	.372	121	FPEDRN	.594
81	SUPVFM	.231	39	LAWYER	.342	164	MCATHB	.372	129	FSECY	.596
47	NRSRYM	.231	64	PSYTST	.344	140	MARTED	.457	99	FDNTAS	.597
56	PHYTHR	.232	65	PSYCCL	.352	152	MENGL	.475	94	FBKMGR	.600
36	INS AG	.240	89	YMCASC	.366				97	FCNSHS	.602
8	BANKER	.241	83	TRKDRV	.386				131	FSOCGR	.612
26	ELECTR	.241	77	SOCPSY	.391				110	FINTDC	.614
34	FLORST	.244	74	SOCCWK	.394				116	FNURSE	.626
54	PHARM	.244	76	SOCWKM	.397				91	FBNKCL	.631
61	POLICE	.245	78	SOCRES	.416				133	FSOCPS	.634
88	X RAY	.251	75	SOCWKG	.416				135	FSTENO	.640
52	PERS M	.252	38	JOURN	.424				92	FBEAUT	.640
42	MATHM	.253	85	U PSTR	.429				130	FSOCCW	.657
82	TRVLAG	.256	40	LIBRAR	.435				113	FLIBR	.666
80	STATCN	.258	25	ENDWSP	.436				120	FOFCLK	.670
70	REALES	.262	79	SOCSCH	.461				132	FSOCMD	.675
41	MCHNST	.265	45	MINIST	.488				134	FSOCSC	.678
86	VETRN	.266	37	INTDEC	.507				123	FPRSCT	.681
12	BRKLYR	.266							127	FRELED	.696
									95	FCTLIB	.705
									100	FDPTSW	.716

TABLE 27

MEAN SCORE DISTANCE OF MALE LIBRARIANS (NO. 40)
FROM OTHER GROUPS

Employed Men						College Men			Employed Women			College Women		
11	BKSMGR	.108	14	BUYER	.325	153	MFRNLG	.159	113	FLIBR	.138	176	GHISTO	.173
39	LAWYER	.149	3	AC CPA	.328	155	MHIST	.185	95	FCTLIB	.157	173	GENGL	.262
42	MATHM	.174	18	CLTH R	.331	152	MENGL	.197	94	FBKMGR	.157	174	GFRNLG	.272
38	JOURN	.184	28	ENGELE	.336	147	MELED	.250	112	FLAWYR	.162	182	GPOLYS	.283
80	STATCN	.188	57	PHYSN	.340	161	MPOLYS	.254	98	F DEAN	.200	185	GSOCSC	.303
25	EDNWSP	.189	31	ENGMCH	.340	165	MSOC	.263	124	FPSY	.215	178	GMATH	.327
45	MINIST	.207	23	DPTSTS	.340	158	MMUSIC	.277	126	FPSYCN	.228	172	GELED	.327
68	PSYPRF	.214	29	ENGHAC	.341	156	MLAW	.284	96	FCMPRG	.235	170	GBUSGN	.333
78	SOCRES	.218	56	PHYTHR	.343	164	MCATHB	.292	131	FSOCGR	.241	183	GPSYCH	.333
74	SOCCWK	.219	34	FLORST	.345	157	MMATH	.320	125	FPSYCL	.244	179	GMUSIC	.349
64	PSYTST	.222	35	FORSTR	.347	160	MPHYSC	.329	130	FSOCCW	.249	186	GSOC	.361
85	U PSTR	.232	8	BANKER	.351	146	MECON	.332	97	FCNSHS	.253	177	GHMEC	.364
77	SOCPSY	.232	54	PHARM	.352	163	MPSY	.350	132	FSOCMD	.253	169	GBIOSC	.378
17	CHEMST	.235	60	PODRST	.356	141	MBIOSC	.360	133	FSOCPS	.259	181	GPHYED	.383
20	COUNHS	.238	46	MTLMGR	.356	139	MARCH	.368	90	FACNT	.260	171	GDRMA	.408
66	PSYCCN	.239	88	X RAY	.364	154	MFORST	.384	134	FSOCSC	.267	175	GHELTH	.411
51	PEDTRN	.242	7	BAKER	.367	143	MBSGEN	.388	121	FPEDRN	.282	180	GNURSE	.428
5	ARCH	.243	4	AC IND	.369	145	MBSMGT	.392	122	FPHYTH	.286	168	GARTED	.433
79	SOCSCH	.245	10	BKKPR	.371	140	MARTED	.392	101	FDTNAD	.286	184	GCATHS	.452
76	SOCWKM	.249	84	TV REP	.379	159	MPHYED	.395	117	FNUTRN	.294			

No.	Code	Value		No.	Code	Value		No.	Code	Value		No.	Code	Value
65	PSYCCL	.252		49	OSTPTH	.389		142	MBUSAC	.400		109	FHOMEC	.300
75	SOCWKG	.257		30	ENGIND	.389		150	MENGEL	.400		104	FDTHOS	.301
19	COMPRG	.262		62	POSTCL	.391		162	MPREMD	.408		128	FSCTHS	.303
2	AC	.263		21	COAGAG	.392		148	MENGCH	.411		103	FDTCOM	.304
73	SCHSUP	.263		9	BARBER	.392		144	MBSMRK	.419		110	FINTDC	.304
82	TRVLAG	.264		86	VETRN	.397		149	MENGCL	.421		114	FMATHS	.305
44	METEOR	.271		24	DRCTFN	.398		167	MWPCAD	.423		123	FPRSCT	.306
48	OPTMST	.276		36	INS AG	.399		137	MAG	.428		127	FRELED	.307
32	ENG MM	.279		13	BDG CN	.418		151	MENGMH	.435		129	FSECY	.312
67	PSYCIN	.286		71	SLSENG	.422		166	MAFCAD	.444		118	FNUTIN	.316
52	PERS M	.291		81	SUPVFM	.423		138	MANLHS	.466		105	FDTSCH	.317
43	MATHHS	.291		33	FARMER	.438						102	FDTCDM	.321
27	ENGCVL	.293		12	BRKLYR	.456						115	FMTLMR	.328
16	CC EX	.295		59	PLMBCN	.465						119	FOCCTH	.336
1	AC AAA	.297		61	POLICE	.468						106	FDTTHR	.337
37	INTDEC	.299		53	PHAR S	.470						108	FHMDEM	.340
55	PHOTOG	.302		50	PNTR H	.478						107	FFLRST	.347
63	PRNTER	.303		26	ELECTR	.490						136	FX RAY	.363
72	SCITHS	.307		58	PLUMBR	.490						111	FKYPCH	.371
47	NRSRYM	.307		87	WELDER	.502						135	FSTENO	.371
69	RADSTA	.308		41	MCHNST	.507						93	FBKKPR	.397
22	DNTIST	.310		6	AUTO M	.524						120	FOFCLK	.400
70	REALES	.317		15	CRPNTR	.532						116	FNURSE	.410
89	YMCASC	.323		83	TRKDRV	.542						99	FDNTAS	.421
												92	FBEAUT	.425
												91	FBNKCL	.431
												100	FDPTSW	.472

TABLE 28

MEAN SCORE DISTANCE OF MALE NEWSPAPER EDITORS (NO. 25)
FROM OTHER GROUPS

Employed Men			College Men			Employed Women			College Women		
38	JOURN	.012	152	MENGL	.264	112	FLAWYR	.309	176	GHISTO	.422
11	BKSMGR	.162	155	MHIST	.271	94	FBKMGR	.351	182	GPOLYS	.443
39	LAWYER	.181	153	MFRNLG	.302	113	FLIBR	.394	173	GENGL	.456
40	LIBRAR	.189	156	MLAW	.303	124	FPSY	.408	170	GBUSGN	.483
63	PRNTER	.205	161	MPOLYS	.305	95	FCTLIB	.412	174	GFRNLG	.494
69	RADSTA	.229	146	MECON	.341	98	F DEAN	.422	185	GSOCSC	.497
16	CC EX	.236	165	MSOC	.343	96	FCMPRG	.425	183	GPSYCH	.515
82	TRVLAG	.249	147	MELED	.360	125	FPSYCL	.432	181	GPHYED	.537
80	STATCN	.268	154	MFORST	.373	126	FPSYCN	.432	186	GSOC	.547
70	REALES	.269	143	MBSGEN	.374	90	FACNT	.432	178	GMATH	.555
27	ENGCVL	.274	157	MMATH	.381	122	FPHYTH	.458	172	GELED	.564
44	METEOR	.283	159	MPHYED	.382	132	FSOCMD	.459	177	GHMEC	.579
73	SCHSUP	.286	145	MBSMGT	.388	130	FSOCCW	.459	169	GBIOSC	.585
2	AC	.286	144	MBSMRK	.389	133	FSOCPS	.462	171	GDRMA	.592
32	ENG MM	.288	164	MCATHB	.391	129	FSECY	.465	179	GMUSIC	.599
68	PSYPRF	.290	142	MBUSAC	.400	131	FSOCGR	.471	175	GHELTH	.613
52	PERS M	.290	160	MPHYSC	.403	115	FMTLMR	.477	180	GNURSE	.613
18	CLTH R	.291	163	MPSY	.414	103	FDTCOM	.479	168	GARTED	.636
46	MTLMGR	.292	137	MAG	.416	97	FCNSHS	.483	184	GCATHS	.646
42	MATHM	.293	149	MENGCL	.419	101	FDTNAD	.485			
84	TV REP	.337									
29	ENGHAC	.338									
36	INS AG	.339									
21	COAGAG	.340									
77	SOCPSY	.341									
3	AC CPA	.343									
7	BAKER	.349									
61	POLICE	.351									
10	BKKPR	.355									
57	PHYSN	.356									
45	MINIST	.358									
76	SOCWKM	.358									
62	POSTCL	.359									
13	BDG CN	.364									
9	BARBER	.367									
43	MATHHS	.368									
4	AC IND	.370									
86	VETRN	.372									
88	X RAY	.376									
30	ENGIND	.376									

No.	Code	Value	No.	Code	Value	No.	Code	Value	No.	Code	Value
1	AC AAA	.299	24	DRCTFN	.376	151	MENGMH	.436	134	FSOCSC	.494
14	BUYER	.299	89	YMCASC	.377	167	MWPCAD	.437	121	FPEDRN	.495
35	FORSTR	.300	56	PHYTHR	.381	158	MMUSIC	.438	117	FNUTRN	.504
55	PHOTOG	.305	85	U PSTR	.381	141	BMIOSC	.443	110	FINTDC	.505
67	PSYCIN	.312	59	PLMBCN	.381	148	MENGCH	.444	111	FKYPCH	.509
66	PSYCCN	.315	79	SOCSCH	.389	150	MENGEL	.444	128	FSCTHS	.510
47	NRSRYM	.315	81	SUPVFM	.391	166	MAFCAD	.448	136	FX RAY	.510
28	ENGELE	.316	75	SOCWKG	.392	138	MANLHS	.449	104	FDTHOS	.512
17	CHEMST	.318	12	BRKLYR	.396	162	MPREMD	.464	135	FSTENO	.517
48	OPTMST	.319	71	SLSENG	.397	139	MARCH	.478	107	FFLRST	.519
51	PEDTRN	.321	72	SCITHS	.397	140	MARTED	.522	105	FDTSCH	.520
5	ARCH	.322	60	PODRST	.398				102	FDTCDM	.532
22	DNTIST	.323	33	FARMER	.402				108	FHMDEM	.532
78	SOCRES	.324	49	OSTPTH	.406				119	FOCCTH	.536
20	COUNHS	.324	58	PLUMBR	.412				114	FMATHS	.539
19	COMPRG	.325	26	ELECTR	.427				123	FPRSCT	.542
23	DPTSTS	.326	53	PHAR S	.438				118	FNUTIN	.548
74	SOCCWK	.331	50	PNTR H	.438				109	FHOMEC	.549
64	PSYTST	.332	87	WELDER	.443				106	FDTTHR	.557
31	ENGMCH	.333	41	MCHNST	.450				127	FRELED	.563
8	BANKER	.333	6	AUTO M	.452				93	FBKKPR	.564
34	FLORST	.335	37	INTDEC	.453				116	FNURSE	.564
54	PHARM	.335	83	TRKDRV	.469				120	FOFCLK	.569
65	PSYCCL	.336	15	CRPNTR	.475				92	FBEAUT	.575
									91	FBNKCL	.584
									99	FDNTAS	.586
									100	FDPTSW	.627

TABLE 29

MEAN SCORE DISTANCE OF FEMALE MUSIC AND MUSIC EDUCATION MAJORS (NO. 179) FROM OTHER GROUPS

Employed Men						College Men			Employed Women			College Women		
37	INTDEC	.301	2	AC	.546	158	MMUSIC	.131	133	FSOCPS	.211	174	GFRNLG	.121
45	MINIST	.323	14	BUYER	.554	153	MFRNLG	.231	127	FRELED	.217	172	GELED	.151
77	SOCPSY	.334	18	CLTH R	.555	164	MCATHB	.307	122	FPHYTH	.218	176	GHISTO	.181
79	SOCSCH	.340	44	METEOR	.559	147	MELED	.326	130	FSOCCW	.223	177	GHMEC	.182
74	SOCCWK	.342	32	ENG MM	.559	165	MSOC	.355	132	FSOCMD	.226	186	GSOC	.183
85	U PSTR	.347	16	CC EX	.560	152	MENGL	.355	98	F DEAN	.227	185	GSOCSC	.184
40	LIBRAR	.349	63	PRNTER	.562	140	MARTED	.367	104	FDTHOS	.230	173	GENGL	.188
76	SOCWKM	.355	73	SCHSUP	.565	155	MHIST	.391	125	FPSYCL	.232	183	GPSYCH	.192
75	SOCWKG	.360	53	PHAR S	.575	139	MARCH	.410	131	FSOCGR	.233	171	GDRMA	.198
64	PSYTST	.360	3	AC CPA	.577	163	MPSY	.430	134	FSOCSC	.233	181	GPHYED	.207
51	PEDTRN	.380	70	REALES	.581	141	MBIOSC	.432	119	FOCCTH	.238	180	GNURSE	.207
5	ARCH	.401	29	ENGHAC	.582	162	MPREMD	.471	111	FKYPCH	.243	178	GMATH	.220
65	PSYCCL	.416	38	JOURN	.582	161	MPOLYS	.474	106	FDTTHR	.245	175	GHELTH	.226
20	COUNHS	.423	84	TV REP	.586	159	MPHYED	.478	123	FPRSCT	.247	169	GBIOSC	.237
56	PHYTHR	.429	46	MTLMGR	.589	156	MLAW	.483	126	FPSYCN	.252	182	GPOLYS	.254
78	SOCRES	.437	27	ENGCVL	.590	157	MMATH	.494	116	FNURSE	.252	168	GARTED	.262
23	DPTSTS	.439	62	POSTCL	.591	160	MPHYSC	.497	121	FPEDRN	.253	170	GBUSGN	.270
11	BKSMGR	.439	1	AC AAA	.596	166	MAFCAD	.532	118	FNUTIN	.256	184	GCATHS	.306
55	PHOTOG	.441	86	VETRN	.598	167	MWPCAD	.544	113	FLIBR	.263			
60	PODRST	.445	25	EDNWSP	.599	146	MECON	.556	94	FBKMGR	.266			

#	Name	Value
48	OPTMST	.447
66	PSYCCN	.448
42	MATHM	.451
22	DNTIST	.456
68	PSYPRF	.477
39	LAWYER	.481
89	YMCASC	.484
82	TRVLAG	.484
88	X RAY	.486
80	STATCN	.487
57	PHYSN	.496
49	OSTPTH	.498
9	BARBER	.503
19	COMPRG	.504
34	FLORST	.510
72	SCITHS	.512
17	CHEMST	.517
24	DRCTFN	.519
54	PHARM	.521
67	PSYCIN	.532
47	NRSRYM	.533
52	PERS M	.533
7	BAKER	.537
69	RADSTA	.539
43	MATHHS	.539

#	Name	Value
28	ENGELE	.599
12	BRKLYR	.603
31	ENGMCH	.605
50	PNTR H	.607
8	BANKER	.608
71	SLSENG	.611
10	BKKPR	.611
81	SUPVFM	.613
36	INS AG	.615
4	AC IND	.621
35	FORSTR	.627
30	ENGIND	.655
61	POLICE	.661
13	BDG CN	.663
21	COAGAG	.670
87	WELDER	.672
26	ELECTR	.695
59	PLMBCN	.697
83	TRKDRV	.703
33	FARMER	.705
41	MCHNST	.705
6	AUTO M	.710
58	PLUMBR	.715
15	CRPNTR	.728

#	Name	Value
150	MENGEL	.574
145	MBSMGT	.576
154	MFORST	.583
148	MENGCH	.600
144	MBSMRK	.608
143	MBSGEN	.609
149	MENGCL	.612
151	MENGMH	.617
138	MANLHS	.625
142	MBUSAC	.627
137	MAG	.639

#	Name	Value
107	FFLRST	.267
101	FDTNAD	.269
97	FCNSHS	.271
103	FDTCOM	.273
96	FCMPRG	.277
115	FMTLMR	.277
124	FPSY	.280
112	FLAWYR	.284
136	FX RAY	.284
129	FSECY	.285
117	FNUTRN	.287
110	FINTDC	.289
99	FDNTAS	.296
105	FDTSCH	.298
108	FHMDEM	.300
102	FDTCDM	.302
135	FSTENO	.314
95	FCTLIB	.317
92	FBEAUT	.336
109	FHOMEC	.347
90	FACNT	.352
120	FOFCLK	.360
91	FBNKCL	.365
93	FBKKPR	.377
114	FMATHS	.381
128	FSCTHS	.383
100	FDPTSW	.400

Score distances from selected groups

In lieu of presenting tables of score distances for all variables in the study, there has been an effort to make the limited number that can be presented as representative as possible. In attempting to do this, variables with high loadings on each of the more specific factors identified in the final factor analysis reported in chapter 5 have been selected for presentation in tables 13 through 28. In the effort to present occupations of more general interest, the occupation chosen is not always the one with the very highest factor loading, although it is always very close. For example, physicians instead of osteopaths represent one factor, and librarians instead of cataloguers represent another. In the case of one factor, it seemed desirable to present two occupations — those of chemist and mathematician. Table 29 for distances from the group of college women majoring in music is also presented, since that group would have had the highest loading on factor 12 if the possibility of reflecting that factor had been carried out.

Sex Differences

1. *The problem of using the same occupational scales for both sexes.* It usually is possible to generate a heated discussion by raising the question of whether separate scoring scales for an occupation should be developed for the two sexes. Some maintain that interests are interests whether held by a man or a woman and that scores should be compared directly, regardless of the sex of the counselee or of the group on which the scoring keys are based.

The problem is a little more involved than might at first appear. There are two important considerations that support the present practice of reporting separately the scores based on data from each sex. In the following discussion the term *masculine score* will be used to designate a score based on data from men and *feminine score* to designate a score based on data from women. It is apparent that under this system a man can receive feminine scores and a woman can receive masculine scores.

One consideration bearing on the question is the anomalous situation that arises in some occupations where the duties of the average female worker are not quite the same as those of the average male worker. The average male librarian's job is not quite equivalent to the average female librarian's job, and the average female florist's job is not quite equivalent to the average male florist's job. If a woman happened to get a higher masculine than feminine score for librarian, perhaps that should be interpreted to mean she should aim for the kind of library work that most male librarians do!

For some occupations, keys developed for one sex work just about as well as they do for the other sex. There is, however, one important qualification: masculine scores must be compared with masculine scores and feminine scores must be compared with feminine scores. On the average, men obtain higher masculine scores than women and women obtain higher feminine scores than men for any occupation on which both kinds of scores are obtained. For example, more male lawyers receive their highest feminine score for the occupation of lawyer than for any other occupation. In a spirit of true reciprocity, more female lawyers receive their highest masculine score for the occupation of lawyer than for any other occupation. But the score distance between men and women lawyers is .143.

There are actually eight groups of women who are closer to female lawyers in their interests than are male lawyers. Similarly, there are some groups of men who are more like male lawyers in their interests than are female lawyers. In order to obtain meaningful reports for individual subjects, it is necessary to get separate orderings of scores for those based on women and those based on men.

TABLE 30

MASCULINE AND FEMININE SCORES OF A MALE SOCIAL
CASE WORKER

Masculine Scores in Order of Magnitude		Feminine Scores in Order of Magnitude	
Social Case Worker	71	Social Case Worker	60
Psychiatric Case Worker	68	Psychiatric Case Worker	58
High School Counselor	68	High School Counselor	58
Physical Therapist	65	Physical Therapist	58
Clinical Psychologist	65	Social Worker-Group	58
Social Worker-Group	64	Clinical Psychologist	57
Lawyer	60	Lawyer	57
X-Ray Technician	59	X-Ray Technician	55
Bookstore Manager	57	Computer Programmer	51
High School Science Teacher	57	Bookstore Manager	48
High School Math Teacher	56	High School Science Teacher	48
Computer Programmer	55	High School Math Teacher	48
Librarian	54	Librarian	46
Florist	50	Florist	46
Bookkeeper	47	Bookkeeper	45
Interior Decorator	41	Interior Decorator	39

TABLE 31

SCORE DISTANCE BETWEEN MALE AND FEMALE GROUPS
IN THE SAME OCCUPATION OR COLLEGE MAJOR

Occupation	Score Distance	College Major	Score Distance
Bookkeeper	.235	Art and Art Education	.099
Bookstore Manager	.179	Biological Science	.157
Computer Programmer	.152	General Business	.302
Counselor, High School	.187	Elementary Education	.226
Department Store Sales	.269	English	.138
Florist	.256	Foreign Languages	.118
Interior Decorator	.069	History	.171
Lawyer	.143	Mathematics	.240
Librarian	.138	Music and Music Ed.	.131
Math Teachers, High School	.222	Physical Education	.208
Pediatrician	.142	Political Science	.164
Physical Therapist	.162	Psychology	.192
Psychologist, Clinical	.134	Sociology	.177
Psychologist, Counseling	.164		
Science Teacher, High School	.149		
Social Case Worker	.140		
Social Worker, Group	.131		
Social Worker, Medical	.166		
Social Worker, Psychiatric	.131		
Social Worker, School	.147		
X-Ray Technician	.168		

The masculine and feminine scores of a male social case worker are listed in table 30 for those occupations scored for both sexes. In this representative case, there is a pronounced correspondence in the actual order of the two sets of scores, though the masculine scores are definitely higher. The extent to which differences exist on the average for groups of men and women in the same occupation or college major is reflected in the score distances between the sexes in corresponding occupations or college majors listed in table 31. These range from .069 for interior decorator to .320 for motel manager. It might be argued that these differences are to some extent a reflection of the relative extent to which these jobs differ for men and women.

As of now, any masculine score a woman receives must be interpreted in terms of its relation to her other masculine scores; any feminine score a man receives must be interpreted in its relation to his other feminine scores. This practice is supported by the existence of the substantial sex factors reported in chapter V, as well as by the considerations noted above. It is apparent that

43 Employed Women in Six Occupations
Median = .81

19 College Women
Median = .77

37 High School Girls
Median = .74

Figure 10. Distributions of correlations between thirteen masculine occupational scores and the feminine scores for the same occupations for individual subjects.

failure to use separate norms for the two sexes would reduce the effectiveness of counseling. If and when the interests of men and women who are in the same job are indistinguishable, it will of course be unnecessary to furnish separate scores. It may be possible to develop a correction formula for making masculine and feminine scores comparable, though the problem is more involved than might at first appear.

At the time the study reported in figure 10 was made, there were thirteen occupations for which both masculine and feminine scores were obtained from the Occupational Interest Survey. That figure reveals a fairly high correspondence in general between the order in which the two sets place the thirteen occupations for groups of women and girls. There are, however, enough exceptions to the rule to indicate the desirability of furnishing both sets of scores.

In only one of the occupations are the interests of the two sexes closer to each other than either is to the interests of some other group of the same sex. This is the occupation of interior decorator. In the case of lawyers, on the other hand, female lawyers are closer to some dieticians and some female social workers, psychologists, and bookstore managers than they are to male lawyers. Male lawyers are closer to male bookstore managers, some accountants, statisticians, school superintendents, and travel agents than they are to female lawyers.

There is more similarity between corresponding college majors groups in general, although there are pronounced exceptions to this rule. In three pairs of majors the two sexes are more like each other than they are like any other major group of the same sex. These pairs are music majors, art majors, and Roman Catholic teaching brothers and sisters. A pair in which the sexes are *not* closest is that of mathematics majors. Male mathematics majors are more like physical science majors, economics majors and, as a matter of fact, almost all other male major groups than they are like female mathematics majors. Female mathematics majors are more like most other female major groups than they are like their corresponding male mathematics majors. Only six female major groups are farther away.

2. *Masculinity-feminity.* The system described in chapter 3 for differentiating between occupational groups is also applicable to the problem of differentiating between the sexes on the basis of their interests. In this case the difference score $M - W$ appears to be appropriate, since the M score is based on a general reference group of men and the W score is based on a general reference group of women. These groups were originally assembled for use as general reference groups for Form D of the Preference Record some time before it became apparent that general reference groups were unnecessary for evaluating occupational interests.

Another difference score, $F - Mo$ (father score minus mother score), appears particularly appropriate since the socioeconomic status of the two groups can be assumed to be practically equivalent. In fact, married couples constitute a large proportion of the father and mother groups. These groups were parents of high school groups used in reliability studies.

It is not surprising that the occupations with high positive difference scores are those that few, if any, women enter. These are in the engineering, construction, and outdoor fields. The converse appears to be true to a lesser degree of the occupations with high negative differences. The results from college major groups appear to be consistent with those from the occupational groups, with engineering and outdoor work at the masculine extreme and elementary education at the feminine extreme.

TABLE 32

MEAN DIFFERENCE SCORES F-Mo and M-W OF
OCCUPATIONAL GROUPS OF MEN AND WOMEN

Occupation	Sex	F-Mo	M-W	Occupation	Sex	F-Mo	M-W
30 ENGIND	M	240	189	72 SCITHS	M	148	109
71 SLSENG	M	229	178	2 AC	M	146	89
31 ENGMCH	M	227	183	7 BAKER	M	144	108
59 PLMBCN	M	223	188	63 PRNTER	M	140	102
27 ENGCVL	M	213	165	34 FLORST	M	138	91
29 ENGHAC	M	213	167	48 OPTMST	M	137	91
35 FORSTR	M	210	174	82 TRVLAG	M	137	81
13 BDG CN	M	208	167	22 DNTIST	M	136	95
4 AC IND	M	206	147	24 DRCTFN	M	134	95
28 ENGELE	M	206	169	55 PHOTOG	M	134	93
32 ENG MM	M	201	154	10 BKKPR	M	130	93
33 FARMER	M	196	157	62 POSTCL	M	129	101
44 METEOR	M	196	151	56 PHYTHR	M	128	86
26 ELECTR	M	193	171	49 OSTPTH	M	127	91
61 POLICE	M	192	165	50 PNTRH	M	127	105
84 TV REP	M	188	156	68 PSYPRF	M	126	77
21 CORGAG	M	187	145	80 STATCN	M	126	70
36 INS AG	M	187	139	88 X RAY	M	126	94
41 MCHNST	M	187	165	38 JOURN	M	123	80
86 VETRN	M	185	147	39 LAWYER	M	123	60
3 AC CPA	M	184	122	25 EDNWSP	M	121	79
6 AUTO M	M	182	166	89 YMCASC	M	119	53
46 MTLMGR	M	182	141	9 BARBER	M	114	88
58 PLUMBR	M	182	160	42 MATHM	M	112	61
53 PHAR S	M	180	135	57 PHYSN	M	112	79
69 RAD STA	M	176	121	60 PODRST	M	109	64
14 BUYER	M	175	128	66 PSYCCN	M	107	55
52 PERS M	M	173	114	5 ARCH	M	106	45
81 SUPVFM	M	173	142	20 COUNHS	M	101	50
8 BANKER	M	172	120	23 DPTSTS	M	99	63
16 CC EX	M	168	104	11 BKSMGR	M	91	42
87 WELDER	M	168	151	65 PSYCCL	M	86	42
15 CRPNTR	M	167	147	78 SOCRES	M	82	24
67 PSYCIN	M	166	113	51 PEDTRN	M	81	35
1 AC AAA	M	164	113	64 PSYTST	M	66	20
17 CHEMST	M	163	114	85 U PSTR	M	63	04
70 REALES	M	163	114	75 SOCWKG	M	60	03
19 COMPRG	M	162	120	74 SOCCWK	M	53	-01
83 TRKDRV	M	154	136	76 SOCWKM	M	53	02
47 NRSRYM	M	153	102	77 SOCPSY	M	45	-02
73 SCHSUP	M	153	100	79 SOCSCH	M	25	-25
18 CLTH R	M	152	95	45 MINIST	M	20	-36
54 PHARM	M	151	106	40 LIBRAR	M	14	-38
12 BRKLYR	M	148	128	96 FCMPRG	F	-07	-55
43 MATHHS	M	148	106	37 INTDEC	M	-29	-85

TABLE 32 (Continued)

Occupation		Sex	F-Mo	M-W	Occupation		Sex	F-Mo	M-W
28	FSCTHS	F	-30	-72	106	FDTTHR	F	-110	-145
112	FLAWYR	F	-47	-112	111	FKYPCH	F	-115	-136
90	FACNT	F	-58	-117	94	FBKMGR	F	-118	-162
124	FPSY	F	-62	-112	107	FFLRST	F	-123	-161
122	FPHYTH	F	-63	-101	97	FCNSHS	F	-123	-176
101	FDTNAD	F	-64	-114	115	FMTLMR	F	-125	-158
109	FHOMEC	F	-73	-119	93	FBKKPR	F	-127	-162
105	FDTSCH	F	-76	-121	99	FDNTAS	F	-129	-160
103	FDTCOM	F	-78	-126	116	FNURSE	F	-134	-165
102	FDTCDM	F	-83	-127	133	FSOCPS	F	-136	-184
126	FPSYCN	F	-84	-137	130	FSOCCW	F	-137	-186
136	FX RAY	F	-85	-114	92	FBEAUT	F	-137	-158
119	FOCCTH	F	-88	-131	100	FDPTSW	F	-140	-160
114	FMATHS	F	-88	-135	127	FRELED	F	-243	-200
104	FDTHOS	F	-88	-135	129	FSECY	F	-146	-187
98	F DEAN	F	-90	-153	134	FSOCSC	F	-149	-196
125	FPSYCL	F	-92	-140	132	FSOCMD	F	-149	-198
117	FNUTRN	F	-92	-139	91	FBNKCL	F	-150	-179
110	FINTDC	F	-99	-162	95	FCTLIB	F	-152	-202
131	FSOCGR	F	-100	-159	113	FLIBR	F	-153	-201
121	FPEDRN	F	-102	-149	135	FSTENO	F	-164	-197
118	FNUTIN	F	-103	-146	120	FOFCLK	F	-166	-194
108	FHMDEM	F	-110	-157	123	FPRSCT	F	-185	-216

These two difference scores (F — Mo and M — W) are reported in table 32 in the order of the F — Mo difference scores. The F — Mo difference score appears to the writer to be a somewhat better index of masculinity-feminity than the M — W difference score. For one reason, as just mentioned, the F and Mo groups can be assumed to be more nearly matched in their characteristics. For another reason, the use of zero as the appropriate cutting point works better for the F — Mo score. All female groups have negative scores and all except one male group have positive scores. On the other hand, the M — W scale misplaces six of the male groups. The same kind of situation is reflected in table 33 for college major groups. On the F — Mo scale all male groups receive positive scores and all female groups receive negative scores. On the M — W scale five of the male groups are misplaced.

In spite of these differences, the orders in which occupations are placed correspond closely. The extremely high and low occupations are identical for both sexes.

TABLE 33
MEAN DIFFERENCE SCORES F - Mo and M - W
OF COLLEGE MAJOR GROUPS OF MEN AND WOMEN

Occupation	Sex	F-Mo	M-W	Occupation	Sex	F-Mo	M-W
151 MENGMH	M	222	189	155 MHIST	M	76	24
149 MENGCL	M	217	183	164 MCATHB	M	22	-09
148 MENGCH	M	210	172	158 MMUSIC	M	19	-26
150 MENGEL	M	202	171	140 MARTED	M	08	-33
137 MAG	M	192	161	152 MENGL	M	04	-38
154 MFORST	M	190	164	153 MFRNLG	M	01	-38
166 MAFCAD	M	190	150	182 GPOLYS	F	-54	-113
143 MBSGEN	M	189	142	169 GBIOSC	F	-61	-94
145 MBSMGT	M	188	140	181 GPHYED	F	-62	-93
144 MBSMRK	M	186	138	178 GMATH	F	-64	-103
138 MANLHS	M	183	154	170 GBUSGN	F	-83	-132
142 MBUSAC	M	183	133	175 GHELTH	F	-85	-112
167 MWPCAD	M	182	139	183 GPSYCH	F	-86	-124
146 MECON	M	178	124	176 GHISTO	F	-94	-140
160 MPHYSC	M	158	125	168 GARTED	F	-107	-146
157 MMATH	M	155	116	184 GCATHS	F	-108	-136
156 MLAW	M	151	91	171 GDRMA	F	-120	-159
159 MPHYED	M	136	105	186 GSOC	F	-122	-159
162 MPREMD	M	130	94	185 GSOCSC	F	-123	-163
161 MPOLYS	M	120	60	177 GHMEC	F	-123	-159
141 MBIOSC	M	115	82	180 GNURSE	F	-128	-155
139 MARCH	M	113	64	179 GMUSIC	F	-135	-181
163 MPSY	M	111	68	174 GFRNLG	F	-140	-177
147 MELED	M	84	41	173 GENGL	F	-146	-187
165 MSOC	M	77	36	172 GELED	F	-151	-189

It is of interest to note that when men and women mark answers they think will make a good impression, they agree with one another far better than when they answer sincerely. This situation and some of its implications are discussed in the next section.

Some Characteristics of Best Impression
Responses to Interest Inventory Items

What happens when people deliberately try to mark answers they believe will make the best possible impression on anyone who might see their choices? In the case of the Occupational Interest Survey, at least, their answers are rather predictable. The answers of people trying to make the best impression agree with each other much better than when they answer the survey in the standard sincere way. This circumstance is partly responsible for the success of the verification key for that inventory. There are also other significant bits of information that can be obtained from a study of best impression answers with respect to both individuals and groups. Some of them will be reported in the following pages.

The immediate reason for giving the Occupational Interest Survey to a number of groups with instructions to fake was to validate and standardize the verification scale that had been developed through use of the earlier experimental forms. Three other considerations led, however, to a somewhat more extensive research than might otherwise have been necessary.

One study mentioned below bears on the possibility of developing a measure of general social approval for a person's set of answers. Another is directed at measuring the extent to which the responses of individuals agree under the two sets of directions. In addition, there is the suggestion that best impression responses might be useful in selection devices and also as a means of moving toward the use of the same norms for both sexes. As is so often the case, the information uncovered to date raises more questions than it answers.

1. *Measuring social approval.* When people mark those answers to the Occupational Interest Survey that they believe would make the best impression, they are in effect judging the items with respect to the social approval attached to the responses. As already noted, people in general tend to agree which answers carry social approval. The replies of groups of people are far more homoge-

TABLE 34
HOMOGENEITIES (Σp^2) OF
"BEST IMPRESSION" GROUPS

Group	N	Σp^2
Accountants	200	107–348
Male Base Group	1000	104–217
County Agricultural Agents	200	104–408
Ministers	300	99–640
Personnel Managers	200	107–695
Salesmen of Pharmaceuticals	400	99–366
YMCA Secretaries	250	105–439
Female Base Group	200	106–140
Female Psychologists	250	107–558

neous when giving best impression answers than when answering sincerely, as revealed in table 34, which lists for the best impression groups the index of homogeneity (Σp^2) previously reported for 217 sincere groups. The homogeneities reported in table 34 are substantially higher than those of the sincere groups reported in table 1.

Furthermore, there is much better agreement between groups in the selection of the actual responses when they are picking out best impression answers. The correlations between the set of proportions of people in nine groups marking the 600 answer positions are given in table 35 for both the standard and best impression administrations. The median intercorrelation for the best impression situation is .929; for the standard situation the median correlation is .742.

The highest agreement in the entire table is represented by a correlation of .974 between best impression responses of the two norm groups. The corresponding correlation between sincere groups is only .697.

In terms of score distances, shown in table 36, the sincere and best impression administrations of county agricultural agents are farthest apart. The score distance is .954, which is larger than any distance found between sincere groups. The salesmen of pharmaceuticals are least far apart on the two administrations, with a score distance of .439. This is still, however, a large distance.

The smallest score distance in the table for best impression responses (.033) is between the male and female norm groups. On the other hand, there are pronounced sex differences in the sincere responses of these same groups, the score distance being .323. Except for ministers, the sincere replies of male groups are closer to all other male groups than they are to females, but in their faked interests men agree about as well with women as they do with other men.

Least alike in their sincere interests are the female norm group and salesmen of pharmaceuticals, with a score distance of .504. The corresponding distance between the two for best impression responses is only .083. The average of the 36 score distances for sincere responses is .294, whereas the corresponding average for the best impression responses is only .111. This small distance of .111 is about the same as that between the sincere replies of medical social workers and clinical psychologists, between sales engineers and electrical engineers, or between YMCA secretaries and personnel managers.

TABLE 35

CORRELATIONS OF RESPONSE PROPORTIONS OF SINCERE (ABOVE THE DIAGONAL INDICATED BY THE BOXES) AND BEST IMPRESSION (BELOW THE DIAGONAL) ADMINISTRATIONS

(Correlations between sincere and best impression proportions for each group are given in the cells on the diagonal.)

Group	1	2	3	4	5	6	7	8	9
Accountants	.377	.905	.793	.656	.829	.718	.724	.665	.629
Male Base Group	.973	.285	.888	.728	.864	.810	.789	.697	.656
County Agricultral Agents	.824	.850	.215	.683	.779	.756	.774	.614	.593
Ministers	.891	.899	.776	.562	.800	.672	.855	.756	.802
Personnel Managers	.967	.967	.846	.909	.566	.866	.887	.637	.718
Pharmaceutical Salesmen	.939	.957	.826	.866	.957	.623	.792	.549	.576
YMCA Secretaries	.947	.969	.855	.912	.971	.952	.492	.675	.688
Female Base Group	.953	.974	.846	.895	.952	.932	.957	.291	.804
Female Psychologists	.934	.925	.794	.894	.940	.898	.920	.944	.568

TABLE 36

SCORE DISTANCES BETWEEN NINE GROUPS FOR SINCERE (ABOVE THE DIAGONAL)
AND BEST IMPRESSION (BELOW THE DIAGONAL INDICATED BY THE BOXES) ADMINISTRATIONS
(Score distances between sincere and best impression mean scores of the same group are given in the cells on the diagonal.)

Group	1	2	3	4	5	6	7	8	9
Accountants	.736	.103	.236	.382	.193	.318	.307	.370	.429
Male Base Group	.034	.810	.122	.291	.148	.207	.227	.323	.384
County Agricultural Agents	.222	.188	.954	.362	.258	.283	.260	.435	.484
Ministers	.131	.122	.273	.500	.226	.370	.162	.266	.229
Personnel Managers	.043	.041	.200	.112	.529	.154	.129	.407	.332
Pharmaceutical Salesmen	.072	.051	.212	.158	.051	.439	.236	.504	.498
YMCA Secretaries	.067	.039	.183	.107	.037	.058	.603	.359	.363
Female Base Group	.060	.033	.197	.129	.061	.083	.055	.840	.222
Female Psychologists	.085	.096	.265	.132	.078	.127	.104	.073	.541

The same procedure described in chapter 3 for developing scales for discriminating between occupational groups is applicable for differentiating between sincere groups and those groups attempting to make the best possible impression.

This has not actually been done. A determination of the mean score distance between the sincere and best impression administrations has been obtained for the above tables, however, on the basis of the response proportions combined with the appropriate formulas for transforming proportion scores to lambda scores. The other distances in the tables were also obtained in this way, but best impression replies have been obtained from only a few groups.

An indirect approach has therefore been used to deal with the problem of measuring social approval. The difference scores used for this purpose are M — MBI for men and W — WBI for women. The symbols refer to experimental scores reported for the Occupational Interest Survey. The M score is based on proportions from a male general reference group developed before the use of such a group was abandoned for the development of occupational scores. The MBI is based on proportions from a sample of the same group when they were given the best impression instructions. The W and WBI scores represent similar scores obtained from a general reference group of women. Thus the difference scores answer the question of the extent to which a person resembles the sincere group more or less than the best impression group.

Average difference scores arranged in order of magnitude are reported in table 37 for groups of men and in table 38 for groups of women. Comparable score distances for college students are presented in tables 39 and 40. The entries represent decimals carried to three places, with the decimal points omitted.

The considerable variation in means affords a basis for speculation as to the significance of these difference scores. Here are some questions that might be raised:

a. Do automobile mechanics answer the inventory more sincerely than do social workers?
b. Do plumbers have less concern for what people think than do university pastors?
c. Are the interests of electricians less like what is generally approved than are the interests of clinical psychologists?
d. Were the county agricultural agents' replies more honest than those of the ministers?

The answers to questions a, b, and d must be that the scores ob-

TABLE 37
AVERAGE DIFFERENCE SCORES (M-MBI)
OF OCCUPATIONAL GROUPS OF MEN

No. and Code	M-MBI	No. and Code	M-MBI	No. and Code	M-MBI
6 AUTO M	480	32 ENG MM	356	51 PEDTRN	256
58 PLUMBR	475	34 FLORST	353	39 LAWYER	255
26 ELECTR	467	47 NRSRYM	347	82 TRVLAG	255
15 CRPNTR	463	36 INS AG	344	4 AC IND	253
41 MCHNST	463	71 SLSENG	337	5 ARCH	247
59 PLMBCN	458	88 X RAY	337	23 DPTSTS	245
33 FARMER	449	24 DRCTFN	335	68 PSYPRF	239
35 FORSTR	442	22 DNTIST	333	20 COUNHS	236
13 BDG CN	432	1 AC AAA	230	80 STATON	235
87 WELDER	427	70 REALES	325	16 CC EX	234
21 COAGAG	405	54 PHARM	324	52 PERS M	233
10 BKKPR	404	9 BARBER	322	3 AC CPA	227
28 ENGELE	396	11 BKSMGR	322	40 LIBRAR	224
81 SUPVFM	395	72 SCITHS	321	89 YMCASC	222
8 BANKER	393	2 AC	319	67 PSYCIN	210
62 POSTCL	393	30 ENGIND	319	53 PHAR S	196
61 POLICE	392	18 CLTH R	313	76 SOCWKM	193
46 MTLMGR	390	25 EDNWSP	312	64 PSYTST	188
83 TRKDRV	389	57 PHYSN	312	66 PSYCCN	187
27 ENGCVL	386	42 MATHM	310	77 SOCPSY	183
44 METEOR	386	73 SCHSUP	309	74 SOCCWK	181
86 VETRN	384	17 CHEMST	307	65 PSYCCL	177
12 BRKLYR	379	49 OSTPTH	300	37 INT DEC	167
63 PRNTER	378	7 BAKER	299	45 MINIST	159
50 PNTR H	376	19 COMPRG	295	60 PODRST	147
84 TV REP	376	38 JOURN	287	75 SOCWKG	133
29 ENGHAC	375	69 RADSTA	286	79 SOCSCH	132
31 ENGMCH	374	56 PHYTHR	284	78 SOCSCH	132
43 MATHHS	369	48 OPTMST	272	85 U PSTR	115
14 BUYER	361	55 PHOTOG	262		

tained have no bearing on these questions, though it is tempting to believe that they do. The answer to question c probably is yes.

The tables are essentially a reflection of the extent to which the inventoried interests of the members of the occupations can be considered to meet with general approval as reflected in the data from the general reference group. There is no basis for concluding, for example, that county agricultural agents are more honest than ministers are in answering the OIS. On the other hand, the data available allow us to classify county agricultural agents as sincere *with more confidence*. This is simply because

TABLE 38

AVERAGE DIFFERENCE SCORES (W - WBI)
OF OCCUPATIONAL GROUPS OF WOMEN

No. and Code	W - WBI	No. and Code	W - WBI	No. and Code	W - WBI
120 FOFCLK	477	94 FBKMGR	355	128 FSCTHS	287
135 FSTENO	467	136 FX RAY	354	110 FINTDC	281
91 FBNKCL	448	102 FDTCDM	349	131 FSOCGR	280
93 FBKKPR	446	90 FACNT	344	98 F DEAN	279
123 FPRSCT	423	134 FSOCSC	339	104 FDTHOS	277
129 FSECY	418	119 FOCCTH	330	96 FCMPRG	276
114 FMATHS	416	97 FCNSHS	327	121 FPEDRN	275
95 FCTLIB	409	105 FDTSCH	321	126 FPSYCN	263
100 FDPTSW	398	132 FSOCMD	321	109 FHOMEC	262
92 FBEAUT	396	122 FPHYTH	320	117 FNUTRN	261
115 FMTLMR	396	130 FSOCCW	321	118 FNUTIN	258
113 FLIBR	393	106 FDTTHR	311	125 FPSYCL	258
107 FFLRST	385	127 FRELED	303	124 FPSY	251
108 FHMDEM	382	133 FSOCPS	302	101 FDTNAD	248
116 FNURSE	371	111 FKYPCH	292	112 FLAWYR	228
99 FDNTAS	364	103 FDTCOM	289		

TABLE 39

AVERAGE DIFFERENCE SCORES (M-MBI)
OF COLLEGE MAJORS GROUPS OF MEN

No. and Code	M - MBI	No. and Code	M - MBI	No. and Code	M - MBI
137 MAG	383	159 MPHYED	256	162 MPREMD	188
154 MFORST	380	145 MBSMGT	244	165 MSOC	163
138 MANLHS	372	144 MBSMRK	237	140 MARTED	158
149 MENGCL	369	166 MAFCAD	232	156 MLAW	154
151 MENGMH	352	139 MARCH	202	158 MMUSIC	151
150 MENGEL	340	147 MELED	201	153 MFRNLG	141
148 MENGCH	286	164 MCATHB	198	163 MPSY	136
142 MBUSAC	270	141 MBIOSC	196	155 MHIST	115
160 MPHYSC	261	167 MWPCAD	194	152 MENGL	104
143 MBSGEN	259	146 MECON	190	161 MPOLYS	94
157 MMATH	257				

they are less like the best impression group in their real interests, and the differentiation is therefore easier to make with confidence. The members of some occupational groups tend to enjoy a greater number of socially approved activities than do the mem-

TABLE 40

AVERAGE DIFFERENCE SCORES (W – WBI)
OF COLLEGE MAJORS GROUPS OF WOMEN

No. and Code	W – WBI	No. and Code	W – WBI
170 GBUSGN	319	186 GSOC	258
178 GMATH	292	185 GSOCSC	257
180 GNURSE	286	168 GARTED	250
177 GHMEC	284	169 GBIOSC	238
172 GELED	283	176 GHISTO	232
181 GPHYED	282	173 GENGL	229
175 GHELTH	275	183 GPSYCH	221
184 GCATHS	269	171 GDRMA	192
174 GFRNLG	268	182 GPOLYS	160
179 GMUSIC	261		

bers of some other occupational groups. Even so, they do not enjoy them to the extent that the difference scores obtained from their sincere answers become negative. This finding is in keeping with one of the principles used by Hartshorne and May (1928) in their celebrated "Studies in Deceit" for detecting attempted deception. There is a limit within which it is plausible for people to say they correspond to the socially approved model. Beyond that limit the odds are great that they are lying.

The general situation discussed above is reflected in figure 11, which pictures the distribution of the M — MBI difference scores of samples of auto mechanics and social case workers.

2. *An index of the extent to which a person meets his or her own standards of what answers are desirable.* People whose answers to an inventory are at considerable variance from those standards they believe are generally approved by their society must surely

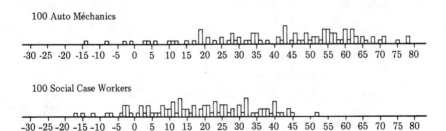

Figure 11. Difference scores (M-MBI) of Auto Mechanics
and Social Case Workers (decimal points omitted).

50—Forester

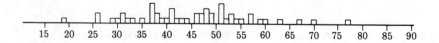

50—Salesman of Pharmaceuticals

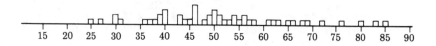

50—Meteorologist

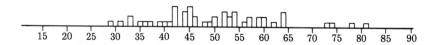

50—Clinical Psychologist

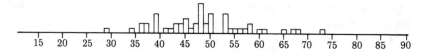

50—Professor of Psychology

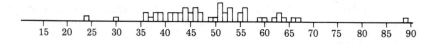

50—County Agricultural Agent

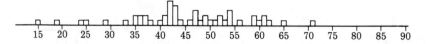

Figure 12. Distributions of B.I indices for eight
occupational groups (decimal points omitted).

142

50—YMCA Secretary

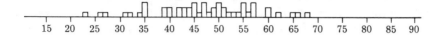

| | | | | | | | | | | | | | | | |
|15|20|25|30|35|40|45|50|55|60|65|70|75|80|85|90|

50—Minister

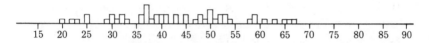

| | | | | | | | | | | | | | | | |
|15|20|25|30|35|40|45|50|55|60|65|70|75|80|85|90|

Figure 12 (Continued).

differ in important ways from people whose answers indicate they are substantially meeting those standards. One attempt to obtain an index of the amount of such agreement has been made by simply counting the number of responses in the first fifty items of the Occupational Interest Survey that are answered the same way under standard directions and then under instructions to answer, so as to make the best impression on anyone who might see the answers. This kind of system would appear to be applicable only if the items involved are fairly evenly distributed in factorial space. Otherwise the index could not be expected to be free from distortion.

Strictly speaking, this index is not a measure of self-approval, since the standard is what the subject thinks others would approve. Nor is it necessarily an index of social approval with respect to an absolute standard. It is essentially an indication of how well a person's interests correspond with what that particular individual thinks people would approve. In the following discussion it will be referred to as the Best Impression Index or B.I. Index.

B.I. indices have been obtained for the first fifty items of the Occupational Interest Survey for 400 subjects from eight occupational groups, and the distributions of the scores obtained are presented in figure 12. It is apparent that the index varies considerably from person to person, and that there are lesser differences in the means of occupational groups.

There is a county agricultural agent in figure 12 who marked only fifteen of the responses in the sincere administration that he judged would later make the best impression. There also is a professor of psychology whose answers agreed 89 percent of the time. Salesmen of pharmaceuticals have the highest average B.I. Index with an average score of 51.1, and ministers have the lowest with an average score of 43.2. A score of 100 represents complete agreement. The difference would seem to justify the conclusion that ministers are more severe in their judgments of themselves than are salesmen of pharmaceuticals of themselves. On the other hand, perhaps it should be said that the salesmen are more self-tolerant or less self-perceptive! Whatever the interpretation, it seems likely that this index will turn out to have some meaningful relation to a number of criteria, which might include performance on some jobs. Further, it is hoped that studies along this line will materialize in time.

3. *On the possibility of using best impression answers for differentiating between groups.* The chief difficulty in using interest inventories in the selection of personnel is that answers can be faked and scores can be slanted in the direction desired. Althought not every applicant attempts to slant the answers, there is reason to believe that a substantial proportion do so when they believe that answering sincerely would not be to their advantage. Although devices can be developed for identifying most of the fakers, the result is simply to eliminate those people from consideration unless they are willing to answer sincerely at a second administration. One way of keeping the influence of faking constant might be to ask all applicants to mark the answers they think would make the best impression.

The success of such an approach would depend, of course, on the extent to which the experimenter is able to make his collections of experimental items representative of a wide range of factors in the faked domain. This would be a challenging task, for the evidence at hand indicates that the "great core" of faked interests that would form a typical response factor is even greater than it is for sincere answers. A great deal of ingenuity would be called for in developing items not high on the common factor.

If the idea of scoring best impression answers for employee selection has any merit at all, it seems likely that the best results would be obtained by trying out a large and varied number of items administered with best impression instructions. Development of the final inventory from these best impression responses would require going through the same rigorous procedures used for development of an inventory answered sincerely. The plan would necessarily call for administering a succession of experimental forms, each new one built upon the experience gained from preceding ones. It is almost certain that inventories developed for sincere and best impression administrations would turn out to be quite different even if the experimental items tried out were identical. Incidentally, a lie scale in reverse would be needed to check on whether an applicant had actually cooperated in giving faked responses!

There is one other possible advantage to using an inventory that calls for best impression replies. As previously noted, sex differences are less, in general, for best impression replies than for sincere responses. Thus there appears a better prospect of developing scales that could have identical norms for the two sexes. This objective is unrealistic for the sincere response administrations of inventories now in use, since, as Campbell (1973) has recently observed, "Males and females respond differently to interest inventories; that is an empirical fact." (p. 179)

Combining two significantly different groups of approximately equal homogeneity has one clear effect: the larger combined group cannot be differentiated as well from other groups as could each of the component groups. Consequently the use of the same norms for both sexes can lead only to lowered validity and the diminution of the usefulness of these inventories in today's counseling. In time it may be possible to develop inventories composed of a wide diversity of items that show only insignificant sex differences when answered sincerely; it may be that this faint possibility will turn to a probability as research proceeds. In the light of the evidence uncovered to date, however, best impression items may be a better bet.

Interests and Satisfaction in Work

Almost all the workers who cooperated in the development of occupational scoring systems by filling out the Occupational Interest Survey also answered a series of five questions bearing on how well they liked their work. Scores based on these questions have a repeat reliability of .85 for a sample of the general reference group originally used. It was quickly discovered that for the purpose of identifying the definitely dissatisfied, one question produced almost exactly the same classification of subjects as did the entire scale. That one question has therefore been used as the simplest means of identifying dissatisfied workers. The question is as follows:

If you had your choice, which of the following would you choose, if each paid the same? (Check one.)

_____ The job you have now.

_____ The same kind of work but with some changes in the working conditions or people you work with.

_____ A different kind of work entirely.

Members of occupational groups who said they would choose a different kind of work entirely were eliminated from the groups used for developing the scoring system for the Occupational Interest Survey.

The information presented in this section about dissatisfied workers can be regarded as a sort of bonus incidental to the main project. It would have been fortunate if enough dissatisfied cases could have been collected to allow scoring for similarity to dissatisfied groups as a supplement to, not a substitute for, the regular scoring system. There is reason to believe, as noted in chapter 2, that counselees generally will be more like the satisfied members of the occupations for which they receive high lambda scores than like the dissatisfied members of those same occupations. Nevertheless, there may be some exceptions to this rule; in that case, it would be useful to know when they occur.

Just how useful it would be to furnish scores derived from dissatisfied workers, as well as those from satisfied workers, is at this point unknown, but it is a question that needs to be explored. Such a project would have to be more extensive than the development of scales based on satisfied workers, even allowing for the fact that a considerable number of returns have already been collected from dissatisfied workers. Since dissatisfied groups are less homogeneous than satisfied groups in the corresponding occupations, it follows that larger numbers than usual are needed to establish stable scoring systems. In some occupations there are not enough dissatisfied workers in existence to serve as subjects for developing a scoring system. In others, the task of locating the necessary number of dissatisfied workers would be a formidable challenge. At present the undertaking is in the dream stage!

It has not been possible to score more than a few of the blanks from dissatisfied workers on the regular scales, much less develop scoring systems for dissatisfaction in specific occupations. There are only two dissatisfied groups of at least 200 in size. A third group numbers 197. These groups happen to be large because special studies called for obtaining large samples of these particular occupations. The fourth largest group of dissatisfied workers consists of 145 painters, and the explanation for this number is simply the high incidence of dissatisfaction among house painters!

TABLE 41

PERCENTAGE DISSATISFIED IN OCCUPATIONAL GROUPS
OF MEN

Occupation	Percent Dis-satisfied	Total N	Occupation	Percent Dis-satisfied	Total N
House Painter	40.4	359	Travel Agent	11.3	230
Postal Clerk	36.2	376	Forester	10.3	390
Welder	31.1	228	Statistician	9.9	284
Bricklayer	30.2	258	High School Math		
Barber	28.9	401	Teacher	9.6	229
Machinist	27.5	404	High School Science		
Pharmacist	25.1	347	Teacher	8.9	382
Auto Mechanic	24.0	458	Heating & Air Condi-		
Dept. Store			tioning Engineer	8.2	851
Salesman	23.4	320	Photographer	7.4	243
Retail Clothier	23.0	344	Radio Station		
Truck Driver	23.0	244	Manager	7.0	284
Carpenter	22.1	393	Interior Decorator	6.8	206
Meterologist	21.5	195	Veterinarian	6.8	429
Baker	21.1	190	Lawyer	6.7	373
Bookkeeper	20.7	208	Chamber of Com-		
Motel Manager	20.2	287	merce Executive	6.5	510
Job Printer	18.8	276	Librarian	6.4	283
Funeral Director	18.5	394	Social Worker	6.3	1775
Plumber	18.0	278	Real Estate Agent	6.0	368
Plumbing Contractor	17.7	243	County Agricultural		
Electrician	16.7	353	Agent	5.6	644
Chemist	15.7	338	Building Contractor	5.4	257
Mechanical Engineer	15.7	415	Mathematician	5.2	287
T.V. Repairman	15.6	377	Nurseryman	4.9	285
Supervisor/Foreman			Pharmaceutical		
Industrial	15.4	293	Salesman	4.7	813
X-Ray Technician	15.1	410	Pediatrician	4.5	443
Florist	14.7	339	Farmer	4.3	184
Banker	13.8	407	Osteopath	4.3	232
Buyer	13.8	276	Architect	3.4	495
Policeman	13.8	232	High School Counselor	3.3	243
Mutual Insurance			Electrical Engineer	3.2	507
Agent	13.3	383	Physician	3.0	329
Industrial Engineer	13.0	509	Psychiatrist	2.8	247
Bookstore Manager	12.4	298	Minister	2.7	370
Civil Engineer	12.1	478	Journalist	2.6	505
Accountant	11.8	1668	Psychologist	2.5	2541
Personnel Manager	11.5	521	School		
Dentist	11.3	388	Superintendent	2.4	292
Mining & Metallurgi-			Optometrist	1.9	514
cal Engineer	11.1	386	YMCA Secretary	1.3	309

TABLE 42

PERCENTAGE DISSATISFIED IN OCCUPATIONAL GROUPS
OF WOMEN

Occupation	Percent Dissatisfied	N
Office Clerk	29.8	356
Secretary	24.2	495
Bookkeeper	21.8	335
Stenographer	21.3	258
Bank Clerk	17.4	298
X-Ray Technician	16.3	245
Dental Assistant	14.9	356
Lawyer	14.0	443
Accountant	12.7	314
Motel Operator	11.8	340
High School Science Teacher	11.1	171
Department Store Saleswoman	10.9	2135
Dietitian	9.8	2230
Beautician	9.4	235
High School Mathematics Teacher	9.3	323
Florist	7.0	313
Bookstore Manager	6.9	175
Librarian	6.8	413
Occupational Therapist	6.5	465
Interior Decorator	6.3	160
Dean of Women	5.5	382
Home Demonstration Agent	5.2	324
Social Worker	4.4	2541
Primary School Teacher	4.1	342
Nurse	4.0	274
Psychologist	2.8	864
High School Counselor	2.1	384

Although scoring systems have not been developed for any of the dissatisfied groups, response counts have been obtained for some of the large groups and certain useful and somewhat tantalizing information can be reported. First is the incidence of dissatisfaction in the groups studied, as shown in tables 41 and 42. These results appear generally consistent with other lists that have appeared in the literature. As might be anticipated, the proportion of dissatisfied workers varies tremendously from occupation to occupation. House painters head the list with 40 percent dissatisfied. On the other hand there are practically no unhappy YMCA secretaries. It is notable that those occupations concerned with being of direct help to people through personal communication — and even physical contact — have the lowest incidence of dissatisfaction.

The following pages report the information available at publication time from a preliminary analysis of data from a few relatively small groups of dissatisfied workers. Studies of the actual overlapping of difference scores for satisfied and dissatisfied groups cannot be made until a project is set up for obtaining scores based on the dissatisfied groups, and then for obtaining distributions of the difference scores.

It has been possible, however, to compute the means of these groups on various scales by using response counts and transformation formulas, although indices of the spread of scores about the means are not available. Furthermore, the correlations of the response proportions for each dissatisfied group with those of other groups in the whole project have been obtained so that we can study various interrelations and trends. In some occupations the number of dissatisfied workers used is less than the number listed in tables 41 and 42 because the study was begun well before all returns were in.

1. *Differences between satisfied and dissatisfied groups.* Is it possible to differentiate between satisfied and dissatisfied groups on the basis of their inventoried interests? The data at hand give only some indication of the answer. The obvious approach is to apply the rationale described in chapter 3. Unfortunately, the numbers of cases in the dissatisfied groups are (with few exceptions) far too few to do this in a systematic fashion, even if the necessary time and resources were available. It is possible, however, to calculate from the response proportions what the mean score distance would be between various groups if scores based on the dissatisfied group data were actually obtained. The score distances between satisfied and dissatisfied members in the groups studied are presented in table 43. These distances are relatively small, the mean being .062.

The correlations of the response proportions of satisfied and dissatisfied groups in the same occupation or college major are also given in table 43. The mean is .94. The message is unmistakable: Large differences between satisfied and dissatisfied workers in the same occupation are not to be expected. The comments made later concerning the fallible criterion are applicable here. Nevertheless, some degree of differentiation is possible. Distributions from other groups with about the average score distance and correlation obtained have ordinarily shown an overlapping in

TABLE 43

CORRELATIONS OF RESPONSE PROPORTIONS AND SCORE
DISTANCES BETWEEN SATISFIED AND DISSATISFIED
GROUPS IN THE SAME OCCUPATION OR COLLEGE MAJOR

Occupational Groups	Correlation	Score Distance
Male		
Accountant	.93	.073
Auto Mechanic	.91	.103
Barber	.96	.046
Bricklayer	.94	.059
Carpenter	.92	.094
Clothier	.95	.056
Electrician	.94	.073
Machinist	.96	.048
Painter	.95	.050
Pharmacist	.95	.055
Plumber	.93	.077
Postal Clerk	.94	.063
Social Worker	.94	.068
Business Management	.94	.056
Engineering	.94	.068
Social Sciences	.93	.074
Female		
Dietician	.94	.067
Office Clerk	.93	.079
Secretary	.93	.077
Social Worker	.95	.056
Elementary Education	.95	.053
English	.96	.040
Foreign Languages	.97	.036
Social Sciences	.96	.048
Sociology	.97	.033

the neighborhood of 50 percent. Although this degree of differentiation is generally regarded as being of some use for counseling purposes, it appears that the practical value of the approach is quite limited.

To what extent do dissatisfied members of an occupation tend to obtain their highest scores in their own occupation? In samples of 224 cases of satisfied and dissatisfied workers matched as to occupational composition, 77* of the satisfied group obtained their highest score in their own occupations, whereas only 36 of the dissatisfied group obtained their highest scores in their own oc-

*This number is consistent with Campbell's observation concerning scores on the SVIB (1971, p. 285): "Most men are not in occupations where they score highest; at best, probably not more than one-third are."

cupations. An inspection of the actual scores along with the other data available suggests that although the dissatisfied workers have in common a degree of interest in their present occupation, they tend to veer individually in many directions in their interests so that

a. the members of the dissatisfied group are much more likely to receive higher scores in some other occupations than are the members of the satisfied group, and
b. the dissatisfied group is less homogeneous than the satisfied group in the same occupation.

2. *Other studies.* For the purpose of evaluating the effectiveness of a counseling program or a specific guidance instrument, one is almost compelled to explore the relation to job satisfaction, however poorly satisfaction can be measured. What is more, if one allows for the probability that the criterion is contaminated by a number of irrelevant factors and that the measure used is far from absolute, it may be acknowledged that any relation found is likely to be a substantial underestimate of the relation between true measures. In view of this situation, the evidence available is particularly indicative of a genuine underlying relation between interests and job satisfaction. As long ago as the fifties, Herzberg was moved to say:

Of all the types of tests used in the counseling process, it appears that the use of interest tests has the strongest factual justification. Evidence based on different populations, using varying lengths of time and different interest tests, shows that the pattern of interests as measured by objective tests has a demonstrable positive relationship to the satisfaction the individual derives from his job. (p. 215)

This quotation from Herzberg and his associates (1957) is well supported by data from nine studies involving the Preference Record. Interests as measured by the Preference Record are related to job satisfaction: the young person who enters an occupation consistent with his or her interests is more likely to be satisfied than the person who does not enter such an occupation.

By far the most comprehensive follow-up study on the relation of measured interests to later job satisfaction has been reported by McRae (1959). He studied 1164 young people who had taken the Preference Record in high school, and who responded some seven to ten years later to a questionnaire concerning how well they liked their work. The group included the former students of 61 secondary schools located in 31 states.

In the group studied, 728 persons were classified as being in work consistent with their interests as measured when they were in high school; 436 were classified as being in work not consistent with their earlier interests. (For purposes of brevity and clarity the terms *consistent* and *inconsistent* will be used in referring to these groups.) McRae also divided his subjects into three levels with respect to job satisfaction on the basis of an extensive series of questions. The members of the high group were definitely satisfied with their work, and those in the low group were definitely dissatisfied. The middle group consisted of subjects whose answers were qualified so that an unequivocal assignment to one of the extreme groups could not be made.

McRae found that 62 percent of the consistent group were satisfied with their work, whereas only 34 percent of the inconsistent group were satisfied. He also found the proportion of dissatisfied workers in the inconsistent group to be about three times as great as in the consistent group; the actual figures were 25 percent and 8 percent respectively.

The results of the McRae study are in remarkable agreement with an earlier, though less extensive, follow-up study made by Lipsett and Wilson (1954). In their study, 22 percent of the inconsistent group disliked their work as compared with 8 percent of the consistent group. Seventy-three percent of the consistent group liked their work very much or thought the work the best possible job, and 41 percent of the inconsistent group felt the same way. The difference is much greater if we consider only those who reported they were in "the best possible job" for them. Only 8 percent of the inconsistent group said this of themselves, although 32 percent of the consistent group gave this answer.

Several investigators have reported studies of specific occupational groups, which are mentioned briefly below.

The earliest study of this type was made by Hahn and Williams (1945), who investigated the relation of the job satisfaction of three clerical groups of women reservists in the Marine Corps to scores on Preference Record scales. Significant differences on the clerical scale were found between the satisfied and dissatisfied workers in all three groups. Brayfield (1953) reported corroborative evidence, namely, that satisfied clerical workers in his studies made significantly higher scores on the clerical scale than did dissatisfied clerical workers.

Brayfield (1946) also studied six groups of workers in an industrial concern and found significant relations between job satisfaction and scores in preference areas logically expected to be related to the jobs of the workers involved.

DiMichael and Dabelstein (1947), in a study of rehabilitation counselors, found certain significant relations between preferences and satisfaction with a job as a whole, as well as with satisfaction with certain aspects of the job. The social service scale was positively related to satisfaction with the job. Workers with high social service and persuasive scores tended to like interviewing clients more than did those with lower scores on these scales. Those with high clerical preference scores tended to like clerical work more than did those with low clerical scores, and the persuasive scores were related to a liking for dealing with employers.

Jacobs and Traxler (1954) and North (1958) reported a comprehensive study of the relation of Preference Record scores to the job satisfaction of accountants. The satisfied group scored significantly higher than the dissatisfied group on the computational and clerical scales; they scored significantly lower on the outdoor, scientific, and artistic scales.

Herzberg and Russell (1953) found that persons desiring to leave an occupation had lower appropriate interest scores than those content to remain in it.

Brayfield and Marsh (1957) found a significant negative correlation between the job satisfaction of farmers and the literary scale. In the same study, a correlation of .40 was found between the performance ratings of these farmers and scores on the scientific scale.

A study of 980 housewives and of several smaller occupational groups was reported by Kuder in the 1953 manual. He found preferences of satisfied housewives significantly higher than those of dissatisfied ones for familiar and stable situations. Satisfied housewives were also more interested in avoiding conflict and less interested in authority and power. Satisfied school superintendents and retail store managers were more interested in group participation than were their dissatisfied counterparts. Satisfied accountants and auditors stood higher in their preference for familiar and stable situations and in avoiding conflict than did the dissatisfied members of the accounting and auditing occupations.

It should also be noted that Campbell (1971) in his *Handbook for the Strong Vocational Interest Blank* reported several studies of the relation of job satisfaction to SVIB scores.

3. *Job satisfaction as a criterion.* In a number of respects, self-

ratings of satisfaction with one's work fall short of the ideal criterion for developing measures of interests and evaluating the results of the use of interest inventories. For one thing, there is no assurance that different people use the same standards in making their judgments. As noted by Clark (1961), there are tremendous variations in the degree to which people find occupations attractive. Some no doubt would enjoy as many as fifty different occupations; others would not like *any* work at all! Some of the variation in the degree of satisfaction reported is no doubt real, but some probably is a matter of individual interpretation and standards.

E. L. Thorndike (1935) once observed that the variance of self-ratings of interest could be divided into two components. One of these emanates from the true variation in the degree of interest different people have in an activity. The other comes from individual differences in interpreting and applying the instructions, including "response set." It would also include error variance attributable to differences in standards from one person to another. Thorndike postulated that the two components were probably about equal in magnitude. This sort of attenuation probably also occurs in ratings of satisfaction with one's work.

Perhaps the most serious shortcoming of job satisfaction as a criterion, as noted earlier, is its severe limitation in range among the members of an occupation. This restriction is especially striking in certain professions, as reflected in tables 41 and 42. Although Strong (1943, p. 385) at one point held the position that there is ". . . no better criterion of a vocational interest test than that of satisfaction enduring over a period of years," he did not use it as a criterion for the construction of his interest scales. He later took the position that job satisfaction is such a complex concept, with the several components differing greatly from person to person, that a good measure of it is unobtainable (1955).

Strong proceeded on the assumption that people who have been in an occupation for a given length of time are likely to be satisfied with it. In his 1955 book (p. 12), however, he frankly admitted that "there are some men who are engaged in work they dislike but for various reasons cannot shift to more congenial activities." This statement is supported by the data in tables 41 and 42, which reveal that the proportion of dissatisfied workers is substantial in a number of occupations. Strong actually conducted one study (1955) using ratings of job satisfaction as a criterion, but his results were disappointing. Quite possibly he might have obtained better results by using a different design. Instead of treating occupational scores as absolute measures, he might better have used a measure of the relative standing of a person's score in relation to that person's entire set of occupational scores.

After all, the form in which the criterion is used must be appropriate to the problem, and the problem is not one of differentiating one person from another. The counselees are not concerned with whether they will get more satisfaction from a particular occupation than will Tom, Dick, Harry, or Mary. Rather, counselees want to know whether they will find occupation A more satisfying than occupations B, C, and D, and all the other occupations that they conceivably might enter. Whether certain other people would like occupation A more or less than our counselees would like it is certainly not their primary concern, even if valid information were available. The distinction noted here is essentially the one made by Horst (1954, 1955) between absolute and differential prediction and treated by a number of others including Tucker (1960) and Carroll (1972) in his "Individual Differences and Multidimensional Scaling."

In this context, ratings of satisfaction in a single occupation are not adequate for the problem. The criterion needed is an indication of the relative degree to which each subject in the validation group likes a large number of specific occupations in which the subject has had experience. In the face of this discouraging situation, the approach described in chapter II offers a more realistic way of handling the problem of the criterion. The reasoning presented there supports the conclusion that the degree of differentiation achieved by a difference scale is an index of the validity of that scale with respect to the criterion of job satisfaction.

Although the rationale described in chapter II appears to be the best available for developing a scoring system, unfortunately it is not practical for follow-up studies of the effectiveness of tests, inventories, or even complete counseling programs. Ratings of satisfaction appear to be the best available criterion in spite of contamination and severe restriction of range. As was to be expected, the highest relations with job satisfaction seem to be found when the design of the study calls for expressing each occupational score in terms of its standing in the individual's set of scores.

Note the difference, for example, between the Strong (1955) and the McRae (1959) studies. Strong obtained for each of 663 subjects the Strong score for the subject's own occupation and each one's rating of satisfaction with the work. Then these two measures were correlated for the group of subjects used. Strong did not consider the relative standing of a person's "own" score to the person's other scores. The procedure did not allow for the fact that the highest score for one person may well be far from the highest score for another. He thus ignored the essential fact that in counseling the frame of reference is the individual rather than the group.

McRae's follow-up study of 1164 subjects, on the other hand, involved a consideration of each person's constellation of scores with respect to that person's occupation. Lipsett and Wilson's earlier (1954) study of 224 subjects used this same approach. These studies are in agreement in the finding that people who entered occupations consistent with the pattern of their interest scores were more satisfied with their work, on the average, than those who did not. These results were obtained in spite of the serious shortcomings of job satisfaction as a criterion.

When the task is to develop and score an interest inventory, it still appears that differentiating between occupational groups is the best way to deal with the problem. When resources are unlimited, some employment of ratings of satisfaction might be made to yield useful results in developing inventories. Such an approach, however, is more likely to supplement than to supplant the fundamental technique of discriminating between groups.

On the other hand, when the task is one of evaluating the use of an inventory over a period of years, the choice inevitably becomes restricted to the type of system used by Lipsett and Wilson and by McRae. The bright spot in the picture is that if any relation at all is revealed between interests and an attenuated measure of satisfaction, the true relation is probably substantially greater.

It must be apparent that the factors contributing to job satisfaction are many and varied. Further, the particular mixture that contributes to one person's satisfaction may be quite different from the mixture that contributes to another's satisfaction. For example, on the basis of his research Friedlander (1965) has observed that "task-centered opportunities for self-actualization are of prime importance to white-collar workers only," whereas "the social environment is of paramount value to blue-collar workers." (p. 1) This observation reflects the fact that the interests of groups differ, the situation on which we capitalize in the development of occupational interest scales.

Score Level

With the subject of score level we enter an intriguingly speculative area. There is just enough information available to make it appear that a consideration of score level can eventually be valuable in counseling; however, a definite picture of its significance remains to be established by careful research. In view of the limited amount of information now available, the following discussion is bound to raise more questions than it can possibly answer.

One cannot use the Occupational Interest Survey very long in counseling or research without noting a striking variation in the general level of scores from one person to another. Even in the same occupation, wide variation in score level can exist. Figure 13 illustrates how it is possible for the absolute values of scores of members of the same occupation to differ greatly, even when each person scores highest in that person's own occupation. The median of 77 occupational scores received by one forester, as tallied in figure 13, is .65; the scores range from .38 to .81. On the other hand, another forester received scores ranging from .15 to .44, with a median of .33. The variations among journalists and carpenters shown in figures 14 and 15 are just as striking.

By the nature of the scoring system, a person who receives generally high occupational scores has more answers in common

M Score = 75

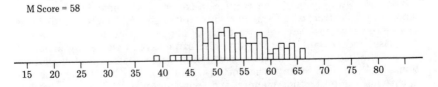

M Score = 40

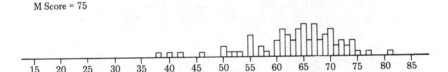

M Score = 58

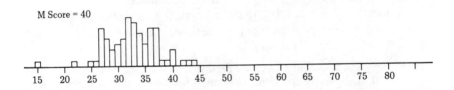

Figure 13. Distributions of the masculine occupational scores of three foresters with high, low, and medium M scores (decimal points omitted).

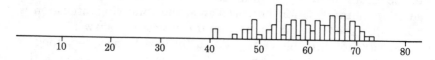

M Score = .66

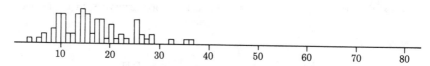

M Score = .60

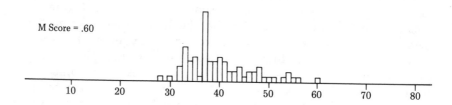

M Score = .15

Figure 14. Distributions of the masculine occupational scores of three journalists (decimal points omitted).

with the people in the occupations involved, on the average, than a person who receives low scores. This circumstance has suggested to Clemans (1968, pp. 53–55) an interesting possibility as set forth in the following excerpt from his article, "Interest Measurement and the Concept of Ipsativity."

Admittedly, the individuals in most occupations have specific interests that tend to set them apart from the general population. But it is perhaps even more clear that people in many diverse occupations tend to have much in common. A medical doctor whose interests agree closely with the interests unique to doctors, but little with the interests of people in other occupations, would be considered an odd-ball not only by people in general but by doctors as well; as a group, doctors have much in common with men in general. The same would be true of a carpenter whose interests agree closely with those unique to carpenters but not with those of people in general. He, too, would be considered an odd character by other carpenters as well as by people in general. Both, however, should receive A ratings on their respective occupational scales on the Strong. The doctor would probably be described as one not having a good bedside manner; and some humorist might say the carpenter doesn't have a good boardside manner. It is interesting to note that if an occupation exists (and research suggests that some do) that has a well-defined

M Score = .73

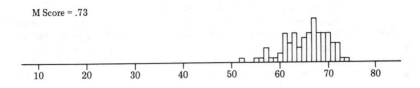

M Score = .47

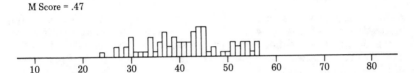

M Score = .13

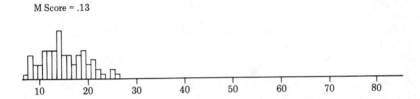

Figure 15. Distributions of the masculine occupational scores
of three carpenters (decimal points omitted).

pattern of interests — but one very like that of men in general — the Strong
technique of interest-scale construction would not result in a set of items.

The question could be posed: Why doesn't someone develop an interest inventory that takes into account, simultaneously, the unique differences and
similarities between occupations? Such an approach would give much more
information about an individual's complete pattern of interests. An instrument that accomplishes this objective has been devised by Kuder; it is his new
Occupational Interest Survey (1966). The technique of scoring this new inventory is unique. Visualize for each of its 156 scales a vector 600 elements
in length composed of the percentages characteristic of each of the 156 criterion groups for each of the 600 possible responses to the items in the inventory. These vectors are stored in the memory of the computer doing the
scoring. The matrix of proportions that is stored is 600 rows in length and
156 columns in width; in all, it contains a total of more than 93,000 values.
When an individual responds to the inventory, he too generates a vector 600
elements long composed of marks and nonmarks that are treated by the
computer-scoring device as ones and zeros. The scores for an individual are
actually coefficients of correlation between the individual's response vector
600 elements in length and the vector of proportions for each of the criterion
groups.

Now, if the theory suggested here is correct, this approach should not only result in identification of those groups with whom an individual's interest pattern is in most agreement; it should also reveal, on the basis of the general level of the scores, to what extent his interests are in common with those of men in general. Further, the intercorrelation matrix of the scales should be almost entirely composed of positive values. Two studies (Kuder, 1966) confirm the latter hypothesis. In one, based on 276 men and 23 scales, only 11 intercorrelations out of the 253 coefficients were negative; in another, based on 280 women and 21 scales, only 12 out of 200 intercorrelations were found to be negative.

Although a tremendous amount of data has been reported by Kuder (1966) illustrating the efficiency with which his new technique differentiates between different occupational groups, no study has been completed that relates to the hypothesis that the general level of scores is determined by a man's breadth of interests.

Using a somewhat clinical approach to make a preliminary check of this hypothesis, I asked an associate of mine to draw three Occupational Interest Survey profiles from our files — one that was generally high, one that was intermediate, and one that was generally low. I also specified that each should be a psychologist well known to me. The "highest" scores for the person with the generally high profile were on the scales for Mathematician, Statistician, and Psychology professor. This individual is a member of the Psychometric Society and has a generally high level of interest in quantitative psychology. He also plays golf and bridge, tinkers with cars, makes furniture, dabbles in electronics, and is a business executive. The generally high profile fits him well.

The intermediate profile clearly identified the respondent as having interests in common with psychologists. It also revealed a pattern of interests in common with those of social workers and psychiatrists. The man's pattern was in considerable agreement with his vocational and avocational activities. In general, however, his breadth of interest is somewhat more restricted than that of the first person, and the intermediate profile fits him well.

The third individual is a psychologist whom I have known for 10 years. He, too, was clearly shown to have a pattern of interests in common with other psychologists. But his generally depressed profile also revealed that his interests in common with people in general are limited. In actual fact, he keeps to himself much more than other individuals. He does not engage in a wide variety of hobbies, eats lunch alone, and rarely drives a car.

Being a quantitative psychologist, I was a little hesitant to discuss these three cases, but my assignment was to consider theoretical problems in interest measurement and, from a theoretical point of view, I think they are very interesting. A more detailed study testing the hypothesis suggested here would, in my opinion, be quite interesting and worthwhile.

In this connection it can be observed that *having interests* similar to those of other people is not the same as *being interested in* other people. It can be assumed from the nature of their work that ministers, for example, are interested in people, although their

160

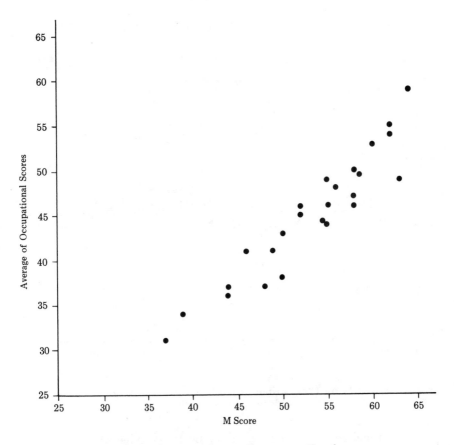

Figure 16. Average of masculine occupational scores
vs. M scores of 25 college men (decimal points omitted).

score level on the average is relatively low. On the other hand, foresters, plumbing contractors, and engineers have relatively high score levels and must be regarded as having interests more typical of men; however, these groups can hardly be said to be extraordinarily interested in people as such. A man with a high level of scores would presumably be at home with other men because he is like a good many of them, but it does not follow that he would particularly enjoy being of obvious, direct help to others. As for women, the picture is different. Social workers and high school counselors, for example, are highly typical of women as revealed by relatively high score levels, and can, from the nature of their occupations, also be presumed to be interested in people.

What index of score level would be most suitable for research studies? One possibility would be to use the mean of a person's

House Painters
N = 55

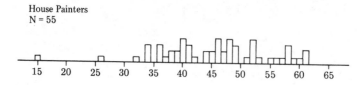

Foresters
N = 100

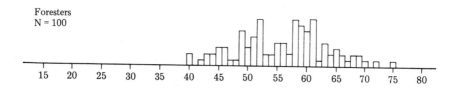

Male Base Group
N = 50

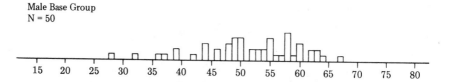

Figure 17. Distributions of M scores for three groups
(decimal points omitted).

occupational scores. Another would be to use a list judged to be a good sample of occupations in general. For reasons of simplicity and convenience, the writer favors using, for the present, the M score for men and the W score for women. These are two of the experimental scores reported for the Occupational Interest Survey. They are based on general reference groups of 1000 men and 400 women well distributed over many occupations, as described in the manual for Form D of the Preference Record.

There is a fairly good correspondence between the M score and the average of all masculine occupational scores as revealed in figure 16. The average M scores range from 368 for interior decorators to 552 for foresters. The average W scores for female occupational groups range from 469 for keypunch operators to 580 for school social workers. The distributions of M scores for sample groups are given in figure 17.

In any case, it appears that investigation of the relation of score level to the type of work enjoyed within an occupation might well produce some interesting results.

Interests and Age

It can be said that interests change with age and also that interests have considerable stability; both statements are true. It also can be said that certain interests are more stable than others. In the development of the Occupational Interest Survey, care was taken to restrict the items to those not highly correlated with age. In the selection of items, consideration was given to two indices of relation to age. One of these was the difference in the proportions of two generations of the same sex (matched groups of fathers and sons and of mothers and daughters) who marked each response. The other was the correlation of each item with age in a sample of the male norm group, which was originally intended for use as a general reference group.

The effect of the item selection has been to restrict the relation of scores to age on the OIS. If one were to undertake the development of a scale highly related to age from a pool of items including those in the OIS, probably few of the OIS items would survive.

The result of this systematic selection of items has been to keep the score distance between young and old to comparatively small amounts. The score distance between fathers and sons is .190, for example, and that between mothers and daughters is .192. Nonetheless, the fact that there is any difference at all raises the question as to whether the difference between a person's Father score and Son score (F — S) or between a person's Mother score and Daughter score (Mo — D) can be regarded as a subtle index of maturity. It is apparent that extensive experimental and clinical data need to be accumulated before the significance of these difference scores and their proper interpretation can become clear.

Career Matching

The traditional task in occupational counseling is that of matching people to occupations. In practice, this task is often transformed into one of matching people to people, and the discussion dealing with principle 1 in chapter 3 supports this practice. Strictly speaking, this approach really involves person-to-people matching, since it consists of trying to match a specific individual to a group of people in an occupation. In the following pages it is planned to explore a possible extension of the reasoning behind person-to-people matching.

Perfect matching does not occur in real life. Even the members of an occupational group do not match their group perfectly.

Actually, considerable variation exists among them, and there is ordinarily a corresponding variation in the extent to which the different members resemble the composite of their group. Thus the success of the matching is a relative matter and needs to be expressed in relative terms.

There are many problems to be solved in the process of determining the degree to which a person resembles various groups of people. One exceedingly important question asks what elements shall be used as the basis of such an index. In the case of psychological tests and inventories, these elements are the separate items or questions that are used. The following discussion proceeds on the assumption that the items actually used are fairly evenly distributed throughout the relevant factorial space, and that they are not substantially correlated with age.

Another important problem calls for deciding which groups shall be used as the basis for obtaining indices of similarity between a person and a number of groups. This requires formulating principles to be followed in selecting specific groups. The term *occupational group* may appear to be a definition in itself, but it is a definition that needs some clarification before it can be made operational. Some occupational titles are much more comprehensive than others. The decision of what constitutes an occupational group for purposes of developing a scoring system has ordinarily been a matter of judgment. Some titles, such as "clerk" or "tradesman," encompass such a wide range of activities as to seem of little promise. Scales ordinarily have been developed for groups that appear to the investigators to be relatively homogeneous.

It is well known that the interests of occupational groups differ, and this fact is recognized as important. It is perhaps less well recognized that the homogeneity of interests of occupational groups differ, and that the differences in homogeneity also are important. Indeed, the most important guiding principle to be kept in mind in settling on the composition of occupational groups is that the more homogeneous a group is the better will be the basis for matching.

It is also apparent that homogeneity is related to the number of cases needed to establish a scoring system. If a group is highly homogeneous, relatively few cases should be enough to establish a stable scoring pattern. Scoring systems based on relatively small samples of the same occupational group would almost certainly be in high agreement. Greater variation within the group could be expected to require larger samples for achieving stable results.

If all the members of a group answered the questions in an inventory in exactly the same way, the ultimate in homogeneity would have been achieved. This is definitely a theoretical situation! In this case there would be reason for considerable confidence in the scoring system developed for the occupation, and the answers of one could represent the answers of all. On the other hand, if a group were composed of such a variety of people that their answers were spread out as much as if they had answered at random, any index of similarity to the group would be meaningless, regardless of the size of the sample.

Actual occupational groups fall between these two extremes. As a rule, specialties within a general occupation are more homogeneous than the occupation as a whole. The interests of catalogers are more homogeneous than those of librarians in general; the interests of clinical psychologists are more homogeneous than those of psychologists in general. This generalization also applies to the fields of social work, medicine, engineering, the skilled trades, and dietetics. There is no reason to suppose that this same rule would not hold true in any other area that might be studied. Other things being equal, it appears that the greater the degree of specialization the more homogeneous the group will be; therefore, the greater the degree of confidence with which similarity of interests to the group can be assessed. This situation may well mean that homogeneity within an occupational group is a reflection of the extent to which members of the group do the same thing. No two people ever do exactly the same thing, of course, and no two careers are ever exactly alike. In a real sense, as observed by Ghiselli (1969, p. 10), "there are as many jobs as there are people."

These considerations lead to the idea that the original objective of matching people to jobs might be achieved most efficiently by person-to-person matching. A young person is looking for more than an occupation in the abstract sense; he or she is looking for a career, which is a highly individual matter. Instead of looking for occupational groups why not look for individuals he or she resembles, particularly individuals who are enthusiastic about their work? After all, if a person goes into law, the person's career will be more like that of one particular lawyer than another. Why not capitalize on this fact? If the items are evenly distributed in factorial space, then the simple count of the number of responses that each member of the pool has in common with the counselee is a good measure of the relative similarity of the various members of the pool to the counselee.

If person-to-person matching is used, one of the problems stated earlier disappears. Of course the composition of the inventory it-self is still of fundamental concern, but no longer is the composi-tion of occupational groups a problem. Instead, the task is to form a pool of records from people in all walks of life with whom to compare the subject. The report to the subject could be much more detailed and suggestive than could occupational scores. The introduction might read something like this:

Here are the personal histories of a number of people whose interests are simi-lar to yours, but who are enough older than you to have spent a substantial amount of time in the world of work. They all have been fortunate enough to get into work that they find highly satisfying. In spite of the fact that you are younger and may live in another part of the country, you may find some ideas that you can apply to your own plans through studying their education-al and work records.

The personal histories presented to the counselee would be as detailed as financial and technological limitations would allow. A supplementary list might be furnished of the occupations of a larger number of people — perhaps a hundred — who appear at the top when scored for resemblance to the counselee. Perhaps a sum-mary statement of the occupations of the top hundred also could be furnished.

Drawing up specifications for the pool of people whose answers would be scanned for similarity to those of the counselee would need to be done with care. In general, members should be those who are enthusiastic about their work, and the entire world of work should be well represented. Perhaps some dissatisfied workers should also be included, with the idea of giving the coun-selee the records of a few people who don't enjoy their work.

Theoretically, the larger the number of people in the pool the better, but of course beyond a certain point the value of additonal cases would not be worth the extra cost of including them. This point might be in the neighborhood of 5000 cases, but the esti-mate is sheer speculation.

The first exploratory research in following up this idea should probably be directed at determining the reliability and stability of the individual results for a number of subjects who have taken an inventory twice. It might at first appear that the correlations between a person and a number of other subjects would be less, on the average, than between a person and a number of occupa-tional groups. The former set of correlations would probably have a wider range, however, and this situation might counteract other influences that would tend to reduce reliability and stability.

Another consideration is that the correlations with people in the pool would probably be positively skewed, and the high scores would tend to be spread out in a thin tail. In this case, there is the likelihood that these high scores would have a greater stability than the lower ones that would not qualify for consideration in the counseling process.

A big advantage of person-to-person matching is that new occupations can be represented in the system as soon as data from a few people in the occupation become available, without waiting until a large number of cases can be collected. Clearly, the line of reasoning behind person-to-person matching does not have to be restricted to the field of interests. Although it is most easily applied to the field of interests, it warrants extension to the whole range of information that can be collected about human beings.

REFERENCES

Brayfield, A. H. The interrelation of measures of ability, aptitude, interests, and job satisfaction among clerical employees. Doctoral dissertation, University of Minnesota, 1946.

Brayfield, A. H. Clerical interest and clerical aptitude. *Personnel and Guidance Journal*, 1953, *31*, 304-306.

Brayfield, A. H., and Marsh, M. M. Aptitudes, interests, and personality characteristics of farmers. *Journal of Applied Psychology*, 1957, *41*, 98-103.

Campbell, D. P. *Handbook for the Strong Vocational Interest Blank.* Minneapolis: University of Minnesota Press, 1971.

Campbell, D. P. Reaction to the AMEG Commission report on sex bias in interest measurement. *Measurement and Evaluation in Guidance*, 1973, *6*, 178-180.

Carroll, J. D. Individual differences and multidimensional scaling. In R. N. Shepard, A. K. Romney, and S. B. Nerlove (eds.), *Multidimensional scaling.* New York: Seminar Press, 1972, 105-155.

Clark, K. E. *Vocational interests of non-professional men.* Minneapolis: University of Minnesota Press, 1961.

Clemans, W. V. Interest measurement and the concept of ipsativity. *Measurement and Evaluation in Guidance*, 1968, *1*, 50-55.

DiMichael, S. G., and Dabelstein, D. H. Work satisfaction and work efficiency of vocational rehabilitation counselors as related to measured interests. (Abstract). *American Psychologist*, 1947, *2*, 342-343.

Friedlander, F. Comparative work value systems. *Personnel Psychology*, 1965, *18*, 1-20.

Ghiselli, E. E. *The validity of occupational aptitude tests.* New York: Wiley, 1966.

Hahn, M. E., and Williams, C. T. The measured interests of Marine Corps women reservists. *Journal of Applied Psychology*, 1945, *29*, 198-211.

Hartshorne, H., and May, M. A. Studies in deceit. In *Studies in the nature of character.* (Volume 1) New York: Macmillan, 1928.

Herzberg, F., Mausner, B., Peterson, R. O., and Capwell, D. F. *Job attitudes: A review of research and opinion.* Pittsburgh: Psychological Service of Pittsburgh, 1957.

Herzberg, F., and Russell, D. The effects of experience and change of job interest on the Kuder Preference Record. *Journal of Applied Psychology*, 1953, *37*, 478-481.

Horst, P. A technique for the development of a differential prediction battery. *Psychological Monographs*, No. 380, 1954.

Horst, P. A technique for the development of a multiple absolute prediction battery. *Psychological Monographs*, No. 390, 1955.

Jacobs, R., and Traxler A. E. Use of the Kuder in counseling with regard to accounting as a career. *Journal of Counseling Psychology*, 1954, *1*, 153-158.

Kuder, G. F. *Examiner manual for the Kuder Preference Record Personal — Form A.* Chicago: Science Research Associates, 1953.

Kuder, G. F. Expected developments in interest and personality inventories. *Educational and Psychological Measurement*, 1954, *14*, 265-271.

Kuder, G. F. *Occupational Interest Survey.* Chicago: Science Research Associates, 1966.

Lipsett, L., and Wilson, J. W. Do suitable interests and mental ability lead to job satisfaction? *Educational and Psychological Measurement*, 1954, *14*, 373-380.

McRae, G. G. The relationship of job satisfaction and earlier measured interests. Doctoral dissertation, University of Florida, 1959.

North, R. D. Tests for the accounting profession. *Educational and Psychological Measurement*, 1958, *18*, 691-713.

Strong, E. K., Jr. *Vocational interests of men and women.* Stanford: University Press, 1943.

Strong, E. K., Jr. *Vocational interests 18 years after college.* Minneapolis: University of Minnesota Press, 1955.

Thorndike, E. L. *Adult interests.* New York: Macmillan, 1935.

Tucker, L. R. Intra-individual and inter-individual multidimensionality. In H. Gulliksen and S. Messick (eds.), *Psychological scaling.* New York: Wiley, 1960, 155-167.

5

The Problem of the Structure of Occupational Interests

In the effort to achieve an orderly picture of the world of work, a number of investigators have used the promising techniques of factor analysis. Notable among the studies in areas other than interest are those of Coombs and Satter (1949), Cardinet and Gendre (1967), and Blau and Duncan (1967).

By far the greatest attention, however, has been given to the field of interests, beginning with the identification of four factors by Thurstone (1931). The number of factor studies of interests is so extensive that it is unrealistic to attempt to present a survey of them here. Let it suffice to note that although a limited amount of agreement exists from one study to another, a definitive structure of interests has not been established. After all, an *appearance* of agreement is possible when agreement is no more than chance. A set of vectors placed in a domain would inevitably have some substantial correlations with the axes of any framework that might have been previously established in the same domain. (For example, an infinite number of vectors placed at random in a two-factor space would have a median absolute correlation of .77 with the nearer of the two factors, assuming all measures involved to have reliabilities of .90.) Indeed, it has not been inappropriate to ask whether the realm of interests is an amorphous domain that has no basic structure as such. Strong (1943, p. 315) stated the issue well some years ago when he asked concerning Thurstone's factors: "Are they really functional unities or are they merely mathematical coordinates in terms of which occupations may be located in space?" In the latter case, the different structures that might be set up are infinite in number.

The search for the best theoretical framework for dealing with interests is further complicated by Guilford's criticism (1952) that most factor analyses of interests are inappropriate. Other complications are that different analyses of the same data by different investigators do not necessarily lead to the same answers. Furthermore, sometimes the limitations of the technique used are overlooked in interpreting the results. As observed by Overall (1964), there is no basis for expecting that the best set of functional factors will necessarily emerge from a factor analysis, although the analysis may furnish a fresh and promising basis for viewing the domain involved.

More recently, Crawford and Ferguson (1970) have shown that the results of a factor analysis can be a function of the relative emphasis placed on test parsimony. The implication is strong in their discussion that a factor analysis cannot be considered complete or satisfactory if the structure includes any ambiguous or undefinable factors.

The discussion, "A Factor Analytic Interpretation Stategy," by Harris and Harris (1971) also illustrates how different methods and researchers can arrive at different results. It is apparent that if factor analyses of the same domain are not in agreement, the choice of one solution over the others must rest on a judgment as to which is most useful for a defined purpose. Differences of opinion are to be expected. It also is pertinent to ask whether the idea of a positive manifold — as assumed in the factor analysis of cognitive measures — is applicable to the field of interests, since in the case of interests one extreme of the scale is not necessarily better or more desirable than the other.

The Domain of Occupational Interests

We can safely state that at this moment no one knows precisely what the domain of occupational interests is. This situation exists partly because no one has defined the domain in operational terms. A general statement that the domain consists of interests in occupations is useful only as a point of departure. It could, in fact, be somewhat misleading if allowed to stand in that form. For the purpose of counseling, probably the most useful point of view is that interests can be regarded as occupational if they are related to occupational choice, regardless of whether the activities involved are occupational in nature. Even this definition needs elaboration, for interests vary considerably in their relation to occupational choice. It therefore follows that some standard of pertinence to occupational choice needs to be established.

The relation of an item to occupational choice might be considered to be the degree to which it is successful in differentiating between occupational groups representing occupations open to the counselees. One index of pertinence might be the number of significant differences found in all the possible comparisons of occupations for which scores are reported. Other things being equal, the larger this index the better the item. This index would, of course, have to be defined in terms of a specific list of occupations. Such an index is unrealistic at the moment since it would be so difficult to obtain, but it may become practical in the future. In the meantime, the standard deviation of the proportions of people in a wide variety of occupations who mark a specific response might be used. They would furnish a good idea of the extent to which differences exist between occupational groups in their reactions to a question.

It can be noted that the application of a standard of pertinence is just one way of implementing the principles listed in chapter I. The kind of measure suggested above was not available for evaluating items for inclusion in the Occupational Interest Survey or in any other inventory in existence, for that matter. An item was included in the Occupational Interest Survey because it fell in an area that had been established as related to vocational choice and because it fit into the general design developed for the inventory.

There are no doubt many considerations that bear upon the possible adequacy of a factor analysis of interests. The following points appear to be of particular importance:

1. The field of interests pertinent to the choice of a career should be covered as well as possible. Other things being equal, the more heterogeneous the sample of items the better. If a factor is not represented in the sample, it cannot be revealed by the analysis.

2. The occupational world should be well represented by the sample of subjects studied. Other things being equal, the more heterogeneous the sample the better. If the particular sample of people studied happens to be homogeneous with respect to a possible factor, that factor cannot be revealed by the analysis.

3. The number of cases studied should be large, in the interest of keeping sampling errors to a minimum. Otherwise, the variance attributable to small factors may be indistinguishable from error variance.

4. The variables used should not have common elements that artificially determine interrelationships. If a particular response is scored positively on one scale and negatively on another, for example, a relation is artificially predetermined and a distorted picture of the factorial structure might be ob-

tained from a factor analysis. This point was first made by Guilford (1952) in his article "When Not to Factor Analyze."

5. There should be as few loose ends as possible; that is, unidentifiable factors or loadings that do not make sense in their context should be kept to a minimum.

By this time it appears that the small number of interest factors revealed in early studies was simply a reflection of the limitations of those studies with respect to one or more of the points mentioned.

From the standpoint of these criteria, by far the most adequate of the factor analyses reported in the literature is the one of Guilford, Christensen, Bond, and Sutton (1954), although certain of its limitations should not be overlooked. The most serious is in the actual subjects used. The airmen and officers studied were all of the same sex and very nearly of the same age, thereby precluding the possibility of obtaining sex or age factors. The subjects were in all probability quite homogeneous in a few other respects, too, so that some factors pertinent to the general population may not have been revealed. Although the content of the inventory used is far more extensive than that of any other studies, it is still appropriate to suggest that some important areas may have been missed because of the way the items were selected, organized, and scored. Even so, the study still must be considered preeminent. It therefore will be used as the basis for comparison with the factor analyses reported later in this chapter.

Guilford's Criticism

Almost all factor analyses of interests published are subject to a criticism presented by Guilford in the article mentioned earlier, "When Not to Factor Analyze." The most important exception is the Guilford, Christensen, Bond, and Sutton study.

In the 1952 article Guilford sharply criticized the factor analysis of scores from inventories in which the same items are scored for more than one scale. At that time the Strong Vocational Interest Blank was the only inventory scored directly for specific occupations that had been factor analyzed. Guilford's point was that the results of a factor analysis of ipsative scores is likely to be misleading because the correlations between any two scales is determined largely by the scoring system, and may therefore be regarded as an artifact.

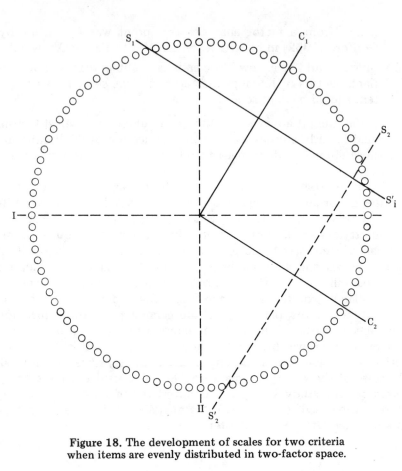

Figure 18. The development of scales for two criteria
when items are evenly distributed in two-factor space.

If a person marks answers that are weighted heavily for life insurance agent on the SVIB, that person inevitably marks responses
that have low weights for chemist. If a subject marks responses
weighted positively for lawyer, many of the subject's answers are
automatically weighted negatively for carpenter, which is reflected
by a large negative correlation between the two scales. It is not
possible to get all high or all low scores on an inventory if the
same set of items is scored differentially on a number of scales.
This generalization applies to all inventories that are scored in this
way.

It is not clear whether Guilford meant to object to the differential scoring of items as such. After all, if a particular response is
positively related to choice of one occupation and negatively related to choice of another, the item must be used for both keys as
a matter of general practice unless the inventory is increased to an

174

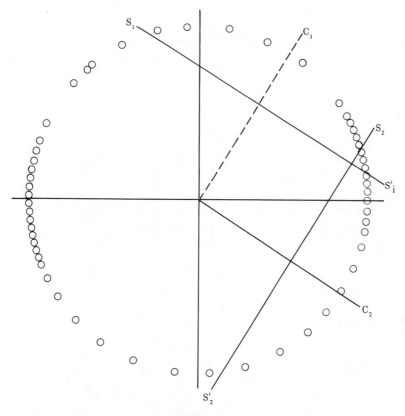

Figure 19. The development of scales for two criteria
when items are unevenly distributed in two-factor space.

unrealistic length. In any case, Guilford feels that for the purpose
of getting meaningful results from factor analyses, such scores are
inappropriate.

It is difficult to evaluate with any certainty the effect of the
multiple scoring of items on the correlations obtained between
scales. It might be held that weights assigned the same item for
different scoring keys simply reflect the relations among the
criteria involved, be they positive or negative, and that the correlations between any two scales would represent the "true" relation between the occupations. This conclusion might or might
not be true, depending on the distribution of items in factorial
space.

Let us consider again a two-space example as shown in figure
18. Let C_1 and C_2 represent the vectors of two uncorrelated criteria, and let us apply a standard for accepting items in tests for

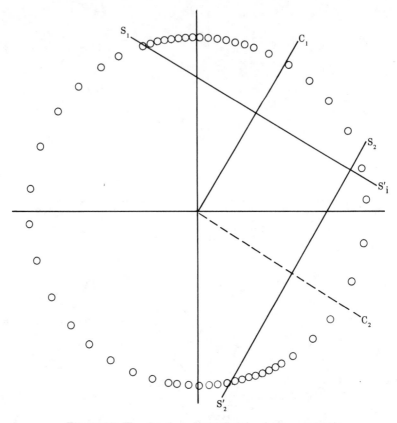

Figure 20. The development of scales for two criteria
when items are unevenly distributed in two-factor space.

those criteria as indicated by lines s_1 - s_i and s_2 - s'_2. If the items
are evenly distributed in space as in figure 18, the centroid of the
items selected for each criterion will coincide with the criterion
vector. Furthermore, tests developed for the two criteria would be
uncorrelated, even though some items would be scored on both
scales.

Now let us consider the instance of a quite uneven distribution
of items as depicted in figure 19.

It is evident that the vector of the test developed for C_1 will be
closer to C_2 than in figure 18, and will be positively correlated
with C_2. In the same manner, the test developed for C_2 will be
closer to C_1 than in figure 18, and will be positively correlated
with C_1. The two tests, T_1 and T_2, will be even more highly correlated. In a similar manner, a different distribution of items in the

same space would produce tests negatively correlated, as illustrated in figure 20. Although the illustration is an oversimplification, the principle involved is clear. Correlations among occupational scores are not a true indication of the relationships among the occupations themselves unless the items in the inventory are evenly distributed in the appropriate factorial space.

Factor analyses that are subject to Guilford's criticism should not be dismissed automatically as worthless. After all, the weights assigned to items have been empirically determined. If the items are evenly distributed throughout factorial space, it is quite likely that the correlations between occupational scales from inventories scored ipsatively will approximate those obtained from inventories not scored ipsatively, assuming that the same general areas are sampled. The key condition here is that the items be evenly distributed in space, a condition that has never been demonstrated to be met precisely and that may not even be met approximately in most cases. Studies subject to Guilford's criticism must therefore be interpreted with the caution so often recommended. They are still useful, however, when comparing results from different inventories and when looking for factors that appear fairly consistently in a variety of situations.

Another limitation of factor analyses of scales based on a general reference group is that the intercorrelations of the occupational scales depend to some extent upon the particular reference group used in developing them. Strong (1943, chapter 21, "Point of Reference," pp. 553–576) discovered that when the scales are developed with the use of a particular reference group, the intercorrelations may be quite different from those obtained among scales developed with another reference group. Factor analyses of the two tables of intercorrelations might therefore produce different pictures for identical lists of occupations.

In the effort to develop an approach not subject to Guilford's objection, a variable was finally found that is independent from one occupation to another and that also avoids the second shortcoming mentioned. That variable was the proportions of the members of an occupation that mark the specific responses in the inventory. Obviously, the proportion of lawyers who mark a particular response does not determine in any way how many physicians or how many welders mark the same response. It cannot be said that the correlation between the proportions of lawyers who mark the 600 responses in the Occupational Interest Survey and the proportions of physicians who mark those responses is in any sense an artifact.

Since there are no identical elements in the entries for the different variables, Guilford's objections would appear to be overcome in this instance. The high correlation of .94 between the proportions of clinical psychologists and the proportions of professors of psychology who marked the 600 responses is not artificial or contrived in any sense. It simply indicates that the interests of the two groups are quite similar to begin with. On the other hand, the low correlation of .33 between carpenters and college men majoring in English probably reflects little more than that these two groups are living in the same milieu and inevitably have some small community of interests. The correlation is not, however, predetermined by the way the variables are set up.

Factor Analyses of Response Proportions

Six factor analyses of response proportions have been made over a period of years, beginning in 1963. That period has been a time of tremendous change in several ways: in the number of groups becoming available for study, in the development of factor-analytic techniques, and in the capacity of electronic computers to apply these techniques efficiently.

Analysis I involved 124 variables, and was conducted under the direction of Dr. William V. Clemans of Science Research Associates. Analyses II, III, and IV involved samples of 99, 97, and 93 variables, respectively, drawn from a total of 217; these three analyses were done at the same time. Analyses V and VI involved 217 variables, but analysis VI was done considerably later when more powerful techniques had been developed. Analyses II, III, IV, and V were conducted under the direction of Dr. William Katzenmeyer of Duke University, and analysis VI was conducted by Dr. Robert J. Wherry of The Ohio State University. All of the analyses involved the principal components approach with rotation of axes. The last analysis, by Wherry, introduced additional techniques, which are described briefly in appendix C. Acknowledgment is made for the substantial contributions of the investigators involved, although responsibility for the identifications, interpretations, and organization of the factors presented in this book belongs to the author.

The first analysis included a number of variables composed of the proportions of various groups who responded under special instruction to mark those answers that would make the best impression on anyone who might see the answers. These best impression variables constituted such a large factor in the analysis that it seemed to have the effect of influencing the interpretation and even determination of other factors.

This situation is similar in principle to that encountered by Guilford, Christensen, Bond, and Sutton (1954, p. 28) who observed that certain large factors tended "to attract into their orbits variance that should perhaps have gone to [other] factors." These authors note elsewhere that strong factors, "by making satellites of score variables related to weaker factors, may weaken the appearance of the latter even to the point at which they vanish

TABLE 44

SUMMARY OF FACTORS FOUND IN
FACTOR ANALYSIS I

Factor	High Groups
1. "Best impression"	All seven groups answering under instructions to make the best possible impression have far higher loadings than any other group
2. Feminity-masculinity	All female groups have higher loadings than all male groups on this factor
3. Skilled trades	Plumber, carpenter, machinest, and auto mechanic
4. Behavioral sciences	Psychologist, high school counselor, lawyer
5. Artistic factor	Interior decorator, photographer, architect
6. Scientific-mathematical	Science teacher, math teacher, chemist
7. Sales	Insurance agent, radio station manager, retail clothier
8. Youth	Sons, daughters
9. Literary	Journalist, librarian
10. Medical	Physician, osteopath, podiatrist, and X-ray technician
11. Religious	Minister, university pastor, YMCA secretary
12. Outdoor	County agricultural agent, farmer
13, 14, 15. Not easily identified	

TABLE 45
FACTOR ANALYSES II, III, and IV

Factor	High Groups		
	Study II	Study III	Study IV
1. Skilled trades	House painter Welder Electrician Building contractor	Machinist Welder Bricklayer Electrician	Automobile mechanic Carpenter Welder
2. Business-Accounting	Accountant 1 Accountant 2 Accountant 3 Industrial engineer	Mathematics major Computer programmer Electrical engineer	Business—accounting major Business—general major Economics major
3. Artistic	Art major Interior decorator Architect major	Art major Architect	Art major Architect major Drama major
4. Social Welfare	Social worker—case Social worker—group Social worker—psychiatric University pastor	Social worker—group Social worker—school Social worker—case Social worker—psychiatric	Social worker—group Social worker—case Social worker—medical Social worker—case
5. Sales	Salesman of pharma- ceuticals Radio station manager Sales engineer	Radio station manager Retail clothier Real estate agent	Chamber of commerce executive Radio station manager Industrial engineer Insurance agent

6. Food	Animal husbandry major Agriculture major Farmer	Agriculture major Forester	Agriculture major Nutritionist Home economist
7. Clerical	Key punch operator Bank clerk Bookkeeper Secretary		Bank clerk Office clerk Department store saleswoman Stenographer
8. Journalism	Journalist		Newspaper editor History major
9. Physical Sciences	Physical sciences major		Mathematician Chemist
10. Medical		Physician Pediatrician X-ray technician	Pre-med major Biological sciences major Physician
11. Nutrition	Science teacher Home economics teacher Nutritionist	School dietician Home demonstration agent Home economics teacher	
12. Library Science		Cataloguer Librarian Bookstore manager	
13. Young Women		Daughters Young women groups	

TABLE 46
FACTORS FOUND IN
FACTOR ANALYSIS V

1. Drive, aggressiveness Youthful and masculine groups	10. Outdoor County agricultural agents
2. Feminity-masculinity All female groups are higher than all male groups	11. Religious Ministers
3. Mechanical Auto mechanics	12. Engineering Engineers
4. Medical Physicians	13. Political science, power Political science majors
5. Literary Journalists	14. Science-mathematics Mathematicians, chemists
6. Social welfare Social workers	15. Accounting-clerical Bookkeepers
7. Artistic Interior decorators	16. Musical Music majors
8. Dietetics Dieticians	17. Physical education Physical education majors
9. Persuasive Chamber of Commerce executive	18. Library science Cataloguers, librarians
	19, 20. Not easily identifiable

from the solution." (p. 30) They suggest that it would be interesting to conduct a factor analysis after eliminating variables involved mainly in the strong factors.

Such considerations, combined with the fact that the best impression factor is essentially an artifical one, led to the decision not to include the best impression variables in later analyses. This decision was made although, as noted later, the relation of these variables to one factor in analysis VI aided in labeling that factor.

The results of the last analysis are reported in detail in later pages. Summaries of the earlier analyses are presented, for purposes of comparison and discussion, in tables 44, 45, and 46.

Note that there was no possibility of complete agreement in analyses II, III, and IV, since the variables in each study were not the same despite considerable overlapping. There are six areas, however, that show up clearly in all three analyses, and all six are rather common in other studies that have been made. Five other areas show up in two of the analyses, and two other areas are revealed in only one. Limiting the number of factors extracted in each case to ten was probably unduly restrictive.

In analysis V twenty factors were extracted. Sixteen are easily identified by more or less specific vocational titles. The two listed at the top in table 46 are group factors that appear to call for more general titles.

Factor 1, Drive, Aggressiveness, is identified by differences in large groupings. In general, young groups have higher loadings than old groups, and male groups have higher loadings than the corresponding female groups.

Femininity-Masculinity appears to be justified as the title for factor 2 by the remarkable situation that perfect discrimination is achieved. All male groups are lower than all female groups on this factor, with no overlapping whatever.

Two of the factors in analysis V are not easily identifiable.

Factor Analysis VI

As noted previously, the entries for each variable in this and the preceding studies were the proportions of people in a group who marked each of the response positions in the Occupational Interest Survey. The set of 600 proportions from each group was correlated with the set of 600 proportions from each of the other groups. In this study and the preceding one, the resulting 217 by 217 correlation matrix was then factor analyzed by the method of principal components with later rotation. In analysis VI, the Wherry-Wherry Hierarchical Rotation Method was applied. Professor Wherry directed the actual analysis, and tribute is due him for his remarkable skill in achieving a set of factors that leaves comparatively few loose ends. His method is to be presented in a forthcoming article by him, and a brief description is contained in appendix C.

The groups studied have already been listed in table 1 (p. 35), together with the numbers of cases in each group and the mnemonic code used for identifying the groups in later tables. The numbers of cases in various major classifications of the groups are given in table 47. Those groups for which scores are reported on the standard report form for the Kuder Occupational Interest Survey are described in the general manual for that survey. There are a few adult groups in the study that were not used as the basis for scores for a number of reasons, of which similarity to other groups and relatively low homogeneity were the principal ones.

TABLE 47

NUMBERS OF CASES IN
FACTOR ANALYSIS STUDY

89 Male occupational groups	20,849
47 Female occupational groups	9,901
31 Male college major groups	7,045
19 Female college major groups	5,291
13 Male dissatisfied occupational groups	1,097
4 Female dissatisfied occupational groups	440
3 Female dissatisfied college major groups	450
5 Female dissatisfied college major groups	550
6 Others (fathers, sons, mothers, daughters, male and female base groups)	2,566
217 Total	48,189

There is one group represented on the standard report form of the survey that is not represented in this study. The sad fact is that the records on file for automobile salesmen are not now intelligible.

The dissatisfied groups were collected at the same time as the others and differ only in that they indicated dissatisfaction with their work. In general these dissatisfied groups are much smaller than the others; they were included only because of the desirability of having dissatisfied groups represented in the analysis. Needless to say, the factor loadings for them are therefore less accurate than for the others.

Perhaps further elaboration is in order for the four groups of accountants in the study. The certified public accountants for whom scores are reported on the standard form are group 3. They are described in the manual for the survey. Groups 2 and 4 were assembled at approximately the same time by Dean Dickens of Duke University. Group 4 is composed of industrial accountants, and group 2 is composed of a sample of other members of a number of accountant associations. Group 1 consists of members of the American Association of Accountants not engaged in teaching. This is the group used as the basis for the Accountant score for the Kuder Preference Record — Occupational.

Twenty-three factors emerged from the study. These are listed in table 48 in the order of the degree of generalization required in identifying them as judged by the writer. The factor loadings for all 217 variables are listed in appendix D. It can be noted that sixteen of these factors are similar to factors in analysis V, although in two or three cases the correspondence is poor. The only identified factors in analysis V that do not have some obvious resemblance to factors in analysis VI are the Musical and Accounting-Clerical factors, which appear to have been absorbed in more general factors in the later study.

Interpretation of Factors

The twenty-three factors are discussed below in the order listed in table 48. Lists of the groups with high and low loadings on each

TABLE 48
FACTORS IN FACTOR ANALYSIS VI

Factor	Similar Factor in Factor Analysis V
1. Typical response	
2. Feminity-masculinity	2. Feminity-masculinity
3. Adult women	
4. Adult men	
5. Young women	
6. Young men	1. Drive, aggressiveness
7. Influencing People — Social Approval	13. Political science, power
8. Occupational dissatisfaction	
9. Agriculture-law-political science	10. Outdoor
10. Skilled trades	3. Mechanical
11. Sales	9. Persuasive
12. Behavioral sciences	
13. Science-mathematics	14. Science-mathematics
14. Literary	5. Literary
15. Medical professions	4. Medical
16. Food-nutrition	8. Dietetics
17. Physical education and therapy	17. Physical education
18. Social welfare	6. Social welfare
19. Religious activities	11. Religious
20. Artistic	7. Artistic
21. Engineering	12. Engineering
22. Library science	18. Library science
23. Journalism	

factor are also presented. In these lists, groups are indentified by number and mnemonic code. Full titles can be found in table 1, p. 36.

1. *Typical Response Factor.* This general factor, representing the interests typical of the groups studied, is weighted in the direction of employed men, as might be expected from the fact that employed men constitute a large proportion of the subjects in the study. In this sense, fathers and the male norm group are highly typical. The female norm group with a loading of .826 is farther down, though still comparatively high on the list.

Least typical of the population studied are female students majoring in art or art education; next to them are male students majoring in the same area. Women students of drama and Roman Catholic teaching sisters are next in line for being different from the mainstream of subjects in the study. Of the employed men, carpenters have the lowest loading on this factor.

HIGH

187	FATHRS	.908	69	RADSTA	.853	64	PSYTST	.829
11	BKSMGR	.894	51	PEDTRN	.851	47	NRSRYM	.828
74	SOCCWK	.892	16	CC EX	.850	25	EDNWSP	.827
191	MALES	.892	52	PERS M	.847	147	MELED	.827
198	DCLTHR	.879	9	BARBER	.846	44	METEOR	.826
14	BUYER	.873	34	FLORST	.844	89	YMCASC	.826
22	DNTIST	.871	63	PRNTER	.842	192	FEMALE	.826
48	OPTMST	.871	55	PHOTOG	.841	29	ENGHAC	.824
82	TRVLAG	.871	77	SOCPSY	.841	38	JOURN	.823
20	COUNHS	.865	36	INS AG	.839	40	LIBRAR	.822
24	DRCTFN	.865	73	SCHSUP	.838	195	DBRBER	.822
23	DPTSTS	.863	202	DPHARM	.838	57	PHYSN	.820
204	DPSTCL	.863	27	ENGCVL	.837	67	PSYCIN	.820
205	DSOCWK	.861	7	BAKER	.836	81	SUPVFM	.813
70	REALES	.860	32	ENG MM	.835	28	ENGELE	.812
18	CLTH R	.859	8	BANKER	.834	31	ENGMCH	.811
46	MTLMGR	.858	84	TV REP	.834	79	SOCSCH	.810
39	LAWYER	.856	2	AC	.831	45	MINIST	.809
56	PHYTHR	.856	60	PODRST	.830	61	POLICE	.809
76	SOCWKM	.855	66	PSYCCN	.830	75	SOCWKG	.809
54	PHARM	.854	49	OSTPTH	.829	122	FPHYTH	.808

LOW

15	CRPNTR	.720	120	FOFCLK	.707	179	GMUSIC	.685
148	MENGCH	.719	152	MENGL	.707	177	GHMEC	.684
93	FBKKPR	.719	178	GMATH	.707	169	GBIOSC	.678
127	FRELED	.719	183	GPSYCH	.707	173	GENGL	.674
128	FSCTHS	.719	92	FBEAUT	.705	190	DGHTRS	.673
166	MAFCAD	.718	174	GFRNLG	.705	175	GHELTH	.668
160	MPHYSC	.717	167	MWPCAD	.704	139	MARCH	.656
186	GSOC	.716	138	MANLHS	.698	184	GCATHS	.650
91	FBNKCL	.715	217	XSOC	.692	171	GDRMA	.632
137	MAG	.715	182	GPOLYS	.691	140	MARTED	.607
214	XENGL	.712	110	FINTDC	.688	168	GARTED	.577

2. *Femininity-Masculinity Factor.* This factor is the best of the factors for discriminating between male and female groups. All except one female group (department store saleswomen) are above .340 on this factor, and all except one male group (foreign language majors) are below .340. This almost perfect discrimination is comparable to that for the Femininity-Masculinity Factor in analysis V and to that for the Femininity-Masculinity Factor in analysis I. There is a tendency for college major groups to be somewhat higher than occupational groups of the same sex, though there is little difference between fathers and sons and between mothers and daughters.

HIGH

174	GFRNLG	.622	216	XSOCSC	.516	132	FSOCMD	.490
215	XFRLNG	.566	169	GBIOSC	.515	127	FRELED	.489
217	XSOC	.547	176	GHISTO	.514	209	XSOCWK	.484
172	GELED	.536	186	GSOC	.513	125	FPSYCL	.482
173	GENGL	.536	213	XELED	.512	113	FLIBR	.479
177	GHMEC	.527	179	GMUSIC	.500	118	FNUTIN	.479
183	GPSYCH	.526	133	FSOCPS	.499	97	FCNSHS	.476
214	XENGL	.523	130	FSOCCW	.495	112	FLAWYR	.476
185	GSOCSC	.518	206	XDT	.493	168	GARTED	.476
178	GMATH	.517	134	FSOCSC	.491	121	FPEDRN	.475

LOW

70	REALES	-.017	196	DBRKLR	-.045	6	AUTO M	-.094
30	ENGIND	-.017	81	SUPVFM	-.049	87	WELDER	-.095
14	BUYER	-.018	71	SLSENG	-.050	15	CRPNTR	-.095
201	DPNTER	-.021	50	PNTR H	-.054	46	MTLMGR	-.096

187 FATHRS	-.022	203 DPLUMB	-.061	61 POLICE	-.099
53 PHAR S	-.031	200 DMACH	-.073	41 MCHNST	-.099
33 FARMER	-.032	197 DCRPNT	-.075	26 ELECTR	-.109
199 DELEC	-.035	36 IN SAG	-.081	59 PLMBCN	-.114
84 TV REP	-.041	13 BDG CN	-.081	58 PLUMBR	-.115
69 RADSTA	-.041	12 BRKLYR	-.083	83 TRKDRV	-.129

3. *Adult Women Factor.* High on this factor are employed women, therefore the name. Although there is considerable overlapping, the averages of major groups are in the following order: Adult women; Women in college; Men in college; Adult men.

There does not appear to be a firm basis for a more precise identification of this factor.

HIGH

100 FDPTSW	.439	106 FDTTHR	.275	104 FDTHOS	.222
92 FBEAUT	.416	207 XOFCLK	.275	208 XSECY	.222
91 FBNKCL	.380	129 FSECY	.272	90 FACNT	.220
120 FOFCLK	.362	114 FMATHS	.268	177 GHMEC	.219
93 FBKKPR	.358	105 FDTSCH	.262	172 GELED	.218
189 MTHRS	.349	103 FDTCOM	.259	109 FHOMEC	.214
107 FFLRST	.324	102 FDTCDM	.257	190 DGHTRS	.206
115 FMTLMR	.324	108 FHMDEM	.252	170 GBUSGN	.205
123 FPRSCT	.321	118 FNUTIN	.244	206 XDT	.199
135 FSTENO	.309	116 FNURSE	.233	83 TRKDRV	.197
111 FKYPCH	.299	192 FEMALE	.225	117 FNUTRN	.196
99 FDNTAS	.284	101 FDTNAD	.223	23 DPTSTS	.195

LOW

154 MFORST	-.121	211 D ENG	-.123	68 PSYPRF	-.144
67 PSYCIN	-.122	160 MPHYSC	-.125	25 EDNWSP	-.154
78 SOCRES	-.122	66 PSYCCN	-.131	65 PSYCCL	-.159
152 MENGL	-.122	163 MPSY	-.138	38 JOURN	-.170

4. *Adult Men Factor.* The one unifying generalization that applies to this factor is simply that all the high loadings are for groups of employed men.

HIGH

68 PSYPRF	.297	8 BANKER	.210	198 DCLTHR	.194
16 CC EX	.291	29 ENGHAC	.207	69 RADSTA	.191
1 AC AAA	.277	2 AC	.206	5 ARCH	.189

30 ENGIND	.274	67 PSYCIN	.206	32 ENG MM	.184
89 YMCASC	.267	39 LAWYER	.201	13 BDG CN	.179
73 SCHSUP	.265	11 BKSMGR	.198	25 EDNWSP	.179
70 REALES	.247	31 ENGMCH	.198	20 COUNHS	.178
21 COAGAG	.223	27 ENGCVL	.196	191 MALES	.177
52 PERS M	.219	36 INS AG	.196	59 PLMBCN	.175
28 ENGELE	.218	46 MTLMGR	.195	82 TRVLAG	.175
71 SLSENG	.218	18 CLTH R	.194	90 FACNT	.174
63 PRNTER	.212				

LOW

56 PHYTHR	-.064	153 MFRNLG	-.085	164 MCATHB	-.122
160 MPHYSC	-.065	92 FBEAUT	-.086	158 MMUSIC	-.123
172 GELED	-.066	122 FPHYTH	-.090	179 GMUSIC	-.133
163 MPSY	-.069	136 FX RAY	-.094	116 FNURSE	-.139
106 FDTTHR	-.075	174 GFRNLG	-.096	184 GCATHS	-.140
183 GPSYCH	-.079	213 XELED	-.097	190 DGHTRS	-.154
167 MWPCAD	-.080	166 MAFCAD	-.098	141 MBIOSC	-.160
171 GDRMA	-.080	159 MPHYED	-.110	169 GBIOSC	-.160
121 FPEDRN	-.083	111 FKYPCH	-.114	175 GHELTH	-.162
99 FDNTAS	-.085	181 GPHYED	-.116	180 GNURSE	-.194

5. *Young Women Factor.* Although there are a few exceptions to the rule, the high entries are mainly groups of college women. The group of daughters has the highest loading of all.

HIGH

190 DGHTRS	.255	176 GHISTO	.139	213 XELED	.123
173 GENGL	.195	208 XSECY	.136	38 JOURN	.121
152 MENGL	.189	155 MHIST	.135	217 XSOC	.121
214 XENGL	.180	182 GPOLYS	.128	215 XFRNLG	.110
185 GSOCSC	.175	172 GELED	.126	127 FRELED	.104
216 XSOCSC	.153	170 GBUSGN	.125	161 MPOLYS	.104
186 GSOC	.151	174 GFRNLG	.123	25 EDNWSP	.103
180 GNURSE	.140	164 MCATHB	.123		

LOW

6 AUTO M	-.133	13 BDG CN	-.140	5 ARCH	-.162
84 TV REP	-.133	139 MARCH	-.145	12 BRKLYR	-.167
37 INTDEC	-.134	81 SUPVFM	-.149	15 CRPNTR	-.173
109 FHOMEC	-.134	41 MCHNST	-.154	7 BAKER	-.181
30 ENGIND	-.135	87 WELDER	-.155	50 PNTR H	-.190
201 DPNTER	-.135				

6. *Young Men Factor.* Groups of college men account for most of the high loadings on this factor, and sons stands high on the list. The fact that the two groups of cadets are particularly high may possibly have some significance. It appears difficult, however, to justify a title more specific than that of "Young Men," unless possibly the quite general one of "Drive, Aggressiveness."

HIGH

142	MBUSAC	.384	146	MECON	.323	212	DSOCSC	.234
167	MWPCAD	.374	145	MBSMGT	.321	30	ENGIND	.229
149	MENGCL	.365	3	AC CPA	.319	1	AC AAA	.226
166	MAFCAD	.361	160	MPHYSC	.317	156	MLAW	.226
148	MENGCH	.359	138	MANLHS	.316	27	ENGCVL	.225
150	MENGEL	.344	210	DBSMNT	.314	61	POLICE	.221
188	SONS	.337	144	MBSMRK	.295	53	PHARS	.220
157	MMATH	.336	159	MPHYED	.288	31	ENGMCH	.217
4	AC IND	.334	19	COMPRG	.273	163	MPSY	.217
151	MENGMH	.334	162	MPREMD	.270	35	FORSTR	.213
154	MFORST	.332	2	AC	.268	70	REALES	.208
137	MAG	.331	68	PSYPRF	.268	32	ENG MM	.206
211	D ENG	.330	141	MBIOSC	.265	44	METEOR	.206
143	MBSGEN	.325	193	DACNT	.251	29	ENGHAC	.201

LOW

37	INTDEC	-.139	189	MTHRS	-.153	119	FOCCTH	-.192
115	FMTLMR	-.139	108	FHMDEM	-.157	209	XSOCWK	-.194
217	XSOC	-.143	107	FFLRST	-.160	130	FSOCCW	-.210
95	FCTLIB	-.144	123	FPRSCT	-.165	132	FSOCMD	-.210
126	FPSYCN	-.144	97	FCNSHS	-.167	127	FRELED	-.213
186	GSOC	-.144	133	FSOCPS	-.168	134	FSOCSC	-.223
113	FLIBR	-.148	98	F DEAN	-.175	110	FINTDC	-.234
94	FBKMGR	-.151	131	FSOCGR	-.191			

7. *Influencing People-Social Approval Factor.* The naming of this factor was influenced by the discovery that it is correlated substantially with response proportions obtained from best impression groups. These are groups who were asked to answer so as to make the best possible impression on anyone who might see the answers. The loadings of nine such groups on this factor range from .490 to .636 — all larger than the largest weight obtained by any group in the analysis.

HIGH

161	MPOLYS	.409	165	MSOC	.306	45	MINIST	.260
85	U PSTR	.401	209	XSOCWK	.302	67	PSYCIN	.253
75	SOCWKG	.352	76	SOCWKM	.294	77	SOCPSY	.252
163	MPSY	.351	60	PODRST	.290	20	COUNHS	.243
155	MHIST	.345	53	PHAR S	.287	182	GPOLYS	.238
156	MLAW	.342	74	SOCCWK	.286	166	MAFCAD	.237
66	PSYCCN	.323	212	DSOCSC	.284	152	MENGL	.231
78	SOCRES	.320	52	PERS M	.278	145	MBSMGT	.230
79	SOCSCH	.320	65	PSYCCL	.273	141	MBIOSC	.228
146	MECON	.307	167	MWPCAD	.273	63	PRNTER	.227
210	DBSMNT	.307	162	MPREMD	.265	16	CC EX	.226

LOW

12	BRKLYR	-.217	87	WELDER	-.241	93	FBKKPR	-.267
10	BKKPR	-.218	92	FBEAUT	-.243	91	FBNKCL	-.280
197	DCRPNT	-.219	26	ELECTR	-.249	58	FLUMBR	-.281
201	DPNTER	-.222	135	FSTENO	-.252	15	CRPNTR	-.290
200	DMACH	-.230	41	MCHNST	-.257	6	AUTO M	-.290
50	PNTR H	-.238						

8. *Occupational Dissatisfaction Factor.* If this factor were a perfect measure of job dissatisfaction (using the term in a very general sense, which includes dissatisfaction with one's area of major study), all dissatisfied groups in the study could be expected to be at the head of the list. This is patently not the case. Even so, these groups are generally high. The fact that, without exception, the dissatisfied groups have higher loadings on this factor than the corresponding satisfied groups indicates that a significant, though small, amount of the variance of this factor is dissatisfaction with work. Efforts to find a better way of identifying this factor have so far proved futile. The title "Occupational Dissatisfaction" is therefore being used, since this variable appears to be the only identifiable portion of the variance of the factor.

It is not plausible that job satisfaction is completely independent of the work one happens to be in. On the other hand, it is reasonable to suppose there are individual differences in a general tendency to be content with one's work.

HIGH

142	MBUSAC	.301	193	DACNT	.210	156	MLAW	.178
143	MBSGEN	.254	211	D ENG	.208	201	DPNTER	.175
10	BKKPR	.241	202	DPHARM	.203	181	GPHYED	.172
210	DBSMNT	.241	4	AC IND	.202	89	YMCASC	.170
146	MECON	.237	62	POSTCL	.195	55	PHOTOG	.169
144	MBSMRK	.235	3	AC CPA	.191	1	AC AAA	.167
157	MMATH	.234	212	DSOCSC	.190	203	DPLUMB	.167
139	MARCH	.229	161	MPOLYS	.188	163	MPSY	.164
195	DBRBER	.221	67	PSYCIN	.186	194	DAUTOM	.163
204	DPSTCL	.219	2	AC	.184	196	DBRKLR	.163
140	MARTED	.215	198	DCLTHR	.183	200	DMACH	.162
145	MBSMGT	.213	9	BARBER	.181	19	COMPRG	.160
9	BARBER	.211	165	MSOC	.181			

LOW

130	FSOCCW	-.070	109	FHOMEC	-.080	117	FNUTRN	-.097
118	FNUTIN	-.072	97	FCNSHS	-.085	121	FPEDRN	-.098
68	PSYPRF	-.075	116	FNURSE	-.090	127	FRELED	-.105
180	GNURSE	-.076	95	FCTLIB	-.090	113	FLIBR	-.113
126	FPSYCN	-.078	131	FSOCGR	-.091	128	FSCTHS	-.121
125	FPSYCL	-.078	134	FSOCSC	-.093	108	FHMDEM	-.150
98	F DEAN	-.078	123	FPRSCT	-.096			

9. *Agriculture-Law-Political Science Factor.* The effort to give this factor a simple title has been unsuccessful. The problem of identifying the factor has been by far the most difficult in the study. Five college major groups head the list: animal husbandry, law, agriculture, political science, and history. These are followed by four occupational groups that form a similar but also bewildering mixture: lawyer, nurseryman, county agricultural agent, and forester.

Any number of titles might be used for this factor. If it is assumed that animal husbandry can be subsumed under agriculture, the cumbersome title given above appears to carry the apparently ambiguous idea involved. The combination is not, however, quite as preposterous as might at first appear. After all, food production has its legal and political angles. The first impulse to abandon this factor as unidentifiable has therefore itself been abandoned, in the hope that its listing may eventually make some contribution to the understanding of the structure of occupational interests.

HIGH

138	MANLHS	.273	19	COMPRG	.214	4	AC IND	.188
156	MLAW	.271	40	LIBRAR	.213	5	ARCH	.187
137	MAG	.268	146	MECON	.213	42	MATHM	.185
161	MPOLYS	.257	38	JOURN	.212	153	MFRNLG	.184
155	MHIST	.255	154	MFORST	.209	144	MBSMRK	.182
39	LAWYER	.254	25	EDNWSP	.206	11	BKSMGR	.182
47	NRSRYM	.243	139	MARCH	.206	182	GPOLYS	.181
21	COAGAG	.239	33	FARMER	.200	2	AC	.178
35	FORSTR	.230	167	MWPCAD	.196	112	FLAWYR	.177
152	MENGL	.226	142	MBUSAC	.194	210	DBSMNT	.173
80	STATCN	.225	212	DSOCSC	.194	140	MARTED	.173
136	FX RAY	.222	143	MBSGEN	.191	44	METEOR	.172
3	AC CPA	.218						

LOW

49	OSTPTH	-.109	88	X RAY	-.136	116	FNURSE	-.217
179	GMUSIC	-.112	111	FKYPCH	-.148	136	FX RAY	-.222
119	FOCCTH	-.118	190	DGHTRS	-.175	99	FDNTAS	-.229
127	FRELED	-.125	180	GNURSE	-.209	184	GCATHS	-.262

10. *Skilled Trades Factor.* This factor corresponds to the mechanical factor so generally found in factor analyses, and could justifiably be given that label.

HIGH

6	AUTO M	.492	138	MANLHS	.427	35	FORSTR	.379
58	PLUMBR	.475	203	DPLUMB	.426	86	VETRN	.363
87	WELDER	.474	199	DELEC	.420	84	TV REP	.356
33	FARMER	.471	13	BDG CN	.414	62	POSTCL	.341
41	MCHNST	.469	59	PLMBCN	.413	61	POLICE	.319
26	ELECTR	.468	137	MAG	.404	46	MTLMGR	.308
194	DAUTOM	.455	196	DBRKLR	.403	191	MALES	.307
197	DCRPNT	.451	81	SUPVFM	.396	88	X RAY	.304
15	CRPNTR	.448	201	DPNTER	.396	149	MENGCL	.304
83	TRKDRV	.438	21	COAGAG	.389	28	ENGELE	.303
200	DMACH	.436	12	BRKLYR	.388	195	DBRBER	.300
50	PNTR H	.427	154	MFORST	.386			

LOW

215	XFRNLG	-.073	179	GMUSIC	-.090	172	GELED	-.118
168	GARTED	-.074	186	GSOC	-.093	152	MENGL	-.125

130 FSOCCW	-.074	125 FPSYCL	-.094	170 GBUSGN	-.130
217 XSOC	-.077	40 LIBRAR	-.095	182 GPOLYS	-.139
132 FSOCMD	-.079	185 GSOCSC	-.097	214 XENGL	-.149
176 GHISTO	-.083	174 GFRNLG	-.105	173 GENGL	-.187
113 FLIBR	-.086	213 XELED	-.108	171 GDRMA	-.254
110 FINTDC	-.088	133 FSOCPS	-.110		

11. *Sales Factor.* "Marketing" or "Business" are other titles that might be used for this factor, which is one that almost always shows up in factor analyses of interests.

HIGH

144 MBSMRK	.318	195 DBRBER	.203	203 DPLUMB	.167
143 MBSGEN	.276	166 MAFCAD	.201	69 RADSTA	.166
145 MBSMGT	.274	30 ENGIND	.198	54 PHARM	.165
53 PHAR S	.260	167 MWPCAD	.195	170 GBUSGN	.162
67 PSYCIN	.257	163 MPSY	.187	162 MPREMD	.161
71 SLSENG	.247	84 TV REP	.186	7 BAKER	.159
188 SONS	.236	20 COUNHS	.184	198 DCLTHR	.157
142 MBUSAC	.225	210 DPSMNT	.182	199 DELEC	.155
148 MENGCH	.220	14 BUYER	.181	23 DPTSTS	.154
151 MENGMH	.219	52 PERS M	.181	55 PHOTOG	.151
36 INS AG	.217	59 PLMBCN	.175	150 MENGEL	.150
18 CLTH R	.213	66 PSYCCN	.174	16 CC EX	.146
9 BARBER	.211	4 AC IND	.173	60 PODRST	.146
159 MPHYED	.207	70 REALES	.172	165 MSOC	.146
146 MECON	.205	46 MTLMGR	.171		

LOW

109 FHOMEC	-.101	113 FLIBR	-.124	40 LIBRAR	-.136
158 MMUSIC	-.103	209 XSOCWK	-.129	121 FPEDRN	-.152
5 ARCH	-.113	112 FLAWYR	-.133	184 GCATHS	-.172

12. *Behavioral Sciences Factor.* The high loadings of psychologists, psychology majors, premeds, and research workers in the field of social welfare appear to justify this title.

HIGH

66 PSYCCN	.219	124 FPSY	.152	60 PODRST	.127
67 PSYCIN	.215	61 POLICE	.148	126 FPSYCN	.124
65 PSYCCL	.208	145 MBSMGT	.148	151 MENGMH	.123
163 MPSY	.189	143 MBSGEN	.144	72 SCITHS	.122

68 PSYPRF	.170	77 SOCPSY	.139	78 SOCRES	.121
20 COUNHS	.158	188 SONS	.132	54 PHARM	.121
162 MPREMD	.156	159 MPHYED	.130	205 DSOCWK	.121

LOW

5 ARCH	-.073	174 GFRNLG	-.089	164 MCATHB	-.149
182 GPOLYS	-.074	127 FRELED	-.090	184 GCATHS	-.204
168 GARTED	-.074	176 GHISTO	-.094	158 MMUSIC	-.221
215 XFRNLG	-.084	171 GDRMA	-.104	179 GMUSIC	-.266
45 MINIST	-.087				

13. *Science-Mathematics Factor.* This is one of the most clear-cut identifications in the study. The factor is one that almost always is found in factor studies of interests.

HIGH

160 MPHYSC	.353	169 GBIOSC	.244	72 SCITHS	.198
17 CHEMST	.340	150 MENGEL	.227	121 FPEDRN	.197
42 MATHM	.322	65 PSYCCL	.216	148 MENGCH	.191
96 FCMPRG	.300	124 FPSY	.214	28 ENGELE	.189
19 COMPRG	.296	158 MMUSIC	.212	64 PSYTST	.189
80 STATCN	.276	68 PSYPRF	.208	163 MPSY	.189
128 FSCTHS	.276	44 METEOR	.202	178 GMATH	.188
141 MBIOSC	.268	51 PEDTRN	.199	1 AC AAA	.186
157 MMATH	.244	211 D ENG	.199		

LOW

16 CC EX	-.100	87 WELDER	-.121	89 YMCASC	-.138
58 PLUMBR	-.101	9 BARBER	-.122	61 POLICE	-.150
100 FDPTSW	-.102	24 DRCTFN	-.123	52 PERS M	-.150
92 FBEAUT	-.109	12 BRKLYR	-.133	15 CRPNTR	-.158
108 FHMDEM	-.115	50 PNTR H	-.137	83 TRKDRV	-.182

14. *Literary Factor.* The identification of this commonly found factor is clear. The single surprising entry in the relatively high loadings — that for dissatisfied automobile mechanics — is one to think about! When the study was set up it was considered important to include a number of dissatisfied groups. Doing so, however, necessitated using some quite small groups that would under no circumstances have been adequate for developing a scale. The group of dissatisfied automobile mechanics was one of those small

groups, and the loadings for it may not be very reliable. Perhaps it should not have been included in this study at all.

HIGH

152	MENGL	.232	171	GDRMA	.133	112	FLAWYR	.109
173	GENGL	.191	155	MHIST	.132	113	FLIBR	.107
38	JOURN	.188	182	GPOLYS	.127	161	MPOLYS	.101
153	MFRNLG	.182	194	DAUTOM	.125	215	XFRNLG	.100
25	EDNWSP	.180	176	GHISTO	.121	95	FCTLIB	.099
214	XENGL	.170	158	MMUSIC	.117	140	MARTED	.099
40	LIBRAR	.152	174	GFRNLG	.111	216	XSOCSC	.097
8	BANKER	.143						

LOW

22	DNTIST	-.100	3	AC CPA	-.122	47	NRSRYM	-.135
72	SCITHS	-.101	90	FACNT	-.129	18	CLTH R	-.139
69	RADSTA	-.104	57	PHYSN	-.130	36	INS AG	-.143
1	AC AAA	-.106	49	OSTPTH	-.130	34	FLORST	-.162
33	FARMER	-.120	24	DRCTFN	-.130	60	PODRST	-.185
54	PHARM	-.122	53	PHAR S	-.135			

15. *Medical Professions Factor.* Aside from the high loadings of high school science teachers, the identification of this factor is clear.

HIGH

49	OSTPTH	.283	56	PHYTHR	.182	99	FDNTAS	.128
57	PHYSN	.275	128	FSCTHS	.176	169	GBIOSC	.128
86	VETRN	.266	48	OPTMST	.174	68	PSYPRF	.121
54	PHARM	.254	162	MPREMD	.169	122	FPHYTH	.121
22	DNTIST	.242	141	MBIOSC	.159	121	FPEDRN	.116
51	PEDTRN	.224	53	PHAR S	.151	21	COAGAG	.112
60	PODRST	.223	17	CHEMST	.151	25	EDNWSP	.112
202	DPHARM	.223	136	FX RAY	.141	195	DBRBER	.104
72	SCITHS	.219	24	DRCTFN	.133	64	PSYTST	.103
88	X RAY	.214						

LOW

126	FPSYCN	-.083	124	FPSY	-.095	145	MBSMGT	-.119
186	GSOC	-.084	151	MENGMH	-.100	131	FSOCGR	-.124
127	FRELED	-.089	149	MENGCL	-.108	170	GBUSGN	-.126
44	METEOR	-.093	142	MBUSAC	-.108	179	GMUSIC	-.147

16. *Food-Nutrition Factor.* The main theme that appears to be characteristic of groups with high loadings in this factor is their relation to food production and preparation. It is, however, food production and preparation with a scientific bent. The high loading for women majors in mathematics is somewhat puzzling.

HIGH

169	GBIOSC	.241	109	FHOMEC	.191	96	FCMPRG	.155
178	GMATH	.225	104	FDTHOS	.187	183	GPSYCH	.150
105	FDTSCH	.222	181	GPHYED	.185	206	XDT	.149
177	GHMEC	.221	117	FNUTRN	.184	186	GSOC	.148
102	FDTCDM	.219	103	FDTCOM	.178	128	FSCTHS	.142
137	MAG	.207	106	FDTTHR	.174	86	VETRN	.136
138	MANLHS	.204	217	XSOC	.169	72	SCITHS	.135
101	FDTNAD	.198	122	FPHYTH	.160	141	MBIOSC	.134
118	FNUTIN	.194						

LOW

94	FBKMGR	-.078	83	TRKDRV	-.089	40	LIBRAR	-.125
5	ARCH	-.079	63	PRNTER	-.092	23	DPTSTS	-.153
16	CC EX	-.081	153	MFRNLG	-.108	152	MENGL	-.160
45	MINIST	-.085	37	INTDEC	-.114	38	JOURN	-.173
204	DPSTCL	-.085	11	BKSMGR	-.115	25	EDNWSP	-.174
70	REALES	-.086	69	RADSTA	-.115			

17. *Physical Education and Therapy Factor.* The above title appears to be logical for identifying this factor. The failure, however, of women physical therapists — with a loading of only .086 — to appear high on the list is puzzling.

HIGH

181	GPHYED	.242	175	GHELTH	.132	116	FNURSE	.110
119	FOCCTH	.191	180	GNURSE	.132	168	GARTED	.110
159	MPHYED	.185	136	FX RAY	.130	41	MCHNST	.109
147	MELED	.166	161	MPOLYS	.127	141	MBIOSC	.109
72	SCITHS	.165	108	FHMDEM	.126	158	MMUSIC	.108
88	X RAY	.162	140	MARTED	.126	128	FSCTHS	.105
56	PHYTHR	.160	154	MFORST	.126	49	OSTPTH	.103
184	GCATHS	.154	164	MCATHB	.126	61	POLICE	.103
151	MENGMH	.146	190	DGHTRS	.122	149	MENGCL	.102
150	MENGEL	.143	139	MARCH	.121	169	GBIOSC	.100
99	FDNTAS	.139	137	MAG	.111			

LOW

68	PSYPRF	-.100	133	FSOCPS	-.111	110	FINTDC	-.139
132	FSOCMD	-.101	38	JOURN	-.116	70	REALES	-.144
69	RADSTA	-.102	124	FPSY	-.118	39	LAWYER	-.144
156	MLAW	-.104	94	FBKMGR	-.126	209	XSOCWK	-.147
155	MHIST	-.107	18	CLTH R	-.127	182	GPOLYS	-.159
25	EDNWSP	-.107	198	DCLTHR	-.128			

18. *Social Welfare Factor.* The consistently high loadings of social workers on this factor almost demanded it be given the "Social Welfare" title. The fact that psychiatrists and psychologists also have relatively high loadings is consistent with the title.

HIGH

77	SOCPSY	.280	64	PSYTST	.198	209	XSOCWK	.146
76	SOCWKM	.267	65	PSYCCL	.196	57	PHYSN	.144
79	SOCSCH	.265	56	PHYTHR	.155	49	OSTPTH	.143
74	SOCCWK	.256	68	PSYPRF	.152	85	U PSTR	.142
75	SOCWKG	.243	130	FSOCCW	.149	62	POSTCL	.131
78	SOCRES	.219	66	PSYCCN	.148	132	FSOCMD	.131
205	DSOCWK	.211	133	FSOCPS	.146	134	FSOCSC	.131

LOW

55	PHOTOG	-.102	102	FDTCDM	-.117	144	MBSMRK	-.130
16	CC EX	-.103	108	FHMDEM	-.120	34	FLORST	-.132
105	FDTSCH	-.108	37	INTDEC	-.123	103	FDTCOM	-.138
18	CLTH R	-.110	168	GARTED	-.125	110	FINTDC	-.143
69	RADSTA	-.112	107	FFLRST	-.125	170	GBUSGN	-.154

19. *Religious Activities Factor.* The identification of this factor is easy. All religious groups in the study except YMCA secretaries have high loadings.

HIGH

184	GCATHS	.314	127	FRELED	.147	38	JOURN	.104
164	MCATHB	.258	165	MSOC	.135	147	MELED	.098
45	MINIST	.213	75	SOCWKG	.126	66	PSYCCN	.097
85	U PSTR	.185	186	GSOC	.114	215	XFRNLG	.097
78	SOCRES	.172	217	XSOC	.109	130	FSOCCW	.091
79	SOCSCH	.149	175	GHELTH	.107	68	PSYPRF	.090

LOW

1	AC AAA	-.132	29	ENGHAC	-.142	110	FINTDC	-.157
144	MBSMRK	-.136	4	AC IND	-.150	3	AC CPA	-.161
28	ENGELE	-.136	151	MENGMH	-.152	37	INTDEC	-.168
193	DACNT	-.138	30	ENGIND	-.154	71	SLSENG	-.188

20. *Artistic Factor.* There are only seven groups in the study that clearly are artistic in nature and all appear in the top eight positions. The only "interloper" consists of women drama majors, and their inclusion in the top ranks is not illogical.

HIGH

140	MARTED	.546	110	FINTDC	.304	119	FOCCTH	.230
168	GARTED	.491	55	PHOTOG	.279	181	GPHYED	.229
139	MARCH	.416	5	ARCH	.270	186	GSOC	.220
37	INTDEC	.399	217	XSOC	.236	213	XELED	.220
171	GDRMA	.375	183	GPSYCH	.235			

LOW

42	MATHM	-.130	8	BANKER	-.137	43	MATHHS	-.203
62	POSTCL	-.132	109	FHOMEC	-.154	93	FBKKPR	-.205
105	FDTSCH	-.132	91	FBNKCL	-.162	90	FACNT	-.215
4	AC IND	-.133	2	AC	-.175	10	BKKPR	-.218
120	FOFCLK	-.135	1	AC AAA	-.186	114	FMATHS	-.244

21. *Engineering Factor.* This factor clearly is engineering.

HIGH

150	MENGEL	.243	27	ENGCVL	.198	211	D ENG	.175
149	MENGCL	.239	148	MENGCH	.193	30	ENGIND	.174
151	MENGMH	.238	166	MAFCAD	.193	4	AC IND	.155
139	MARCH	.234	28	ENGELE	.191	56	PHYTHR	.155
167	MWPCAD	.229	42	MATHM	.191	160	MPHYSC	.155
31	ENGMCH	.223	5	ARCH	.184	71	SLSENG	.154
29	ENGHAC	.212	3	AC CPA	.176	17	CHEMST	.151
19	COMPRG	.200	32	ENG MM	.175	96	FCMPRG	.150
157	MMATH	.199						

LOW

207	XOFCLK	-.090	129	FSECY	-.107	107	FFLRST	-.124
91	FBNKCL	-.091	111	FKYPCH	-.115	92	FBEAUT	-.127
127	FRELED	-.095	135	FSTENO	-.118	100	FDPTSW	-.137

118 FNUTIN -.096	117 FNUTRN -.124	21 COAGAG -.168
189 MTHRS -.097		

22. *Library Science Factor.* The three groups of librarians in the study head the list and clearly justify the title given to this factor. The high loadings for the two groups of bookstore managers tend to support this general classification. Why men music majors are high on this factor is mystifying. The loading for women music majors is only .082.

HIGH

95 FCTLIB	.208	114 FMATHS	.120	34 FLORST	.102
40 LIBRAR	.181	18 CLTH R	.112	69 RADSTA	.102
113 FLIBR	.174	72 SCITHS	.107	45 MINIST	.101
11 BKSMGR	.161	127 FRELED	.105	155 MHIST	.101
158 MMUSIC	.159	43 MATHHS	.103	82 TRVLAG	.100
94 FBKMGR	.137	55 PHOTOG	.103		

LOW

51 PEDTRN	-.053	121 FPEDRN	-.060	175 GHELTH	-.096
83 TRKDRV	-.054	169 GBIOSC	-.062	183 GPSYCH	-.101
214 XENGL	-.054	217 XSOC	-.067	116 FNURSE	-.106
125 FPSYCL	-.055	186 GSOC	-.072	180 GNURSE	-.121
135 FSTENO	-.055	65 PSYCCL	-.074	190 DGHTRS	-.169
99 FDNTAS	-.058	207 XOFCLK	-.085	111 FKYPCH	-.169

23. *Journalism Factor.* There is a wide gap in the loadings between the two groups at the head of the list and the others. This factor is the most specific on the list. It is interesting that dissatisfied English majors with a loading of .071 are higher on this factor than both the male and female satisfied English majors whose loadings are approximately zero.

HIGH

25 EDNWSP	.183	119 FOCCTH	.089	76 SOCWKM	.070
38 JOURN	.179	102 FDTCDM	.076	131 FSOCGR	.068
63 PRNTER	.102	122 FPHYTH	.072	130 FSOCCW	.066
117 FNUTRN	.095	103 FDTCOM	.071	104 FDTHOS	.065
158 MMUSIC	.092	214 XENGL	.071	125 FPSYCL	.065
179 GMUSIC	.092				

LOW

100	FDPTSW	-.080	92	FBEAUT	-.084	157	MMATH	-.100
120	FOFCLK	-.082	143	MBSGEN	-.084	178	GMATH	-.102
91	FBNKCL	-.083	72	SCITHS	-.095	68	PSYPRF	-.105
170	GBUSGN	-.083	93	FBKKPR	-.099	114	FMATHS	-.116
188	SONS	-.083	148	MENGCH	-.100	142	MBUSAC	-.123

A Comparison of Factor Analysis VI with the Guilford, Christensen, Bond, and Sutton Study

The study by Guilford, Christensen, Bond, and Sutton (1954) is by far the most extensive and elaborate of the factor analyses of interests reported in the literature. It also meets Guilford's own requirement (1952) that the different variables used in a factor analysis should have no items in common that tend to predetermine correlations. For these reasons, the study by Guilford, Christensen, Bond, and Sutton (sometimes referred to later as "GCBS") has been chosen for comparison with the factors in analysis VI.

It can be noted in passing that the possibilities of the GCBS study have yet to be exploited fully regarding those factors that may appear on the surface to have no vocational significance, but that may be found to have such significance if only given the chance.

Before comparing the factors found in analysis VI with those identified by GCBS, it is in order to consider the substantial differences between the ways the two studies were conducted.

1. Perhaps the most striking difference is that factor loadings are given for occupational groups in the case of the Occupational Interest Survey and for hypothetical measures of human interests in the other. The identification of factors is thus automatically oriented around occupations in the one case and around traits in the other. On the face of it, this situation would seem to make inevitable a substantial lack of correspondence in the results. It is difficult to imagine a group of occupations that would suggest the general title of "Autistic Thinking" or of "Need for Diversion," for example, although occupations can be expected to differ in the extent to which these two characteristics might be involved.

2. The GCBS study was concerned with the whole range of human interests and was not confined to occupational interests even in the broad sense of having some relation to occu-

pational choice. In addition to activity items there were attitude and belief items. It is apparent that the range of items is considerably wider, and many more questions were actually used.

3. On the other hand, the GCBS study was confined to two fairly homogeneous groups: 898 airmen and 720 officers and officer candidates in the U. S. Air Force. There were no women in the Guilford study, and the age range was intentionally restricted. The possibility of identifying sex or age factors was therefore automatically eliminated.

4. Scores of individuals were the basis for the analysis in the GCBS study as compared with proportions of groups marking each response in analysis VI.

Factors Identified by Guilford, Christensen, Bond, and Sutton

GCBS made separate factor studies of the airmen and of the officers. Seventeen of the identifiable factors were the same for both groups and are represented by factors through the letter O in table 49. Six additional factors were identified for airmen only, and five others were identified for officers only. These factors also are listed in table 49.

A Comparison

On one hand, some of the GCBS factors appear to correspond closely to a number of the Occupational Interest Survey factors. On the other hand, there is nothing in the OIS data that can be held to correspond more than remotely to such factors as cultural conformity or need for sympathetic environment. It should also be noted that even those factors assigned identical titles cannot be presumed to be in fact identical. Furthermore, there is no way of determining from the data at hand the extent of their actual relation. The job of estimating similarities becomes one that each person familiar with the data must make on his own. For what it may be worth, the writer's speculations concerning the extent to which analysis VI factors may be related to those of GCBS are presented below, starting with those which appear most closely related.

TABLE 49

INTEREST FACTORS
IDENTIFIED BY GUILFORD, CHRISTENSEN,
BOND, AND SUTTON

A.	Mechanical interest		AIRMEN ONLY
B.	Scientific interest	Ra	Thinking
C.	Adventure vs. security	Sa	Expressiveness vs. restraint
D.	Social welfare	Ta	Sociability
E.	Aesthetic appreciation	Ua	Sympathetic environment, need for
F.	Cultural conformity		
G.	Self-reliance vs. dependence	Va	Precision
H.	Aesthetic expression	Wa	Social initiative
I.	Clerical interest		OFFICERS ONLY
J.	Need for diversion	Ro	Cultural interest
K.	Autistic thinking	So	Orderliness vs. disorderliness
L.	Attention, need for	To	Physical fitness interest
M.	Resistance to restriction	Uo	Ambition
N.	Business interest	Vo	Variety, need for
O.	Outdoor-work interest		
P.	Physical drive		
Q.	Aggression		

High Correspondence

A. Mechanical Interest Factor   10. Skilled Trades Factor

Of all interest factors, the mechanical one is probably most commonly found, and the correspondence between the two studies appears clear-cut. The policy of using occupationally oriented titles when possible has been followed in analysis VI. Otherwise the title "Mechanical" would have been assigned to this factor.

B. Scientic Interest Factor   13. Science-Mathematics Factor

This is another factor that is almost always clearly indicated in factor studies. An inspection of variables with high loadings suggests a high correspondence between these factors in the two studies.

D. Social Welfare Factor   18. Social Welfare Factor

The extremely high loading on Altruism in the GCBS study is consistent with the prevalence of social workers in the high loadings of analysis VI.

203

N. Business Interest Factor   11. Sales Factor

The correspondence here is marked. The analysis VI factor might have been titled "Business" almost as appropriately as "Sales."

Moderate Correspondence

P. Physical Drive Factor   6. Young Men Factor

Among the titles considered for the Young Men factor were "Drive" and "Aggressiveness." It seems reasonable to suppose that physical drive is an important component of the Young Men factor and that therefore there is a moderate degree of correspondence with the Guilford factor.

E. Aesthetic Appreciation Factor   20. Artistic Factor
H. Aesthetic Expression Factor

GCBS note a relation in their study between aesthetic appreciation and aesthetic expression, and the variables with high loadings on these factors reflect this situation. The GCBS aesthetic factors represent a fair balance among the graphic arts, literature, drama, and music. On the other hand, the OIS factor is predominantly the graphic arts, although drama and literary activities have high loadings. Musical activities, however, do not qualify for the top list.

To Physical Fitness Interest Factor   17. Physical Education
                                                  and Therapy Factor

The high factor To loadings for interest in athletics and healing appear to be consistent with high factor 17 loadings in physical education and physical therapy.

Some Small Correspondence Worth Noting

O. Outdoor-Work Interest Factor   9. Agriculture-Law-Political
                                            Science Factor

A number of the high loadings on factor 9 are consistent with the outdoor category, but many are not. The correspondence must therefore be rated as low.

Q. Aggression Factor   6. Young Men Factor
                              7. Influencing People-Social
                                 Approval Factor

The degree of aggression implied by the high variables in factor Q is considerably greater than indicated by those high on the factors in analysis VI. Nevertheless, the possibility that a significant relation exists should be recognized.

Ro   Cultural Interest Factor   23. Journalism Factor

Factor Ro might justifiably be labeled "Verbal Expression with a Bent toward Social Science." The journalism factor might be labeled "Verbal Expression with a Bent toward Music." There probably is a significant relation between the two.

Commentary

GCBS express surprise at not finding a verbal or linguistic interest factor in their study. It is puzzling that GCBS do not mention that their factor Ro for the officer group only, which they label "Cultural Interest," comes close to qualifying for the literary label. The verbal expression doublet shares honors with civics for the top three loadings. Five of the nine high loadings reported for this factor are definitely literary and include all tests in the battery that might reasonably be classified as literary.

The failure of a literary factor to show up among the enlisted airmen possibly may be explained by a small variation on this characteristic in that group. Airmen are, after all, a selected and relatively homogeneous group. It is not unlikely that they are particularly homogeneous in their low literary interests, as are engineers and members of the skilled trades. A lack of variation in this characteristic would eliminate the possibility of detecting it as a factor.

Another clue to the apparent absence of a literary factor is given by GCBS themselves in another connection when they note (1954, p. 30) as quoted previously, how strong factors, "by making satellites of score variables related to weaker factors, may weaken the appearance of the latter even to the point at which they vanish from the solution." This sort of suppression may also have happened to some extent with literary variables in the GCBS study. Such variables have shown up as "satellites" of the aesthetic expression and aesthetic appreciation variables, which are heavily represented in the experimental battery and show up as "strong."

Still another consideration is that the Verbal Expression area is represented by only two tests in the experimental battery as compared, for example, with six for Need for Diversion, five for Aesthetic Appreciation, and four for Aesthetic Expression. This keeps at a minimum the possibility of revealing a literary factor.

Conclusion

Clearly, as long as there is variation in a number of circumstances from one study to another, the reports of factor analyses of interests are bound to differ in greater or lesser degree. Variations in the content of the inventories and in the nature of the subjects are probably the major influences involved. But even if these variables are controlled, the report that reaches the printed page is bound to be influenced by the particular philosophy and technique involved in the factor analysis itself. It also will be influenced by the judgment of the investigators who interpret the factor loadings that come from the computer.

There appears to be substantial agreement among factorial studies with respect to a number of fundamental factors. It also is evident that interest factors cover a wide range, from very general to very specific; furthermore, the factors are "genuine psychological unities," to use the phrasing of Guilford, Christensen, Bond, and Sutton. In addition, it appears likely that more and more specific factors will be identified as factor studies become more extensive and heterogeneous with respect to the subjects and activities sampled.

The implications of the analysis of the Occupational Interest Survey are at some variance from the conclusions of Guilford, Christensen, Bond, and Sutton. Furthermore, the variance is in the direction that might be expected from the nature of the studies. GCBS concluded that "the structure of the interest domain, then, can be conceived as having a large number of basic, generalized dimensions that cut across many vocational lines, superimposed upon which are a few social stereotypes of broad job families whose existence as unities rests upon knowledge of vocations [p. 29]."

The following statement seems to be more in keeping with our findings and observations: The structure of the interest domain can be conceived as having a limited number of basic, generalized dimensions that cut across many vocational lines, superimposed upon which are many specific factors. Although these specific factors are generally consistent with social stereotypes of families of occupations, there is no evidence that their existence as unities rests upon knowledge of vocations.

As this book goes to press, a report of a factor analysis that takes into proper account the nature of KOIS scores has just been shown to the writer. The technique is notable for the fact that before the factor analysis, each person's scores are converted into standard scores in terms of the distribution of that particular subject's scores. The 56 feminine scores yielded nine factors, and the 106 masculine scores yielded eleven factors. The report, by Donald G. Zytowski, has been accepted for publication in *Measurement and Evaluation in Guidance.*

REFERENCES

Blau, P. M., and Duncan, O. D. *The American Occupational Structure.* New York: Wiley, 1967.

Cardinet, J., and Gendre, F. Structure psychometrique des professions. *Revue de Psychologie Appliqué,* 1967, *17,* 91–114.

Coombs, C. H., and Satter, G. A. A factorial approach to job families. *Psychometrika,* 1949, *14,* 33–42.

Crawford, C. B., and Ferguson, G. A. A general rotation criterion and its use in orthogonal rotation. *Psychometrika,* 1970, *35,* 331-332.

Guilford, J. P. When not to factor analyze. *Psychological Bulletin,* 1952, *49,* 26-37.

Guilford, J. P., Christensen, P. R., Bond, N. A., Jr., and Sutton, M. A. A factor analysis of human interests. *Psychological Monographs,* 1954, *68,* 4 (Whole Number 375).

Harris, M. L., and Harris, C. W. A factor analytic interpretation strategy. *Educational and Psychological Measurement,* 1971, *31,* 589-606.

Hartshorne, H., and May, M. A. Studies in deceit. In *Studies in the nature of character.* (Volume I) New York: Macmillan, 1928.

Overall, J. E. Note on the scientific status of factors. *Psychological Bulletin,* 1964, *61,* 270-276.

Strong, E. K., Jr. *The vocational interests of men and women.* Palo Alto: Stanford University Press, 1943.

Thurstone, L. L. A multiple factor study of vocational interests. *Personnel Journal,* 1931, *10,* 202-206.

Zytowski, D. G. Factor analysis of the Kuder Occupational Interest Survey. *Measurement and Evaluation in Guidance.* (In press.)

6

A Few Remarks

The time has come to gather everything into a compact little package, wrap it securely, and add a beautiful bow with a flourish. Somehow, however, the contents of this book do not seem to be amenable to such a neat disposition. Instead, perhaps it will be useful to emphasize a few particularly important points. For those "backward" readers who turn to the end of a book first, as does the writer, this chapter can serve as a sort of introduction.

This book revolves around the general objective of helping young people enter careers they are likely to find most satisfying. To solve this problem it would be convenient if a classic prediction situation could be set up, with criteria consisting of absolute measures of job satisfaction obtained for many different jobs from each of many different people. In view of the apparent impossibility of fulfilling this specification, an alternative rationale has been developed and is presented in chapters 2 and 3. This rationale capitalizes on the fact that in occupational counseling the problem is not to tell a counselee whether he or she will derive more or less satisfaction than someone else from a particular occupation. Rather, it is to point out which of a multitude of possible careers are most promising for the individual. The prediction in each case is within the person rather than within the group. When carried to its logical conclusion, the rationale indicates that the validity of an interest inventory with respect to job satisfaction rests on the extent to which that inventory can discriminate between occupational groups.

The extent to which discrimination between two occupational groups is achieved by an interest inventory can be expressed in terms of the proportion of each group that is classified correctly in its own occupation. An average of the two proportions obtained can be used as an index of the accuracy of discrimination of this particular comparison. When a third group is added to the study, it is possible to compare it with each of the other two groups in turn and to obtain an accuracy of classification figure for each of the two new comparisons. Then an average of all three indices can be obtained to yield an overall index for the three groups. The study could be extended indefinitely to obtain an overall index of accuracy of classification, based on all possible pairings of occupational groups within any number of groups.

The proposition that validity with respect to job satisfaction cannot exist without a high proportion of correct classifications is supported in chapter 2. The question of just what the standard should be must be considered open for the present. Data presented in earlier pages indicate that for a quite heterogeneous collection of occupational groups, the average accuracy of classification can be well over 90 percent. A high degree of accuracy is possible only if the inventory used meets a number of important requirements. One of these is that the items should be evenly scattered throughout the pertinent factorial space.

There are other important criteria that an interest inventory should meet. One is that the items should be concerned with activities with which almost everyone is familiar. Occupational titles or little-known activities specific to jobs are inappropriate in interest inventories intended for the guidance of young people with limited experience. Other desirable characteristics of an interest inventory are mentioned in chapter 2.

The question of the structure of occupational interests can be expected to intrigue researchers for many years to come. A number of interesting observations can be made on the basis of the factor analyses considered in chapter 5. One in particular is that a large proportion of the factors are related to age and sex. Although there is no apparent disposition to disregard age in counseling, there have been frequent suggestions that sex is not a pertinent consideration. The data at hand do not support these suggestions with respect to current practice. Perhaps in time it will become practical to ignore in counseling whether the subject is a boy or a girl. To do so at the present time, however, can serve only to undermine counseling effectiveness.

The elimination of both the subtle and overt biases against women in our society is long overdue, and it may be that interest inventories can be used as a gentle influence against bias. One step in that direction is to furnish both feminine and masculine scores to all subjects regardless of their sex. Other possibilities are noted below. On the other hand, such influence might easily become inoperative if we resort to the extreme measure of treating our data as though sex differences in interests do not now exist. We already know that ignoring the differences between the men and women in an occupation reduces the degree with which people in that occupation can be differentiated from people in other occupations. Yet good differentiation is the heart and soul of validity. If an inventory cannot differentiate among occupational groups, it is useless in occupational counseling. If the validity of occupational interest scores were allowed to be substantially eroded, the effectiveness of the counseling based on them would suffer, and there would be less and less reason to use interest inventories. It may well be questioned whether reducing or destroying the usefulness of interest inventories can contribute to the elimination of sex bias in our society.

It may be that the possibility of scoring best-impression answers suggested in chapter 5 will prove to be a good way of reducing sex bias, as would the application of the career matching technique described in chapter 4. There is also a need for, and a good possibility of, working out reference scales on which scores for the two sexes are comparable.

These possibilities for future research and development are a small sample of the many intriguing possibilities that are bound to be explored sooner or later in the measurement of interests. Little could Kelley (1914) have foreseen, when he produced his pioneer interest questionnaire, the substantial developments that have since occurred. The next sixty years should be equally exciting in ways yet undreamed of!

REFERENCE

Kelley, T. L. *Educational guidance.* An experimental study in the analysis and prediction of ability of high school pupils. Teachers College, Columbia University. *Contributions to Education*, No. 71, 1914, p. 116.

Appendix A

The Criterion Vector Method
of Test Construction

On occasion the writer has referred briefly in articles and manuals to what he calls the criterion vector method of test construction, an approach appropriate for the construction of a composite test for the prediction of a criterion. Since the method is a fundamental part of the evolution of the Occupational Interest Survey, a more detailed account of it, together with a description of its specific application in the development of the survey, will be presented here.

The purpose of the method is to construct a test whose vector coincides in factor space with the criterion vector. Let us suppose we have a number of reference variables that have been found to have some relation to the criterion. Let us suppose, further, that we want to develop a relatively short test for predicting the criterion. As a start we have obtained the product-moment correlations of all the tests in the battery. These data can be used to check on the relative merits of different sets of items. The more valid a test we are able to construct, of course, the closer to each other the vectors representing the criterion and the new test will be. If they actually coincide, the new test will have the same relative correlations with the reference variables as the criterion has with them. The following technique is designed to help in selecting the particular combination of items that will bring the resulting test as close as possible to the criterion.

As a starting point, let us list the items in the order of their correlation with the criterion, and let us consider as many items down the list as we estimate will produce a test of the desired reliability. We can then score these particular items and find the correlations with the criterion and the original tests in the battery. Since we are almost certain to have to obtain the same information for quite a number of combinations of items before settling on a particular one, it is desirable to work out a more efficient way of getting the answers we need.

The correlation of the tentative test with another variable can be expressed as a relatively simple function of the items in the test as follows:

$$r_{tc} = \frac{\Sigma r_{ic}\, \sigma_i}{\sigma_t}$$

in which

r_{tc} = the correlation between the selected variable and the test (t) composed of the selected items,

σ_t = the standard deviation of the test, and

$\Sigma r_{ic}\sigma_i$ = the sum of the products of the correlation of each item with the criterion and that item's standard deviation, the summation being over the items in the tentative test.

The same method is appropriate for obtaining the correlation of this set of items with any other variable, such as a test. The formulas for the correlations of the composite set of items with the other tests, a, b, c, and so forth, can be written as follows:

$$r_{ta} = \frac{\Sigma r_{ia}\, \sigma_i}{\sigma_t}\,,$$

$$r_{tb} = \frac{\Sigma r_{ib}\, \sigma_i}{\sigma_t}\,,$$

$$\vdots$$

$$r_{tn} = \frac{\Sigma r_{in}\, \sigma_i}{\sigma_t}\,.$$

In each case the summation is over the items in the tentative test.

One significant fact becomes immediately apparent. The denominator in each formula is the same. For the purpose of determining the relative magnitudes of the correlations of our set of items with a number of other variables, it is unnecessary to know the standard deviation of the composite. The simple sum of the item covariances will do for each variable. In practice, it is desirable to check on the actual standard deviation when a test that appears promising is worked out. The standard deviation is indispensable, of course, when the time comes to compute the actual reliability and validity achieved. In the trial-and-error process along the way, however, the scoring and computation of standard deviations for a multitude of experimental sets of items can be dispensed with.

Although the writer considers this approach to be promising for developing a test for the prediction of any criterion, he has used it for only one special situation — and that an adaptation — namely, the development of a test with low correlations with all reference variables except one. It should be pointed out that the procedure is practical only when fairly large numbers of cases are included so that the correlations involved are fairly stable.

The starting point is the list of items in the order of their validities, as noted earlier. On the basis of experience the testmaker goes as far down the list as he or she thinks necessary to obtain a test of satisfactory reliability. When the summations are made for the first set of items chosen tentatively, it is almost certain that the relative magnitude of the summations will not correspond to the relative sizes of the correlations desired. Certain adjustments therefore will have to be made. Items too highly related to certain variables will have to be eliminated, and others will have to be added to achieve summations that approximate the relative amounts desired. The iteration process can be extended until practical considerations bring it to an end. The system is self-correcting, but a start has to be made at some arbitrary point, and time is saved if the first guess is a good one.

Appendix B

Intercorrelations

TABLE OF INTERCORRELATIONS OF THE PROPORTIONS OF 217 GROUPS
MARKING EACH OF THE 600 ITEM RESPONSE POSITIONS IN
THE KUDER OCCUPATIONAL INTEREST SURVEY
(Please refer to table 1 p. 36 for identification of the variables.)

	1	2	3	4	5	6	7	8	9	10	11	12	13	14	15	16	17	18	19	20	21	22	23	24	25
1	1.00																								
2	.96	1.00																							
3	.90	.94	1.00																						
4	.92	.93	.98	1.00																					
5	.77	.80	.75	.73	1.00																				
6	.72	.70	.59	.63	.74	1.00																			
7	.83	.84	.80	.83	.68	.32	1.00																		
8	.91	.91	.84	.87	.73	.88	.89	1.00																	
9	.77	.78	.72	.75	.68	.36	.91	.88	1.00																
10	.89	.88	.77	.80	.68	.36	.86	.93	.87	1.00															
11	.86	.88	.80	.79	.83	.72	.82	.86	.79	.83	1.00														
12	.74	.74	.67	.70	.68	.94	.88	.84	.92	.87	.74	1.00													
13	.84	.82	.74	.77	.78	.71	.88	.91	.87	.88	.81	.91	1.00												
14	.90	.91	.88	.90	.78	.83	.92	.95	.91	.91	.87	.87	.90	1.00											
15	.67	.67	.57	.61	.63	.76	.81	.81	.87	.85	.70	.95	.92	.89	1.00										
16	.84	.84	.66	.86	.78	.62	.81	.84	.77	.73	.84	.68	.76	.89	.61	1.00									
17	.82	.78	.75	.76	.75	.77	.88	.85	.79	.80	.82	.83	.81	.91	.76	.73	1.00								
18	.87	.81	.75	.78	.72	.83	.89	.90	.92	.84	.87	.86	.87	.94	.69	.68	.73	1.00							
19	.85	.87	.71	.85	.72	.60	.85	.71	.66	.68	.82	.64	.68	.80	.71	.84	.90	.73	1.00						
20	.90	.91	.85	.87	.67	.61	.85	.76	.89	.75	.85	.69	.94	.90	.63	.79	.92	.80	.77	1.00					
21	.79	.78	.70	.81	.86	.77	.82	.79	.79	.71	.90	.81	.91	.84	.61	.89	.69	.79	.71	.79	1.00				
22	.80	.83	.75	.74	.68	.84	.86	.85	.80	.78	.87	.82	.88	.91	.76	.89	.84	.81	.89	.80	.80	1.00			
23	.76	.78	.62	.76	.64	.77	.85	.87	.79	.80	.84	.80	.81	.86	.80	.83	.84	.85	.69	.75	.76	.81	1.00		
24	.80	.81	.78	.76	.81	.83	.83	.86	.92	.84	.79	.74	.84	.94	.70	.86	.68	.84	.86	.80	.77	.90	.88	1.00	
25	.74	.75	.79	.76	.72	.60	.85	.90	.66	.68	.79	.86	.87	.65	.69	.81	.72	.82	.91	.79	.80	.87	.70	.67	1.00
26	.76	.74	.81	.69	.67	.61	.67	.71	.89	.75	.83	.64	.68	.73	.74	.69	.63	.70	.62	.66	.84	.71	.75	.67	.63
27	.71	.78	.86	.83	.86	.77	.80	.79	.80	.78	.86	.66	.75	.91	.83	.84	.89	.84	.73	.74	.86	.89	.80	.84	.77
28	.90	.87	.81	.84	.80	.79	.82	.82	.78	.83	.84	.79	.88	.91	.78	.79	.90	.81	.89	.78	.81	.83	.79	.89	.73
29	.87	.89	.84	.86	.78	.43	.83	.87	.79	.83	.84	.80	.81	.86	.80	.83	.84	.85	.84	.75	.82	.85	.79	.84	.71
30	.88	.87	.88	.91	.73	.83	.85	.90	.86	.52	.79	.74	.84	.94	.70	.86	.72	.94	.72	.80	.79	.81	.76	.82	.68
31	.90	.87	.84	.86	.88	.60	.85	.71	.65	.80	.83	.79	.87	.65	.69	.81	.63	.78	.62	.66	.80	.66	.76	.83	.75
32	.79	.91	.86	.87	.73	.77	.85	.88	.79	.83	.86	.81	.85	.90	.74	.84	.94	.79	.73	.74	.84	.72	.78	.84	.68
33	.78	.78	.70	.73	.65	.84	.83	.82	.82	.84	.77	.76	.89	.84	.83	.74	.72	.68	.82	.86	.93	.89	.75	.81	.76
34	.84	.84	.78	.80	.81	.79	.90	.89	.86	.83	.86	.82	.88	.91	.78	.86	.77	.92	.76	.78	.85	.83	.88	.89	.70
35	.84	.84	.77	.80	.78	.73	.82	.86	.79	.83	.84	.82	.90	.86	.80	.78	.84	.80	.69	.75	.90	.85	.76	.82	.74
36	.86	.86	.84	.85	.73	.72	.83	.93	.86	.83	.83	.80	.88	.94	.76	.91	.72	.94	.93	.80	.85	.81	.88	.90	.72
37	.61	.64	.61	.56	.88	.48	.67	.59	.59	.52	.74	.55	.67	.65	.48	.69	.63	.70	.87	.66	.52	.66	.71	.62	.61
38	.73	.75	.72	.69	.73	.58	.70	.70	.65	.66	.85	.62	.75	.73	.56	.80	.68	.74	.73	.72	.72	.72	.69	.66	.99
39	.89	.89	.86	.83	.82	.61	.78	.82	.73	.75	.90	.66	.62	.83	.60	.86	.84	.84	.82	.85	.81	.81	.74	.76	.84
40	.73	.77	.71	.68	.78	.53	.65	.69	.63	.66	.87	.57	.75	.71	.52	.80	.80	.70	.76	.79	.66	.72	.68	.64	.83
41	.75	.72	.62	.67	.64	.73	.84	.84	.87	.88	.72	.95	.91	.85	.96	.64	.71	.71	.69	.63	.76	.79	.77	.83	.61
42	.83	.86	.78	.76	.81	.65	.83	.74	.67	.75	.86	.66	.73	.76	.62	.68	.94	.70	.93	.77	.71	.82	.65	.69	.75
43	.87	.88	.79	.82	.74	.76	.72	.86	.80	.86	.83	.77	.83	.86	.74	.74	.88	.78	.87	.84	.82	.87	.73	.82	.68
44	.67	.87	.81	.83	.80	.76	.83	.85	.78	.81	.86	.76	.85	.86	.78	.78	.79	.79	.90	.82	.86	.89	.74	.81	.76
45	.66	.63	.63	.62	.54	.54	.67	.66	.68	.60	.77	.59	.62	.68	.55	.74	.72	.68	.66	.86	.68	.76	.72	.74	.68
46	.88	.87	.84	.84	.76	.77	.95	.92	.92	.90	.87	.88	.94	.96	.85	.87	.77	.92	.77	.81	.88	.86	.89	.92	.72
47	.86	.87	.82	.83	.82	.76	.88	.89	.82	.82	.87	.79	.88	.90	.75	.85	.82	.89	.81	.79	.83	.83	.76	.83	.61
48	.63	.87	.84	.84	.73	.70	.83	.82	.81	.77	.83	.74	.78	.87	.66	.83	.90	.83	.87	.88	.94	.94	.90	.87	.72
49	.73	.75	.68	.70	.72	.74	.77	.77	.82	.73	.75	.76	.76	.79	.70	.84	.84	.73	.77	.77	.77	.96	.75	.87	.65
50	.68	.67	.58	.62	.68	.74	.84	.80	.90	.83	.72	.95	.90	.82	.95	.63	.63	.72	.64	.65	.74	.79	.81	.84	.59

216

	26	27	28	29	30	31	32	33	34	35	36	37	38	39	40	41	42	43	44	45	46	47	48	49	50
26	1.00																								
27	.85	1.00																							
28	.84	.96	1.00																						
29	.84	.97	.97	1.00																					
30	.78	.93	.93	.95	1.00																				
31	.83	.97	.96	.98	.97	1.00																			
32	.82	.97	.80	.80	.94	.97	1.00																		
33	.86	.84	.84	.87	.76	.78	.83	1.00																	
34	.82	.87	.90	.91	.83	.84	.86	.84	1.00																
35	.85	.87	.84	.87	.85	.71	.92	.88	.86	1.00															
36	.82	.64	.60	.65	.86	.84	.86	.85	.91	.85	1.00														
37	.51	.64	.72	.71	.68	.63	.64	.48	.75	.58	.61	1.00													
38	.61	.76	.80	.82	.79	.72	.75	.64	.69	.74	.81	.61	1.00												
39	.65	.85	.80	.70	.66	.80	.87	.76	.79	.79	.81	.69	.85	1.00											
40	.56	.74	.70	.81	.74	.70	.75	.61	.68	.70	.64	.73	.84	.87	1.00										
41	.98	.82	.82	.81	.76	.81	.79	.82	.78	.82	.78	.47	.59	.63	.54	1.00									
42	.68	.67	.85	.84	.78	.85	.89	.71	.72	.80	.68	.63	.75	.86	.85	.67	1.00								
43	.81	.90	.89	.88	.85	.88	.91	.83	.79	.85	.80	.54	.68	.81	.74	.78	.89	1.00							
44	.80	.94	.93	.72	.88	.93	.95	.84	.83	.92	.82	.59	.75	.85	.76	.77	.90	.92	1.00						
45	.57	.68	.65	.66	.65	.67	.70	.64	.67	.64	.66	.68	.70	.81	.76	.56	.74	.73	.70	1.00					
46	.90	.91	.88	.90	.87	.88	.89	.89	.93	.89	.95	.63	.73	.81	.67	.87	.74	.85	.87	.68	1.00				
47	.80	.89	.84	.88	.84	.85	.89	.87	.95	.89	.89	.72	.71	.84	.72	.75	.78	.82	.87	.67	.92	1.00			
48	.75	.88	.88	.89	.86	.89	.90	.75	.82	.82	.83	.66	.73	.85	.76	.71	.86	.87	.90	.76	.83	.83	1.00		
49	.77	.80	.81	.81	.76	.83	.84	.79	.79	.79	.75	.57	.66	.75	.66	.74	.77	.83	.84	.75	.79	.75	.91	1.00	
50	.94	.77	.75	.76	.69	.75	.74	.79	.80	.78	.76	.57	.58	.61	.55	.94	.62	.73	.72	.60	.85	.76	.70	.75	1.00

	25	24	23	22	21	20	19	18	17	16	15	14	13	12	11	10	9	8	7	6	5	4	3	2	1
51	.73	.78	.73	.92	.74	.83	.83	.71	.90	.71	.61	.74	.77	.68	.80	.69	.73	.72	.74	.64	.79	.71	.72	.79	.74
52	.75	.84	.73	.92	.78	.83	.76	.87	.78	.93	.62	.83	.71	.69	.82	.70	.77	.83	.81	.63	.79	.87	.87	.83	.83
53	.62	.84	.84	.80	.76	.80	.66	.86	.70	.87	.59	.83	.71	.68	.71	.64	.78	.76	.80	.62	.66	.80	.79	.73	.72
54	.70	.91	.84	.95	.81	.83	.79	.86	.85	.80	.73	.85	.83	.80	.83	.83	.88	.86	.88	.78	.78	.79	.77	.84	.81
55	.72	.81	.79	.85	.72	.79	.81	.86	.79	.84	.68	.85	.80	.76	.83	.72	.80	.78	.84	.70	.88	.78	.78	.80	.78
56	.67	.82	.77	.95	.75	.86	.80	.75	.83	.74	.70	.81	.76	.77	.76	.74	.82	.76	.80	.73	.75	.75	.74	.77	.73
57	.69	.86	.79	.94	.75	.82	.67	.72	.66	.70	.68	.86	.94	.73	.77	.88	.79	.86	.85	.76	.64	.67	.69	.73	.76
58	.63	.85	.79	.79	.80	.64	.74	.75	.73	.67	.96	.92	.96	.94	.75	.88	.88	.91	.89	.92	.74	.78	.62	.81	.75
59	.67	.90	.84	.90	.84	.73	.74	.84	.79	.79	.91	.91	.96	.72	.80	.88	.78	.72	.78	.66	.74	.75	.74	.75	.83
60	.64	.85	.79	.90	.70	.85	.72	.78	.79	.80	.57	.82	.76	.67	.73	.64	.76	.72	.78	.60	.57	.72	.75	.75	.70
61	.69	.87	.80	.82	.75	.73	.71	.77	.67	.73	.85	.87	.86	.91	.74	.83	.89	.83	.85	.87	.66	.75	.71	.75	.75
62	.68	.88	.82	.82	.78	.71	.72	.79	.71	.70	.90	.79	.88	.93	.78	.94	.91	.89	.87	.91	.76	.85	.71	.70	.80
63	.82	.82	.79	.82	.77	.74	.74	.81	.75	.79	.77	.85	.84	.81	.86	.82	.81	.82	.81	.80	.76	.77	.70	.81	.80
64	.72	.71	.69	.86	.83	.87	.81	.69	.86	.72	.52	.68	.63	.59	.75	.61	.68	.66	.69	.54	.80	.72	.73	.76	.71
65	.72	.66	.65	.82	.78	.89	.79	.74	.83	.73	.46	.73	.64	.57	.78	.63	.63	.62	.70	.52	.74	.72	.73	.72	.68
66	.73	.72	.69	.82	.82	.94	.79	.78	.83	.80	.50	.66	.57	.71	.80	.74	.68	.69	.78	.25	.76	.57	.76	.76	.74
67	.73	.73	.78	.84	.89	.90	.69	.67	.82	.86	.51	.67	.56	.54	.78	.80	.81	.73	.81	.60	.72	.72	.70	.69	.80
68	.75	.76	.74	.80	.69	.93	.73	.76	.76	.75	.52	.79	.60	.60	.73	.62	.73	.69	.71	.54	.73	.75	.75	.78	.76
69	.80	.72	.79	.76	.64	.91	.77	.72	.76	.77	.63	.70	.93	.94	.85	.92	.68	.83	.85	.66	.70	.64	.73	.77	.68
70	.66	.71	.70	.82	.70	.92	.59	.75	.58	.74	.74	.89	.81	.91	.88	.78	.74	.91	.89	.90	.82	.71	.73	.73	.68
71	.66	.63	.74	.80	.81	.90	.82	.81	.82	.94	.67	.82	.91	.90	.69	.88	.62	.87	.92	.86	.57	.47	.72	.84	.68
72	.75	.70	.72	.81	.77	.74	.78	.75	.84	.79	.70	.91	.73	.52	.83	.53	.81	.88	.83	.93	.75	.75	.74	.77	.68
73	.71	.85	.78	.76	.81	.86	.69	.67	.82	.86	.70	.86	.81	.72	.74	.77	.66	.86	.81	.70	.72	.68	.70	.63	.64
74	.71	.76	.74	.84	.63	.79	.76	.76	.84	.79	.55	.74	.63	.61	.67	.76	.81	.70	.71	.54	.63	.67	.67	.69	.82
75	.72	.72	.70	.81	.71	.64	.72	.81	.66	.77	.92	.77	.70	.60	.67	.79	.68	.65	.85	.74	.59	.43	.70	.71	.86
76	.67	.77	.74	.75	.81	.83	.73	.75	.82	.94	.66	.64	.93	.84	.72	.41	.74	.73	.89	.97	.73	.55	.61	.75	.67
77	.77	.71	.72	.89	.77	.90	.77	.95	.70	.66	.79	.57	.81	.91	.78	.68	.62	.63	.86	.63	.64	.47	.64	.85	.74
78	.65	.63	.63	.78	.81	.74	.66	.72	.71	.79	.63	.66	.57	.61	.80	.79	.70	.58	.77	.62	.72	.45	.74	.59	.81
79	.67	.70	.68	.73	.63	.86	.69	.67	.73	.73	.55	.67	.56	.54	.67	.53	.66	.67	.66	.46	.55	.53	.70	.66	.62
80	.68	.68	.74	.67	.71	.79	.93	.76	.92	.77	.59	.65	.60	.60	.67	.77	.72	.71	.69	.45	.59	.46	.47	.59	.67
81	.60	.90	.79	.84	.81	.64	.73	.81	.72	.75	.92	.81	.91	.94	.67	.87	.76	.65	.81	.78	.73	.56	.58	.77	.72
82	.67	.85	.80	.81	.77	.83	.77	.95	.76	.94	.66	.85	.81	.91	.67	.41	.83	.82	.85	.97	.64	.55	.51	.63	.74
83	.67	.84	.79	.75	.81	.77	.84	.72	.70	.79	.79	.81	.73	.90	.78	.68	.81	.81	.77	.62	.72	.47	.74	.60	.67
84	.62	.80	.79	.89	.65	.74	.78	.84	.71	.70	.63	.76	.91	.67	.80	.79	.76	.88	.72	.25	.64	.45	.74	.84	.81
85	.68	.85	.78	.73	.86	.86	.58	.67	.84	.75	.46	.67	.56	.52	.67	.64	.61	.64	.66	.46	.65	.58	.53	.68	.85
86	.67	.76	.74	.92	.76	.79	.71	.76	.66	.72	.74	.81	.60	.68	.67	.62	.81	.64	.69	.71	.59	.46	.47	.71	.70
87	.67	.72	.79	.80	.79	.64	.68	.72	.72	.64	.96	.85	.62	.96	.67	.71	.68	.64	.81	.97	.64	.56	.58	.72	.74
88	.62	.90	.80	.95	.78	.90	.77	.75	.77	.88	.79	.81	.91	.67	.65	.63	.76	.64	.85	.80	.72	.47	.51	.75	.74
89	.69	.85	.79	.78	.65	.74	.66	.81	.58	.70	.63	.81	.73	.61	.64	.55	.69	.64	.77	.60	.54	.45	.47	.63	.81
90	.74	.73	.70	.72	.73	.77	.70	.75	.75	.70	.55	.76	.57	.49	.58	.67	.73	.64	.72	.54	.50	.49	.74	.80	.75
91	.67	.70	.78	.63	.63	.86	.58	.66	.50	.55	.60	.67	.56	.54	.67	.60	.61	.64	.65	.45	.65	.58	.61	.66	.62
92	.77	.72	.74	.67	.71	.61	.93	.72	.51	.57	.63	.81	.60	.49	.67	.57	.81	.82	.69	.62	.59	.46	.82	.59	.67
93	.65	.72	.79	.67	.81	.63	.73	.75	.55	.64	.49	.85	.56	.62	.65	.65	.66	.83	.84	.43	.73	.56	.86	.69	.70
94	.78	.63	.69	.67	.54	.70	.77	.68	.67	.88	.46	.65	.50	.54	.84	.67	.62	.81	.77	.58	.64	.47	.67	.60	.64
95	.65	.57	.58	.67	.56	.65	.66	.61	.60	.56	.56	.57	.56	.49	.78	.61	.71	.63	.63	.60	.72	.45	.74	.63	.57
96	.63	.64	.69	.61	.54	.73	.70	.64	.45	.54	.61	.76	.57	.62	.80	.67	.73	.58	.54	.55	.64	.45	.74	.60	.72
97	.59	.69	.65	.69	.61	.84	.58	.66	.64	.68	.46	.65	.53	.51	.67	.60	.64	.64	.62	.45	.65	.58	.61	.67	.62
98	.51	.68	.66	.70	.57	.68	.55	.67	.68	.71	.44	.65	.54	.49	.67	.57	.62	.61	.61	.43	.59	.49	.47	.68	.63
99	.69	.76	.69	.76	.55	.57	.63	.61	.67	.57	.56	.65	.56	.62	.65	.71	.71	.64	.65	.58	.50	.45	.58	.60	.56
100	.46	.69	.75	.58	.54	.57	.41	.64	.45	.54	.61	.64	.57	.64	.64	.67	.73	.64	.66	.60	.50	.45	.45	.56	.54

	50	49	48	47	46	45	44	43	42	41	40	39	38	37	36	35	34	33	32	31	30	29	28	27	26
51	.66	.93	.91	.77	.74	.82	.86	.82	.87	.64	.79	.84	.74	.67	.70	.79	.73	.70	.84	.80	.74	.80	.79	.81	.67
52	.65	.77	.85	.81	.85	.80	.81	.77	.72	.65	.74	.87	.76	.67	.87	.77	.81	.73	.85	.84	.90	.85	.82	.84	.68
53	.64	.78	.82	.80	.82	.67	.74	.69	.58	.62	.58	.73	.63	.59	.88	.75	.81	.71	.78	.76	.80	.78	.74	.75	.67
54	.78	.91	.82	.78	.89	.77	.87	.86	.78	.77	.68	.80	.70	.79	.81	.83	.86	.81	.87	.85	.83	.86	.83	.81	.81
55	.74	.77	.86	.85	.84	.69	.81	.76	.75	.71	.72	.77	.73	.79	.82	.81	.87	.69	.84	.85	.74	.83	.83	.85	.75
56	.75	.95	.93	.75	.79	.76	.84	.83	.79	.74	.70	.79	.68	.62	.76	.80	.76	.73	.83	.84	.74	.81	.81	.82	.76
57	.72	.96	.89	.80	.78	.56	.85	.84	.80	.72	.70	.65	.70	.56	.81	.85	.74	.76	.80	.80	.75	.82	.82	.81	.74
58	.94	.73	.70	.80	.90	.60	.78	.77	.66	.96	.55	.76	.61	.51	.90	.89	.83	.86	.80	.80	.75	.91	.89	.91	.95
59	.89	.78	.79	.86	.95	.76	.85	.83	.69	.92	.58	.76	.65	.64	.76	.71	.89	.87	.88	.77	.76	.77	.89	.91	.65
60	.64	.90	.79	.74	.75	.60	.77	.74	.70	.61	.67	.76	.66	.64	.90	.71	.75	.65	.79	.77	.76	.77	.75	.75	.65
61	.87	.78	.78	.80	.87	.60	.78	.84	.65	.89	.58	.72	.69	.52	.82	.82	.80	.80	.79	.81	.76	.80	.79	.82	.70
62	.90	.78	.78	.82	.86	.63	.80	.79	.73	.93	.64	.76	.80	.64	.81	.84	.82	.84	.81	.83	.73	.83	.84	.83	.73
63	.79	.75	.84	.70	.68	.67	.81	.78	.74	.82	.72	.83	.74	.66	.80	.71	.83	.76	.82	.75	.73	.75	.75	.94	.83
64	.58	.86	.88	.66	.66	.80	.78	.74	.84	.56	.80	.80	.75	.69	.66	.68	.67	.61	.80	.74	.73	.84	.84	.76	.55
65	.52	.79	.84	.68	.68	.84	.80	.79	.80	.49	.78	.83	.76	.65	.64	.70	.64	.57	.76	.70	.73	.76	.75	.73	.53
66	.55	.80	.86	.70	.72	.84	.80	.79	.80	.54	.79	.83	.76	.61	.71	.68	.69	.63	.80	.67	.79	.68	.76	.76	.57
67	.54	.76	.85	.76	.71	.79	.83	.79	.79	.56	.75	.89	.75	.58	.78	.74	.74	.65	.85	.81	.74	.65	.63	.85	.60
68	.55	.80	.81	.74	.88	.70	.87	.84	.89	.59	.81	.84	.77	.69	.68	.76	.69	.66	.74	.67	.72	.68	.72	.72	.51
69	.66	.75	.85	.66	.90	.69	.80	.79	.71	.66	.70	.86	.72	.70	.90	.80	.87	.73	.70	.68	.75	.71	.67	.68	.70
70	.75	.82	.81	.70	.94	.73	.81	.81	.74	.75	.71	.78	.76	.69	.94	.81	.91	.83	.74	.64	.73	.84	.67	.67	.72
71	.71	.73	.85	.75	.80	.87	.85	.87	.57	.74	.63	.83	.57	.65	.92	.84	.77	.76	.72	.69	.73	.76	.71	.73	.78
72	.69	.74	.81	.63	.72	.69	.70	.77	.78	.72	.65	.80	.76	.70	.74	.85	.76	.78	.73	.67	.79	.68	.68	.86	.74
73	.70	.80	.85	.85	.71	.89	.86	.87	.79	.71	.77	.89	.75	.58	.85	.83	.82	.86	.69	.66	.74	.65	.63	.85	.74
74	.60	.79	.81	.66	.71	.56	.70	.70	.76	.56	.81	.84	.73	.69	.71	.67	.69	.64	.71	.66	.59	.65	.63	.72	.59
75	.56	.75	.85	.70	.88	.73	.87	.77	.65	.51	.85	.71	.69	.66	.67	.67	.69	.59	.69	.82	.71	.86	.66	.68	.54
76	.63	.82	.81	.66	.84	.87	.82	.75	.62	.58	.67	.81	.72	.67	.71	.68	.69	.66	.74	.45	.79	.85	.71	.87	.61
77	.59	.73	.85	.70	.80	.69	.81	.71	.73	.54	.71	.80	.76	.70	.71	.81	.87	.83	.72	.57	.80	.84	.84	.86	.50
78	.49	.73	.81	.75	.72	.75	.70	.74	.71	.47	.63	.83	.66	.62	.60	.65	.74	.84	.73	.76	.83	.76	.70	.72	.50
80	.54	.76	.85	.85	.74	.74	.70	.70	.57	.48	.77	.80	.69	.66	.64	.61	.62	.58	.69	.76	.74	.65	.62	.66	.51
81	.56	.80	.86	.79	.92	.74	.87	.86	.55	.59	.65	.71	.78	.54	.71	.85	.72	.86	.71	.56	.59	.68	.83	.86	.62
82	.92	.80	.79	.83	.92	.72	.81	.76	.62	.95	.61	.76	.64	.76	.86	.81	.85	.83	.85	.82	.83	.86	.80	.87	.65
83	.69	.73	.85	.74	.84	.77	.70	.71	.73	.68	.67	.61	.57	.76	.92	.76	.77	.77	.86	.84	.76	.85	.85	.86	.42
85	.91	.71	.80	.86	.80	.69	.79	.87	.71	.92	.71	.80	.69	.72	.80	.87	.87	.83	.77	.73	.87	.76	.71	.90	.93
86	.76	.74	.73	.78	.71	.59	.81	.79	.57	.61	.62	.81	.65	.61	.61	.63	.67	.58	.62	.66	.80	.68	.62	.68	.62
87	.95	.76	.72	.74	.84	.64	.85	.85	.70	.64	.65	.78	.68	.68	.61	.64	.68	.58	.65	.82	.77	.79	.83	.84	.65
88	.83	.80	.89	.78	.84	.77	.85	.76	.59	.97	.86	.73	.59	.79	.63	.73	.68	.86	.64	.85	.84	.84	.80	.60	.85
90	.66	.95	.80	.89	.80	.69	.70	.77	.73	.64	.71	.83	.62	.70	.61	.70	.70	.72	.50	.76	.87	.73	.70	.73	.60
91	.71	.76	.61	.74	.65	.71	.62	.64	.57	.61	.62	.58	.60	.61	.62	.54	.64	.58	.69	.56	.48	.58	.57	.59	.62
92	.76	.67	.64	.66	.67	.64	.65	.59	.55	.64	.65	.57	.59	.68	.62	.57	.68	.58	.55	.60	.47	.54	.53	.60	.65
93	.95	.64	.67	.69	.63	.77	.60	.68	.62	.50	.86	.76	.69	.61	.60	.82	.68	.57	.60	.50	.47	.58	.57	.62	.64
94	.83	.61	.61	.74	.55	.69	.49	.65	.73	.58	.83	.76	.64	.60	.59	.58	.68	.57	.64	.57	.52	.59	.57	.57	.72
95	.66	.62	.80	.61	.66	.69	.79	.79	.71	.59	.63	.61	.62	.70	.61	.70	.70	.58	.79	.51	.44	.52	.52	.77	.47
96	.58	.72	.73	.74	.64	.61	.62	.56	.88	.56	.58	.54	.62	.72	.62	.65	.67	.60	.50	.76	.70	.77	.76	.77	.57
97	.71	.67	.61	.66	.62	.84	.62	.64	.67	.46	.62	.58	.60	.65	.62	.54	.64	.57	.62	.56	.57	.58	.57	.59	.47
98	.50	.68	.73	.66	.63	.69	.65	.68	.70	.58	.65	.57	.48	.68	.62	.57	.66	.57	.65	.60	.46	.57	.57	.62	.46
99	.63	.75	.71	.62	.64	.69	.60	.65	.59	.58	.67	.59	.43	.61	.60	.49	.67	.58	.59	.51	.60	.50	.49	.56	.60
001	.65	.54	.55	.62	.64	.61	.49	.56	.48	.59	.58	.54	.43	.61	.62	.49	.67	.58	.50	.45	.44	.50	.49	.47	.60

	51	52	53	54	55	56	57	58	59	60	61	62	63	64	65	66	67	68	69	70	71	72	73	74	75
51	1.00																								
52	.77	1.00																							
53	.73	.87	1.00																						
54	.86	.81	.84	1.00																					
55	.78	.81	.80	.84	1.00																				
56	.92	.81	.81	.88	.82	1.00																			
57	.94	.76	.64	.90	.72	.72	1.00																		
58	.64	.67	.76	.79	.72	.75	.72	1.00																	
59	.67	.79	.87	.84	.81	.81	.75	.95	1.00																
60	.87	.83	.87	.87	.82	.91	.86	.61	.70	1.00															
61	.70	.75	.74	.82	.78	.81	.75	.88	.89	.72	1.00														
62	.72	.69	.66	.79	.76	.77	.82	.92	.89	.68	.89	1.00													
63	.74	.75	.68	.81	.83	.76	.72	.82	.85	.69	.80	.83	1.00												
64	.94	.81	.72	.80	.85	.79	.87	.54	.62	.86	.64	.63	.68	1.00											
65	.87	.83	.71	.75	.86	.83	.80	.50	.59	.82	.61	.55	.68	.95	1.00										
66	.85	.88	.76	.78	.81	.83	.80	.54	.64	.84	.65	.59	.69	.92	.97	1.00									
67	.79	.88	.78	.85	.75	.79	.83	.56	.67	.82	.75	.78	.70	.91	.92	.85	1.00								
68	.88	.87	.75	.79	.76	.85	.82	.49	.63	.74	.67	.64	.67	.85	.85	.84	.83	1.00							
69	.73	.65	.69	.83	.72	.80	.75	.67	.80	.75	.77	.58	.72	.64	.59	.64	.75	.76	1.00						
70	.72	.72	.72	.84	.75	.86	.73	.76	.83	.73	.83	.67	.80	.72	.69	.77	.66	.74	.91	1.00					
71	.71	.67	.71	.75	.75	.76	.69	.53	.64	.70	.81	.76	.81	.70	.70	.84	.83	.74	.93	.90	1.00				
72	.88	.79	.78	.90	.70	.88	.80	.91	.87	.76	.77	.90	.87	.94	.94	.92	.86	.88	.72	.73	.78	1.00			
73	.80	.82	.75	.85	.76	.82	.83	.74	.81	.79	.78	.84	.73	.77	.76	.83	.86	.82	.75	.77	.75	.85	1.00		
74	.84	.76	.72	.76	.72	.76	.74	.56	.59	.85	.67	.73	.80	.91	.91	.89	.78	.80	.67	.76	.77	.89	.80	1.00	
75	.81	.77	.65	.70	.70	.75	.75	.46	.54	.78	.57	.62	.63	.92	.94	.93	.76	.72	.70	.73	.64	.92	.77	.87	1.00
76	.86	.85	.73	.74	.70	.86	.77	.53	.64	.76	.68	.65	.67	.91	.91	.84	.73	.57	.67	.76	.73	.79	.81	.98	.96
77	.86	.81	.65	.79	.76	.81	.73	.58	.61	.74	.77	.56	.67	.57	.55	.66	.74	.78	.75	.78	.81	.89	.84	.80	.77
78	.83	.83	.71	.71	.74	.80	.80	.53	.54	.78	.76	.54	.63	.76	.64	.68	.65	.75	.70	.81	.78	.73	.82	.71	.67
79	.83	.79	.66	.71	.70	.82	.77	.49	.55	.82	.60	.57	.61	.91	.92	.92	.83	.85	.69	.67	.63	.75	.78	.59	.52
80	.84	.76	.66	.78	.77	.77	.77	.59	.67	.74	.62	.67	.72	.85	.85	.85	.87	.91	.77	.76	.77	.83	.80	.61	.56
81	.76	.89	.73	.85	.81	.80	.73	.94	.94	.72	.90	.94	.83	.64	.59	.64	.66	.65	.76	.83	.81	.78	.84	.60	.54
82	.76	.76	.76	.83	.76	.71	.73	.72	.81	.80	.76	.76	.80	.75	.73	.77	.83	.74	.93	.93	.88	.73	.73	.72	.53
83	.61	.65	.67	.75	.67	.60	.69	.47	.87	.63	.81	.68	.73	.52	.46	.52	.53	.51	.66	.86	.88	.66	.84	.69	.70
84	.77	.79	.73	.90	.85	.84	.81	.90	.94	.78	.89	.90	.87	.71	.67	.72	.76	.74	.83	.81	.88	.84	.82	.73	.87
85	.81	.82	.71	.70	.70	.79	.73	.48	.55	.78	.56	.54	.61	.86	.86	.88	.81	.82	.71	.67	.66	.74	.77	.58	.52
86	.69	.76	.79	.68	.76	.87	.91	.46	.61	.81	.59	.80	.75	.77	.72	.74	.74	.78	.75	.78	.77	.89	.84	.72	.67
87	.88	.66	.65	.79	.81	.76	.73	.64	.61	.64	.59	.73	.80	.57	.51	.55	.57	.57	.67	.76	.73	.72	.71	.61	.54
88	.88	.88	.52	.79	.66	.93	.92	.58	.62	.80	.50	.62	.81	.72	.73	.75	.73	.76	.75	.76	.87	.71	.75	.60	.53
89	.75	.76	.41	.76	.68	.80	.85	.61	.74	.80	.70	.68	.73	.75	.75	.84	.81	.75	.75	.81	.78	.86	.86	.72	.70
90	.73	.69	.56	.72	.66	.66	.64	.59	.64	.65	.68	.72	.68	.76	.76	.68	.65	.80	.64	.74	.68	.78	.75	.73	.69
91	.63	.51	.47	.64	.56	.58	.59	.55	.59	.55	.58	.58	.62	.54	.46	.49	.44	.46	.53	.62	.66	.55	.59	.58	.52
92	.63	.53	.51	.66	.61	.62	.61	.64	.61	.60	.59	.56	.63	.57	.49	.51	.45	.48	.55	.62	.50	.56	.59	.61	.67
93	.63	.54	.48	.66	.68	.60	.62	.64	.62	.56	.50	.68	.66	.72	.48	.52	.48	.51	.55	.64	.52	.59	.65	.60	.54
94	.73	.61	.52	.66	.63	.63	.53	.52	.53	.62	.59	.62	.59	.67	.67	.68	.60	.68	.65	.67	.54	.63	.67	.72	.70
95	.69	.54	.41	.58	.56	.57	.62	.47	.45	.54	.53	.64	.59	.60	.60	.61	.52	.63	.54	.57	.43	.62	.64	.67	.63
96	.81	.66	.55	.72	.73	.73	.74	.55	.61	.67	.56	.64	.64	.76	.76	.74	.72	.80	.64	.74	.68	.78	.70	.73	.69
97	.73	.72	.57	.66	.62	.69	.68	.48	.52	.70	.52	.58	.59	.75	.75	.79	.69	.72	.63	.62	.55	.68	.59	.58	.52
98	.77	.72	.53	.71	.71	.71	.69	.46	.52	.72	.51	.56	.60	.81	.78	.81	.73	.75	.65	.62	.58	.69	.65	.61	.56
99	.74	.58	.59	.72	.63	.73	.73	.58	.59	.73	.59	.68	.62	.68	.59	.61	.53	.57	.56	.64	.52	.67	.67	.68	.63
100	.54	.51	.51	.61	.54	.53	.54	.61	.57	.53	.53	.69	.57	.49	.41	.45	.40	.41	.53	.62	.49	.51	.58	.56	.51

	76	77	78	79	80	81	82	83	84	85	86	87	88	89	90	91	92	93	94	95	96	97	98	99	100
76	1.00																								
77	.97	1.00																							
78	.90	.92	1.00																						
79	.97	.97	.93	1.00																					
80	.77	.78	.88	.78	1.00																				
81	.68	.62	.57	.59	.68	1.00																			
82	.77	.75	.71	.72	.80	.78	1.00																		
83	.59	.54	.44	.50	.53	.90	.68	1.00																	
84	.71	.67	.64	.62	.76	.93	.83	.85	1.00																
85	.90	.89	.88	.92	.78	.57	.73	.48	.62	1.00															
86	.74	.72	.66	.67	.74	.81	.76	.74	.85	.66	1.00														
87	.60	.56	.48	.51	.58	.95	.70	.93	.91	.49	.79	1.00													
88	.78	.74	.67	.70	.73	.87	.70	.78	.74	.89	.89	.84	1.00												
89	.87	.92	.76	.84	.71	.73	.83	.66	.67	.68	.72	.64	.76	1.00											
90	.70	.67	.67	.69	.77	.68	.75	.56	.67	.84	.63	.57	.64	.69	1.00										
91	.59	.54	.45	.54	.53	.67	.62	.63	.61	.64	.54	.61	.65	.56	.87	1.00									
92	.63	.57	.48	.58	.50	.69	.62	.68	.64	.51	.56	.66	.69	.60	.80	.93	1.00								
93	.61	.56	.50	.57	.58	.70	.64	.65	.60	.64	.57	.64	.68	.60	.90	.97	.91	1.00							
94	.71	.71	.69	.71	.72	.57	.71	.49	.64	.69	.58	.51	.59	.60	.86	.80	.81	.80	1.00						
95	.66	.65	.64	.67	.67	.53	.61	.45	.60	.65	.54	.46	.64	.64	.83	.78	.77	.79	.93	1.00					
96	.72	.73	.75	.71	.86	.62	.70	.49	.68	.69	.69	.56	.71	.62	.84	.68	.66	.72	.80	.77	1.00				
97	.83	.80	.75	.84	.68	.58	.69	.49	.57	.78	.59	.47	.65	.78	.85	.79	.79	.80	.86	.85	.75	1.00			
98	.85	.84	.80	.87	.72	.56	.71	.46	.56	.85	.61	.46	.65	.80	.83	.72	.73	.74	.87	.85	.78	.96	1.00		
99	.71	.66	.55	.66	.55	.66	.61	.61	.64	.59	.65	.60	.78	.65	.80	.89	.91	.88	.79	.76	.70	.83	.78	1.00	
100	.56	.52	.41	.53	.46	.65	.60	.67	.59	.47	.50	.61	.60	.59	.76	.90	.94	.88	.78	.73	.58	.75	.69	.83	1.00

	25	24	23	22	21	20	19	18	17	16	15	14	13	12	11	10	9	8	7	6	5	4	3	2	1
101	.58	.75	.69	.74	.67	.81	.66	.70	.71	.71	.51	.71	.59	.58	.72	.64	.68	.69	.72	.51	.70	.67	.67	.72	.67
102	.54	.73	.68	.72	.66	.73	.63	.67	.68	.64	.57	.70	.62	.61	.72	.67	.68	.70	.71	.56	.67	.61	.61	.69	.66
103	.58	.74	.71	.72	.65	.76	.63	.72	.68	.70	.52	.71	.59	.59	.73	.65	.69	.70	.73	.52	.68	.64	.66	.70	.66
104	.56	.74	.69	.76	.65	.78	.64	.66	.71	.65	.52	.68	.58	.58	.71	.63	.68	.66	.70	.56	.69	.61	.62	.68	.63
105	.55	.75	.68	.74	.68	.76	.65	.69	.70	.67	.56	.72	.62	.61	.72	.64	.70	.71	.72	.56	.67	.65	.65	.73	.63
106	.55	.73	.67	.75	.62	.75	.54	.63	.68	.60	.53	.67	.57	.59	.68	.64	.69	.67	.68	.53	.63	.58	.59	.66	.61
107	.54	.73	.67	.68	.59	.67	.54	.69	.57	.63	.58	.67	.57	.64	.73	.67	.72	.65	.70	.59	.69	.52	.53	.65	.61
108	.52	.72	.68	.73	.67	.73	.66	.64	.75	.65	.49	.66	.56	.60	.69	.62	.67	.63	.66	.55	.67	.53	.54	.62	.60
109	.54	.69	.62	.59	.66	.76	.57	.61	.60	.62	.41	.64	.53	.53	.70	.62	.62	.63	.66	.49	.66	.59	.60	.68	.64
110	.57	.55	.64	.73	.48	.62	.57	.65	.63	.63	.56	.58	.55	.46	.72	.48	.72	.54	.57	.39	.83	.51	.57	.61	.57
111	.54	.70	.75	.69	.54	.67	.51	.59	.56	.57	.56	.65	.55	.64	.68	.68	.72	.63	.67	.56	.61	.55	.56	.64	.57
112	.73	.66	.69	.69	.62	.80	.70	.62	.73	.76	.43	.69	.57	.50	.80	.62	.62	.67	.66	.43	.76	.69	.74	.77	.71
113	.66	.59	.61	.63	.54	.68	.58	.57	.63	.59	.45	.59	.50	.49	.79	.59	.56	.73	.55	.45	.67	.49	.53	.63	.58
114	.55	.70	.64	.71	.64	.72	.55	.58	.70	.64	.58	.70	.63	.60	.76	.76	.67	.73	.67	.58	.65	.61	.62	.75	.72
115	.58	.76	.75	.70	.60	.69	.59	.67	.58	.64	.62	.72	.63	.66	.75	.74	.76	.72	.71	.61	.66	.57	.57	.69	.64
116	.52	.72	.69	.74	.58	.69	.70	.58	.58	.60	.57	.61	.55	.61	.64	.61	.69	.60	.62	.57	.59	.46	.47	.57	.52
117	.57	.68	.65	.71	.54	.76	.62	.64	.70	.62	.46	.63	.54	.57	.70	.62	.62	.62	.65	.52	.62	.58	.60	.67	.61
118	.54	.70	.59	.72	.59	.76	.61	.59	.66	.63	.46	.60	.52	.46	.67	.58	.60	.61	.67	.46	.64	.59	.60	.65	.60
119	.64	.58	.59	.70	.54	.71	.65	.58	.66	.61	.54	.61	.56	.49	.68	.53	.62	.56	.54	.54	.76	.49	.50	.58	.54
120	.63	.70	.62	.63	.59	.58	.50	.66	.51	.51	.61	.64	.57	.47	.67	.74	.69	.66	.59	.60	.55	.47	.48	.63	.59
121	.53	.67	.61	.78	.55	.75	.72	.60	.75	.55	.42	.54	.50	.45	.69	.73	.56	.54	.62	.44	.71	.52	.55	.63	.56
122	.57	.62	.60	.83	.69	.76	.62	.67	.75	.60	.58	.62	.57	.54	.73	.63	.69	.64	.67	.59	.73	.57	.59	.67	.61
123	.60	.74	.65	.64	.56	.66	.51	.59	.56	.54	.53	.68	.57	.60	.70	.62	.68	.66	.58	.52	.62	.46	.47	.60	.55
124	.54	.60	.59	.72	.58	.67	.56	.57	.58	.64	.40	.60	.52	.46	.71	.58	.60	.57	.59	.41	.68	.60	.63	.68	.63
125	.65	.60	.68	.70	.59	.79	.58	.62	.64	.61	.45	.58	.51	.49	.71	.47	.56	.52	.54	.38	.71	.55	.59	.62	.56
126	.64	.58	.62	.63	.54	.82	.59	.59	.61	.66	.42	.61	.48	.47	.71	.54	.54	.58	.59	.41	.64	.52	.62	.66	.62
127	.63	.62	.63	.78	.59	.78	.59	.61	.63	.62	.39	.54	.48	.47	.65	.49	.56	.52	.57	.40	.65	.53	.48	.74	.50
128	.53	.67	.61	.66	.56	.66	.59	.60	.64	.61	.54	.62	.46	.45	.72	.62	.61	.54	.56	.53	.66	.51	.59	.67	.64
129	.57	.70	.68	.67	.55	.67	.51	.63	.53	.62	.50	.68	.57	.60	.68	.72	.68	.66	.65	.55	.63	.56	.57	.69	.65
130	.60	.62	.65	.84	.58	.78	.84	.61	.86	.63	.57	.66	.52	.59	.76	.70	.69	.65	.67	.41	.59	.50	.56	.61	.54
131	.62	.62	.59	.73	.62	.76	.83	.61	.69	.66	.61	.58	.48	.68	.76	.73	.72	.82	.79	.55	.68	.51	.51	.63	.57
132	.60	.65	.70	.75	.55	.82	.80	.87	.72	.66	.45	.82	.51	.69	.74	.75	.75	.77	.81	.63	.71	.80	.77	.80	.55
133	.62	.64	.75	.71	.53	.78	.75	.85	.71	.62	.42	.84	.48	.47	.75	.67	.71	.76	.80	.63	.73	.75	.73	.83	.54
134	.59	.59	.76	.74	.56	.79	.80	.83	.64	.61	.39	.87	.46	.45	.76	.73	.75	.81	.77	.58	.73	.68	.70	.83	.54
135	.55	.68	.66	.64	.55	.61	.51	.63	.53	.56	.54	.84	.50	.49	.78	.71	.71	.78	.78	.56	.78	.80	.76	.78	.61
136	.56	.78	.69	.81	.62	.71	.61	.61	.69	.57	.57	.66	.56	.61	.74	.70	.70	.76	.77	.55	.71	.51	.52	.63	.59
137	.63	.79	.70	.79	.89	.74	.79	.69	.73	.73	.61	.82	.61	.66	.77	.68	.75	.65	.79	.62	.68	.51	.51	.79	.79
138	.61	.76	.68	.77	.86	.71	.80	.72	.74	.69	.74	.78	.82	.76	.74	.78	.76	.82	.81	.63	.71	.80	.77	.74	.74
139	.58	.58	.63	.69	.53	.66	.75	.64	.71	.64	.72	.66	.79	.75	.71	.73	.74	.77	.80	.75	.73	.68	.70	.67	.64
140	.54	.47	.56	.59	.41	.57	.65	.53	.59	.53	.52	.50	.65	.47	.63	.40	.48	.43	.78	.56	.82	.48	.51	.51	.46
141	.61	.68	.62	.84	.67	.78	.84	.62	.86	.63	.50	.66	.61	.59	.68	.58	.64	.62	.68	.55	.71	.80	.76	.64	.66
142	.65	.68	.71	.73	.69	.76	.83	.84	.79	.75	.60	.86	.74	.68	.76	.79	.72	.65	.79	.62	.68	.95	.94	.90	.88
143	.66	.74	.75	.75	.72	.79	.80	.87	.72	.85	.61	.87	.76	.69	.77	.75	.75	.82	.81	.63	.71	.94	.93	.86	.85
144	.66	.73	.76	.71	.67	.82	.75	.85	.81	.86	.61	.84	.71	.65	.74	.67	.72	.76	.78	.58	.71	.88	.88	.80	.78
145	.70	.78	.73	.74	.69	.82	.80	.83	.72	.85	.61	.87	.75	.70	.75	.73	.75	.81	.81	.63	.73	.93	.92	.85	.84
146	.66	.72	.73	.82	.71	.77	.83	.73	.75	.85	.54	.84	.70	.63	.76	.71	.71	.78	.77	.56	.75	.93	.94	.86	.83
147	.67	.68	.62	.84	.72	.78	.82	.76	.79	.75	.50	.82	.71	.71	.78	.70	.68	.76	.78	.55	.78	.80	.80	.78	.74
148	.62	.74	.71	.73	.72	.89	.90	.76	.87	.75	.60	.82	.75	.68	.74	.72	.70	.76	.78	.62	.73	.88	.86	.83	.82
149	.64	.77	.75	.81	.75	.77	.89	.76	.81	.72	.72	.84	.84	.78	.75	.78	.78	.74	.80	.75	.76	.86	.83	.83	.82
150	.62	.75	.73	.83	.71	.75	.92	.73	.87	.71	.66	.82	.79	.73	.74	.75	.71	.77	.77	.71	.75	.84	.82	.83	.83

222

	26	27	28	29	30	31	32	33	34	35	36	37	38	39	40	41	42	43	44	45	46	47	48	49	50
101	.56	.66	.64	.66	.66	.65	.70	.62	.71	.62	.66	.72	.57	.74	.74	.53	.70	.71	.69	.79	.67	.73	.77	.73	.57
102	.60	.65	.64	.66	.62	.63	.69	.64	.72	.63	.64	.69	.53	.69	.72	.57	.68	.71	.69	.72	.68	.73	.71	.69	.61
103	.56	.65	.65	.66	.63	.63	.69	.62	.72	.61	.63	.73	.57	.72	.73	.53	.67	.68	.67	.73	.68	.74	.75	.69	.58
104	.56	.64	.63	.64	.61	.62	.68	.61	.69	.61	.63	.71	.56	.71	.74	.53	.70	.71	.68	.80	.65	.70	.76	.75	.59
105	.60	.67	.66	.67	.65	.65	.71	.65	.73	.63	.66	.70	.54	.72	.72	.57	.71	.74	.70	.74	.70	.75	.75	.71	.60
106	.57	.61	.61	.61	.57	.59	.65	.61	.66	.59	.61	.66	.51	.68	.70	.54	.69	.71	.66	.76	.63	.68	.75	.71	.59
107	.60	.59	.57	.59	.53	.59	.60	.61	.70	.57	.65	.81	.53	.64	.69	.58	.60	.61	.58	.70	.68	.71	.65	.62	.66
108	.60	.61	.60	.62	.59	.59	.63	.61	.70	.60	.66	.73	.53	.64	.70	.56	.61	.64	.63	.79	.66	.68	.67	.64	.61
109	.53	.64	.64	.64	.61	.62	.70	.62	.64	.61	.58	.64	.54	.72	.74	.50	.75	.74	.70	.79	.62	.67	.61	.64	.61
110	.42	.58	.54	.58	.54	.55	.59	.44	.67	.51	.55	.94	.58	.68	.74	.39	.62	.52	.54	.67	.56	.67	.68	.73	.49
111	.57	.55	.55	.56	.51	.54	.57	.53	.65	.59	.60	.66	.54	.61	.66	.57	.60	.62	.57	.68	.62	.61	.68	.68	.63
112	.48	.67	.63	.64	.63	.63	.70	.58	.68	.57	.66	.76	.74	.88	.86	.45	.77	.68	.69	.82	.65	.72	.76	.65	.49
113	.47	.67	.54	.63	.47	.52	.59	.52	.60	.55	.52	.73	.66	.72	.88	.55	.70	.63	.60	.76	.56	.62	.64	.58	.49
114	.62	.68	.66	.66	.60	.63	.69	.67	.69	.63	.64	.63	.53	.70	.74	.61	.76	.81	.70	.71	.68	.70	.71	.66	.59
115	.64	.61	.60	.61	.55	.57	.62	.61	.73	.58	.67	.74	.56	.67	.70	.62	.63	.66	.70	.69	.70	.69	.68	.66	.68
116	.57	.54	.55	.55	.48	.52	.56	.55	.62	.56	.61	.64	.51	.59	.64	.56	.59	.62	.58	.74	.60	.59	.69	.75	.64
117	.50	.62	.61	.62	.59	.60	.67	.59	.62	.59	.61	.70	.58	.73	.75	.47	.71	.68	.67	.80	.62	.69	.74	.71	.52
118	.50	.59	.59	.60	.57	.58	.65	.58	.66	.57	.59	.67	.53	.70	.79	.52	.68	.61	.65	.79	.60	.67	.74	.72	.52
119	.56	.62	.57	.60	.57	.63	.63	.50	.64	.58	.54	.77	.55	.62	.71	.41	.67	.64	.62	.78	.58	.60	.72	.73	.61
120	.61	.54	.53	.52	.45	.48	.54	.53	.64	.52	.57	.63	.48	.57	.65	.38	.58	.64	.54	.61	.54	.61	.58	.58	.61
121	.47	.61	.60	.60	.51	.59	.65	.51	.59	.58	.61	.70	.60	.72	.76	.42	.76	.69	.59	.80	.52	.62	.75	.77	.50
122	.62	.54	.67	.68	.62	.67	.70	.62	.68	.68	.61	.71	.62	.71	.75	.41	.75	.73	.73	.80	.65	.68	.77	.78	.64
123	.53	.54	.51	.52	.52	.50	.60	.54	.62	.52	.54	.69	.53	.64	.73	.52	.63	.62	.55	.72	.62	.61	.63	.60	.58
124	.45	.59	.59	.60	.50	.53	.59	.53	.61	.59	.55	.73	.63	.78	.81	.41	.79	.70	.71	.74	.58	.65	.76	.72	.50
125	.42	.60	.64	.60	.57	.56	.61	.48	.57	.55	.52	.67	.62	.74	.79	.38	.73	.63	.65	.60	.58	.60	.73	.73	.51
126	.42	.54	.60	.59	.49	.52	.58	.53	.56	.51	.74	.65	.65	.73	.78	.42	.73	.69	.54	.58	.54	.64	.74	.69	.48
127	.40	.51	.49	.51	.48	.53	.54	.48	.57	.56	.52	.68	.54	.73	.74	.39	.60	.59	.59	.89	.52	.55	.74	.63	.46
128	.56	.68	.67	.68	.62	.67	.70	.64	.68	.68	.57	.59	.58	.71	.75	.43	.80	.62	.59	.85	.57	.68	.77	.78	.54
129	.56	.59	.51	.52	.52	.50	.60	.57	.62	.56	.59	.69	.53	.60	.72	.58	.58	.61	.55	.63	.63	.61	.62	.63	.60
130	.44	.55	.52	.53	.50	.53	.58	.51	.58	.51	.54	.73	.63	.76	.79	.63	.74	.71	.60	.74	.66	.64	.76	.67	.50
131	.44	.58	.55	.55	.49	.52	.61	.53	.61	.54	.74	.73	.62	.74	.79	.76	.68	.82	.62	.66	.56	.84	.79	.67	.51
132	.42	.54	.52	.53	.47	.53	.58	.51	.58	.51	.52	.73	.63	.73	.78	.73	.63	.76	.59	.58	.58	.61	.76	.65	.50
133	.42	.55	.52	.54	.51	.53	.58	.48	.57	.56	.52	.64	.64	.73	.64	.55	.68	.63	.59	.84	.56	.60	.69	.66	.47
134	.40	.52	.52	.53	.50	.52	.57	.52	.59	.52	.57	.73	.60	.71	.78	.41	.73	.62	.59	.85	.57	.60	.68	.66	.52
135	.58	.55	.54	.53	.47	.50	.55	.56	.66	.54	.59	.66	.53	.60	.67	.58	.58	.61	.55	.63	.63	.63	.62	.59	.62
136	.60	.63	.62	.63	.56	.62	.66	.62	.67	.63	.60	.74	.64	.64	.68	.63	.74	.71	.74	.74	.66	.64	.76	.83	.68
137	.79	.85	.88	.83	.87	.83	.84	.89	.82	.90	.81	.49	.63	.72	.68	.76	.68	.82	.85	.60	.84	.87	.79	.83	.72
138	.77	.81	.80	.79	.83	.79	.80	.85	.79	.88	.77	.50	.61	.70	.61	.73	.69	.76	.81	.58	.80	.84	.76	.74	.71
139	.57	.83	.75	.83	.89	.84	.83	.50	.68	.68	.84	.87	.64	.76	.58	.55	.71	.63	.68	.62	.83	.80	.74	.62	.58
140	.44	.57	.67	.80	.85	.81	.82	.36	.57	.53	.45	.83	.58	.55	.65	.41	.60	.48	.53	.59	.79	.69	.59	.53	.51
141	.59	.75	.74	.75	.72	.77	.79	.62	.65	.76	.62	.70	.56	.76	.72	.56	.72	.61	.55	.56	.64	.70	.62	.59	.56
142	.63	.83	.81	.83	.85	.82	.82	.70	.80	.83	.81	.64	.66	.76	.79	.65	.68	.71	.81	.82	.66	.80	.76	.66	.59
143	.67	.83	.80	.79	.87	.83	.82	.70	.77	.89	.85	.67	.68	.76	.79	.66	.72	.82	.77	.59	.81	.82	.81	.68	.63
144	.64	.78	.75	.83	.83	.79	.78	.65	.79	.74	.84	.60	.65	.76	.62	.60	.68	.76	.72	.57	.83	.80	.78	.63	.59
145	.63	.83	.80	.80	.89	.84	.83	.69	.80	.78	.84	.60	.67	.81	.64	.66	.68	.75	.77	.62	.83	.81	.82	.67	.63
146	.63	.72	.76	.80	.85	.81	.82	.68	.75	.75	.80	.58	.72	.81	.70	.59	.73	.75	.77	.65	.79	.78	.82	.67	.56
147	.68	.75	.74	.77	.77	.80	.80	.69	.75	.77	.75	.70	.72	.79	.64	.66	.77	.80	.79	.82	.75	.76	.87	.81	.68
148	.71	.88	.88	.89	.89	.90	.90	.71	.77	.83	.79	.53	.63	.74	.64	.68	.80	.84	.87	.59	.78	.80	.86	.76	.62
149	.90	.92	.89	.91	.91	.92	.90	.77	.79	.89	.79	.54	.64	.72	.63	.77	.79	.84	.87	.57	.82	.82	.83	.75	.71
150	.76	.90	.91	.92	.89	.93	.91	.71	.75	.85	.75	.54	.63	.71	.65	.74	.83	.87	.88	.59	.79	.78	.86	.78	.66

	75	74	73	72	71	70	69	68	67	66	65	64	63	62	61	60	59	58	57	56	55	54	53	52	51
101	.79	.81	.74	.74	.63	.67	.65	.71	.70	.75	.72	.78	.62	.64	.56	.77	.59	.54	.73	.75	.68	.72	.67	.74	.78
102	.69	.72	.71	.71	.61	.65	.60	.64	.62	.65	.63	.70	.61	.67	.56	.68	.61	.60	.69	.69	.64	.70	.60	.66	.73
103	.71	.75	.71	.70	.66	.66	.66	.66	.62	.70	.67	.72	.62	.64	.56	.74	.61	.55	.68	.70	.68	.72	.66	.71	.74
104	.77	.80	.71	.74	.59	.63	.62	.70	.66	.73	.72	.79	.61	.64	.56	.76	.57	.54	.75	.76	.66	.73	.65	.69	.81
105	.71	.74	.73	.73	.63	.68	.62	.67	.61	.69	.65	.72	.63	.68	.56	.72	.62	.58	.71	.71	.66	.72	.62	.69	.75
106	.72	.76	.69	.73	.56	.61	.62	.61	.61	.68	.67	.75	.59	.65	.55	.74	.56	.55	.75	.76	.62	.73	.62	.64	.79
107	.61	.66	.63	.59	.57	.67	.62	.54	.53	.58	.55	.62	.66	.68	.58	.62	.61	.61	.62	.63	.68	.67	.56	.60	.66
108	.61	.72	.68	.66	.59	.64	.58	.61	.59	.65	.60	.66	.63	.63	.50	.65	.54	.51	.64	.66	.64	.64	.59	.65	.68
109	.73	.76	.73	.77	.57	.61	.58	.74	.66	.73	.70	.77	.58	.61	.42	.73	.48	.43	.75	.72	.62	.71	.59	.65	.81
110	.63	.66	.56	.52	.58	.64	.63	.60	.60	.63	.63	.66	.58	.47	.59	.58	.57	.43	.52	.54	.71	.56	.51	.61	.63
111	.64	.68	.61	.61	.52	.60	.52	.71	.67	.61	.61	.68	.63	.69	.50	.67	.57	.56	.66	.68	.63	.67	.57	.58	.71
112	.81	.84	.76	.66	.57	.73	.72	.76	.74	.79	.77	.80	.63	.59	.53	.72	.53	.47	.69	.68	.69	.68	.62	.77	.77
113	.68	.71	.65	.62	.46	.60	.63	.65	.56	.65	.64	.70	.61	.59	.46	.58	.56	.47	.62	.59	.59	.59	.50	.57	.70
114	.62	.67	.74	.73	.58	.66	.61	.66	.58	.63	.60	.67	.64	.58	.54	.60	.57	.60	.69	.65	.60	.70	.56	.60	.71
115	.63	.69	.62	.61	.57	.69	.57	.56	.55	.60	.57	.64	.67	.72	.62	.64	.61	.57	.69	.65	.66	.70	.56	.57	.67
116	.68	.72	.67	.65	.49	.55	.63	.58	.65	.62	.63	.71	.59	.66	.59	.72	.56	.57	.74	.75	.59	.69	.58	.57	.76
117	.78	.80	.71	.71	.57	.63	.62	.72	.67	.74	.73	.78	.58	.58	.49	.74	.52	.49	.72	.72	.64	.65	.57	.68	.77
118	.76	.78	.70	.71	.56	.60	.59	.69	.64	.72	.70	.82	.60	.51	.50	.75	.51	.48	.72	.73	.61	.69	.58	.72	.77
119	.75	.76	.60	.68	.57	.58	.56	.67	.61	.71	.72	.81	.57	.47	.47	.71	.49	.54	.72	.77	.63	.66	.55	.70	.78
120	.51	.57	.58	.71	.45	.55	.50	.47	.41	.48	.45	.54	.55	.52	.51	.52	.46	.44	.60	.57	.54	.61	.42	.68	.60
121	.76	.80	.65	.54	.52	.59	.57	.74	.65	.76	.79	.86	.54	.49	.44	.64	.44	.41	.63	.67	.64	.68	.55	.66	.67
122	.78	.81	.69	.78	.60	.61	.61	.73	.65	.74	.76	.85	.55	.63	.54	.72	.56	.53	.84	.86	.70	.76	.63	.68	.89
123	.64	.68	.61	.59	.46	.58	.52	.56	.49	.58	.57	.65	.59	.64	.50	.58	.51	.53	.62	.62	.58	.60	.47	.52	.68
124	.83	.85	.72	.74	.58	.62	.60	.82	.76	.88	.89	.88	.60	.51	.49	.72	.49	.43	.74	.72	.67	.69	.58	.72	.84
125	.84	.86	.66	.68	.55	.58	.63	.69	.77	.86	.89	.89	.57	.47	.50	.75	.46	.46	.71	.72	.66	.63	.57	.70	.81
126	.85	.87	.73	.71	.57	.61	.61	.65	.61	.86	.86	.85	.59	.52	.49	.71	.49	.40	.71	.71	.66	.62	.60	.74	.77
127	.80	.88	.80	.62	.47	.60	.55	.67	.60	.72	.69	.81	.53	.49	.44	.72	.46	.44	.63	.67	.57	.61	.54	.71	.71
128	.68	.87	.73	.73	.58	.55	.57	.74	.66	.77	.72	.84	.62	.63	.54	.64	.56	.41	.80	.76	.65	.62	.59	.67	.69
129	.61	.67	.65	.88	.58	.61	.61	.50	.71	.80	.83	.87	.66	.70	.57	.82	.61	.53	.85	.88	.75	.80	.73	.71	.89
130	.86	.88	.72	.59	.50	.58	.60	.66	.79	.79	.80	.86	.59	.52	.49	.76	.75	.57	.80	.80	.76	.76	.75	.80	.66
131	.89	.89	.66	.64	.53	.59	.59	.69	.76	.80	.79	.82	.56	.53	.50	.72	.78	.66	.76	.80	.82	.77	.82	.85	.66
132	.84	.87	.71	.66	.49	.61	.58	.73	.66	.77	.77	.81	.57	.53	.49	.74	.74	.61	.71	.71	.84	.75	.83	.84	.62
133	.86	.88	.67	.63	.51	.60	.59	.71	.69	.80	.82	.84	.55	.49	.48	.76	.78	.66	.72	.77	.82	.77	.80	.86	.67
134	.84	.87	.68	.64	.50	.58	.59	.74	.66	.74	.76	.79	.54	.54	.50	.73	.81	.59	.76	.74	.79	.75	.79	.86	.70
135	.55	.62	.59	.55	.47	.61	.54	.50	.46	.58	.50	.57	.64	.70	.56	.56	.56	.58	.60	.59	.58	.63	.46	.52	.63
136	.67	.72	.66	.74	.55	.60	.58	.66	.58	.66	.66	.75	.66	.72	.64	.76	.63	.66	.81	.80	.65	.76	.60	.80	.82
137	.62	.65	.80	.79	.79	.74	.73	.67	.76	.65	.62	.68	.72	.77	.78	.68	.83	.77	.75	.77	.74	.78	.75	.85	.72
138	.70	.63	.76	.82	.86	.77	.71	.67	.83	.70	.68	.66	.70	.73	.76	.68	.79	.75	.74	.76	.73	.77	.75	.84	.72
139	.68	.67	.58	.65	.72	.64	.67	.68	.86	.60	.66	.72	.65	.54	.59	.73	.74	.54	.61	.70	.84	.77	.80	.86	.67
140	.74	.62	.46	.54	.55	.52	.58	.61	.87	.62	.72	.67	.59	.42	.46	.76	.47	.41	.52	.74	.79	.75	.80	.86	.70
141	.62	.76	.71	.88	.69	.62	.67	.84	.79	.81	.83	.86	.62	.60	.65	.82	.61	.64	.85	.88	.75	.80	.79	.83	.89
142	.75	.68	.76	.71	.83	.81	.81	.81	.82	.81	.67	.66	.72	.72	.73	.84	.75	.65	.66	.71	.76	.76	.75	.79	.66
143	.67	.72	.77	.85	.87	.85	.85	.80	.84	.74	.67	.68	.69	.69	.71	.76	.78	.66	.66	.74	.82	.77	.82	.85	.66
144	.70	.70	.73	.82	.86	.77	.73	.70	.83	.70	.68	.70	.72	.77	.77	.70	.74	.61	.67	.71	.84	.75	.84	.88	.62
145	.74	.75	.78	.73	.87	.77	.73	.74	.86	.77	.72	.74	.71	.64	.77	.73	.78	.66	.67	.77	.82	.77	.83	.86	.67
146	.76	.77	.79	.72	.86	.73	.73	.72	.81	.74	.76	.74	.67	.69	.71	.76	.81	.59	.67	.74	.79	.75	.80	.86	.70
147	.88	.88	.80	.84	.76	.81	.76	.84	.82	.80	.84	.86	.72	.72	.74	.84	.71	.64	.80	.89	.83	.80	.79	.83	.89
148	.66	.72	.76	.85	.87	.85	.77	.80	.84	.76	.74	.75	.70	.69	.72	.76	.77	.66	.76	.80	.80	.82	.77	.79	.75
149	.63	.69	.74	.82	.86	.77	.73	.74	.77	.70	.68	.70	.74	.77	.81	.70	.85	.66	.74	.80	.80	.79	.72	.76	.74
150	.65	.67	.73	.86	.86	.73	.73	.69	.81	.74	.72	.74	.74	.73	.75	.73	.81	.72	.76	.81	.80	.80	.71	.75	.77

	76	77	78	79	80	81	82	83	84	85	86	87	88	89	90	91	92	93	94	95	96	97	98	99	100
101	.81	.77	.73	.80	.72	.65	.74	.54	.64	.75	.67	.54	.73	.78	.86	.78	.79	.81	.81	.79	.80	.90	.90	.85	.75
102	.73	.68	.63	.70	.66	.67	.70	.56	.64	.66	.65	.59	.71	.70	.86	.82	.81	.81	.81	.81	.79	.87	.85	.84	.79
103	.76	.72	.67	.74	.69	.65	.70	.56	.65	.69	.64	.55	.69	.72	.85	.81	.82	.82	.83	.79	.79	.88	.87	.85	.78
104	.81	.77	.71	.80	.70	.64	.70	.55	.64	.75	.68	.56	.74	.75	.84	.80	.82	.82	.83	.81	.81	.90	.90	.89	.77
105	.75	.70	.66	.73	.70	.67	.72	.56	.67	.68	.67	.58	.72	.72	.88	.84	.85	.84	.81	.80	.79	.88	.86	.85	.77
106	.77	.73	.66	.75	.66	.64	.65	.56	.63	.69	.67	.56	.74	.69	.83	.90	.93	.89	.80	.82	.79	.84	.80	.89	.80
107	.66	.64	.54	.63	.57	.65	.70	.60	.63	.58	.57	.60	.68	.66	.84	.90	.94	.83	.80	.81	.72	.88	.86	.86	.89
108	.76	.68	.59	.70	.59	.64	.67	.61	.62	.66	.59	.57	.68	.75	.82	.82	.84	.83	.81	.81	.72	.88	.87	.86	.81
109	.76	.72	.73	.77	.75	.61	.69	.50	.62	.74	.68	.52	.72	.71	.83	.73	.74	.77	.81	.81	.81	.87	.81	.82	.70
110	.64	.67	.61	.65	.64	.47	.65	.38	.51	.63	.46	.40	.52	.60	.75	.73	.71	.77	.86	.77	.75	.77	.81	.67	.65
111	.70	.68	.59	.67	.59	.58	.60	.62	.64	.60	.58	.59	.70	.61	.81	.88	.89	.88	.80	.89	.73	.88	.84	.89	.84
112	.82	.82	.82	.83	.81	.57	.79	.45	.60	.80	.62	.45	.62	.74	.87	.70	.69	.72	.83	.83	.82	.88	.91	.71	.57
113	.71	.72	.67	.71	.67	.53	.63	.57	.52	.61	.54	.46	.60	.62	.83	.79	.79	.82	.82	.86	.77	.88	.88	.79	.75
114	.66	.62	.62	.65	.72	.67	.66	.57	.65	.59	.64	.58	.69	.65	.92	.87	.81	.90	.84	.83	.82	.86	.82	.81	.79
115	.67	.66	.56	.66	.60	.70	.70	.64	.60	.59	.59	.63	.71	.67	.89	.95	.95	.95	.88	.76	.74	.83	.80	.91	.91
116	.75	.71	.58	.71	.54	.62	.58	.60	.60	.64	.64	.59	.76	.65	.76	.83	.88	.83	.78	.76	.69	.89	.80	.93	.82
117	.80	.77	.74	.80	.72	.58	.69	.48	.59	.76	.65	.49	.69	.74	.82	.73	.76	.75	.83	.81	.79	.89	.90	.82	.72
118	.79	.87	.71	.79	.69	.59	.64	.50	.59	.75	.62	.50	.70	.71	.82	.76	.73	.71	.82	.80	.78	.89	.89	.85	.75
119	.78	.77	.67	.76	.62	.59	.62	.49	.60	.72	.62	.56	.75	.69	.73	.69	.64	.65	.79	.76	.68	.79	.73	.82	.64
120	.58	.54	.46	.54	.52	.66	.58	.43	.59	.46	.53	.61	.65	.55	.85	.67	.64	.69	.81	.82	.84	.84	.86	.89	.90
121	.77	.80	.77	.81	.73	.53	.61	.43	.55	.74	.67	.47	.72	.64	.76	.67	.70	.68	.83	.80	.84	.84	.85	.81	.62
122	.83	.81	.73	.81	.71	.66	.67	.57	.66	.77	.75	.61	.76	.71	.78	.75	.78	.75	.82	.79	.84	.83	.80	.87	.69
123	.68	.64	.58	.68	.72	.65	.60	.54	.55	.57	.54	.53	.63	.61	.83	.88	.89	.95	.87	.85	.73	.88	.84	.90	.86
124	.84	.87	.81	.88	.69	.51	.62	.39	.52	.80	.64	.44	.66	.69	.78	.62	.64	.65	.86	.84	.85	.88	.90	.88	.68
125	.85	.88	.87	.88	.81	.52	.67	.37	.52	.82	.60	.41	.64	.68	.73	.60	.64	.69	.83	.83	.76	.93	.90	.72	.57
126	.86	.86	.84	.89	.75	.54	.68	.42	.53	.85	.58	.44	.63	.72	.80	.74	.69	.74	.87	.85	.75	.94	.95	.76	.63
127	.80	.77	.70	.82	.60	.49	.61	.43	.51	.80	.58	.41	.60	.70	.76	.67	.77	.74	.81	.81	.76	.91	.93	.78	.70
128	.73	.81	.73	.72	.75	.66	.62	.51	.65	.77	.76	.55	.63	.67	.79	.73	.78	.74	.87	.78	.83	.80	.79	.79	.62
129	.68	.64	.57	.64	.61	.65	.67	.58	.62	.57	.57	.58	.67	.66	.90	.94	.91	.95	.87	.85	.74	.86	.82	.90	.85
130	.88	.88	.81	.90	.68	.51	.64	.43	.52	.82	.73	.44	.62	.73	.78	.70	.75	.71	.86	.84	.76	.93	.94	.79	.68
131	.87	.87	.81	.90	.69	.54	.67	.45	.53	.85	.69	.46	.64	.80	.80	.68	.72	.74	.83	.83	.75	.93	.96	.77	.67
132	.86	.86	.79	.88	.67	.52	.65	.44	.52	.80	.71	.44	.63	.72	.80	.74	.77	.74	.87	.85	.76	.94	.95	.81	.71
133	.87	.89	.82	.90	.69	.48	.65	.40	.51	.81	.71	.41	.60	.70	.76	.67	.71	.68	.85	.84	.77	.91	.93	.75	.65
134	.86	.86	.78	.88	.65	.53	.64	.46	.52	.80	.58	.46	.63	.74	.79	.73	.78	.74	.86	.84	.74	.95	.95	.81	.73
135	.63	.59	.50	.58	.54	.65	.62	.54	.60	.51	.54	.58	.65	.59	.86	.96	.92	.95	.83	.82	.70	.81	.76	.90	.87
136	.74	.71	.62	.73	.62	.73	.76	.73	.82	.82	.73	.65	.85	.66	.79	.83	.86	.79	.86	.78	.76	.82	.80	.96	.77
137	.66	.63	.59	.66	.71	.74	.62	.71	.79	.67	.85	.77	.77	.71	.61	.51	.48	.55	.50	.46	.66	.53	.54	.52	.46
138	.64	.63	.57	.64	.68	.75	.73	.71	.77	.68	.86	.75	.75	.66	.57	.47	.45	.51	.58	.48	.65	.51	.53	.52	.44
139	.66	.70	.68	.70	.72	.58	.70	.63	.80	.69	.71	.67	.70	.61	.64	.40	.44	.42	.52	.40	.61	.52	.60	.46	.34
140	.61	.67	.62	.61	.61	.70	.64	.57	.53	.62	.47	.60	.66	.52	.66	.47	.49	.41	.64	.53	.68	.53	.63	.49	.37
141	.78	.75	.71	.76	.79	.62	.67	.61	.71	.85	.78	.58	.80	.82	.58	.44	.49	.47	.87	.52	.70	.61	.78	.61	.38
142	.67	.66	.67	.63	.68	.74	.64	.59	.78	.67	.69	.64	.76	.68	.70	.53	.45	.56	.52	.45	.66	.56	.56	.47	.44
143	.70	.70	.68	.66	.69	.75	.67	.62	.80	.66	.71	.66	.78	.73	.61	.49	.44	.48	.52	.45	.64	.54	.57	.52	.43
144	.74	.73	.70	.64	.76	.69	.65	.59	.77	.69	.71	.61	.70	.77	.59	.45	.44	.52	.51	.40	.61	.54	.56	.45	.42
145	.66	.70	.68	.70	.72	.75	.65	.63	.80	.62	.71	.67	.66	.74	.64	.50	.46	.51	.52	.43	.66	.59	.61	.50	.43
146	.75	.67	.62	.73	.82	.70	.64	.57	.76	.74	.69	.60	.66	.77	.66	.47	.42	.41	.50	.46	.68	.60	.63	.46	.40
147	.78	.88	.82	.86	.79	.73	.62	.61	.77	.85	.78	.67	.80	.82	.70	.60	.61	.62	.68	.63	.77	.75	.78	.68	.55
148	.69	.69	.70	.64	.62	.74	.62	.59	.78	.67	.79	.68	.76	.68	.79	.45	.42	.48	.50	.43	.75	.53	.56	.47	.38
149	.65	.65	.64	.60	.78	.80	.77	.67	.85	.62	.73	.76	.78	.67	.61	.48	.44	.51	.50	.45	.73	.49	.52	.49	.39
150	.67	.67	.68	.63	.82	.78	.74	.62	.86	.65	.79	.72	.80	.66	.62	.47	.44	.51	.50	.45	.77	.52	.54	.52	.38

	101	102	103	104	105	106	107	108	109	110	111	112	113	114	115	116	117	118	119	120	121	122	123	124	125
101	1.00																								
102	.95	1.00																							
103	.94	.94	1.00																						
104	.97	.96	.95	1.00																					
105	.96	.96	.95	.96	1.00																				
106	.94	.92	.86	.96	.94	1.00																			
107	.84	.86	.92	.85	.86	.85	1.00																		
108	.91	.91	.86	.89	.91	.89	.89	1.00																	
109	.94	.92	.90	.94	.94	.92	.78	.86	1.00																
110	.75	.73	.75	.75	.74	.70	.83	.77	.70	1.00															
111	.80	.79	.81	.83	.80	.85	.86	.80	.75	.68	1.00														
112	.85	.79	.84	.84	.82	.80	.77	.77	.82	.82	.74	1.00													
113	.81	.82	.83	.81	.81	.81	.84	.83	.81	.80	.77	.85	1.00												
114	.84	.87	.82	.84	.88	.85	.83	.83	.86	.69	.78	.80	.84	1.00											
115	.85	.87	.82	.86	.88	.88	.95	.88	.79	.77	.90	.70	.85	.87	1.00										
116	.83	.83	.88	.88	.83	.90	.85	.86	.80	.66	.89	.79	.82	.78	.88	1.00									
117	.95	.91	.92	.96	.93	.92	.80	.88	.96	.75	.76	.86	.83	.82	.92	.81	1.00								
118	.82	.92	.93	.97	.94	.95	.82	.88	.95	.72	.80	.84	.87	.82	.73	.82	.96	1.00							
119	.77	.79	.73	.85	.79	.81	.80	.84	.77	.78	.76	.81	.87	.77	.72	.76	.81	.80	1.00						
120	.82	.82	.80	.79	.82	.83	.80	.83	.74	.67	.88	.88	.86	.71	.77	.77	.89	.76	.72	1.00					
121	.85	.81	.80	.86	.82	.87	.91	.85	.88	.78	.73	.86	.88	.78	.78	.82	.87	.88	.84	.90	1.00				
122	.87	.85	.84	.88	.85	.89	.77	.82	.86	.66	.75	.84	.85	.76	.82	.86	.84	.86	.81	.67	.83	1.00			
123	.82	.84	.82	.86	.86	.86	.91	.87	.81	.89	.81	.78	.81	.84	.92	.80	.82	.83	.76	.71	.80	.83	1.00		
124	.84	.81	.80	.88	.82	.85	.72	.83	.84	.78	.71	.88	.87	.86	.73	.74	.86	.84	.84	.86	.88	.88	.91	1.00	
125	.82	.78	.79	.84	.84	.84	.72	.86	.85	.78	.72	.86	.86	.76	.72	.77	.85	.84	.81	.67	.87	.87	.85	.97	1.00
129	.82	.81	.81	.89	.80	.87	.76	.84	.81	.78	.75	.73	.88	.78	.77	.76	.88	.82	.85	.70	.88	.88	.83	.80	.96
130	.88	.83	.80	.90	.84	.83	.80	.83	.81	.67	.79	.84	.85	.71	.78	.77	.90	.84	.86	.75	.89	.87	.87	.96	.95
131	.85	.79	.82	.87	.81	.86	.79	.80	.80	.78	.76	.71	.84	.76	.83	.82	.90	.88	.84	.72	.88	.88	.87	.90	.92
132	.87	.83	.80	.90	.84	.87	.81	.85	.80	.80	.79	.74	.78	.78	.78	.80	.87	.89	.83	.70	.86	.86	.83	.93	.95
133	.85	.79	.84	.87	.81	.83	.77	.82	.78	.78	.76	.84	.85	.76	.84	.84	.89	.86	.85	.69	.87	.87	.88	.89	.91
134	.87	.83	.89	.85	.84	.86	.82	.85	.83	.78	.78	.74	.88	.84	.73	.84	.84	.83	.75	.88	.87	.88	.89	.89	.91
135	.79	.82	.82	.82	.82	.84	.91	.86	.74	.70	.89	.74	.84	.86	.95	.86	.76	.77	.74	.71	.78	.80	.90	.67	.76
136	.84	.84	.83	.89	.84	.90	.84	.83	.79	.65	.77	.72	.79	.82	.87	.94	.82	.85	.86	.86	.92	.85	.85	.76	.76
137	.63	.63	.62	.61	.64	.59	.53	.57	.60	.42	.52	.56	.47	.59	.53	.51	.58	.57	.51	.49	.52	.63	.47	.54	.51
138	.61	.60	.60	.60	.61	.57	.52	.54	.58	.44	.51	.54	.45	.55	.51	.52	.56	.52	.52	.46	.53	.63	.49	.55	.50
139	.58	.55	.54	.57	.54	.51	.55	.51	.44	.72	.54	.62	.58	.49	.50	.48	.54	.52	.69	.44	.60	.65	.42	.59	.54
140	.52	.50	.53	.56	.51	.50	.49	.53	.47	.78	.56	.61	.58	.45	.53	.52	.59	.59	.73	.62	.64	.54	.54	.64	.65
141	.68	.64	.70	.65	.63	.67	.65	.69	.63	.51	.71	.65	.67	.57	.67	.70	.74	.75	.66	.76	.78	.58	.51	.74	.69
142	.62	.57	.61	.61	.62	.74	.47	.50	.47	.47	.52	.60	.67	.60	.49	.44	.56	.54	.47	.47	.54	.78	.45	.56	.51
143	.62	.57	.62	.60	.61	.53	.50	.51	.52	.52	.53	.64	.60	.54	.53	.42	.53	.54	.48	.46	.52	.54	.44	.56	.54
144	.59	.60	.54	.56	.60	.50	.52	.49	.55	.53	.51	.63	.54	.48	.51	.42	.54	.52	.44	.44	.52	.52	.42	.55	.54
145	.65	.64	.57	.61	.62	.56	.53	.54	.53	.54	.54	.65	.66	.54	.52	.47	.56	.57	.52	.49	.58	.58	.45	.59	.57
146	.65	.64	.60	.60	.61	.56	.49	.51	.54	.54	.54	.71	.71	.55	.55	.45	.59	.59	.49	.53	.58	.58	.45	.64	.61
147	.77	.71	.77	.77	.73	.74	.65	.69	.63	.47	.76	.52	.67	.68	.67	.70	.74	.75	.57	.76	.78	.81	.67	.74	.77
148	.63	.58	.61	.60	.62	.58	.47	.50	.47	.52	.60	.60	.45	.59	.49	.47	.56	.53	.41	.54	.62	.62	.42	.56	.57
149	.59	.57	.57	.60	.59	.55	.49	.56	.56	.46	.55	.55	.45	.58	.51	.48	.52	.52	.55	.53	.53	.65	.44	.57	.53
150	.61	.60	.60	.60	.61	.58	.48	.52	.60	.47	.53	.56	.47	.60	.51	.49	.55	.56	.58	.44	.57	.65	.45	.61	.57

Appendix B: Intercorrelations

	126	127	128	129	130	131	132	133	134	135	136	137	138	139	140	141	142	143	144	145	146	147	148	149	150
126	1.00																								
127	.88	1.00																							
128	.80	.76	1.00																						
129	.77	.78	.73	1.00																					
130	.94	.91	.80	.80	1.00																				
131	.93	.94	.76	.97	.96	1.00																			
132	.93	.90	.76	.83	.99	.99	1.00																		
133	.94	.88	.74	.77	.99	.95	.98	1.00																	
134	.93	.93	.77	.82	.99	.97	.98	.97	1.00																
135	.71	.74	.69	.97	.76	.73	.79	.73	.78	1.00															
136	.78	.79	.85	.80	.78	.78	.82	.77	.81	.85	1.00														
137	.53	.46	.65	.53	.51	.51	.48	.48	.48	.51	.59	1.00													
138	.53	.46	.64	.50	.46	.51	.47	.49	.48	.47	.58	.96	1.00												
139	.61	.52	.54	.49	.57	.60	.54	.60	.54	.44	.52	.64	.64	1.00											
140	.62	.57	.53	.51	.62	.63	.59	.65	.59	.48	.53	.48	.51	.90	1.00										
141	.63	.59	.79	.52	.63	.63	.63	.66	.61	.47	.70	.77	.78	.74	.64	1.00									
142	.55	.42	.52	.55	.51	.49	.49	.50	.48	.50	.49	.81	.77	.68	.50	.71	1.00								
143	.56	.44	.50	.53	.48	.50	.52	.52	.50	.48	.48	.82	.79	.73	.56	.69	.96	1.00							
144	.55	.43	.47	.51	.55	.52	.50	.52	.49	.45	.45	.78	.76	.74	.61	.74	.91	.96	1.00						
145	.60	.48	.52	.54	.62	.57	.53	.55	.53	.48	.51	.82	.79	.75	.58	.75	.98	.95	.95	1.00					
146	.63	.50	.54	.52	.63	.59	.56	.59	.55	.46	.49	.79	.76	.73	.57	.86	.95	.93	.93	.84	1.00				
147	.78	.74	.74	.66	.78	.78	.74	.76	.75	.61	.72	.78	.77	.79	.71	.85	.79	.81	.79	.87	.89	1.00			
148	.57	.44	.66	.49	.51	.51	.48	.51	.47	.44	.57	.85	.82	.75	.56	.89	.85	.88	.85	.89	.89	.82	1.00		
149	.53	.42	.61	.49	.53	.49	.47	.47	.45	.46	.57	.88	.85	.78	.57	.87	.84	.86	.84	.87	.87	.81	.93	1.00	
150	.56	.45	.67	.50	.48	.51	.46	.49	.47	.46	.61	.84	.80	.77	.58	.85	.81	.84	.79	.85	.85	.81	.96	.95	1.00

	1	2	3	4	5	6	7	8	9	10	11	12	13	14	15	16	17	18	19	20	21	22	23	24	25
151	.82	.82	.83	.86	.76	.74	.78	.79	.73	.75	.74	.75	.81	.84	.70	.74	.82	.75	.89	.74	.73	.81	.69	.76	.62
152	.58	.63	.65	.59	.71	.35	.52	.49	.50	.47	.74	.42	.45	.55	.33	.65	.66	.59	.69	.70	.50	.60	.58	.48	.76
153	.63	.69	.69	.65	.74	.47	.63	.59	.61	.56	.78	.54	.55	.64	.46	.65	.75	.64	.78	.77	.57	.72	.66	.60	.72
154	.78	.77	.74	.71	.74	.76	.78	.78	.74	.75	.77	.77	.82	.79	.73	.71	.82	.72	.85	.73	.81	.81	.71	.76	.68
155	.70	.75	.80	.76	.73	.45	.67	.65	.63	.59	.78	.53	.57	.70	.44	.76	.76	.72	.76	.80	.62	.70	.69	.63	.76
156	.75	.79	.88	.85	.74	.48	.71	.69	.64	.60	.75	.56	.63	.75	.47	.81	.81	.77	.81	.82	.65	.72	.69	.66	.74
157	.83	.86	.86	.86	.75	.63	.76	.75	.69	.76	.77	.67	.72	.79	.59	.70	.87	.73	.94	.78	.68	.81	.66	.70	.66
158	.62	.65	.65	.62	.77	.49	.60	.57	.60	.55	.70	.55	.55	.62	.45	.61	.72	.60	.76	.69	.51	.69	.65	.60	.61
159	.72	.75	.78	.80	.68	.62	.80	.76	.82	.71	.72	.78	.69	.81	.56	.76	.72	.77	.75	.82	.72	.83	.78	.68	.65
160	.75	.78	.76	.77	.74	.62	.72	.67	.65	.67	.74	.64	.69	.72	.56	.64	.92	.65	.93	.75	.68	.62	.62	.68	.65
161	.68	.74	.82	.79	.70	.41	.66	.63	.60	.55	.74	.49	.55	.70	.40	.78	.72	.73	.75	.79	.60	.67	.66	.61	.73
162	.70	.74	.76	.77	.68	.53	.73	.67	.71	.63	.68	.63	.64	.73	.53	.68	.84	.69	.82	.81	.67	.87	.66	.65	.60
163	.67	.71	.77	.75	.72	.48	.68	.60	.64	.55	.70	.55	.58	.68	.44	.71	.79	.68	.82	.83	.60	.77	.66	.65	.64

	26	27	28	29	30	31	32	33	34	35	36	37	38	39	40	41	42	43	44	45	46	47	48	49	50
151	.79	.91	.91	.92	.91	.74	.90	.72	.78	.86	.79	.55	.63	.70	.61	.76	.78	.83	.86	.56	.81	.79	.84	.74	.70
152	.38	.57	.55	.56	.54	.58	.61	.43	.53	.57	.51	.68	.81	.75	.82	.35	.69	.55	.60	.72	.51	.58	.66	.57	.70
153	.50	.68	.63	.65	.60	.67	.70	.53	.62	.65	.58	.74	.75	.78	.85	.49	.78	.66	.69	.80	.60	.67	.76	.69	.40
154	.75	.88	.85	.86	.81	.87	.87	.79	.80	.94	.77	.56	.69	.73	.66	.84	.77	.80	.87	.62	.81	.84	.80	.77	.53
155	.50	.70	.64	.66	.66	.68	.72	.59	.65	.66	.66	.66	.79	.86	.83	.47	.75	.67	.70	.78	.65	.70	.77	.66	.49
156	.54	.76	.70	.72	.76	.75	.69	.61	.68	.71	.72	.63	.77	.85	.75	.50	.87	.69	.75	.71	.70	.74	.81	.68	.51
157	.61	.87	.84	.85	.84	.87	.87	.68	.71	.81	.71	.54	.69	.77	.71	.66	.86	.87	.86	.65	.75	.76	.86	.68	.60
158	.51	.67	.65	.67	.61	.67	.68	.48	.62	.62	.56	.73	.63	.68	.75	.50	.75	.65	.67	.72	.59	.63	.73	.66	.52
159	.74	.78	.74	.78	.77	.79	.79	.71	.76	.79	.79	.57	.68	.72	.64	.64	.77	.75	.77	.69	.79	.76	.85	.80	.72
160	.66	.84	.84	.83	.79	.86	.87	.66	.69	.82	.65	.54	.67	.74	.71	.64	.88	.84	.87	.65	.70	.74	.85	.80	.59
161	.47	.69	.64	.66	.68	.68	.71	.56	.63	.64	.67	.61	.77	.82	.77	.44	.71	.64	.69	.73	.64	.69	.76	.62	.45
162	.63	.76	.70	.77	.76	.79	.80	.64	.67	.74	.69	.54	.63	.72	.64	.59	.76	.78	.79	.70	.69	.71	.90	.89	.59
163	.53	.72	.71	.72	.74	.75	.75	.54	.65	.68	.65	.62	.68	.73	.69	.49	.74	.70	.74	.72	.65	.67	.83	.76	.51

	51	52	53	54	55	56	57	58	59	60	61	62	63	64	65	66	67	68	69	70	71	72	73	74	75
151	.72	.78	.73	.78	.82	.80	.72	.74	.84	.72	.78	.73	.75	.70	.70	.72	.80	.75	.75	.77	.89	.82	.73	.65	.64
152	.71	.67	.57	.56	.68	.63	.60	.35	.42	.64	.49	.44	.58	.78	.80	.77	.72	.75	.67	.58	.53	.59	.60	.76	.75
153	.81	.71	.62	.66	.75	.76	.70	.47	.52	.72	.58	.57	.64	.85	.82	.80	.74	.79	.68	.63	.60	.71	.67	.83	.81
154	.77	.73	.74	.79	.80	.81	.77	.77	.82	.70	.80	.75	.75	.70	.66	.81	.77	.74	.74	.75	.80	.85	.75	.66	.62
155	.76	.79	.71	.68	.73	.72	.68	.47	.55	.75	.60	.58	.61	.82	.81	.81	.80	.78	.75	.72	.65	.69	.75	.85	.83
156	.77	.85	.76	.72	.77	.75	.69	.51	.62	.77	.65	.58	.63	.80	.82	.84	.86	.79	.80	.76	.75	.70	.76	.83	.82
157	.75	.75	.67	.79	.78	.80	.77	.63	.72	.74	.70	.72	.70	.79	.78	.71	.68	.83	.73	.71	.79	.85	.58	.72	.71
158	.78	.64	.59	.63	.74	.72	.65	.47	.52	.68	.56	.56	.62	.77	.75	.71	.68	.72	.67	.59	.64	.68	.76	.74	.73
159	.78	.82	.83	.80	.80	.90	.81	.61	.69	.83	.68	.75	.71	.81	.79	.78	.80	.86	.69	.75	.77	.79	.76	.79	.78
160	.64	.70	.68	.80	.77	.82	.81	.61	.69	.75	.84	.67	.68	.78	.80	.81	.82	.77	.76	.71	.76	.90	.72	.70	.68
161	.71	.81	.73	.66	.72	.70	.64	.44	.54	.74	.58	.53	.59	.78	.80	.81	.82	.77	.76	.67	.68	.66	.72	.82	.83
162	.86	.77	.80	.85	.76	.91	.86	.57	.66	.89	.69	.65	.64	.87	.84	.83	.82	.82	.72	.67	.74	.87	.74	.79	.77
163	.81	.79	.76	.74	.76	.82	.75	.48	.59	.82	.64	.55	.62	.87	.90	.89	.88	.86	.74	.67	.72	.77	.70	.83	.82

	100	99	98	97	96	95	94	93	92	91	90	89	88	87	86	85	84	83	82	81	80	79	78	77	76
151	.37	.48	.51	.49	.72	.40	.47	.48	.43	.45	.58	.68	.78	.75	.77	.62	.86	.65	.77	.79	.78	.60	.64	.66	.66
152	.39	.50	.73	.67	.68	.66	.73	.45	.46	.44	.59	.60	.53	.37	.54	.78	.52	.35	.66	.43	.74	.76	.80	.80	.75
153	.51	.63	.79	.74	.80	.72	.78	.57	.58	.56	.67	.67	.66	.50	.64	.84	.62	.47	.72	.55	.79	.83	.83	.86	.82
154	.41	.53	.54	.51	.70	.49	.54	.50	.47	.46	.58	.69	.80	.76	.85	.64	.83	.68	.75	.78	.74	.61	.63	.67	.67
155	.44	.52	.76	.70	.70	.65	.70	.50	.48	.48	.65	.71	.61	.49	.66	.85	.63	.48	.79	.57	.81	.83	.85	.85	.82
156	.37	.46	.70	.64	.71	.52	.60	.55	.41	.42	.62	.73	.63	.52	.69	.81	.67	.50	.82	.60	.82	.81	.84	.83	.81
157	.40	.53	.61	.58	.82	.53	.59	.54	.46	.51	.70	.65	.76	.65	.77	.71	.80	.57	.75	.73	.89	.69	.77	.72	.71
158	.49	.60	.71	.64	.78	.48	.68	.55	.55	.54	.63	.61	.66	.51	.59	.75	.62	.45	.66	.56	.73	.72	.72	.76	.72
159	.49	.63	.63	.62	.64	.48	.54	.55	.55	.55	.59	.78	.81	.74	.81	.72	.80	.71	.79	.77	.68	.75	.69	.80	.80
160	.36	.54	.59	.55	.81	.53	.57	.48	.43	.44	.61	.62	.78	.64	.81	.71	.79	.54	.69	.68	.86	.68	.76	.72	.70
161	.37	.44	.71	.65	.66	.56	.62	.42	.40	.40	.60	.71	.58	.46	.62	.83	.62	.45	.80	.54	.80	.81	.84	.82	.80
162	.43	.65	.65	.63	.73	.48	.56	.50	.51	.49	.61	.70	.83	.62	.83	.76	.76	.57	.71	.67	.78	.78	.78	.81	.81
163	.37	.56	.69	.65	.73	.49	.59	.45	.44	.42	.59	.70	.71	.52	.71	.81	.70	.47	.73	.58	.80	.83	.85	.86	.83

	101	102	103	104	105	106	107	108	109	110	111	112	113	114	115	116	117	118	119	120	121	122	123	124	125
151	.58	.56	.56	.55	.58	.53	.48	.51	.54	.47	.50	.54	.42	.55	.49	.46	.50	.51	.56	.41	.50	.60	.41	.56	.53
152	.61	.53	.60	.61	.53	.55	.54	.53	.58	.68	.61	.77	.71	.50	.54	.55	.62	.60	.61	.46	.69	.66	.58	.76	.78
153	.72	.66	.71	.73	.67	.69	.65	.64	.70	.72	.70	.81	.76	.63	.65	.66	.73	.72	.74	.79	.79	.80	.68	.81	.83
154	.59	.58	.58	.58	.59	.56	.53	.54	.58	.47	.53	.56	.50	.55	.52	.53	.55	.55	.57	.46	.57	.67	.47	.58	.55
155	.69	.60	.67	.68	.62	.62	.55	.56	.65	.64	.60	.84	.68	.57	.57	.55	.68	.68	.59	.46	.68	.68	.58	.74	.75
156	.66	.56	.62	.63	.59	.57	.49	.52	.59	.60	.59	.79	.56	.51	.51	.48	.62	.62	.57	.48	.62	.63	.47	.71	.70
157	.65	.61	.62	.64	.64	.61	.50	.52	.65	.51	.59	.67	.54	.66	.54	.64	.66	.61	.72	.48	.63	.68	.50	.69	.64
158	.67	.63	.65	.69	.63	.64	.62	.61	.63	.68	.67	.70	.66	.60	.61	.64	.60	.62	.64	.53	.72	.74	.62	.72	.74
159	.66	.61	.64	.64	.63	.64	.57	.58	.58	.49	.56	.61	.51	.55	.60	.64	.61	.62	.59	.51	.60	.72	.53	.62	.61
160	.63	.60	.60	.64	.62	.62	.48	.50	.67	.59	.56	.63	.53	.60	.49	.53	.63	.63	.59	.43	.68	.70	.48	.70	.66
161	.65	.55	.63	.71	.58	.56	.48	.50	.60	.49	.53	.59	.59	.50	.49	.46	.63	.63	.53	.37	.61	.61	.48	.70	.70
162	.70	.62	.66	.66	.65	.70	.52	.54	.70	.57	.63	.65	.51	.58	.55	.65	.67	.70	.64	.45	.73	.77	.51	.72	.70
163	.67	.57	.63	.66	.60	.61	.51	.52	.64	.64	.61	.70	.54	.52	.52	.57	.64	.64	.63	.40	.69	.70	.49	.78	.77

	126	127	128	129	130	131	132	133	134	135	136	137	138	139	140	141	142	143	144	145	146	147	148	149	150
151	.52	.41	.59	.48	.44	.48	.43	.47	.43	.44	.55	.86	.82	.79	.60	.79	.87	.88	.84	.89	.85	.80	.95	.96	.97
152	.74	.66	.60	.59	.74	.71	.72	.77	.70	.52	.55	.52	.54	.72	.75	.73	.61	.63	.66	.64	.72	.77	.61	.56	.58
153	.79	.74	.72	.67	.80	.79	.79	.82	.78	.62	.68	.63	.63	.79	.80	.82	.66	.68	.68	.69	.75	.87	.70	.66	.69
154	.55	.47	.68	.51	.50	.52	.48	.51	.49	.48	.61	.91	.90	.74	.60	.83	.77	.78	.75	.79	.76	.80	.86	.91	.88
155	.74	.67	.62	.59	.73	.74	.73	.75	.71	.52	.56	.66	.65	.72	.65	.77	.76	.78	.77	.78	.87	.85	.73	.68	.68
156	.70	.57	.57	.51	.66	.67	.66	.69	.63	.44	.50	.72	.71	.75	.64	.79	.84	.86	.86	.88	.92	.86	.81	.76	.75
157	.71	.57	.71	.56	.55	.57	.55	.57	.54	.58	.61	.80	.77	.77	.60	.87	.89	.84	.79	.84	.88	.85	.94	.91	.94
158	.71	.68	.66	.61	.69	.70	.68	.71	.67	.58	.66	.57	.58	.79	.76	.75	.61	.62	.62	.64	.67	.79	.67	.66	.71
159	.62	.58	.63	.51	.61	.63	.60	.62	.60	.55	.66	.81	.81	.71	.60	.83	.81	.83	.82	.86	.82	.83	.82	.83	.80
160	.63	.51	.77	.51	.55	.56	.54	.57	.53	.46	.64	.80	.79	.76	.63	.94	.77	.75	.72	.76	.79	.83	.93	.88	.93
161	.70	.60	.56	.51	.68	.69	.67	.70	.65	.44	.48	.65	.64	.72	.63	.75	.79	.82	.82	.82	.90	.83	.75	.68	.80
162	.69	.58	.75	.54	.63	.63	.64	.65	.62	.49	.71	.76	.77	.69	.58	.95	.76	.77	.75	.79	.81	.87	.88	.81	.84
163	.75	.61	.67	.52	.68	.67	.66	.71	.65	.45	.62	.69	.71	.78	.70	.90	.77	.80	.81	.82	.85	.88	.84	.76	.80

	151	152	153	154	155	156	157	158	159	160	161	162	163
151	1.00												
152	.57	1.00											
153	.66	.92	1.00										
154	.88	.63	.71	1.00									
155	.67	.89	.90	.69	1.00								
156	.76	.81	.83	.72	.92	1.00							
157	.90	.70	.78	.84	.78	.82	1.00						
158	.66	.77	.86	.68	.78	.72	.75	1.00					
159	.82	.66	.75	.83	.76	.91	.80	.69	1.00				
160	.88	.70	.79	.88	.75	.77	.94	.76	.78	1.00			
161	.68	.85	.86	.67	.96	.95	.78	.71	.75	.74	1.00		
162	.81	.69	.78	.79	.77	.81	.87	.71	.87	.90	.77	1.00	
163	.79	.82	.85	.76	.85	.88	.85	.77	.82	.86	.85	.91	1.00

Appendix B: Intercorrelations

	26	27	28	29	30	31	32	33	34	35	36	37	38	39	40	41	42	43	44	45	46	47	48	49	50
164	.65	.69	.67	.68	.62	.68	.70	.65	.68	.70	.66	.61	.65	.71	.72	.62	.71	.73	.70	.81	.68	.67	.76	.76	.64
165	.57	.72	.68	.71	.71	.73	.73	.60	.67	.68	.68	.67	.73	.79	.76	.53	.74	.71	.73	.81	.69	.71	.81	.75	.57
166	.64	.79	.77	.80	.80	.82	.80	.63	.71	.77	.73	.58	.64	.71	.60	.60	.70	.70	.76	.61	.72	.74	.81	.74	.60
167	.62	.78	.74	.78	.80	.79	.78	.63	.69	.74	.73	.56	.64	.72	.61	.58	.68	.69	.74	.61	.71	.73	.79	.69	.57
168	.37	.47	.45	.49	.43	.48	.47	.31	.52	.43	.38	.82	.49	.50	.63	.34	.55	.43	.45	.61	.41	.50	.54	.49	.45
169	.61	.61	.61	.62	.55	.61	.65	.53	.70	.57	.49	.65	.52	.62	.67	.46	.72	.66	.59	.70	.53	.63	.75	.75	.45
170	.51	.62	.59	.62	.61	.79	.62	.53	.71	.62	.67	.74	.57	.67	.70	.48	.61	.62	.59	.64	.65	.70	.69	.75	.51
171	.23	.42	.39	.44	.41	.43	.44	.29	.51	.57	.67	.78	.52	.54	.64	.26	.50	.39	.42	.64	.41	.48	.56	.56	.52
172	.43	.52	.50	.53	.49	.51	.54	.45	.59	.49	.54	.73	.53	.64	.71	.41	.54	.57	.54	.75	.53	.58	.68	.48	.36
173	.30	.47	.44	.46	.43	.46	.50	.35	.50	.45	.44	.74	.64	.65	.77	.27	.60	.47	.50	.73	.44	.52	.68	.61	.48
174	.40	.52	.50	.52	.46	.51	.55	.49	.55	.50	.48	.77	.59	.65	.76	.37	.60	.55	.50	.75	.50	.52	.60	.52	.36
175	.53	.57	.57	.61	.54	.61	.62	.53	.61	.59	.52	.64	.66	.59	.66	.49	.67	.66	.64	.71	.50	.58	.66	.60	.46
176	.53	.55	.52	.55	.50	.54	.58	.48	.59	.53	.58	.76	.50	.73	.80	.39	.67	.57	.58	.78	.55	.61	.75	.77	.55
177	.48	.55	.55	.58	.55	.57	.58	.49	.65	.53	.59	.67	.50	.61	.67	.44	.59	.76	.57	.72	.54	.63	.68	.60	.46
178	.57	.68	.67	.68	.63	.67	.69	.57	.66	.63	.57	.67	.53	.66	.71	.54	.77	.76	.70	.69	.62	.68	.75	.68	.52
179	.39	.50	.49	.51	.44	.49	.52	.40	.55	.50	.46	.74	.50	.59	.69	.38	.56	.53	.51	.72	.48	.54	.62	.57	.55
180	.42	.50	.52	.53	.47	.50	.52	.49	.57	.52	.52	.62	.49	.57	.63	.48	.58	.59	.55	.75	.53	.55	.69	.75	.55
181	.58	.55	.58	.58	.56	.61	.61	.55	.66	.61	.60	.69	.54	.62	.66	.55	.62	.64	.62	.73	.61	.64	.74	.73	.62
182	.73	.89	.88	.89	.87	.88	.90	.72	.76	.81	.78	.51	.65	.73	.75	.34	.74	.59	.58	.68	.53	.61	.68	.57	.41
183	.73	.82	.82	.83	.80	.83	.81	.44	.56	.52	.59	.57	.59	.65	.71	.38	.67	.59	.58	.66	.52	.58	.71	.66	.45
184	.20	.45	.45	.47	.42	.45	.57	.57	.51	.48	.46	.57	.44	.51	.59	.39	.56	.45	.51	.76	.49	.49	.89	.66	.53
185	.42	.52	.50	.53	.49	.51	.55	.47	.59	.50	.55	.51	.60	.68	.73	.39	.61	.56	.51	.78	.55	.59	.69	.57	.44
186	.42	.50	.52	.51	.48	.50	.52	.45	.57	.48	.52	.72	.56	.63	.68	.38	.58	.54	.53	.75	.53	.55	.69	.75	.55
187	.88	.86	.88	.89	.87	.88	.90	.87	.76	.86	.91	.66	.74	.85	.73	.85	.58	.68	.62	.75	.95	.64	.74	.73	.62
188	.73	.86	.82	.83	.79	.83	.81	.72	.82	.81	.82	.51	.68	.85	.76	.75	.70	.77	.79	.75	.81	.79	.88	.84	.65
189	.94	.82	.82	.54	.78	.83	.79	.56	.83	.52	.79	.72	.54	.68	.60	.96	.74	.63	.79	.57	.87	.80	.79	.84	.87
190	.92	.85	.80	.80	.73	.85	.87	.83	.83	.83	.81	.71	.71	.71	.71	.93	.72	.82	.82	.72	.91	.80	.84	.76	.87
191	.73	.84	.84	.84	.79	.83	.82	.83	.84	.83	.81	.59	.62	.79	.59	.78	.69	.79	.82	.66	.88	.81	.78	.83	.92
192	.77	.87	.87	.85	.83	.84	.67	.78	.84	.85	.83	.61	.75	.80	.74	.88	.81	.80	.80	.61	.91	.84	.75	.78	.89
193	.73	.76	.74	.74	.79	.76	.78	.82	.71	.61	.70	.72	.79	.85	.84	.58	.76	.87	.79	.86	.73	.73	.85	.80	.73
194	.73	.81	.85	.86	.86	.89	.88	.84	.69	.61	.62	.76	.61	.74	.77	.50	.70	.81	.79	.80	.90	.79	.86	.82	.90
195	.79	.85	.81	.80	.77	.78	.83	.55	.66	.55	.59	.71	.56	.69	.70	.56	.74	.71	.69	.70	.89	.80	.76	.73	.92
196	.55	.59	.57	.58	.54	.57	.61	.53	.63	.56	.56	.76	.67	.76	.75	.51	.66	.63	.59	.66	.88	.81	.88	.89	.95
197	.48	.60	.58	.83	.79	.83	.63	.53	.63	.56	.59	.56	.62	.76	.82	.46	.72	.80	.80	.61	.91	.81	.78	.80	.78
198	.77	.87	.84	.86	.83	.84	.86	.78	.90	.83	.83	.69	.75	.80	.74	.62	.76	.81	.83	.70	.90	.84	.85	.76	.90
199	.73	.86	.87	.85	.79	.84	.83	.82	.82	.84	.81	.56	.63	.70	.77	.58	.70	.81	.81	.63	.73	.73	.80	.82	.73
200	.73	.85	.86	.84	.86	.89	.82	.84	.83	.86	.82	.53	.64	.67	.59	.93	.70	.80	.81	.57	.90	.80	.76	.80	.90
201	.74	.82	.80	.80	.73	.79	.79	.82	.83	.83	.79	.61	.66	.69	.62	.93	.70	.78	.79	.64	.89	.81	.75	.76	.95
202	.74	.84	.84	.85	.79	.85	.87	.83	.84	.83	.84	.59	.71	.79	.67	.78	.79	.85	.79	.68	.88	.84	.88	.89	.78
203	.74	.84	.83	.83	.80	.83	.82	.82	.85	.83	.83	.56	.62	.69	.58	.92	.69	.80	.80	.61	.91	.81	.78	.80	.90
204	.87	.89	.87	.87	.83	.86	.67	.82	.84	.85	.83	.61	.75	.80	.74	.88	.81	.87	.86	.70	.90	.84	.85	.82	.86
205	.61	.76	.74	.74	.73	.76	.78	.78	.71	.61	.70	.72	.73	.85	.77	.58	.76	.81	.79	.86	.73	.73	.86	.80	.63
206	.53	.57	.64	.66	.62	.64	.70	.58	.69	.61	.62	.76	.61	.74	.68	.56	.74	.71	.69	.78	.65	.79	.76	.73	.56
207	.52	.57	.56	.55	.49	.53	.58	.55	.65	.55	.59	.71	.56	.69	.78	.51	.66	.63	.59	.70	.62	.75	.67	.66	.62
208	.48	.59	.57	.58	.52	.56	.61	.53	.66	.56	.56	.76	.67	.69	.70	.46	.72	.62	.64	.66	.60	.65	.70	.68	.54
209	.48	.60	.58	.58	.54	.57	.82	.53	.63	.56	.59	.78	.67	.76	.82	.62	.69	.64	.64	.74	.60	.65	.72	.72	.54
210	.66	.82	.79	.82	.84	.83	.83	.67	.78	.79	.80	.63	.73	.79	.70	.62	.81	.87	.85	.66	.79	.80	.85	.82	.61
211	.68	.67	.86	.87	.86	.89	.88	.67	.75	.82	.75	.59	.70	.77	.68	.65	.82	.73	.77	.64	.73	.79	.86	.72	.63
212	.57	.78	.74	.76	.77	.78	.78	.62	.71	.73	.73	.65	.79	.83	.78	.56	.82	.81	.77	.74	.73	.75	.83	.76	.61
213	.43	.54	.51	.55	.51	.54	.56	.44	.59	.56	.53	.75	.56	.64	.70	.40	.62	.57	.55	.72	.53	.59	.70	.62	.48

	51	52	53	54	55	56	57	58	59	60	61	62	63	64	65	66	67	68	69	70	71	72	73	74	75
164	.81	.68	.68	.73	.69	.81	.77	.62	.64	.73	.68	.70	.68	.76	.70	.71	.64	.68	.67	.64	.62	.75	.70	.77	.74
165	.80	.83	.74	.78	.78	.82	.74	.53	.62	.80	.66	.60	.65	.87	.89	.89	.84	.84	.75	.71	.70	.75	.75	.91	.90
166	.74	.80	.80	.75	.80	.81	.72	.60	.71	.77	.72	.62	.64	.77	.76	.76	.82	.74	.76	.72	.82	.75	.70	.72	.72
167	.70	.80	.79	.71	.77	.78	.67	.58	.69	.75	.70	.61	.61	.73	.73	.73	.80	.71	.71	.73	.80	.71	.70	.72	.72
168	.63	.48	.42	.47	.66	.56	.48	.34	.38	.54	.36	.37	.51	.63	.61	.57	.64	.54	.49	.44	.45	.49	.40	.60	.60
169	.83	.57	.59	.69	.66	.77	.76	.45	.49	.72	.49	.53	.54	.80	.74	.71	.64	.73	.53	.51	.54	.78	.61	.71	.69
170	.62	.68	.61	.63	.69	.63	.57	.49	.57	.71	.54	.60	.63	.65	.62	.65	.59	.59	.56	.69	.63	.57	.65	.70	.67
171	.53	.65	.54	.46	.63	.57	.46	.26	.33	.60	.37	.33	.45	.66	.66	.63	.59	.56	.56	.47	.45	.46	.44	.68	.68
172	.70	.62	.58	.60	.60	.68	.61	.41	.45	.67	.47	.52	.52	.74	.70	.69	.61	.62	.56	.56	.52	.61	.60	.77	.76
173	.67	.59	.51	.51	.60	.59	.54	.28	.33	.60	.37	.38	.48	.73	.72	.69	.62	.65	.56	.50	.44	.53	.53	.74	.73
174	.72	.59	.53	.58	.64	.66	.61	.38	.41	.64	.43	.48	.52	.76	.72	.69	.61	.65	.56	.53	.48	.60	.57	.76	.75
175	.81	.59	.61	.70	.65	.80	.76	.49	.52	.74	.53	.57	.56	.79	.72	.70	.62	.68	.61	.52	.54	.74	.61	.74	.72
176	.73	.65	.60	.59	.66	.67	.62	.40	.52	.68	.44	.50	.55	.76	.75	.73	.65	.68	.61	.52	.52	.60	.62	.80	.79
177	.63	.64	.57	.62	.66	.69	.69	.46	.51	.68	.48	.53	.55	.71	.74	.72	.63	.61	.58	.59	.57	.62	.61	.75	.74
178	.70	.61	.61	.69	.68	.72	.66	.47	.45	.66	.52	.63	.60	.75	.67	.67	.55	.59	.58	.60	.63	.73	.66	.71	.69
179	.63	.54	.50	.54	.60	.63	.57	.36	.39	.61	.42	.48	.50	.69	.65	.62	.55	.59	.53	.49	.48	.56	.51	.71	.69
180	.77	.58	.60	.66	.59	.77	.74	.48	.49	.73	.53	.56	.53	.75	.68	.66	.60	.66	.59	.50	.50	.66	.59	.75	.73
181	.61	.65	.65	.69	.70	.81	.71	.48	.49	.68	.52	.62	.61	.76	.69	.69	.63	.63	.59	.58	.59	.69	.62	.77	.76
182	.67	.68	.60	.58	.65	.64	.59	.35	.41	.68	.44	.45	.51	.76	.75	.73	.69	.67	.63	.60	.54	.57	.62	.80	.80
183	.76	.65	.57	.62	.58	.72	.66	.38	.44	.71	.47	.46	.53	.83	.83	.80	.75	.75	.76	.55	.54	.66	.60	.81	.80
184	.70	.48	.43	.59	.49	.67	.64	.47	.45	.59	.49	.58	.51	.64	.55	.56	.43	.53	.43	.44	.39	.62	.55	.65	.62
185	.72	.68	.60	.62	.63	.70	.64	.41	.45	.70	.49	.50	.52	.78	.76	.75	.66	.66	.59	.59	.52	.60	.63	.84	.83
186	.71	.66	.59	.60	.63	.70	.63	.40	.45	.73	.48	.47	.52	.77	.73	.75	.66	.66	.59	.56	.50	.59	.60	.83	.82
187	.81	.87	.83	.92	.85	.85	.83	.87	.92	.83	.86	.90	.86	.76	.72	.78	.80	.77	.87	.92	.87	.84	.89	.78	.74
188	.71	.74	.77	.82	.77	.79	.75	.74	.80	.77	.80	.77	.75	.68	.67	.68	.74	.69	.76	.75	.81	.77	.72	.64	.61
189	.63	.74	.68	.66	.77	.64	.59	.56	.55	.64	.54	.67	.62	.66	.59	.61	.53	.57	.51	.63	.50	.59	.64	.70	.65
190	.75	.58	.67	.57	.51	.72	.76	.39	.42	.64	.47	.50	.50	.64	.60	.58	.52	.51	.51	.49	.46	.53	.51	.66	.65
191	.62	.86	.81	.91	.86	.83	.86	.89	.94	.81	.88	.90	.89	.77	.74	.78	.81	.80	.87	.92	.90	.87	.90	.76	.71
192	.73	.65	.56	.69	.66	.67	.63	.59	.60	.65	.57	.69	.68	.71	.65	.67	.60	.65	.64	.69	.58	.66	.70	.73	.68
193	.79	.88	.80	.84	.83	.81	.80	.68	.78	.80	.76	.76	.75	.79	.80	.81	.86	.80	.71	.84	.87	.79	.83	.79	.76
194	.73	.70	.67	.83	.76	.79	.81	.90	.89	.70	.86	.91	.82	.65	.60	.64	.65	.67	.78	.77	.76	.80	.79	.79	.59
195	.73	.78	.77	.89	.81	.79	.77	.86	.88	.78	.87	.90	.81	.71	.66	.70	.71	.65	.78	.84	.79	.79	.82	.74	.69
196	.72	.72	.70	.63	.80	.79	.73	.92	.92	.63	.89	.73	.83	.64	.59	.63	.65	.60	.69	.78	.78	.77	.78	.64	.54
197	.61	.68	.66	.78	.75	.75	.77	.76	.84	.78	.79	.90	.78	.60	.54	.57	.60	.60	.69	.78	.78	.73	.73	.59	.54
198	.77	.86	.81	.87	.87	.85	.77	.87	.93	.81	.88	.81	.85	.74	.72	.75	.81	.75	.74	.80	.87	.75	.85	.75	.71
199	.67	.67	.70	.84	.78	.79	.78	.92	.93	.66	.89	.91	.81	.66	.62	.65	.61	.66	.72	.81	.80	.81	.77	.66	.61
200	.67	.63	.68	.81	.77	.80	.75	.94	.90	.72	.89	.93	.83	.60	.55	.59	.66	.62	.73	.79	.79	.73	.74	.60	.54
201	.72	.69	.67	.82	.73	.79	.76	.93	.84	.73	.82	.84	.94	.64	.58	.62	.61	.73	.81	.80	.74	.74	.75	.65	.59
202	.73	.73	.77	.95	.81	.36	.89	.80	.93	.81	.88	.91	.82	.78	.73	.75	.76	.78	.75	.83	.81	.85	.82	.73	.67
203	.70	.73	.72	.84	.78	.78	.77	.93	.84	.76	.88	.94	.81	.63	.58	.63	.66	.63	.77	.83	.80	.75	.81	.63	.59
204	.76	.76	.76	.87	.84	.83	.82	.87	.84	.78	.88	.94	.86	.73	.68	.71	.71	.66	.78	.84	.79	.81	.82	.72	.68
205	.87	.94	.73	.79	.80	.86	.75	.59	.65	.83	.68	.66	.71	.93	.88	.92	.86	.89	.77	.74	.71	.81	.76	.95	.93
206	.81	.70	.64	.73	.70	.75	.81	.51	.55	.76	.55	.63	.62	.81	.75	.76	.70	.74	.72	.66	.62	.80	.75	.80	.77
207	.71	.63	.63	.67	.63	.56	.74	.51	.55	.62	.56	.68	.63	.67	.59	.60	.52	.58	.56	.60	.49	.62	.71	.68	.63
208	.73	.61	.56	.67	.66	.68	.67	.51	.53	.68	.56	.65	.63	.72	.65	.65	.58	.61	.62	.64	.54	.62	.63	.73	.68
209	.69	.69	.56	.67	.66	.71	.71	.48	.50	.69	.52	.60	.60	.82	.79	.78	.68	.74	.62	.54	.54	.66	.69	.85	.82
210	.74	.85	.81	.78	.84	.79	.72	.62	.73	.78	.74	.68	.70	.77	.78	.80	.86	.78	.83	.81	.84	.75	.76	.76	.75
211	.78	.80	.76	.79	.82	.31	.75	.64	.74	.74	.72	.68	.70	.78	.78	.79	.85	.82	.77	.76	.85	.82	.75	.73	.72
212	.78	.78	.78	.76	.81	.80	.74	.56	.66	.80	.73	.64	.67	.84	.85	.85	.87	.80	.80	.73	.76	.74	.77	.85	.83
213	.72	.64	.61	.62	.68	.69	.62	.40	.45	.69	.48	.50	.52	.76	.74	.71	.65	.65	.59	.56	.55	.62	.59	.77	.77

	76	77	78	79	80	81	82	83	84	85	86	87	88	89	90	91	92	93	94	95	96	97	98	99	100
164	.77	.75	.69	.75	.67	.68	.68	.62	.70	.78	.72	.64	.78	.71	.67	.64	.65	.66	.69	.67	.69	.71	.72	.73	.62
165	.90	.91	.89	.90	.80	.62	.76	.53	.69	.86	.70	.56	.70	.78	.65	.50	.53	.52	.67	.59	.75	.73	.78	.59	.46
166	.72	.75	.70	.69	.74	.66	.77	.49	.75	.71	.70	.62	.71	.68	.53	.38	.39	.40	.47	.37	.68	.51	.56	.47	.35
167	.71	.73	.68	.68	.73	.65	.78	.55	.72	.70	.71	.60	.66	.68	.52	.38	.37	.39	.46	.37	.65	.52	.57	.43	.33
168	.57	.64	.57	.61	.54	.38	.51	.29	.43	.61	.41	.36	.50	.49	.57	.52	.59	.51	.72	.63	.71	.63	.69	.61	.48
169	.74	.69	.69	.73	.69	.52	.57	.43	.59	.71	.53	.48	.71	.59	.68	.62	.65	.71	.79	.69	.84	.74	.76	.61	.56
170	.66	.71	.61	.67	.64	.58	.74	.49	.39	.67	.53	.49	.59	.66	.84	.82	.76	.82	.73	.72	.76	.81	.80	.75	.73
171	.71	.78	.68	.69	.53	.34	.58	.29	.51	.73	.40	.28	.46	.55	.56	.54	.60	.51	.81	.77	.66	.69	.74	.62	.52
172	.77	.78	.71	.79	.61	.50	.63	.43	.42	.76	.53	.43	.60	.66	.77	.76	.77	.75	.83	.77	.72	.87	.87	.81	.73
173	.77	.78	.71	.76	.63	.37	.59	.30	.49	.76	.46	.30	.49	.58	.68	.60	.63	.59	.57	.77	.72	.79	.84	.67	.57
174	.76	.78	.71	.78	.65	.45	.62	.51	.55	.71	.53	.40	.57	.60	.73	.69	.71	.73	.73	.71	.80	.83	.86	.75	.65
175	.76	.75	.66	.75	.63	.56	.58	.55	.62	.70	.64	.52	.75	.62	.71	.67	.72	.71	.71	.67	.75	.77	.78	.84	.64
176	.76	.81	.76	.81	.69	.56	.68	.47	.59	.70	.69	.41	.56	.65	.73	.69	.66	.56	.76	.69	.77	.77	.87	.69	.61
177	.75	.84	.78	.83	.60	.54	.65	.40	.51	.70	.55	.47	.63	.68	.77	.76	.78	.60	.77	.74	.91	.82	.86	.82	.67
178	.75	.70	.64	.66	.75	.61	.57	.46	.63	.68	.63	.54	.68	.62	.84	.76	.72	.76	.78	.74	.76	.81	.79	.76	.67
179	.70	.71	.63	.71	.58	.46	.66	.38	.48	.70	.49	.40	.60	.58	.70	.69	.71	.68	.81	.65	.75	.77	.81	.75	.65
180	.78	.76	.63	.76	.55	.55	.55	.51	.55	.71	.63	.51	.73	.65	.70	.74	.78	.73	.73	.71	.70	.82	.81	.77	.72
181	.77	.77	.64	.76	.60	.61	.65	.55	.62	.78	.66	.58	.73	.71	.69	.72	.75	.71	.71	.67	.75	.78	.79	.88	.67
182	.77	.81	.78	.81	.70	.44	.70	.37	.49	.80	.53	.37	.73	.64	.55	.56	.57	.56	.68	.60	.75	.77	.83	.61	.61
183	.81	.84	.78	.83	.69	.46	.62	.51	.53	.78	.58	.41	.52	.63	.86	.60	.64	.60	.77	.69	.81	.81	.84	.61	.74
184	.83	.82	.76	.66	.78	.53	.47	.37	.49	.67	.56	.50	.66	.59	.66	.76	.72	.68	.77	.68	.63	.73	.72	.72	.67
185	.83	.85	.76	.85	.64	.49	.66	.42	.51	.79	.56	.43	.60	.69	.73	.70	.65	.69	.81	.75	.74	.88	.89	.75	.65
186	.63	.84	.74	.85	.60	.48	.62	.42	.50	.78	.55	.42	.59	.68	.70	.67	.71	.66	.77	.70	.73	.85	.87	.75	.64
187	.65	.71	.71	.72	.80	.92	.89	.85	.84	.78	.85	.86	.88	.83	.75	.67	.69	.59	.68	.60	.71	.68	.68	.68	.66
188	.65	.65	.60	.72	.80	.77	.74	.72	.94	.88	.86	.76	.79	.65	.55	.50	.48	.51	.49	.42	.64	.49	.50	.54	.45
189	.67	.68	.59	.69	.59	.62	.59	.59	.60	.61	.56	.57	.66	.64	.86	.93	.94	.92	.90	.85	.73	.88	.84	.91	.91
190	.67	.68	.54	.67	.48	.46	.55	.46	.48	.63	.50	.43	.59	.59	.66	.75	.75	.71	.90	.65	.64	.76	.75	.61	.61
191	.77	.74	.70	.70	.81	.92	.88	.83	.95	.69	.88	.87	.89	.81	.73	.64	.64	.67	.66	.60	.73	.65	.66	.65	.67
192	.74	.72	.64	.71	.66	.64	.62	.63	.63	.66	.62	.57	.70	.68	.70	.67	.71	.66	.68	.63	.72	.63	.68	.62	.64
193	.77	.78	.77	.74	.84	.77	.89	.64	.83	.73	.77	.67	.75	.70	.75	.57	.69	.59	.77	.69	.78	.80	.84	.64	.60
194	.73	.62	.58	.58	.68	.92	.73	.86	.91	.88	.82	.92	.86	.68	.64	.50	.53	.65	.65	.56	.86	.90	.90	.86	.60
195	.73	.72	.68	.68	.69	.89	.80	.86	.91	.75	.83	.88	.87	.75	.70	.62	.64	.65	.58	.55	.76	.85	.81	.91	.66
196	.60	.62	.57	.57	.67	.94	.77	.90	.93	.63	.81	.94	.86	.69	.65	.69	.72	.67	.58	.56	.64	.84	.84	.84	.63
197	.60	.58	.51	.52	.64	.71	.72	.90	.90	.56	.79	.93	.82	.64	.59	.65	.67	.61	.55	.45	.60	.79	.72	.79	.54
198	.74	.73	.70	.69	.80	.81	.92	.71	.86	.69	.78	.74	.78	.78	.74	.64	.70	.66	.72	.62	.71	.67	.68	.62	.61
199	.63	.65	.58	.72	.60	.93	.75	.88	.92	.78	.81	.94	.87	.70	.71	.62	.61	.66	.57	.50	.63	.55	.54	.64	.60
200	.61	.58	.51	.59	.60	.94	.74	.90	.92	.57	.80	.95	.84	.65	.88	.62	.80	.64	.54	.49	.62	.49	.48	.64	.60
201	.67	.64	.55	.69	.65	.93	.74	.91	.90	.51	.80	.94	.85	.69	.85	.66	.72	.68	.62	.55	.62	.56	.55	.66	.66
202	.74	.72	.68	.68	.64	.84	.81	.74	.90	.56	.88	.80	.89	.72	.81	.63	.65	.65	.66	.57	.73	.63	.63	.66	.59
203	.67	.62	.54	.57	.64	.73	.77	.89	.93	.54	.80	.93	.86	.70	.73	.64	.67	.66	.55	.48	.61	.54	.53	.64	.62
204	.75	.78	.74	.72	.80	.72	.92	.71	.93	.73	.78	.74	.78	.72	.74	.64	.70	.66	.72	.62	.72	.63	.63	.62	.64
205	.94	.96	.77	.94	.84	.93	.75	.88	.93	.88	.75	.61	.87	.70	.71	.57	.60	.59	.76	.69	.78	.80	.84	.69	.53
206	.80	.79	.75	.80	.84	.94	.79	.90	.64	.75	.65	.52	.84	.65	.88	.80	.80	.81	.76	.83	.86	.90	.90	.86	.75
207	.69	.67	.58	.67	.60	.93	.73	.91	.61	.60	.58	.57	.85	.69	.85	.91	.86	.91	.87	.84	.76	.85	.81	.91	.84
208	.73	.73	.68	.72	.64	.84	.63	.58	.61	.60	.61	.53	.70	.72	.81	.73	.76	.74	.88	.83	.78	.85	.84	.79	.88
209	.84	.86	.79	.85	.72	.73	.69	.45	.56	.77	.61	.48	.65	.63	.85	.64	.65	.61	.89	.85	.80	.91	.93	.79	.69
210	.75	.78	.75	.72	.80	.72	.85	.78	.78	.73	.73	.64	.71	.72	.74	.49	.70	.53	.58	.48	.71	.60	.64	.69	.61
211	.73	.74	.76	.70	.85	.71	.79	.57	.81	.73	.77	.65	.75	.69	.71	.44	.70	.46	.54	.46	.63	.55	.60	.51	.53
212	.83	.86	.84	.82	.83	.65	.82	.54	.87	.82	.72	.58	.70	.74	.88	.49	.80	.50	.65	.57	.73	.67	.72	.54	.75
213	.77	.80	.70	.78	.64	.49	.65	.41	.53	.75	.55	.43	.60	.64	.72	.69	.71	.67	.71	.71	.77	.81	.83	.75	.65

234

Appendix B: Intercorrelations

	.101	102	103	104	105	106	107	108	109	110	111	112	113	114	115	116	117	118	119	120	121	122	123	124	125
164	.72	.70	.70	.76	.70	.75	.68	.68	.71	.56	.76	.68	.69	.67	.69	.77	.70	.74	.72	.65	.73	.81	.71	.68	.70
165	.72	.63	.69	.71	.70	.66	.59	.60	.68	.63	.65	.78	.64	.58	.60	.62	.70	.70	.69	.65	.72	.81	.58	.81	.82
166	.59	.53	.58	.58	.55	.54	.45	.47	.53	.50	.52	.59	.42	.46	.45	.49	.53	.54	.55	.34	.56	.63	.40	.61	.60
167	.59	.53	.58	.57	.55	.53	.43	.46	.52	.48	.49	.60	.42	.46	.44	.46	.53	.54	.51	.33	.53	.59	.40	.58	.57
168	.63	.60	.77	.66	.61	.61	.69	.65	.58	.83	.64	.65	.68	.63	.63	.64	.63	.62	.83	.55	.70	.73	.67	.70	.75
169	.79	.76	.77	.83	.77	.82	.70	.71	.81	.66	.75	.71	.71	.71	.68	.78	.79	.82	.80	.63	.88	.89	.72	.83	.83
170	.81	.79	.83	.79	.81	.78	.83	.78	.70	.77	.81	.80	.77	.77	.84	.73	.74	.76	.72	.79	.68	.74	.79	.73	.74
171	.60	.60	.68	.68	.61	.63	.68	.64	.58	.76	.68	.71	.69	.51	.64	.65	.65	.67	.74	.53	.68	.70	.67	.72	.78
172	.84	.80	.83	.86	.81	.85	.82	.82	.78	.77	.84	.81	.83	.76	.82	.84	.82	.85	.83	.75	.78	.86	.76	.82	.85
173	.74	.68	.74	.74	.75	.72	.71	.70	.70	.79	.74	.82	.83	.76	.82	.72	.75	.76	.75	.62	.78	.77	.76	.80	.87
174	.80	.76	.81	.83	.77	.80	.78	.76	.76	.81	.80	.83	.84	.71	.77	.79	.81	.82	.83	.70	.84	.86	.82	.84	.88
175	.82	.79	.80	.86	.80	.87	.74	.75	.81	.65	.74	.70	.72	.73	.74	.86	.81	.84	.85	.69	.87	.93	.77	.80	.82
176	.80	.75	.79	.81	.75	.76	.74	.74	.75	.80	.82	.88	.84	.69	.73	.73	.80	.81	.79	.65	.81	.82	.79	.80	.87
177	.82	.82	.89	.90	.87	.88	.84	.88	.82	.79	.80	.78	.76	.85	.83	.84	.86	.88	.85	.76	.79	.86	.84	.80	.82
178	.77	.74	.76	.80	.83	.83	.77	.77	.80	.71	.80	.76	.78	.85	.76	.77	.79	.81	.80	.75	.80	.81	.79	.81	.79
179	.77	.78	.80	.80	.74	.79	.77	.75	.71	.76	.78	.75	.78	.68	.76	.78	.76	.78	.80	.69	.79	.81	.79	.76	.80
180	.82	.78	.80	.88	.79	.88	.78	.76	.79	.63	.85	.80	.75	.70	.78	.94	.81	.86	.85	.75	.81	.92	.93	.77	.80
181	.79	.76	.78	.83	.77	.81	.78	.77	.72	.67	.81	.70	.71	.70	.65	.85	.75	.78	.85	.71	.78	.89	.78	.82	.77
182	.76	.72	.76	.76	.71	.71	.65	.66	.70	.77	.67	.87	.74	.61	.64	.75	.76	.77	.71	.60	.75	.76	.69	.74	.84
183	.73	.71	.76	.81	.73	.77	.70	.70	.74	.75	.79	.62	.71	.65	.69	.85	.72	.78	.75	.72	.84	.85	.79	.89	.92
184	.82	.76	.82	.79	.78	.82	.78	.72	.76	.77	.79	.85	.81	.70	.73	.80	.82	.84	.81	.69	.82	.81	.79	.65	.67
185	.80	.74	.79	.82	.75	.82	.75	.75	.73	.75	.78	.80	.81	.66	.76	.80	.80	.81	.82	.67	.81	.84	.78	.84	.89
186	.73	.71	.73	.72	.73	.70	.70	.68	.69	.60	.69	.72	.61	.71	.72	.66	.68	.68	.63	.65	.64	.71	.62	.65	.61
187	.54	.51	.55	.54	.54	.57	.50	.47	.50	.42	.58	.52	.44	.44	.53	.53	.47	.50	.51	.47	.50	.62	.54	.54	.51
188	.85	.86	.87	.88	.87	.90	.93	.87	.82	.77	.92	.81	.87	.86	.96	.89	.83	.86	.78	.94	.80	.83	.94	.76	.76
189	.83	.69	.69	.78	.71	.78	.76	.72	.67	.64	.86	.68	.65	.65	.78	.84	.71	.75	.74	.73	.73	.71	.89	.69	.73
190	.69	.69	.69	.68	.71	.79	.67	.67	.66	.58	.65	.69	.61	.62	.70	.63	.65	.63	.65	.62	.62	.71	.60	.66	.61
191	.87	.87	.88	.89	.88	.88	.93	.90	.83	.81	.88	.85	.91	.89	.95	.88	.85	.85	.83	.92	.82	.86	.93	.81	.81
192	.70	.65	.69	.67	.68	.64	.59	.58	.65	.61	.62	.76	.73	.65	.72	.55	.64	.64	.57	.53	.62	.67	.57	.69	.65
193	.60	.62	.60	.62	.63	.64	.61	.59	.61	.45	.62	.56	.57	.65	.65	.59	.57	.57	.58	.62	.55	.65	.54	.54	.49
194	.63	.68	.69	.69	.70	.69	.68	.65	.63	.52	.70	.63	.53	.67	.67	.68	.63	.64	.63	.66	.59	.71	.62	.59	.57
195	.60	.63	.61	.61	.64	.61	.65	.62	.58	.49	.65	.55	.45	.59	.73	.61	.56	.56	.58	.64	.53	.65	.50	.52	.48
196	.55	.57	.53	.54	.57	.54	.57	.55	.50	.43	.55	.49	.45	.60	.60	.54	.48	.48	.54	.57	.46	.60	.50	.46	.42
197	.73	.65	.70	.66	.68	.63	.68	.63	.62	.65	.65	.75	.64	.63	.76	.59	.63	.62	.60	.61	.61	.66	.57	.65	.66
198	.58	.61	.60	.61	.62	.57	.61	.60	.56	.49	.64	.54	.51	.61	.67	.59	.54	.55	.60	.62	.54	.62	.54	.53	.51
199	.53	.61	.57	.56	.60	.58	.49	.57	.53	.45	.60	.50	.49	.63	.64	.58	.50	.51	.56	.67	.48	.72	.57	.47	.44
200	.61	.64	.61	.62	.63	.57	.68	.63	.57	.53	.66	.56	.57	.69	.71	.68	.56	.56	.62	.67	.55	.82	.54	.53	.51
201	.68	.67	.69	.69	.69	.62	.65	.60	.67	.54	.67	.66	.57	.69	.68	.66	.65	.65	.63	.61	.66	.74	.58	.66	.62
202	.63	.61	.60	.69	.69	.69	.64	.60	.56	.48	.63	.54	.49	.62	.67	.61	.54	.54	.58	.63	.51	.63	.55	.51	.47
203	.68	.68	.68	.69	.69	.60	.69	.64	.66	.55	.71	.67	.63	.72	.67	.66	.63	.63	.64	.69	.62	.72	.61	.61	.58
204	.76	.68	.74	.69	.73	.73	.66	.69	.74	.69	.69	.83	.73	.67	.68	.70	.77	.75	.64	.58	.80	.82	.68	.87	.87
205	.53	.71	.44	.96	.94	.88	.85	.87	.93	.81	.84	.88	.85	.84	.86	.85	.94	.94	.84	.79	.89	.82	.88	.88	.87
206	.61	.92	.84	.87	.84	.86	.91	.84	.80	.75	.92	.78	.84	.80	.91	.86	.80	.83	.80	.93	.80	.84	.91	.75	.80
207	.83	.84	.86	.88	.83	.86	.88	.82	.78	.79	.91	.84	.86	.80	.83	.89	.82	.84	.86	.87	.82	.85	.89	.78	.80
208	.87	.83	.86	.88	.84	.82	.82	.83	.84	.83	.77	.90	.82	.80	.83	.82	.88	.87	.86	.75	.88	.88	.91	.91	.93
209	.65	.58	.64	.62	.61	.57	.53	.53	.57	.57	.58	.69	.52	.55	.55	.51	.58	.59	.55	.44	.57	.63	.48	.61	.64
210	.64	.59	.62	.62	.63	.58	.49	.51	.61	.53	.55	.65	.49	.49	.50	.49	.58	.59	.57	.46	.60	.66	.68	.53	.63
211	.69	.61	.68	.67	.63	.61	.61	.56	.63	.61	.62	.77	.61	.56	.56	.56	.65	.65	.61	.66	.66	.69	.53	.74	.74
212	.80	.75	.80	.83	.76	.80	.77	.75	.74	.78	.81	.80	.78	.69	.76	.79	.78	.81	.80	.68	.80	.84	.80	.82	.85
213	.80	.75	.80	.83	.76	.80	.77	.75	.74	.78	.81	.80	.78	.69	.76	.79	.78	.81	.80	.68	.80	.84	.80	.82	.85

	126	127	128	129	130	131	132	133	134	135	136	137	138	139	140	141	142	143	144	145	146	147	148	149	150
164	.70	.76	.73	.69	.71	.72	.70	.70	.71	.67	.78	.69	.68	.63	.59	.77	.63	.63	.59	.65	.66	.85	.68	.69	.70
165	.80	.70	.67	.60	.78	.79	.77	.80	.76	.54	.64	.70	.71	.78	.73	.84	.77	.80	.79	.82	.85	.92	.78	.74	.74
166	.58	.48	.57	.43	.52	.54	.51	.56	.50	.38	.53	.79	.80	.77	.61	.85	.83	.86	.85	.88	.87	.86	.88	.87	.86
167	.56	.47	.53	.42	.51	.54	.50	.55	.49	.38	.48	.79	.78	.77	.61	.80	.85	.88	.86	.90	.90	.85	.88	.86	.84
168	.68	.69	.58	.62	.71	.71	.70	.74	.70	.59	.63	.39	.42	.80	.92	.57	.39	.44	.48	.46	.45	.65	.45	.45	.47
169	.79	.74	.63	.70	.77	.75	.77	.79	.76	.66	.82	.63	.58	.64	.68	.86	.53	.53	.53	.56	.57	.75	.67	.63	.67
170	.76	.72	.54	.86	.76	.76	.78	.77	.77	.83	.71	.61	.58	.64	.63	.57	.72	.72	.72	.73	.71	.75	.62	.60	.59
171	.74	.73	.72	.82	.76	.76	.75	.79	.74	.60	.71	.37	.41	.61	.65	.57	.43	.49	.55	.53	.53	.80	.44	.41	.43
172	.85	.87	.66	.73	.89	.87	.89	.90	.89	.60	.79	.50	.50	.61	.65	.64	.54	.55	.55	.58	.58	.80	.62	.60	.43
173	.82	.81	.72	.82	.86	.83	.86	.89	.84	.67	.67	.42	.44	.64	.73	.63	.48	.51	.54	.53	.58	.72	.48	.50	.45
174	.79	.84	.82	.73	.80	.86	.81	.81	.80	.75	.76	.61	.51	.63	.75	.68	.51	.53	.55	.56	.56	.80	.52	.50	.52
175	.84	.77	.82	.74	.88	.78	.88	.90	.87	.71	.76	.61	.62	.67	.70	.80	.53	.59	.60	.61	.60	.80	.63	.61	.64
176	.79	.83	.69	.75	.86	.86	.81	.81	.80	.75	.87	.53	.53	.64	.63	.68	.57	.58	.59	.62	.60	.79	.56	.53	.54
177	.83	.84	.80	.82	.86	.76	.86	.90	.87	.70	.70	.56	.56	.69	.67	.73	.56	.63	.60	.65	.66	.80	.63	.54	.55
178	.79	.73	.68	.79	.77	.76	.77	.78	.76	.76	.79	.64	.62	.64	.65	.77	.68	.63	.60	.62	.66	.80	.71	.69	.71
179	.79	.82	.77	.79	.81	.82	.81	.82	.81	.73	.75	.44	.52	.69	.68	.62	.45	.46	.47	.49	.51	.71	.48	.47	.51
180	.80	.84	.77	.78	.84	.80	.85	.83	.85	.77	.90	.52	.53	.53	.57	.71	.53	.47	.46	.51	.49	.76	.52	.50	.52
181	.76	.79	.73	.76	.79	.82	.79	.79	.79	.75	.83	.63	.64	.67	.68	.73	.58	.60	.59	.64	.60	.84	.62	.62	.62
182	.81	.75	.62	.67	.84	.80	.84	.87	.81	.61	.62	.51	.52	.72	.70	.67	.61	.64	.65	.66	.60	.73	.54	.53	.54
183	.88	.79	.73	.70	.87	.83	.87	.90	.87	.75	.75	.53	.56	.58	.76	.77	.56	.58	.60	.62	.64	.81	.62	.57	.60
184	.69	.82	.74	.72	.77	.76	.73	.69	.75	.72	.83	.48	.48	.72	.46	.61	.38	.36	.33	.39	.39	.67	.62	.57	.47
185	.83	.86	.69	.78	.92	.90	.93	.94	.92	.74	.77	.51	.52	.63	.67	.67	.56	.58	.59	.62	.64	.80	.54	.51	.51
186	.87	.85	.67	.68	.91	.89	.90	.92	.90	.72	.76	.50	.52	.64	.69	.67	.53	.56	.58	.60	.61	.80	.53	.53	.52
187	.66	.59	.69	.61	.86	.65	.63	.61	.63	.65	.71	.82	.80	.68	.50	.72	.81	.82	.78	.82	.80	.73	.80	.81	.62
188	.50	.43	.58	.51	.45	.46	.45	.47	.45	.49	.59	.81	.80	.60	.47	.79	.82	.83	.81	.84	.81	.79	.87	.87	.54
189	.60	.42	.74	.94	.54	.46	.87	.83	.87	.94	.87	.49	.47	.52	.52	.52	.50	.49	.47	.49	.50	.67	.46	.45	.46
190	.72	.78	.64	.78	.76	.74	.77	.77	.76	.78	.79	.46	.47	.68	.49	.61	.47	.48	.50	.52	.50	.72	.48	.46	.47
191	.65	.57	.70	.66	.60	.62	.60	.59	.61	.63	.71	.86	.83	.59	.53	.74	.81	.82	.79	.82	.79	.77	.83	.86	.85
192	.84	.85	.69	.66	.87	.85	.88	.85	.88	.94	.87	.55	.54	.64	.59	.58	.55	.54	.53	.55	.55	.81	.52	.53	.53
193	.60	.54	.63	.61	.61	.63	.62	.63	.60	.56	.60	.79	.75	.73	.58	.77	.92	.91	.87	.90	.92	.84	.71	.85	.84
194	.53	.48	.66	.61	.50	.52	.51	.48	.52	.60	.68	.78	.76	.58	.46	.66	.69	.70	.65	.69	.67	.73	.88	.78	.77
195	.61	.55	.64	.68	.61	.61	.61	.59	.62	.66	.73	.79	.76	.59	.50	.69	.75	.74	.70	.70	.69	.73	.74	.77	.77
196	.52	.47	.61	.63	.50	.51	.50	.48	.51	.62	.67	.80	.78	.62	.49	.64	.72	.70	.66	.70	.69	.77	.74	.80	.77
197	.46	.39	.55	.61	.44	.46	.43	.42	.45	.55	.67	.78	.76	.61	.46	.60	.70	.70	.66	.73	.64	.77	.73	.82	.51
198	.66	.76	.62	.68	.62	.62	.63	.62	.62	.64	.74	.79	.74	.67	.57	.67	.84	.86	.85	.84	.84	.78	.78	.78	.76
199	.53	.49	.61	.61	.52	.53	.51	.50	.53	.61	.72	.80	.76	.61	.50	.65	.69	.72	.68	.72	.67	.73	.73	.81	.77
200	.47	.42	.57	.65	.54	.46	.46	.44	.47	.60	.66	.80	.78	.60	.47	.62	.71	.72	.67	.71	.66	.69	.72	.59	.62
201	.53	.20	.60	.65	.54	.55	.54	.52	.55	.65	.70	.76	.75	.62	.54	.61	.65	.67	.64	.67	.62	.72	.67	.49	.50
202	.64	.78	.72	.61	.49	.59	.61	.59	.59	.62	.74	.78	.76	.61	.53	.77	.75	.75	.72	.74	.73	.77	.80	.78	.53
203	.51	.46	.58	.61	.49	.50	.49	.47	.50	.60	.67	.78	.76	.59	.47	.62	.71	.73	.69	.72	.67	.75	.73	.51	.51
204	.61	.56	.69	.77	.59	.60	.60	.57	.62	.69	.74	.79	.76	.66	.55	.71	.77	.77	.72	.76	.75	.80	.78	.82	.53
205	.85	.83	.74	.67	.86	.85	.84	.87	.83	.62	.72	.81	.67	.74	.70	.81	.70	.73	.68	.72	.95	.88	.73	.79	.84
206	.89	.83	.84	.86	.89	.88	.90	.89	.88	.82	.86	.83	.78	.82	.65	.83	.88	.88	.85	.89	.90	.85	.90	.86	.94
207	.78	.81	.76	.95	.82	.81	.84	.80	.83	.94	.88	.74	.73	.78	.69	.83	.86	.88	.87	.89	.93	.89	.84	.92	.79
208	.81	.81	.74	.93	.85	.81	.87	.84	.85	.79	.81	.78	.75	.73	.73	.70	.57	.59	.81	.62	.63	.81	.58	.54	.53
209	.92	.86	.77	.83	.96	.93	.96	.96	.95	.79	.67	.51	.52	.62	.66	.65	.53	.55	.54	.57	.60	.75	.53	.50	.52
210	.64	.52	.62	.55	.58	.60	.57	.61	.56	.49	.54	.81	.80	.79	.55	.81	.92	.94	.95	.76	.75	.80	.78	.86	.85
211	.61	.48	.65	.50	.54	.56	.53	.57	.52	.45	.57	.83	.81	.82	.70	.87	.88	.88	.87	.89	.90	.85	.95	.92	.94
212	.72	.61	.62	.58	.70	.70	.69	.72	.66	.51	.59	.74	.73	.78	.73	.83	.86	.88	.87	.89	.93	.89	.84	.79	.79
213	.82	.81	.70	.76	.83	.83	.85	.88	.84	.72	.55	.51	.53	.77	.73	.70	.57	.59	.81	.62	.63	.81	.58	.54	.55

	151	152	153	154	155	156	157	158	159	160	161	162	163	164	165	166	167	168	169	170	171	172	173	174	175
164	.65	.69	.80	.73	.74	.68	.73	.74	.78	.74	.68	.77	.74	1.00											
165	.74	.85	.90	.74	.89	.91	.81	.77	.84	.79	.89	.85	.93	.78	1.00										
166	.88	.68	.75	.83	.77	.86	.85	.71	.88	.85	.79	.87	.87	.71	.84	1.00									
167	.86	.66	.73	.79	.79	.88	.84	.67	.87	.87	.82	.83	.84	.69	.82	.97	1.00								
168	.47	.69	.76	.48	.59	.54	.51	.72	.52	.53	.54	.52	.61	.60	.66	.53	.49	1.00							
169	.62	.68	.81	.68	.67	.64	.72	.74	.78	.69	.62	.81	.77	.76	.76	.67	.62	.75	1.00						
170	.60	.66	.73	.55	.68	.69	.64	.65	.67	.56	.66	.62	.66	.68	.73	.62	.63	.70	.72	1.00					
171	.44	.74	.79	.43	.67	.65	.49	.74	.58	.49	.64	.56	.67	.62	.72	.58	.56	.83	.70	.76	1.00				
172	.47	.70	.80	.50	.70	.65	.58	.71	.57	.56	.65	.66	.68	.76	.75	.58	.58	.78	.84	.76	.84	1.00			
173	.43	.88	.88	.48	.78	.69	.57	.73	.57	.56	.72	.61	.71	.70	.77	.56	.55	.82	.79	.87	.88	.89	1.00		
174	.47	.80	.89	.53	.76	.68	.56	.78	.68	.61	.70	.66	.66	.75	.79	.60	.54	.85	.87	.84	.88	.94	.95	1.00	
175	.60	.82	.77	.63	.72	.60	.65	.70	.71	.70	.58	.80	.72	.79	.75	.66	.69	.73	.95	.76	.83	.88	.77	.87	1.00
176	.52	.62	.86	.54	.85	.77	.64	.75	.64	.62	.80	.65	.72	.75	.82	.63	.65	.80	.81	.80	.83	.85	.89	.90	.81
177	.54	.64	.75	.54	.65	.63	.58	.72	.66	.56	.62	.72	.71	.73	.74	.60	.64	.78	.76	.79	.86	.94	.91	.91	.88
178	.61	.63	.77	.63	.66	.66	.78	.61	.67	.73	.45	.60	.63	.75	.74	.66	.64	.73	.61	.61	.57	.78	.64	.73	.80
179	.46	.68	.79	.50	.65	.58	.57	.71	.57	.57	.59	.59	.63	.72	.68	.54	.51	.78	.80	.85	.85	.95	.91	.94	.86
180	.48	.61	.73	.55	.61	.55	.56	.68	.68	.56	.54	.73	.66	.81	.70	.57	.54	.69	.87	.84	.86	.94	.90	.94	.87
181	.62	.64	.78	.64	.65	.64	.65	.73	.81	.64	.60	.74	.71	.80	.77	.68	.65	.76	.86	.67	.46	.59	.51	.56	.62
182	.80	.80	.86	.51	.87	.82	.65	.72	.85	.81	.86	.67	.75	.68	.84	.69	.63	.75	.76	.59	.45	.52	.47	.51	.60
183	.38	.81	.87	.58	.76	.74	.68	.77	.83	.72	.72	.76	.83	.72	.86	.65	.66	.82	.90	.79	.67	.86	.76	.82	.88
184	.40	.50	.64	.50	.54	.43	.51	.61	.56	.69	.45	.60	.53	.75	.59	.42	.42	.58	.75	.61	.57	.78	.64	.73	.80
185	.50	.76	.84	.52	.78	.73	.60	.71	.74	.58	.59	.69	.74	.75	.84	.61	.51	.77	.82	.85	.85	.95	.91	.94	.86
186	.50	.61	.82	.51	.73	.70	.58	.71	.68	.56	.70	.68	.74	.74	.70	.60	.60	.79	.83	.84	.86	.94	.90	.94	.87
187	.81	.64	.68	.64	.72	.75	.58	.64	.81	.64	.60	.74	.71	.75	.77	.74	.65	.76	.86	.67	.46	.59	.51	.56	.62
188	.53	.30	.67	.84	.69	.82	.85	.65	.85	.83	.86	.82	.75	.73	.84	.85	.83	.45	.76	.80	.83	.85	.89	.90	.84
189	.43	.58	.68	.48	.59	.51	.52	.61	.57	.49	.52	.56	.63	.71	.59	.42	.42	.64	.90	.79	.67	.86	.76	.82	.88
190	.86	.60	.71	.86	.60	.74	.81	.66	.82	.79	.68	.77	.72	.73	.67	.56	.54	.69	.72	.80	.45	.57	.50	.55	.62
191	.85	.64	.73	.56	.64	.57	.59	.65	.60	.71	.56	.58	.58	.74	.65	.49	.48	.50	.62	.65	.69	.86	.79	.84	.78
192	.85	.70	.75	.79	.83	.88	.88	.71	.82	.82	.83	.81	.82	.70	.82	.84	.85	.49	.71	.71	.53	.61	.59	.61	.60
193	.77	.47	.58	.78	.59	.59	.74	.56	.75	.73	.55	.69	.61	.67	.63	.65	.63	.39	.57	.52	.32	.48	.38	.46	.57
194	.76	.52	.64	.77	.66	.68	.74	.56	.83	.75	.63	.74	.67	.71	.73	.72	.66	.44	.52	.65	.44	.59	.48	.56	.65
195	.79	.48	.59	.80	.58	.61	.73	.59	.78	.66	.55	.68	.61	.68	.63	.68	.66	.41	.54	.57	.36	.49	.39	.47	.56
196	.77	.41	.52	.81	.52	.57	.78	.54	.74	.68	.55	.63	.55	.62	.58	.66	.64	.37	.54	.51	.29	.42	.32	.40	.51
197	.78	.66	.69	.76	.76	.79	.78	.64	.78	.71	.75	.72	.72	.70	.75	.74	.74	.50	.57	.73	.51	.61	.57	.59	.58
198	.79	.47	.58	.78	.57	.60	.72	.58	.77	.70	.54	.69	.62	.69	.65	.68	.65	.42	.55	.56	.36	.50	.39	.48	.58
199	.79	.55	.65	.77	.56	.57	.71	.58	.69	.66	.52	.64	.57	.65	.60	.66	.61	.48	.55	.54	.32	.45	.35	.43	.58
200	.80	.44	.60	.79	.56	.57	.67	.58	.76	.66	.52	.64	.57	.68	.63	.64	.60	.39	.56	.57	.39	.51	.42	.51	.58
201	.73	.48	.66	.77	.66	.69	.79	.63	.76	.67	.69	.82	.72	.74	.72	.73	.69	.48	.67	.67	.44	.57	.49	.56	.68
202	.78	.57	.66	.79	.55	.59	.70	.55	.76	.67	.52	.67	.59	.66	.62	.66	.64	.40	.52	.56	.35	.48	.35	.44	.56
203	.78	.43	.54	.77	.59	.59	.70	.68	.80	.78	.66	.74	.69	.76	.72	.71	.69	.48	.61	.64	.44	.58	.51	.57	.62
204	.80	.60	.70	.81	.70	.69	.81	.68	.80	.78	.66	.81	.86	.77	.91	.76	.60	.71	.85	.70	.70	.76	.78	.79	.75
205	.70	.82	.88	.72	.86	.84	.78	.73	.80	.78	.68	.73	.71	.73	.75	.61	.44	.69	.77	.83	.72	.88	.81	.87	.85
206	.58	.69	.77	.59	.73	.68	.69	.69	.66	.67	.50	.58	.56	.74	.63	.46	.44	.69	.82	.82	.68	.85	.76	.83	.80
207	.46	.60	.71	.52	.59	.51	.56	.72	.59	.54	.62	.63	.64	.74	.70	.54	.52	.73	.77	.76	.76	.88	.84	.88	.81
208	.56	.70	.78	.54	.69	.61	.60	.71	.62	.59	.69	.64	.68	.69	.77	.55	.54	.75	.79	.79	.76	.87	.86	.89	.80
209	.50	.74	.82	.54	.75	.68	.70	.73	.74	.71	.69	.64	.68	.70	.64	.54	.54	.54	.62	.72	.51	.62	.63	.64	.62
210	.88	.76	.79	.82	.85	.91	.89	.73	.83	.87	.81	.85	.89	.70	.87	.92	.90	.48	.61	.72	.59	.57	.51	.57	.62
211	.93	.72	.78	.87	.79	.86	.95	.76	.85	.93	.81	.88	.92	.74	.84	.91	.89	.59	.85	.64	.53	.57	.57	.61	.66
212	.86	.86	.88	.77	.94	.94	.87	.77	.85	.83	.93	.85	.92	.73	.93	.88	.89	.59	.70	.72	.66	.69	.73	.73	.67
213	.54	.76	.84	.55	.75	.70	.64	.75	.69	.62	.70	.70	.75	.74	.80	.64	.64	.83	.86	.85	.87	.95	.92	.95	.87

Appendix B: Intercorrelations

	176	177	178	179	180	181	182	183	184	185	186	187	188	189	190	191	192	193	194	195	196	197	198	199	200
176	1.00																								
177	.83	1.00																							
178	.82	.87	1.00																						
179	.84	.84	.81	1.00																					
180	.77	.88	.80	.82	1.00																				
181	.81	.89	.85	.82	.90	1.00																			
182	.96	.83	.78	.78	.72	.76	1.00																		
183	.90	.87	.85	.83	.84	.85	.88	1.00																	
184	.67	.74	.72	.73	.86	.76	.72	.68	1.00																
185	.94	.92	.82	.84	.87	.86	.92	.93	.73	1.00															
186	.92	.91	.82	.84	.88	.88	.89	.95	.72	.97	1.00														
187	.61	.62	.67	.54	.61	.66	.59	.59	.57	.61	.58	1.00													
188	.74	.53	.63	.48	.55	.64	.53	.58	.48	.53	.52	.81	1.00												
189	.73	.85	.79	.78	.83	.78	.70	.74	.53	.80	.80	.69	.50	1.00											
190	.71	.86	.77	.81	.90	.87	.73	.82	.57	.86	.87	.55	.59	.82	1.00										
191	.57	.60	.67	.52	.58	.66	.56	.59	.53	.58	.56	.95	.85	.64	.53	1.00									
192	.30	.86	.83	.81	.82	.80	.72	.77	.74	.83	.80	.71	.54	.75	.80	.71	1.00								
193	.67	.62	.71	.57	.56	.63	.70	.65	.47	.64	.61	.88	.81	.60	.54	.88	.65	1.00							
194	.49	.50	.60	.44	.54	.59	.45	.48	.53	.48	.47	.88	.79	.60	.47	.90	.62	.75	1.00						
195	.58	.61	.66	.53	.63	.69	.55	.59	.57	.61	.60	.91	.80	.68	.58	.90	.76	.81	.89	1.00					
196	.47	.53	.60	.47	.54	.61	.39	.48	.51	.49	.47	.90	.79	.65	.50	.92	.72	.76	.93	.90	1.00				
197	.42	.46	.56	.41	.47	.56	.43	.44	.44	.42	.41	.85	.77	.52	.39	.89	.64	.73	.84	.86	.92	1.00			
198	.65	.61	.66	.53	.55	.63	.65	.61	.48	.63	.60	.91	.80	.66	.55	.91	.72	.90	.78	.85	.81	.76	1.00		
199	.43	.53	.61	.47	.56	.62	.45	.51	.53	.50	.50	.89	.79	.61	.49	.93	.63	.75	.92	.90	.93	.91	.76	1.00	
200	.49	.49	.58	.43	.50	.59	.45	.51	.53	.45	.44	.88	.81	.57	.50	.91	.74	.92	.68	.89	.95	.93	.68	.91	1.00
201	.51	.55	.60	.49	.57	.64	.47	.51	.55	.51	.52	.89	.76	.65	.54	.90	.60	.93	.72	.90	.94	.93	.60	.95	.94
202	.57	.58	.68	.52	.63	.66	.56	.62	.62	.59	.58	.90	.80	.65	.54	.91	.66	.91	.84	.89	.84	.80	.63	.85	.87
203	.46	.52	.56	.44	.54	.60	.43	.47	.51	.49	.47	.90	.79	.61	.49	.91	.62	.76	.91	.91	.94	.91	.76	.93	.94
204	.57	.58	.68	.56	.61	.67	.56	.59	.59	.58	.56	.92	.82	.68	.55	.93	.71	.84	.92	.91	.92	.88	.92	.91	.91
205	.82	.74	.74	.71	.73	.77	.81	.84	.62	.83	.81	.79	.70	.70	.57	.80	.74	.82	.68	.77	.68	.64	.86	.69	.65
206	.85	.90	.87	.82	.84	.81	.82	.85	.74	.87	.84	.72	.57	.88	.79	.69	.90	.72	.60	.68	.60	.52	.80	.59	.55
207	.78	.84	.82	.78	.84	.80	.69	.77	.78	.81	.79	.67	.52	.95	.82	.65	.94	.60	.62	.68	.63	.55	.70	.63	.59
208	.84	.86	.82	.84	.84	.82	.78	.82	.75	.87	.84	.68	.56	.93	.85	.65	.93	.66	.60	.68	.60	.52	.69	.60	.56
209	.89	.86	.79	.81	.81	.79	.85	.87	.68	.91	.88	.66	.50	.86	.74	.65	.89	.55	.55	.64	.55	.49	.67	.55	.51
210	.68	.63	.69	.57	.55	.67	.72	.70	.43	.67	.65	.81	.86	.52	.57	.82	.59	.92	.69	.76	.73	.69	.69	.69	.70
211	.64	.60	.73	.57	.65	.65	.67	.69	.45	.60	.59	.80	.87	.48	.52	.83	.55	.68	.72	.74	.73	.71	.85	.72	.72
212	.71	.67	.71	.63	.70	.70	.67	.78	.50	.76	.73	.78	.80	.57	.62	.78	.63	.66	.66	.74	.67	.62	.82	.66	.64
213	.92	.91	.86	.87	.86	.88	.88	.93	.71	.94	.94	.60	.58	.80	.88	.58	.81	.49	.49	.60	.49	.43	.63	.52	.47

	201	202	203	204	205	206	207	208	209	210	211	212	213	214	215	216	217
201	1.00																
202	.83	1.00															
203	.92	.84	1.00														
204	.91	.88	.90	1.00													
205	.63	.78	.66	.77	1.00												
206	.61	.71	.61	.69	.88	1.00											
207	.67	.67	.59	.71	.81	.89	1.00										
208	.64	.66	.59	.71	.70	.70	.94	1.00									
209	.59	.66	.54	.64	.75	.71	.85	.87	1.00								
210	.67	.77	.70	.77	.80	.67	.54	.62	.62	1.00							
211	.67	.79	.71	.79	.79	.71	.51	.58	.58	.93	1.00						
212	.64	.75	.65	.76	.88	.73	.59	.68	.72	.94	.90	1.00					
213	.52	.59	.43	.59	.79	.86	.81	.87	.85	.69	.65	.76	1.00				

	1	2	3	4	5	6	7	8	9	10	11	12	13	14	15	16	17	18	19	20	21	22	23	24	25
214	.52	.57	.60	.54	.69	.33	.53	.48	.52	.46	.69	.41	.41	.54	.33	.60	.60	.59	.62	.70	.46	.60	.60	.52	.63
215	.53	.59	.55	.51	.70	.41	.56	.51	.55	.51	.69	.48	.47	.55	.42	.55	.61	.57	.62	.68	.49	.64	.61	.56	.57
216	.58	.65	.65	.61	.73	.43	.61	.57	.60	.53	.72	.50	.50	.62	.42	.63	.66	.65	.67	.76	.53	.70	.65	.62	.63
217	.48	.54	.54	.50	.66	.38	.55	.49	.56	.46	.63	.45	.44	.53	.39	.54	.57	.57	.58	.71	.48	.63	.60	.57	.53

	26	27	28	29	30	31	32	33	34	35	36	37	38	39	40	41	42	43	44	45	46	47	48	49	50
214	.37	.53	.50	.52	.49	.52	.55	.40	.55	.50	.49	.76	.66	.68	.77	.33	.64	.53	.55	.73	.50	.57	.65	.56	.42
215	.44	.55	.52	.54	.47	.53	.56	.46	.59	.53	.49	.76	.60	.65	.76	.42	.66	.57	.57	.75	.52	.59	.65	.60	.49
216	.46	.61	.57	.60	.55	.59	.62	.49	.63	.57	.56	.77	.66	.72	.78	.43	.69	.61	.62	.77	.58	.64	.72	.62	.51
217	.41	.51	.49	.51	.47	.50	.53	.44	.56	.49	.49	.74	.55	.61	.69	.38	.60	.54	.54	.73	.51	.57	.65	.60	.47

	51	52	53	54	55	56	57	58	59	60	61	62	63	64	65	66	67	68	69	70	71	72	73	74	75
214	.67	.63	.55	.56	.65	.63	.58	.35	.40	.63	.43	.45	.53	.75	.75	.73	.66	.68	.60	.56	.50	.57	.57	.77	.76
215	.72	.57	.50	.58	.64	.66	.62	.42	.44	.61	.46	.52	.56	.74	.74	.68	.60	.65	.55	.54	.48	.60	.58	.74	.73
216	.75	.67	.60	.65	.70	.72	.67	.44	.49	.71	.51	.54	.58	.80	.78	.76	.70	.72	.63	.62	.57	.65	.65	.82	.80
217	.70	.61	.55	.58	.64	.67	.61	.40	.43	.65	.46	.47	.52	.75	.74	.72	.63	.65	.55	.54	.49	.59	.57	.78	.78

	76	77	78	79	80	81	82	83	84	85	86	87	88	89	90	91	92	93	94	95	96	97	98	99	100
214	.76	.79	.73	.78	.67	.43	.64	.35	.48	.76	.50	.36	.53	.62	.71	.63	.65	.63	.82	.76	.77	.81	.84	.69	.59
215	.74	.76	.70	.76	.65	.48	.62	.41	.51	.73	.54	.44	.59	.61	.76	.72	.73	.72	.85	.81	.82	.82	.85	.75	.67
216	.81	.83	.77	.82	.71	.52	.69	.43	.56	.79	.59	.46	.62	.67	.75	.68	.69	.68	.82	.76	.81	.84	.87	.73	.61
217	.78	.80	.71	.80	.61	.46	.60	.39	.50	.74	.53	.42	.57	.64	.69	.67	.70	.66	.78	.72	.76	.83	.85	.74	.63

	101	102	103	104	105	106	107	108	109	110	111	112	113	114	115	116	117	118	119	120	121	122	123	124	125
214	.76	.70	.77	.78	.71	.74	.73	.71	.71	.80	.76	.84	.81	.65	.73	.72	.76	.76	.76	.64	.79	.79	.76	.84	.87
215	.80	.78	.79	.82	.77	.80	.80	.78	.76	.80	.80	.82	.85	.74	.79	.79	.80	.81	.83	.73	.83	.86	.83	.84	.86
216	.81	.76	.81	.83	.77	.79	.76	.75	.76	.79	.78	.86	.81	.71	.76	.77	.80	.81	.81	.67	.82	.85	.78	.86	.88
217	.79	.75	.79	.82	.75	.79	.76	.75	.74	.77	.77	.79	.78	.67	.75	.78	.79	.80	.82	.67	.81	.84	.78	.84	.88

	126	127	128	129	130	131	132	133	134	135	136	137	138	139	140	141	142	143	144	145	146	147	148	149	150
214	.84	.80	.66	.76	.86	.83	.86	.89	.84	.70	.69	.48	.49	.69	.75	.67	.56	.58	.60	.60	.64	.77	.55	.51	.52
215	.83	.83	.73	.81	.87	.85	.87	.88	.86	.77	.77	.52	.52	.69	.79	.67	.57	.54	.54	.56	.58	.77	.54	.53	.54
216	.86	.81	.71	.78	.88	.86	.88	.90	.87	.73	.75	.57	.58	.73	.75	.73	.62	.64	.65	.67	.70	.83	.63	.59	.60
217	.85	.82	.69	.76	.89	.86	.88	.91	.87	.72	.75	.51	.52	.67	.73	.67	.52	.55	.56	.58	.59	.78	.53	.51	.52

	151	152	153	154	155	156	157	158	159	160	161	162	163	164	165	166	167	168	169	170	171	172	173	174	175
214	.51	.87	.89	.53	.80	.73	.63	.75	.63	.61	.75	.66	.76	.71	.82	.62	.61	.82	.81	.83	.86	.90	.96	.95	.80
215	.51	.77	.86	.55	.74	.67	.62	.75	.62	.61	.68	.63	.69	.75	.78	.59	.57	.85	.86	.85	.85	.93	.92	.97	.86
216	.59	.82	.89	.60	.82	.78	.68	.77	.70	.67	.78	.72	.79	.76	.86	.68	.67	.82	.86	.86	.84	.92	.92	.95	.85
217	.50	.75	.84	.52	.72	.68	.59	.72	.65	.58	.68	.66	.73	.72	.82	.61	.59	.83	.85	.84	.86	.93	.90	.95	.88

	176	177	178	179	180	181	182	183	184	185	186	187	188	189	190	191	192	193	194	195	196	197	198	199	200
214	.94	.86	.81	.84	.78	.81	.90	.93	.65	.93	.91	.56	.53	.77	.82	.56	.80	.65	.44	.54	.46	.38	.63	.46	.41
215	.94	.90	.88	.87	.83	.86	.88	.92	.74	.93	.92	.58	.52	.82	.83	.58	.85	.61	.49	.58	.51	.44	.61	.50	.47
216	.96	.90	.86	.85	.83	.86	.93	.94	.70	.96	.94	.64	.60	.79	.83	.63	.83	.71	.53	.63	.53	.47	.68	.54	.50
217	.92	.92	.84	.85	.85	.87	.89	.95	.71	.95	.97	.57	.52	.79	.85	.55	.81	.60	.47	.58	.47	.41	.59	.49	.44

	201	202	203	204	205	206	207	208	209	210	211	212	213	214	215	216	217
214	.48	.55	.43	.56	.80	.34	.79	.86	.87	.69	.63	.78	.93	1.00			
215	.54	.58	.48	.60	.84	.86	.84	.88	.88	.63	.61	.72	.92	.95	1.00		
216	.56	.63	.52	.64	.84	.87	.81	.87	.89	.73	.70	.82	.94	.95	.95	1.00	
217	.52	.57	.46	.56	.79	.85	.80	.84	.88	.64	.60	.72	.93	.92	.95	.94	1.00

Appendix C

The Wherry-Wherry Hierarchial Rotation Method

Notes on Hierarchical Rotation
Robert J. Wherry

Early factor extraction methods (Spearman g, Holzinger Bi-Factor) resulted in immediately interpretable factors that explained the entire correlation table. In the Holzinger case, group factors had nearly zero loadings on all variables except their marker variables. The only difficulty was the fact that these models did not fit most correlation tables very accurately.

Later extraction methods (centroid, principal factor, minimum residual, maximum likelihood) will fit any table of correlations, but interpretation of the loadings as extracted is not possible until after rotation. The concept of simple structure has been used to achieve rotations that are both meaningful and objective. The application of this principle to rotation has resulted, however, in three competing rotation techniques: (1) varimax (2) oblique, and (3) hierarchical.

Varimax Rotation. Factors remain orthogonal, and the loadings explain the entire correlation matrix. The marker variables for the group factors are usually discernible. Marker variables for *other* factors are likely, however, to have definitely nonzero loadings as well as the true loadings. This overlap sometimes makes interpretation difficult. The factors are both statistically and linearly independent.

Oblique Rotation. Factors become correlated, and the loadings alone will no longer reproduce the correlation matrix. Group factor loadings are clean. Marker variables for *other* factors no longer have nonzero loadings. The overlap loadings removed are now accounted for only by the table of correlations among the factor reference vectors. Unless higher order factors are extracted and presented, the analysis is incomplete. The factors are linearly independent but are not statistically independent.

Hierarchical Rotation. This concept was first proposed by Thompson as a basis for bringing the various methods back together. The method was extended by Lieman-Schmid (using oblique loadings and factor intercorrelations as a starting point) and by Wherry-Wherry (using varimax loadings as a starting point). The method adds general and subgeneral factors *as needed* to make the group factors really clean (keep all nonmarker loadings near zero). Final factor loadings do reproduce the entire correlation matrix. The final factors are statistically independent but are not linearly independent.

Steps in the Wherry-Wherry Hierarchical Rotation Method

The computer program used to carry out the Wherry-Wherry rotation is based on the following steps:

1. Factors are extracted by the principal factor method. This is followed by the minimal residual method to ensure correct communalities.

2. Initial rotation is carried out by the usual varimax rotation technique. Variables are then assigned to clusters representing each factor on the basis of the variables' highest absolute loading.

3. Using the above clusters, the usual multiple group centroid method is carried out to obtain the correct cluster intercorrelation matrix.

4. The cluster intercorrelation matrix is then factored as in (1) above, and uniqueness loadings are appended to represent the clusters.

5. The above extended factor matrix is then converted into a transformation matrix whose transpose is its own inverse.

6. The multiplication of the original varimax loadings by the above transformation matrix yields the hierarchical loadings.

7. The computer output is such that the user can choose the most meaningful final result (that is, can accept or reject various hierarchical levels produced by the program).

8. As in any machine rotation the user may want to make minor further orthogonal rotations between some of the factors to ensure more meaningfulness, but this is rarely needed.

Appendix D

Factor Loadings, Factor Analysis VI

APPENDIX D

FACTOR LOADINGS, FACTOR ANALYSIS VI

NO.	CODE	1	2	3	4	5	6	7	8	9	10	11
001	AC AAA	802	056	023	277	-030	226	001	167	167	158	069
002	AC	831	112	051	206	-033	268	013	184	178	086	048
003	AC CPA	786	078	030	151	-005	319	200	191	218	002	153
004	AC IND	772	043	025	165	-036	334	184	202	188	078	178
005	ARCH	800	181	-026	189	-162	-005	046	098	187	095	-087
006	AUTO M	736	-094	068	035	-133	107	-290	094	005	492	107
007	BAKER	836	008	134	057	-181	101	016	211	028	268	156
008	BANKER	834	-010	100	210	-024	177	-087	118	107	240	122
009	BARBER	846	-009	149	005	-082	077	-065	181	-051	289	192
010	BKKPR	793	035	129	183	-056	181	-218	241	052	291	052
011	BKSMGR	894	145	031	198	079	089	-076	056	182	064	015
012	BRKLYR	789	-083	112	-016	-167	151	-217	141	000	388	087
013	BDG CN	793	-081	029	179	-140	123	-156	103	125	414	081
014	BUYER	873	-018	093	164	-071	184	-017	146	055	202	178
015	CRPNTR	720	-095	110	064	-173	064	-290	081	058	448	083
016	CC EX	850	-014	024	291	023	143	226	015	120	035	162
017	CHEMST	795	166	-072	111	-096	174	102	-001	145	196	-036
018	CLTH R	859	-006	101	194	-002	153	027	136	079	058	226
019	COMPRG	765	172	-092	079	-120	273	056	160	214	155	-003
020	COUNHS	865	193	-018	178	-001	066	243	-006	034	076	117
021	COAGAG	774	010	014	223	006	151	000	-065	239	389	069
022	DNTIST	871	107	-002	031	-025	103	005	074	-036	233	035
023	DPTSTS	863	-008	195	029	-061	076	016	090	-021	158	221
024	DRCTFN	865	016	107	107	-021	087	008	070	-105	280	137
025	EDNWSP	827	057	-154	179	103	151	-039	046	206	-035	-104
026	ELECTR	758	-109	066	060	-221	122	-249	116	000	468	105
027	ENGCVL	837	020	-060	196	-074	225	-019	059	167	281	041
028	ENGELE	812	014	-083	218	-070	188	-010	047	057	303	080

029	ENGHAC	824	009	-043	207	-097	201	012	019	095	273	129
030	ENGIND	783	-017	-043	274	-135	229	158	040	101	221	170
031	ENGMCH	811	012	-100	118	-094	207	-004	045	101	282	106
032	ENG MM	835	052	-135	184	-082	206	055	021	147	277	054
033	FARMER	732	-032	055	161	007	146	-106	028	200	471	078
034	FLORST	844	020	101	162	-076	125	-072	088	106	232	152
035	FORSTR	801	006	-071	114	010	213	-089	-002	230	379	012
036	INS AG	839	-041	094	196	015	186	031	030	077	214	247
037	INTDEC	738	281	132	103	-134	-134	031	031	131	-064	-030
038	JOURN	823	057	-170	171	121	155	006	059	212	-041	-096
039	LAWYER	856	144	009	201	043	098	142	014	254	055	-037
040	LIBRAR	822	294	034	130	002	043	121	-032	213	-095	-151
041	MCHNST	739	-099	069	069	-154	113	-257	128	-007	469	085
042	MATHM	791	233	-048	115	-128	159	-008	055	185	116	-073
043	MATHHS	803	117	012	174	-102	189	-042	057	060	255	070
044	METEOR	826	076	-068	154	-066	206	-002	001	172	276	035
045	MINIST	809	291	021	142	016	-092	260	-065	-035	101	-051
046	MTLMGR	858	-096	059	195	-034	130	-056	113	064	308	166
047	NRSRYM	828	064	092	145	-082	172	-019	090	243	258	091
048	OPTMST	871	136	013	055	-039	176	125	050	030	106	093
049	OSTPTH	829	114	-016	-039	-007	102	075	042	-109	261	-019
050	PNTR H	759	-054	124	004	-190	024	-238	143	-002	427	068
051	PEDTRN	851	238	-021	-037	-022	105	099	-007	027	132	-106
052	PERS M	847	041	-035	219	010	093	278	-013	077	081	151
053	PHAR S	797	-031	065	013	037	220	287	-021	-008	141	276
054	PHARM	854	055	041	040	-014	132	007	132	-051	229	118
055	PHOTOG	841	068	-002	095	-125	115	060	169	075	098	123
056	PHYTHR	856	136	-025	-064	-025	151	108	039	-064	181	041
057	PHYSN	820	140	-034	-006	041	101	039	034	-044	257	-070
058	PLUMBR	755	-115	067	095	-125	095	-281	095	026	475	084

Note: The factors are identified in table 48, p. 185.

NO.	CODE	1	2	3	4	5	6	7	8	9	10	11
059	PLMBCN	800	-114	023	175	-087	146	-140	089	033	413	154
060	PODRST	830	116	057	-036	-037	109	290	036	-079	072	091
061	POLICE	809	-099	-014	-015	-024	221	-110	152	-011	319	063
062	POSTCL	806	-001	148	037	-092	-205	008	195	006	341	053
063	PRNTER	842	-002	-060	212	-077	-196	227	148	018	160	029
064	PSYTST	829	269	-064	-004	-040	068	212	-017	040	-002	-049
065	PSYCCL	808	245	-159	058	-021	073	273	-021	045	-041	020
066	PSYCCN	830	214	-131	163	-019	055	323	-017	041	000	065
067	PSYCIN	820	121	-122	206	-034	168	253	186	097	008	168
068	PSYPRF	786	189	-144	297	-082	268	151	-075	-008	101	-049
069	RADSTA	853	-041	-030	191	022	164	136	102	067	052	178
070	REALES	860	-017	074	247	008	102	032	091	140	183	181
071	SLSENG	803	-050	-010	218	-076	208	104	023	069	209	269
072	SCITHS	776	154	-025	070	-068	170	089	-047	060	284	050
073	SCHSUP	838	087	039	265	035	084	128	-013	153	236	091
074	SOCCWK	892	254	-025	-009	-012	-088	286	-001	026	-022	013
075	SOCWKG	809	260	-042	076	-036	-002	352	003	014	-051	061
076	SOCWKM	855	255	-020	045	-004	003	294	-013	-001	016	012
077	SOCPSY	841	268	-065	002	023	006	252	-008	047	-040	022
078	SOCRES	777	278	-122	106	-076	051	320	068	100	-065	-042
079	SOCSCH	810	312	-039	052	002	-035	320	-024	010	-043	016
080	STATCN	794	218	-043	176	-128	180	151	099	225	029	-020
081	SUPVFM	813	-049	101	087	-149	134	-135	136	-019	396	104
082	TRVLAG	871	039	085	175	-029	148	115	100	160	043	149
083	TRKDRV	733	-129	197	016	-107	103	-183	081	015	438	147
084	TV REP	834	-041	033	095	-133	164	-054	159	-011	356	145
085	U PSTR	776	282	-059	095	036	-016	401	-047	019	043	028

086	VETRN	792	046	-034	-010	052	177	-023	006	091	363	030
087	WELDER	753	-095	085	003	-156	113	-241	133	-015	474	096
088	X RAY	851	076	014	-006	-059	111	-026	056	-136	304	-008
089	YMCASC	826	112	013	267	-011	005	204	170	-006	130	114
090	FACNT	769	401	220	174	-009	-035	086	110	051	064	-055
091	FBNKCL	715	370	380	-003	020	-041	-280	091	-105	032	012
092	FBEAUT	705	346	416	-086	022	-080	-243	043	-096	081	056
093	FBKKPR	719	378	358	054	-013	-054	-267	102	-065	080	-021
094	FBKMGR	780	436	194	067	024	-051	-097	013	073	-057	-116
095	FCTLIB	721	470	189	066	060	-144	-106	-090	092	-037	-219
096	FCMPRG	748	439	038	057	-086	052	-052	102	132	038	-023
097	FCNSHS	773	476	170	114	071	-167	121	-085	-045	-019	-025
098	F DEAN	787	473	098	135	073	-175	180	-078	002	-027	-049
099	FDNTAS	752	393	284	085	043	-106	-091	-025	-229	104	-049
100	FDPTSW	740	289	439	-053	-040	-060	-144	-032	-091	078	124
101	FDTNAD	785	441	223	037	-106	-043	170	-029	-021	048	-051
102	FDTCDM	756	426	257	020	-126	-051	-001	-056	-017	117	-055
103	FDTCOM	781	419	259	009	-078	-047	096	-013	-013	044	-002
104	FDTHOS	785	467	222	-030	-068	-067	118	-039	-071	085	-069
105	FDTSCH	768	431	262	042	-121	-041	044	-026	-020	100	-037
106	FDTTHR	754	466	275	-075	-055	-053	051	-049	-104	091	-042
107	FFLRST	766	377	324	031	-053	-165	-163	008	-058	049	-003
108	FHMDEM	751	405	252	122	-074	-157	-009	-150	-031	106	-047
109	FHOMEC	728	465	214	025	-134	-061	163	-080	-012	143	-130
110	FINTDC	688	401	177	135	-094	-234	023	017	148	-088	-063
111	FKYPCH	758	397	299	-114	033	-019	092	100	-148	017	036
112	FLAWYR	754	476	056	057	048	-076	133	116	177	-018	-170
113	FLIBR	746	479	187	062	020	-148	-114	-113	083	-086	-152
114	FMATHS	727	422	268	128	-053	-050	-037	-010	011	084	-023
115	FMTLMR	788	377	324	037	001	-139	058	048	-093	040	000
116	FNURSE	767	399	233	-117	076	-090	-095	-090	-217	087	-061
117	FNUTRN	759	458	196	029	-093	-106	-044	-097	-005	055	-099
118	FNUTIN	749	479	244	-048	-068	-066	-026	-072	-056	024	-069

NO.	CODE	1	2	3	4	5	6	7	8	9	10	11
119	FOCCTH	753	426	054	037	-058	-192	-097	-054	-118	024	-092
120	FOFCLK	707	398	362	034	020	-085	054	061	-080	072	-072
121	FPEDRN	755	475	022	-083	-011	-088	-110	-098	-026	022	-184
122	FPHYTH	808	429	093	-070	024	-054	-071	-026	-070	088	-076
123	FPRSCT	732	471	321	-019	034	-165	-107	-096	-042	-014	-067
124	FPSY	767	470	-021	075	-009	-100	-059	-062	049	-066	061
125	FPSYCL	761	482	-040	034	044	-125	-079	-078	004	-094	047
126	FPSYCN	787	468	023	072	016	-144	-056	-078	-013	-060	045
127	FRELED	719	489	117	070	104	-213	-118	-105	-125	052	-058
128	FSCTHS	719	415	108	000	-022	007	038	-121	014	194	-105
129	FSECY	755	443	272	066	093	-112	-174	096	-048	007	-070
130	FSOCCW	770	495	079	016	056	-210	115	-070	016	-074	-093
131	FSOCGR	761	470	079	098	007	-191	200	-091	007	-032	-081
132	FSOCMD	774	490	118	003	077	-210	108	-056	026	-079	-105
133	FSOCPS	767	499	062	-005	068	-168	131	-066	018	-110	-051
134	FSOCSC	758	491	122	-026	057	-223	093	-093	034	-039	-073
135	FSTENO	728	414	309	017	082	-099	-252	072	069	017	-067
136	FX RAY	784	384	170	-094	041	-069	-098	-032	222	170	-102
137	MAG	715	071	-034	016	039	331	005	094	268	404	093
138	MANLHS	698	079	-047	-025	059	316	010	092	273	427	077
139	MARCH	656	229	-108	056	-145	100	129	229	206	096	020
140	MARTED	607	322	-082	021	-116	-058	066	215	173	-032	-033
141	MBIOSC	722	264	-102	-160	050	265	228	067	089	192	-001
142	MBUSAC	727	089	006	097	034	384	136	301	194	080	192
143	MBSGEN	747	041	-018	167	032	325	194	254	191	095	235
144	MBSMRK	735	029	-022	092	048	295	218	235	182	045	274
145	MBSMGT	761	063	-029	104	021	321	230	213	156	089	230

146	MECON	755	110	-036	096	045	323	307	237	213	061	173
147	MELED	827	266	014	-029	017	166	202	092	090	101	118
148	MENGCH	719	106	-068	036	-016	359	182	134	134	239	173
149	MENGCL	732	059	-096	039	-034	365	009	139	167	304	114
150	MENGEL	739	103	-114	048	-068	344	075	126	077	271	112
151	MENGMH	723	085	-119	077	-056	334	059	134	138	282	178
152	MENGL	707	338	-122	-025	189	093	231	105	226	-125	-087
153	MFRNLG	751	386	-034	-085	091	075	094	128	184	-029	-040
154	MFORST	750	071	-121	-019	039	332	001	057	209	386	000
155	MHIST	762	268	-027	-013	135	142	345	159	255	-023	003
156	MLAW	758	172	-079	045	095	226	342	178	271	-024	110
157	MMATH	736	207	-082	016	-027	336	126	234	135	160	089
158	MMUSIC	742	316	-088	-123	-028	108	125	141	-027	-008	021
159	MPHYED	802	088	-013	-110	084	288	117	110	061	151	163
160	MPHYSC	717	208	-125	-065	-024	317	143	114	124	248	008
161	MPOLYS	726	213	-059	020	104	186	409	188	257	-053	072
162	MPREMD	754	206	-044	-150	055	270	265	099	-014	163	091
163	MPSY	741	252	-138	-069	055	219	351	164	057	042	100
164	MCATHB	791	281	059	-122	123	171	078	032	-101	176	-007
165	MSOC	781	291	-100	-007	064	116	306	181	113	029	100
166	MAFCAD	718	093	-087	-098	041	361	237	116	149	141	193
167	MWPCAD	704	089	-050	-080	054	374	273	115	196	118	194
168	GARTED	577	476	024	016	-042	-203	-006	133	074	-074	-008
169	GBIOSC	678	515	063	-160	076	016	-053	011	021	117	030
170	GBUSGN	731	439	205	089	125	028	-039	105	086	-130	178
171	GDRMA	632	459	075	-080	091	-095	122	002	054	-254	192
172	GELED	722	536	218	-066	126	-098	035	-031	-020	-118	129
173	GENGL	674	536	072	-049	195	-106	135	002	113	-187	014
174	GFRNLG	705	622	112	-096	123	-110	070	059	081	-105	053
175	GHELTH	668	444	107	-162	086	007	-019	-004	097	073	057
176	GHISTO	725	514	095	-024	139	-101	133	076	146	-083	039
177	GHMEC	684	527	219	-021	026	-097	051	001	-018	-036	122
178	GMATH	707	517	163	001	-015	037	-069	129	040	018	140

NO.	CODE	1	2	3	4	5	6	7	8	9	10	11
179	GMUSIC	685	500	089	-133	064	-094	039	028	-112	-090	056
180	GNURSE	727	467	166	-194	140	-055	034	-076	-209	054	008
181	GPHYED	755	372	129	-116	093	011	-039	172	-060	004	118
182	GPOLYS	691	467	067	-014	128	-074	238	146	181	-139	095
183	GPSYCH	707	526	-006	-079	101	-075	139	080	014	-070	095
184	GCATHS	650	422	184	-140	088	-028	005	-048	-262	161	-073
185	GSOCSC	735	518	117	-062	175	-133	138	041	004	-097	095
186	GSOC	716	513	078	-056	151	-144	118	052	-031	-093	139
187	FATHRS	908	-022	103	136	-088	120	027	129	046	271	122
188	SONS	744	012	-061	-059	094	337	-138	108	026	279	196
189	MTHRS	762	441	349	-035	031	-153	-122	005	-089	013	-023
190	DGHTRS	673	461	206	-154	255	-025	023	-008	-175	-042	151
191	MALES	892	008	-010	177	-021	144	-052	087	078	307	105
192	FEMALE	826	453	225	060	085	-064	-070	-011	-126	-059	-048
193	DACNT	830	102	002	113	017	251	166	210	168	090	128
194	DAUTOM	769	-011	055	064	-091	087	-123	163	012	455	063
195	DBRBER	822	038	084	026	-030	089	-077	221	-024	300	169
196	DBRKLR	803	-045	080	040	-128	136	-166	163	038	403	095
197	DCRPNT	746	-075	023	054	-105	142	-219	147	082	451	078
198	DCLTHR	879	-006	032	194	070	136	-014	183	093	090	132
199	DELEC	796	-035	051	064	-086	077	-147	147	-023	420	120
200	DMACH	777	-073	050	050	-096	125	-230	162	036	436	111
201	DPNTER	806	-021	085	037	-135	048	-222	175	030	396	062
202	DPHARM	838	060	-011	051	-006	128	-056	203	-044	251	086
203	DPLUMB	789	-061	091	074	-103	088	-140	167	-030	426	135
204	DPSTCL	863	057	053	049	-057	145	-069	219	017	287	037
205	DSOCWK	861	269	-079	044	014	020	184	062	088	001	017
206	XDT	789	493	199	-013	-054	-062	114	041	-014	006	-047
207	XOFCLK	745	472	275	-026	073	-135	-161	095	-069	055	-067

NO.	CODE	12	13	14	15	16	17	18	19	20	21	22	23
208	XSECY		774	473	222	-045	136	-111	-050	112	-046	-026	-034
209	XSOCWK		788	484	135	027	009	-194	302	027	021	-064	-159
210	DBSMNT		778	125	-049	-012	065	314	307	241	173	088	156
211	D ENG		746	147	-123	012	-007	320	211	208	149	189	128
212	DSOCSC		805	215	-074	-034	096	234	284	190	194	009	091
213	XELED		720	512	148	-097	123	-076	099	061	014	-108	155
214	XENGL		712	523	059	-018	180	-073	129	077	103	-149	039
215	XFRNLG		749	566	110	-042	110	-120	-012	093	072	-073	023
216	XSOCSC		746	516	062	-034	153	-075	109	125	088	-071	067
217	XSOC		692	547	068	-056	121	-143	068	088	013	-077	106

NO.	CODE	12	13	14	15	16	17	18	19	20	21	22	23
001	AC AAA	020	186	-106	-028	-039	-009	-020	-132	-186	105	004	-068
002	AC	014	079	-122	004	-020	-041	-001	-117	-175	137	008	-062
003	AC CPA	011	001	-088	-056	006	-066	-002	-161	-110	176	-008	-053
004	AC IND	043	-012	-094	-049	042	-013	-003	-150	-133	155	000	-060
005	ARCH	-073	161	-062	-035	-079	000	-045	-120	270	184	004	011
006	AUTO M	069	-099	057	005	-040	063	070	-006	020	084	-007	030
007	BAKER	051	009	-055	008	005	-058	-033	-016	-005	-014	050	-004
008	BANKER	014	-079	143	-062	-006	005	022	-102	-137	039	074	-027
009	BARBER	092	-122	-007	074	-035	023	130	-031	006	-043	060	-012
010	BKKPR	031	-041	-045	-016	-061	024	020	-041	-218	047	015	-069
011	BKSMGR	037	083	020	047	-115	-074	-030	020	-010	055	161	001
012	BRKLYR	053	-133	033	-018	-058	078	072	-010	052	082	-007	036
013	BDG CN	029	036	-087	-040	-016	-005	026	-057	048	108	016	011
014	BUYER	057	-073	-051	013	-028	-010	-029	-118	-060	085	057	-001

NO.	CODE	12	13	14	15	16	17	18	19	20	21	22	23
015	CRPNTR	056	-158	045	-021	-036	081	105	029	039	094	-019	014
016	CC EX	018	-100	-052	052	-081	-030	-103	-103	012	-025	054	056
017	CHEMST	056	340	006	151	052	-013	036	-034	-066	151	035	001
018	CLTH R	043	-069	-139	053	-046	-127	-110	-081	021	028	112	-009
019	COMPRG	025	296	048	-017	047	035	032	-054	-037	200	003	-031
020	COUNHS	158	011	-064	027	047	082	129	076	-028	-024	064	008
021	COAGAG	-020	-028	-096	112	111	054	026	040	-048	-168	018	043
022	DNTIST	105	109	-100	242	054	076	079	-040	060	138	019	007
023	DPTSTS	-057	-074	-037	042	-153	-057	005	-020	111	-036	021	-077
024	DRCTFN	044	-123	-130	133	019	091	004	-060	-008	039	044	021
025	EDNWSP	046	-011	180	112	-174	-107	-060	074	-030	013	-017	183
026	ELECTR	087	-079	039	-002	-017	075	041	003	006	116	-005	007
027	ENGCVL	023	135	-041	015	008	029	-011	-105	-023	198	006	015
028	ENGELE	068	189	007	021	019	040	-048	-136	-059	191	-015	020
029	ENGHAC	038	160	-038	000	027	037	-056	-142	014	212	-003	009
030	ENGIND	101	090	-037	-021	035	076	-068	-154	-035	174	-035	-011
031	ENGMCH	082	157	-001	-005	027	091	-045	-124	017	223	-002	019
032	ENG MM	038	171	-018	051	032	-001	-019	-118	-056	175	021	009
033	FARMER	-029	-057	-120	061	-004	-022	070	070	-094	-065	064	-005
034	FLORST	-015	-005	-162	037	008	-039	-132	-093	112	-054	102	006
035	FORSTR	008	081	-054	026	053	060	-012	-043	036	053	045	032
036	INS AG	018	-087	-143	019	-034	-046	-048	-105	-007	-004	071	-012
037	INTDEC	-065	081	-065	-066	-114	-048	-123	-168	399	036	065	006
038	JOURN	051	011	188	102	-173	-116	-031	104	010	008	-014	179
039	LAWYER	-031	052	-049	071	-077	-144	094	-012	-084	088	058	015
040	LIBRAR	-068	092	152	013	-125	-037	033	071	-060	082	181	040

041	MCHNST	068	-091	087	-009	-040	109	079	-022	-029	139	-005	019
042	MATHM	002	322	050	031	010	-017	100	035	-130	191	053	000
043	MATHHS	086	168	-091	-012	030	088	074	059	-203	115	103	-027
044	METEOR	048	202	-021	-093	083	025	056	-042	-081	099	043	031
045	MINIST	-087	006	023	006	-085	084	120	213	018	045	101	008
046	MTLMGR	059	-041	-062	060	-010	-057	-012	-067	-008	-056	062	017
047	NRSRYM	-026	033	-135	053	061	-091	-096	-081	055	-053	096	000
048	OPTMST	105	131	-052	174	061	064	080	-081	-010	142	005	-003
049	OSTPTH	113	105	-130	283	067	103	143	-018	035	102	-039	021
050	PNTR H	078	-137	034	-022	-048	074	101	015	132	058	-016	020
051	PEDTRN	024	199	-092	224	042	022	125	055	043	115	-053	041
052	PERS M	099	-150	-031	-016	-021	-014	052	-055	027	068	-005	049
053	PHAR S	053	-050	-135	151	067	-022	-040	-071	126	-035	050	010
054	PHARM	121	101	-122	254	044	-035	017	-029	-009	047	073	-021
055	PHOTOG	087	098	-011	071	-056	053	-102	-100	279	048	103	000
056	PHYTHR	093	035	-083	182	088	160	155	012	097	155	-011	044
057	PHYSN	102	136	-130	275	017	038	144	031	-013	107	-047	030
058	PLUMBR	069	-101	003	-002	-020	013	030	000	015	095	005	042
059	PLMBCN	086	-053	-050	-042	-009	029	-026	-083	034	102	-003	010
060	PODRST	127	-026	-185	223	039	057	088	-072	087	066	-007	015
061	POLICE	148	-150	003	048	-048	103	063	-051	042	060	017	058
062	POSTCL	034	-102	007	052	-058	068	131	-015	-132	069	031	-015
063	PRNTER	062	-003	012	099	-092	087	-041	052	041	015	011	102
064	PSYTST	118	189	-032	103	029	-004	198	066	081	128	-057	037
065	PSYCCL	208	216	-023	-009	018	-035	196	089	092	039	-074	034
066	PSYCCN	219	147	-033	007	019	013	148	097	037	002	-024	006
067	PSYCIN	215	175	033	-041	029	-020	027	-027	026	017	-038	030
068	PSYPRF	170	208	-055	121	038	-100	152	090	032	-013	002	-105
069	RADSTA	030	-001	-104	096	-115	-102	-112	-083	089	-054	102	025
070	REALES	037	-008	-032	-018	-086	-144	-040	-113	019	006	066	012
071	SLSENG	039	104	-060	-044	014	-019	-094	-188	074	154	034	010
072	SCITHS	122	198	-101	219	135	165	066	059	-077	062	107	-095

NO.	CODE	12	13	14	15	16	17	18	19	20	21	22	23
073	SCHSUP	066	036	-002	055	031	-013	100	070	-125	-014	070	015
074	SOCCWK	074	-048	-046	-034	011	011	256	087	040	137	019	048
075	SOCWKG	077	-075	-057	-038	046	053	243	126	061	077	098	051
076	SOCWKM	106	-054	-055	001	037	047	267	080	047	035	-005	070
077	SOCPSY	139	006	-033	-026	013	005	280	076	129	046	-010	042
078	SOCRES	121	134	066	-019	002	-059	219	172	-026	076	-024	036
079	SOCSCH	104	-016	-053	-035	040	006	265	149	047	044	005	041
080	STATCN	032	276	016	028	000	-076	054	031	-123	133	-008	-020
081	SUPVFM	076	-007	012	004	-017	073	049	-044	-069	081	016	015
082	TRVLAG	-001	-067	-108	008	-051	082	-072	-122	061	022	100	024
083	TRKDRV	022	-182	058	042	-089	060	122	040	-025	-034	-054	-018
084	TV REP	118	060	042	068	-032	035	-004	-065	-011	067	017	-012
085	U PSTR	-064	003	036	-020	-027	033	142	185	056	128	092	033
086	VETRN	071	063	-079	266	136	023	102	017	015	017	050	028
087	WELDER	075	-121	071	007	-034	066	086	000	021	084	-008	029
088	X RAY	097	069	-061	214	024	162	062	-040	022	099	-014	039
089	YMCASC	016	-138	-093	062	012	-056	039	060	020	-028	093	038
090	FACNT	-013	012	-129	-067	031	-008	-026	-111	-215	-031	003	-076
091	FBNKCL	016	-063	-055	-052	-006	067	-062	-106	-162	-091	-027	-083
092	FBEAUT	039	-109	043	-036	-025	-010	-054	-075	-094	-127	-037	-084
093	FBKKPR	008	-068	-053	-055	008	084	-048	-087	-205	-080	-047	-099
094	FBKMGR	013	094	053	019	-078	-126	-085	030	015	-032	137	-022
095	FCTLIB	-005	045	099	006	-042	040	-047	016	-113	013	208	006
096	FCMPRG	-027	300	007	-029	155	-016	-014	-060	-020	150	-008	-010
097	FCNSHS	107	-045	-056	-074	068	003	033	042	-080	-066	085	-036
098	F DEAN	013	-027	-028	-056	067	-012	037	038	-014	007	099	025
099	FDNTAS	068	-016	-065	128	046	139	-043	-095	-009	-073	-058	-034
100	FDPTSW	-022	-102	-004	-070	-061	-051	-071	-007	-066	-137	016	-080

#	Variable	1	2	3	4	5	6	7	8	9	10	11	12
101	FDTNAD	010	-056	-065	019	198	018	-081	-053	-076	-040	003	063
102	FDTCDM	-006	-045	-055	-029	219	-005	-117	-059	-104	-035	054	076
103	FDTCOM	013	-055	-009	021	178	-051	-138	-104	-054	-078	016	071
104	FDTHOS	-017	-020	-052	044	187	026	-051	-030	-047	-035	007	065
105	FDTSCH	005	-033	-068	002	222	-002	-108	-081	-132	-037	219	053
106	FDTTHR	-008	019	-064	068	174	043	-019	-034	-101	-024	-021	-001
107	FFLRST	-006	-041	-063	-045	-019	011	-125	-091	092	-124	040	-034
108	FHMDEM	-008	-115	-015	-061	124	126	-120	-068	007	-075	009	067
109	FHOMEC	015	084	-036	086	191	-009	-065	049	-184	-018	027	017
110	FINTDC	-036	092	-034	-075	-056	-139	-143	-157	304	037	065	-018
111	FKYPCH	-027	011	032	-015	-065	090	-012	-013	-005	-115	-169	-079
112	FLAWYR	017	003	109	-053	031	-102	124	005	-082	072	-030	020
113	FLIBR	006	033	107	-019	-041	-025	-047	054	-049	017	174	012
114	FMATHS	026	105	-090	-028	094	029	-001	022	-244	090	120	-116
115	FMTLMR	026	-072	-037	-030	-021	021	-001	-106	-047	020	000	-042
116	FNURSE	-005	-043	-077	060	049	110	033	015	047	-032	-106	046
117	FNUTRN	-020	007	-042	059	184	-056	-097	004	-066	-124	011	095
118	FNUTIN	-042	-013	-044	062	194	-025	-077	020	-084	-096	004	060
119	FOCCTH	022	037	-031	027	113	191	-011	-010	230	141	012	089
120	FOFCLK	012	039	-059	-044	-036	083	037	-080	-135	009	-053	-087
121	FPEDRN	004	197	-072	116	106	-051	025	042	051	-001	-060	057
122	FPHYTH	-026	068	-064	121	160	086	057	040	094	100	-018	072
123	FPRSCT	-003	-029	000	-058	-013	032	-005	033	-016	047	059	-055
124	FPSY	152	214	-060	-095	112	-118	041	085	030	-057	-041	000
125	FPSYCL	108	174	-006	-071	092	-096	048	080	118	-053	-055	065
126	FPSYCN	124	072	-040	-083	093	-073	026	081	001	-113	027	-002
127	FRELED	-090	-032	-037	-089	021	091	-040	147	039	-095	105	015
128	FSCTHS	058	276	-011	176	142	105	-018	087	-096	-017	095	-059
129	FSECY	025	-061	013	-014	-016	065	-075	-122	-108	-107	-042	-046
130	FSOCCW	068	-028	-025	-076	074	-072	149	081	059	-023	019	066
131	FSOCGR	015	-075	-046	-124	091	001	020	091	047	012	070	068
132	FSOCMD	062	-052	-028	-022	077	-101	131	045	026	-021	015	061

NO.	CODE	12	13	14	15	16	17	18	19	20	21	22	23
133	FSOCPS	080	032	-064	-082	086	-111	146	059	104	-010	-012	064
134	FSOCSC	063	-050	-034	-074	073	-026	131	087	041	-028	061	044
135	FSTENO	023	-083	001	-037	-028	089	-064	-118	-099	-118	-055	-047
136	FX RAY	045	060	-049	141	073	130	-024	-021	-010	067	-053	017
137	MAG	028	-023	-008	-001	207	111	-036	008	003	-039	049	-067
138	MANLHS	025	000	-090	010	204	073	-011	007	102	-077	035	-021
139	MARCH	-027	166	029	-081	-011	121	-062	-087	416	234	035	-038
140	MARTED	-010	112	099	-078	-061	126	-096	-011	546	086	027	-025
141	MBIOSC	092	268	-014	159	134	109	076	045	119	082	-007	-058
142	MBUSAC	118	-029	-066	-108	062	-007	-061	-101	-111	143	040	-123
143	MBSGEN	144	-026	-043	-082	054	-009	-094	-126	030	109	061	-084
144	MBSMRK	101	-063	-007	-066	022	-039	-130	-136	140	041	087	-069
145	MBSMGT	148	-095	-033	-119	070	045	-065	-118	049	118	032	-062
146	MECON	102	001	-005	-080	034	-065	-023	-074	-019	130	033	-072
147	MELED	052	-001	008	-022	066	166	096	098	127	118	065	-063
148	MENGCH	138	191	017	-009	125	059	-068	-100	-019	193	027	-100
149	MENGCL	076	101	-024	-108	120	102	-039	-081	035	239	009	-037
150	MENGEL	103	227	032	-006	105	143	-060	-102	-016	243	026	-049
151	MENGMH	123	133	025	-100	091	146	-066	-152	057	238	-002	-047
152	MENGL	035	125	232	-048	-160	-046	026	083	183	-022	020	-004
153	MFRNLG	-037	123	182	-030	-108	031	076	088	180	063	063	-013
154	MFORST	035	120	-016	-028	080	126	-032	-033	119	036	070	-010
155	MHIST	-023	-015	132	012	-067	-107	098	065	067	094	101	-028
156	MLAW	034	-014	045	-015	031	-104	092	-009	080	129	014	-003
157	MMATH	076	244	062	-037	075	073	005	-018	-090	199	034	-100
158	MMUSIC	-221	212	117	-148	-066	108	093	-114	155	014	159	092
159	MPHYED	130	-107	-029	036	074	185	104	-002	157	079	031	-021
160	MPHYSC	095	353	080	044	083	080	003	022	003	155	039	-069

161	MPOLYS	016	-043	101	008	-023	127	065	053	050	109	089	-007
162	MPREMD	156	178	-050	169	124	078	080	011	065	120	-044	-077
163	MPSY	189	189	031	-024	032	023	063	043	165	034	-049	-077
164	MCATHB	-149	037	019	-017	-061	126	-033	258	054	111	-005	-032
165	MSOC	115	022	037	-084	051	-003	076	135	165	041	-001	-035
166	MAFCAD	073	070	-014	-042	095	039	001	-049	208	193	-022	-035
167	MWPCAD	059	-015	001	-076	096	013	-007	-053	155	229	000	-071
168	GARTED	-074	141	097	-052	034	110	-125	008	491	105	-017	-014
169	GBIOSC	-015	244	031	128	241	100	-008	076	154	032	-062	-069
170	GBUSGN	024	-085	-031	-126	117	038	-154	-076	053	-024	-048	-083
171	GDRMA	-104	056	133	-074	019	071	-016	-051	375	-035	-018	025
172	GELED	-034	-026	032	-064	118	054	-003	060	134	062	-027	-044
173	GENGL	-049	-019	191	-056	-002	-047	-031	066	207	-012	-027	004
174	GFRNLG	-089	075	111	-032	086	009	002	046	195	022	-004	001
175	GHELTH	013	131	-032	092	-027	132	004	107	133	089	-096	-005
176	GHISTO	-094	008	121	-021	086	-084	019	088	162	110	040	013
177	GHMEC	-019	-035	014	-042	221	085	-033	-004	164	028	-053	017
178	GMATH	-056	188	-004	-061	225	081	-042	037	-010	131	-040	-102
179	GMUSIC	-266	141	077	-147	043	080	059	-120	141	-037	082	092
180	GNURSE	-028	-009	-052	058	127	132	042	080	113	028	-121	016
181	GPHYED	-035	-037	-011	021	185	242	040	058	229	048	-034	-012
182	GPOLYS	-074	-045	127	-003	116	-159	041	050	160	122	004	025
183	GPSYCH	064	115	059	-051	150	-027	098	078	235	015	-101	-017
184	GCATHS	-204	017	-079	019	-006	154	-036	314	-010	071	-053	-042
185	GSOCSC	026	-064	041	054	117	-055	069	082	156	029	-028	-012
186	GSOC	019	-043	013	-084	148	-004	086	114	220	-001	-072	000
187	FATHRS	034	-014	-045	089	-050	-032	031	-010	-033	041	012	-023
188	SONS	132	081	086	006	-020	077	-039	-031	073	077	-002	-083
189	MTHRS	020	-043	001	-014	-033	-023	-030	-026	-046	-097	-046	-065
190	DGHTRS	-067	013	049	-030	020	122	-067	040	154	-035	-169	-068
191	MALES	074	039	-012	065	-022	018	014	-048	-013	045	027	015
192	FEMALE	004	-040	007	-033	-014	-003	-041	-070	-036	-052	011	-052

257

NO.	CODE	12	13	14	15	16	17	18	19	20	21	22	23
193	DACNT	028	063	-041	-001	-021	-079	030	-138	-053	142	010	-053
194	DAUTOM	116	001	125	092	-061	056	071	-002	-061	078	040	-029
195	DBRBER	112	-078	005	104	022	019	115	-025	-015	-011	048	-014
196	DBRKLR	083	-007	084	019	-052	058	055	-050	004	-031	033	-002
197	DCRPNT	064	-044	001	-040	001	054	124	-104	025	106	009	009
198	DCLTHR	085	-004	-070	070	-021	-128	-066	-040	016	052	096	-058
199	DELEC	100	-015	030	018	-055	049	105	-046	034	098	-022	-031
200	DMACH	081	-048	084	014	-035	043	050	-050	016	089	-004	013
201	DPNTER	057	-066	048	041	-069	048	092	007	090	013	-002	015
202	DPHARM	112	137	-098	223	030	-059	031	-021	-024	037	026	-009
203	DPLUMB	098	-046	011	034	-050	029	057	-059	021	062	-017	-032
204	DPSTCL	040	001	066	064	-085	057	051	-033	-074	067	056	-024
205	DSOCWK	121	070	026	009	008	-014	211	085	094	026	032	040
206	XDT	012	064	-011	038	149	-046	-065	-061	-029	-018	-027	026
207	XOFCLK	006	003	022	022	-011	051	-036	-039	-013	-090	-085	-074
208	XSECY	-032	006	073	020	-036	013	-027	-121	034	-056	-052	-039
209	XSOCWK	009	-015	006	002	065	-147	146	-038	024	020	039	044
210	DBSMNT	093	006	016	-075	021	-032	-018	-048	087	111	051	-078
211	D ENG	059	199	052	-044	081	037	-030	-086	053	175	015	-048
212	DSOCSC	025	011	082	-032	048	-069	068	-008	103	125	023	-024
213	XELED	-027	051	082	-031	104	021	012	023	220	054	-044	-053
214	XENGL	-013	060	170	-070	028	-052	-022	041	199	005	-054	071
215	XFRNLG	-084	046	100	-061	103	015	-028	097	179	048	-025	-017
216	XSOCSC	-003	020	097	-037	112	-034	015	032	179	078	-020	-018
217	XSOC	011	010	062	-079	169	-001	029	109	236	-001	-067	002

Appendix E

Interest Profiles of Occupational Groups

APPENDIX TABLE E-1

PERCENTILE RANKS OF THE MEAN SCORES OF MEN IN VARIOUS OCCUPATIONAL GROUPS

(Percentile ranks are based on form C of the Kuder Preference Record. Italicized figures represent scores based on the median)

Uses Occupational Code	Occupation	No. of Cases	Scales									
			0 Out	1 Mec	2 Com	3 Sci	4 Per	5 Art	6 Lit	7 Mus	8 Soc	9 Cle
0-01	Accountants and Auditors	581 (93)	42	27	94	43	53	34	63	56	36	83
0-01.10	Cost Accountants	28		31	96	39	56	42	60	51	29	78
0-01.20	General Accountants	92 (31)	43	30	98	48	54	33	63	54	34	79
0-97.05	Controllers	24		59	92	78	35	29	51	35	18	68
0-02	Actors	27	30	11	7	16	48	72	87	90	62	16
0-06	Authors, Editors, and Reporters	113 (19)		10	22	23	59	41	97	69	43	60
0-06.94	Copy Writers, Mail Order Company	25		15	12	18	76	61	96	71	40	28
0-07	Chemists	54		48	57	93	24	53	64	59	37	14
0-08.10	Clergymen	43		21	35	40	29	33	76	60	91	42
0-11	College Presidents, Professors, and Instructors	42 (21)	64	24	48	47	32	37	78	60	58	52
0-12.20	County Agricultural Agents	53		41	35	64	39	40	53	26	59	37
0-15 to 0-19	All Professional Engineers	653 (82)	43	64	68	73	49	51	54	47	34	38
0-15	Chemical Engineers	73		58	72	86	36	46	62	49	29	27
0-16	Civil Engineers	31 (16)	65	57	71	66	18	67	55	42	25	55
0-17	Electrical Engineers	96		64	63	85	30	50	57	55	32	33
0-18	All Industrial Engineers	217		60	77	68	57	46	54	40	37	42
0-18.01	Industrial Engineers	65		68	77	77	59	40	56	26	39	33
0-18.01	Methods Engineers	52		57	81	71	55	45	53	46	35	48
0-18.01	Time Study Engineers	35		57	80	71	55	45	51	50	34	40
0-19	Mechanical Engineers	136		79	61	74	45	58	44	50	34	31
0-19	Sales Engineers	34		63	40	57	83	45	50	33	39	25

Code	Occupation	N										
0-19	Fire Protection Engineers	118	—	57	54	63	65	52	52	42	34	26
0-22	Lawyers and Judges	331 (274)	41	19	48	36	57	43	82	61	61	48	61
0-24	Musicians and Music Teachers	77	—	19	21	22	35	63	65	98	55	39
	Music Teachers	24	—	19	22	24	37	62	70	99	56	41
0-24.3	Drugstore Managers and Pharmacists	140	—	33	55	73	62	46	43	46	47	49
0-25	All Physicians and Surgeons	260	60	37	32	79	26	61	62	58	60	27
0-26	Physicians	45	56	33	31	85	29	52	64	54	61	27
	Physicians, General Practice	73	64	37	35	83	26	59	57	48	70	27
	Surgeons	52	68	45	25	75	27	61	66	62	48	25
0-27	Social and Welfare Workers	53	—	24	38	44	50	37	71	36	91	43
0-27.40	Camp Counselors, Y.M.C.A.	83	—	24	23	46	62	61	67	67	69	28
0-31.01	All Secondary School Teachers	225 (33)	59	28	52	51	34	40	63	51	68	48
	High School Teachers of Commercial Subjects	25	—	19	71	32	52	40	61	52	55	86
	High School Teachers of Mathematics	30	—	37	84	81	25	43	48	47	58	33
	High School Teachers of Social Studies	23	—	15	51	41	45	28	70	40	84	38
0-31.10	School Administrators	65	—	26	53	47	44	34	57	41	77	48
0-32.30	Vocational Training Teachers	35	—	73	50	60	23	68	48	33	54	42
0-35.07	Forest Service, Junior Professionals	130	88	49	51	70	24	55	63	40	44	31
	Professional Personnel of a Region, U.S. Forest Service	259	87	51	55	55	28	55	60	39	47	26
	Professional Office Staff	16	84	40	56	48	28	59	78	33	40	27
	National Forest Staff	34	81	43	58	44	31	51	63	45	55	30
	National Forest Technicians	22	87	52	53	64	24	66	65	45	37	18
	Forest Supervisors	17	91	39	46	44	45	46	62	28	47	36
	District Rangers	102	84	50	56	54	32	55	54	36	53	29
	Assistant District Rangers	28	92	70	51	58	23	49	48	40	46	24
	Research Technicians, Forest Service Experiment Station	23	93	57	63	73	9	66	62	45	35	17
0-35.68	Meteorologists	185	—	53	52	83	23	48	66	49	36	34
0-36.21 to 0-36.26	All Psychologists	111	—	28	67	84	13	56	84	52	60	30

APPENDIX TABLE E-1 (Continued)

Uses Occupational Code	Occupation	No. of Cases	Scales									
			0 Out	1 Mec	2 Com	3 Sci	4 Per	5 Art	6 Lit	7 Mus	8 Soc	9 Cle
0-36.22	Clinical Psychologists	27	—	29	57	76	6	83	78	53	75	18
0-36.23	Consulting and Guidance Psychologists	26	—	19	65	79	22	30	84	44	89	29
0-36.24	Theoretical Psychologists	29	—	32	72	92	6	64	86	68	27	32
0-36.25	Industrial Psychologists	29	—	35	74	84	34	39	86	39	46	42
0-36.23	District Supervisors of Vocational Rehabilitation	20	—	35	54	67	56	26	63	15	95	39
0-39.8	Rehabilitation Counselors	146	—	56	34	43	56	25	60	38	91	42
0-39.83	Personnel Managers and Vocational Counselors	140 (21)	29	26	45	42	69	29	63	53	72	49
0-41	Personnel Managers	50 (14)	30	25	54	43	73	26	59	56	73	54
0-41	Aviators	34	—	80	39	86	24	49	51	65	29	56
0-44	Commercial Artists	31	—	27	37	22	47	94	63	63	32	54
0-48	Draftsmen	216	—	65	56	57	32	80	44	47	36	45
0-50	Laboratory Technicians	90	—	41	49	77	30	56	52	49	44	44
0-56	Photographers	38	—	36	35	49	57	71	58	51	38	53
0-57.41	Physical Education Instructors	60	—	59	28	52	32	33	53	51	89	16
0-61.50	Radio Field Engineers	33	—	66	50	85	69	45	54	57	28	20
0-66.88	Weather Observers	99	—	50	69	83	14	48	61	54	35	54
0-68.50	Production Planners	46	—	69	61	63	52	65	41	53	31	39
0-68.7	Employment and Personnel Relations Occupations	39	—	40	56	44	71	39	41	46	64	55
0-72	Retail Managers	265 (78)	35	32	53	42	75	46	52	51	46	62
0-72.71	Farm Supply Store Managers	41	—	47	62	53	59	40	35	49	46	67
0-72.91	Retail Store Managers	49	—	32	60	33	78	34	44	51	51	62
0-74	Buyers, Mail Order Company	69	—	33	47	42	75	55	64	54	39	30

Code	Occupation											N
0-74	Control Buyers, Mail Order Company	62	42	53	65	40	71	43	66	31	—	159
0-74.12	Assistant Buyers, Department Stores	51	49	55	47	37	84	27	41	24	—	59
0-75.10	Floor and Section Managers, Department Stores	51	65	59	67	37	84	29	33	21	—	74
0-81	Advertising Agents	34	38	69	88	43	83	28	9	14	—	26
	Retail Assistants in Advertising Department, Mail Order Company	50	31	52	60	53	76	42	43	39	—	28
	Mail Order and Retail Sales Managers, Mail Order Company	39	45	59	80	46	86	22	29	22	—	55
0-91	Purchasing Agents and Buyers	65	44	60	67	41	71	39	64	28	—	103
	Unit Managers in Financing and Accounting Department, Oil Company	75	49	53	53	40	35	31	86	28	—	23
0-97.0	Presidents, Vice Presidents, Secretaries, and Treasurers	65	32	60	67	33	65	43	58	29	43	88 (48)
0-97.01	Presidents	53	32	60	63	52	71	35	53	29	53	20
0-97.12 to 0-97.13	Office Managers and Chief Clerks	66	43	55	65	45	57	39	77	29	37	138 (39)
0-97.14	Junior Executives	76	45	63	67	40	71	31	58	17	—	103
0-97.4	Industrial Organization Managers	49	50	45	48	36	73	55	54	41	—	45
0-97.45	Branch Managers, Radio Company	38	50	46	47	30	62	77	75	44	—	27
0-97.5	Production Managers	51	45	39	64	48	56	60	64	58	42	139 (19)
0-97.6	Sales Managers	43	47	59	57	41	87	38	32	30	32	230 (33)
0-98	Banking, Finance, and Insurance Officials	60	43	67	57	53	73	32	53	26	42	42
0-98.07	Insurance Office Managers	57	40	72	56	55	84	25	44	22	32	24
0-98.41	Filling Station Managers	46	48	50	37	47	78	50	46	63	46	210 (171)
0-99	Managers and Officials	62	48	41	63	43	58	37	63	37	59	72 (25)
1-01	Bookkeepers and Cashiers	88	40	59	58	44	51	43	85	26	50	136 (23)
1-05	General Office Clerks	80	42	59	61	42	54	49	74	28	41	110 (20)
1-06	Financial Institution Clerks	64	60	54	54	43	50		83	37	—	25
1-18 to 1-19	General Industry Clerks	78	57	54	59	59	46	36	71	84	52	26 (15)

APPENDIX TABLE E-1 (continued)

Uses Occupational Code	Occupation	No. of Cases	0 Out	1 Mec	2 Com	3 Sci	4 Per	5 Art	6 Lit	7 Mus	8 Soc	9 Cle
1-26	Paymasters, Payroll Clerks, and Timekeepers	44	—	26	83	52	39	51	62	50	37	84
1-27 to 1-28	Post Office Clerks and Mail Carriers	35	55	38	60	53	38	54	61	55	49	66
1-27	Post Office Clerks	23	53	45	54	51	46	51	57	48	53	64
1-34	Shipping and Receiving Clerks	69	—	37	51	34	57	47	47	57	48	77
1-36	Accounting and Statistical Clerks	25	—	29	83	34	43	53	62	65	37	84
1-37.34	Clerk-typists	24	—	24	55	30	44	58	57	73	38	88
1-38	Stock Clerks	78	—	31	62	32	48	43	59	53	46	78
1-48.07	National Service Officers, Veterans Organization	39	—	18	33	36	59	32	56	46	90	61
1-57	Insurance Salesmen	165 (119)	33	26	35	31	84	41	54	61	52	58
1-57.10	Life Insurance Salesmen	*50*	*—*	*20*	*26*	*35*	*89*	*37*	*42*	*57*	*56*	*41*
1-65	Stock and Bond Salesmen	118	—	24	39	27	82	41	54	59	65	55
1-75	Salespersons	82 (44)	36	37	42	39	80	52	43	55	47	63
1-75	Regular Salespersons, Department Stores	*184*	*—*	*17*	*41*	*27*	*76*	*48*	*59*	*69*	*48*	*62*
	Extra Salespersons, Department Stores	95	—	21	45	31	74	50	52	63	55	51
1-80	Salesmen, to Consumers	353 (17)	35	32	31	40	85	40	53	50	49	45
1-85 to 1-87	Salesmen and Sales Agents, Except to Consumers	293 (97)	36	29	38	48	84	40	55	58	49	57
1-87	Paper Container Salesmen	58	—	27	14	27	94	37	52	60	59	23

Code	Occupation	N										
1-87.21	Subscription Salesmen	96	21	17	27	25	85	42	74	66	47	47
	Sales Trainees	528	—	20	17	27	90	34	61	69	61	34
2-61 to 2-68	Protective Service Occupations	23	53	48	48	52	45	50	59	56	59	42
3-06	Farmers	129 (107)	86	54	47	51	40	41	41	40	51	57
4-48	Printers and Pressmen	32	—	38	54	43	43	53	61	69	35	73
4-75	Machinists	117	—	74	54	59	35	62	37	48	39	48
4-76	Toolmakers and Die Sinkers and Setters	60	—	85	58	64	24	66	40	50	39	36
4-78	Machine Shop Occupations, n.e.c.	43	—	54	41	52	41	57	48	56	42	54
4-85	Welders	34	—	61	46	48	35	64	50	51	39	53
4-97	Electricians	37 (16)	60	78	54	67	24	57	46	36	53	40
5-21	Miners	51	—	58	55	49	38	54	47	46	44	65
5-25	Carpenters	124 (93)	70	74	40	41	35	72	31	43	51	44
5-27	Painters, Construction and Maintenance	30	—	40	44	37	39	70	44	40	60	58
5-30	Plumbers and Pipefitters	28	—	60	44	50	38	64	39	38	44	50
5-53	Linemen and Servicemen, Telegraph, Telephone, and Power	23	62	76	45	69	41	49	47	54	44	39
5-80 to 5-83	Mechanics and Repairmen	195 (47)	61	65	44	62	36	59	45	54	47	50
5-92	Manufacturing Foremen	345 (40)	54	68	85	60	39	57	36	40	46	51
	Steel Manufacturing Foremen	54	—	73	60	67	35	60	33	31	43	51
5-92.3	Supervisors (Foremen), Radio Company	406	—	65	61	62	51	50	37	46	50	34
5-92.6	Pipe Line Foremen	64	—	63	11	48	37	55	30	52	55	49
	Assistant Foremen	21	—	77	45	62	25	77	30	40	47	28
5-95.08	Supervisors in Marketing Department, Oil Company	30	—	51	55	53	77	48	42	32	49	48
	Supervisors in Refinery, Oil Company	30	—	68	61	70	41	53	41	47	43	42

APPENDIX TABLE E-1 (Continued)

Uses Occupational Code	Occupation	No. of Cases	0 Out	1 Mec	2 Com	3 Sci	4 Per	5 Art	6 Lit	7 Mus	8 Soc	9 Cle
7-35	Route Salesmen	104	—	39	34	42	79	49	46	55	57	45
7-36	Truck Drivers and Chauffeurs	63	—	59	41	41	48	54	40	48	50	60
7-60	Filling Station Attendants	30	—	67	43	51	54	52	35	58	54	50
7-93	Apprentice Carpenters	41	—	72	44	55	24	74	39	56	41	31
	Mechanical Trade Apprentices	71	—	89	40	65	23	63	31	43	52	34
7-94	Apprentice Machinists	28	—	94	28	72	25	77	30	44	46	20
7-99.025	Apprentice Millwrights	34	—	86	76	58	20	50	33	41	54	46
7-96	Apprentice Plumbers	66	—	79	48	66	28	73	33	39	45	28
	Unskilled Workers, Department Stores	51	—	36	41	31	47	58	49	59	32	62

Reprinted from Kuder Preference Record, examiner's manual, Vocational form C. © 1951, 1953, 1956, G. Frederic Kuder.

APPENDIX TABLE E-2

PERCENTILE RANKS OF THE MEAN SCORES OF WOMEN IN VARIOUS OCCUPATIONAL GROUPS

(Percentile ranks are based on form C of the Kuder Preference Record. Italicized figures represent scores based on the median)

Uses Occupational Code	Occupation	No. of Cases	Scales									
			0 Out	1 Mec	2 Com	3 Sci	4 Per	5 Art	6 Lit	7 Mus	8 Soc	9 Cle
0-04	Artists and Art Teachers	22	—	70	15	27	54	97	69	56	32	10
0-06	Journalists	31	—	44	31	46	65	66	85	58	33	22
0-06.94	Copy Writers, Mail Order Company	19	—	60	27	38	88	72	91	67	18	13
0-12.3	Home Demonstration Agents	24	—	60	37	43	57	64	35	56	65	25
0-23	Librarians	39 (14)	41	46	30	35	44	66	83	52	29	38
0-24	Musicians and Music Teachers	68 (18)	56	40	30	25	45	70	54	96	49	32
0-26	Physicians	43	84	77	47	86	22	60	58	45	63	11
0-27	Social and Welfare Workers	26	51	43	31	43	54	59	70	46	81	25
0-27	Social Workers	50	—	*27*	*22*	*33*	*69*	*51*	*72*	*57*	*92*	*20*
0-30	Primary School and Kindergarten Teachers	544 (459)	54	42	49	35	40	63	56	62	65	38
0-31.0	All Secondary School Teachers	476 (139)	49	45	52	46	48	56	59	53	50	40
	High School Teachers of Commercial Subjects	64 (22)	35	44	76	34	66	52	45	54	33	72
	High School Teachers of English	110 (19)	49	33	36	30	48	55	88	63	47	33
	High School Teachers of Home Economics	136 (34)	54	63	45	59	41	64	49	48	52	29
	High School Teachers of Languages	42	—	35	29	30	51	52	76	73	48	40
	High School Teachers of Mathematics	47	—	67	91	69	31	55	35	44	43	46
	High School Teachers of Social Studies	56 (27)	45	39	43	35	57	47	71	39	66	38
0-32.04	Occupational Therapists	70	70	88	32	58	26	81	45	61	58	14

267

APPENDIX TABLE E-2 (continued)

Uses Occupational Code	Occupation	No. of Cases	0 Out	1 Mec	2 Com	3 Sci	4 Per	5 Art	6 Lit	7 Mus	8 Soc	9 Cle
0-32.30	Synthetic Training Device Instructors, Marine Corps	60	—	71	48	69	52	65	66	59	31	20
0-32.86	Women's Reserve	31	—	37	21	33	38	50	66	57	93	33
0-33	Religious Workers	1071 (20)	51	57	43	69	33	58	46	54	75	26
0-33.26	All Trained Nurses	154	—	56	45	65	34	55	43	55	66	32
0-33.15	General Staff Nurses	144	—	55	49	70	27	60	51	55	76	23
0-33.28	Nurse Educators	159	—	59	45	70	35	56	47	52	76	30
0-33.42	Private Duty Nurses	157	—	56	38	62	43	57	45	50	84	19
0-33.17	Public Health Nurses	196	—	61	46	63	33	56	45	57	73	31
0-39.83	Supervisors and Head Nurses	34	—	36	27	30	93	53	59	58	59	33
0-39.33	Personnel Managers, Mail Order Company	31	—	57	69	77	41	50	53	56	47	29
0-50	Hospital Dietitians	31	—	84	57	93	38	60	35	53	38	23
0-50.07	Laboratory Technicians	35	—	53	27	78	46	67	41	57	81	14
0-71.23	Dental Hygienists	20	—	61	78	74	59	61	52	34	24	40
0-74.11	Tearoom and Restaurant Managers	29	—	50	57	42	93	52	63	71	24	39
0-74.12	Retail Buyers	58	—	39	48	27	94	49	75	60	53	31
0-75.10	Assistant Buyers, Department Stores	25	—	33	55	32	92	31	57	45	57	49
0-97.12 to 0-97.13	Floor and Section Managers, Department Stores	29	—	61	70	47	73	45	64	59	33	57
1-01	Office Managers, Chief Clerks	67	—	42	73	50	79	53	57	62	42	46
1-01.0	Executives in a Mail Order Company	142	—	34	77	45	62	55	61	65	42	59
1-01.5	Bookkeepers and Cashiers											
1-01.5	Bookkeepers	62	—	36	91	46	52	53	61	56	39	70
	Cashiers	43	—	29	60	44	75	61	65	77	35	53
	Tube Room Cashiers, Department Stores	111	—	39	48	34	68	54	45	67	33	54

Scales

268

Code	Occupation	1	2	3	4	5	6	7	8	9	—	N
1-04	Junior Clerks	65	50	51	37	55	66	41	65	60	—	25
1-05	General Office Clerks	61	41	57	50	58	57	51	66	57	—	136
	General Office Clerks, Marine Corps Women's Reserve	32	41	63	55	60	57	56	46	65	—	143
	Office Clerks, Department Stores (Customer Service)	54	63	56	53	45	82	34	48	35	—	88
	Office Clerks, Department Stores (No Customer Contacts)	64	46	64	38	44	68	40	55	35	—	85
1-18.3	Personnel Clerks	35	73	54	63	63	83	52	33	48	—	24
	Personnel Workers other than Managers	43	77	46	56	42	89	36	54	47	—	27
1-25	All Office Machine Operators	53	50	48	43	55	48	64	77	67	—	62
1-25.6	I.B.M. Operators	59	59	44	33	53	39	64	85	72	—	26
1-33.01	Secretaries	58	39	61	64	50	64	41	49	43	51	121 (40)
	Graduates of Secretarial School	59	33	66	64	49	72	46	55	47	—	57
1-36	Statistical Clerks	40	44	57	61	60	54	62	77	48	—	27
1-37	Stenographers and Typists	62	37	61	52	53	46	54	49	47	37	235 (16)
1-37.12	Stenographers, Marine Corps Women's Reserve	44	34	58	63	52	57	60	42	57	—	76
1-37.34	Clerk-typists, Marine Corps Women's Reserve	32	38	62	63	56	46	64	47	64	—	167
1-42.3	Telephone Operators	65	53	55	40	58	66	44	46	50	—	22
1-70	Sales Clerks	58	74	54	51	31	72	45	42	51	—	26
1-75	Salespersons	55	52	51	57	62	64	40	56	51	—	25
1-75	Salespersons, Department Stores (Regular)	45	50	56	43	52	84	40	41	39	—	617
1-75	Salespersons, Department Stores (Extra)	45	44	60	48	58	80	34	41	38	—	342
2-26	Cooks and Bakers	25	48	54	62	48	54	58	41	73	—	31
2-68	Line Officers, Marine Corps Women's Reserve	16	62	48	66	52	50	62	40	71	—	23

APPENDIX TABLE E-2 (continued)

Uses Occupa-tional Code	Occupation	Number of Cases	0 Out	1 Mec	2 Com	3 Sci	4 Per	5 Art	6 Lit	7 Mus	8 Soc	9 Cle
2-68	Staff Officers, Marine Corps Women's Reserve	20	—	62	51	70	52	64	66	55	37	18
2-68	Aviation Assembly and Repair Workers, Marine Corps Women's Reserve	75	—	87	39	74	36	67	40	46	42	18
2-68	Motor Vehicle Operators, Marine Corps Women's Reserve	20	—	69	48	70	42	45	39	61	60	31
	Lawyers' Wives	35	38	32	46	31	47	71	72	57	49	45
	Farmers' Wives	15	90	61	56	18	27	52	44	64	49	59
	Physicians' Wives	51	55	38	50	41	37	69	58	54	50	48

Reprinted from Kuder Preference Record, examiner's manual, Vocational form C. © 1951, 1953, 1956, G. Frederic Kuder.

APPENDIX TABLE E-3
MEAN SCORES AND CORRESPONDING PERCENTILE RANKS OF MEN WHO LIKE THEIR WORK IN VARIOUS OCCUPATIONS†

(The first figure under each scale is the mean raw score; the second figure is the corresponding percentile, based on form A of the Kuder Preference Record)

Uses Occupational Code	OCCUPATION	Number of Cases	A	B††	C	D††	E
					SCALES		
0-01	All Accountants and Auditors	97	30.07 / 48	38.01 / 41	32.03 / 54	**42.59 / 65	**45.47 / 60
0-01.20	General Accountants	30	30.97 / 50	39.80 / 48	33.37 / 59	**45.10 / 75	44.07 / 55
0-06	Authors, Editors, and Reporters	29	31.14 / 51	35.41 / 33 —	**37.62 / 73	38.07 / 46	**49.14 / 71
0-08	Clergymen	33	*37.39 / 70	42.64 / 60	**42.55 / 87	**43.88 / 70	43.67 / 54
0-11	College Professors	20	30.40 / 49	40.95 / 53	**40.65 / 81	**46.50 / 80	45.85 / 61
0-14 to 0-19	All Professional Engineers	107	31.08 / 51	39.93 / 48	31.60 / 52	**41.37 / 61	43.18 / 52
0-16	Civil Engineers	22	26.36 / 36	39.09 / 46	29.41 / 43	42.50 / 65	43.18 / 52

271

Appendix Table E-3 (continued)

Uses Occupational Code	OCCUPATION	Number of Cases	SCALES				
			A	B††	C	D††	E
0-18	Industrial Engineers	24	**38.67 74	39.54 47	34.21 62	40.13 56	44.29 56
0-22	Lawyers and Judges	231	31.82 53	⁻35.28 32	**37.58 73	39.05 51	**53.00 83
0-26	All Physicians and Surgeons	210	⁻28.11 42	39.27 46	**35.01 65	**42.20 64	– 40.18 43
0-26.10	Physicians, General Practice	77	⁻26.82 38	39.90 48	**35.97 68	**44.13 71	– 39.08 40
0-26.10	Surgeons	28	29.50 46	37.00 38	30.82 49	38.32 47	43.54 53
0-31	Secondary School Teachers and Principals	82	*34.00 60	*41.66 56	31.66 52	**44.63 73	42.09 49
0-31.10	Public School Superintendents	215	**34.84 63	40.17 49	**38.51 76	**44.18 70	**50.00 73
0-72	Retail Managers	84	**35.48 65	37.91 41	31.74 52	39.58 53	*44.70 57
0-73	Wholesale Managers	26	33.27 58	37.42 39	29.85 45	35.96 37	*47.39 66

Code	Occupation	N					
0-97.01 to 0-97.14	Presidents, Vice-Presidents, Secretaries, Treasurers, etc.	116	32.46 / 55	— 36.99 / 38	31.77 / 53	39.65 / 54	** 47.38 / 66
0-97.01	Presidents	23	* 36.48 / 68	— 34.30 / 29	* 35.74 / 67	37.96 / 46	** 50.22 / 74
0-97.02	Vice-Presidents	20	31.55 / 52	— 34.30 / 29	30.90 / 49	— 34.75 / 32	* 49.25 / 71
0-97.12	Office Managers	45	32.91 / 56	39.27 / 46	31.69 / 52	41.18 / 60	** 46.11 / 62
0-97.41	Managers, Industrial Organizations	31	30.90 / 50	39.84 / 48	30.39 / 47	37.61 / 44	45.58 / 60
0-97.51	Production Managers	20	32.25 / 54	34.65 / 30	32.20 / 54	40.00 / 55	46.60 / 63 **
0-97.6	Sales and Distribution Managers	62	** 37.90 / 72	— 35.66 / 34	32.08 / 54	39.40 / 52	47.63 / 66
0-98.01 to 0-98.11	Banking, Finance, and Insurance Officials	26	** 36.73 / 69	36.23 / 36	31.15 / 50	38.00 / 46	** 48.77 / 69
0-99.21	Contractors	22	29.86 / 47	36.64 / 37	28.96 / 41	37.91 / 45	43.41 / 53
1-01	Bookkeepers and Cashiers, except Bank Cashiers	30	31.80 / 53	39.13 / 46	33.10 / 58	41.87 / 63	42.70 / 51
1-28	Mail Carriers	20	29.40 / 46	— 39.50 / 47 —	30.40 / 47	36.40 / 39	39.55 / 41

APPENDIX TABLE E-3 (continued)

Uses Occupational Code	OCCUPATION	Number of Cases	SCALES				
			A	B††	C	D††	E
1-57	Insurance Salesmen	117	**37.44 71	36.22 36	31.99 54	37.79 45	**48.34 68
1-63	Real Estate Salesmen	20	32.25 54	35.80 34	31.30 51	38.95 50	**49.35 71
1-75	Salespersons	35	33.77 59	36.43 36	30.06 46	40.29 57	41.69 48
1-86.01 to 1-86.47	Wholesale Salesmen of Metals, Machinery, Equipment, and Supplies	20	32.95 57	37.20 39	31.25 50	37.85 45	*48.25 68
2-61 to 2-68	All Protective Service Occupations	53	31.72 53	38.13 42	30.60 48	⁻34.47 31	**46.36 63
2-68	Soldiers, Sailors, Marines, and Coast Guard	23	30.61 49	39.91 48	30.78 48	38.35 47	**48.35 68
3-01 to 3-37	Farmers	59	⁻27.70 40	**45.32 71	⁻26.80 32	38.27 47	40.61 44
4-76	Toolmakers and Die Sinkers and Setters	20	30.55 49	*43.60 64	28.10 38	35.85 37	⁻35.75 30

	N					
All Mechanics and Repairmen 5-79 to 5-83	54	31.32 51	41.35 54	- - 26.82 32	37.96 46	- 38.28 38
Motor Vehicle Mechanics and Repairmen 5-81	26	** 30.50 49	42.50 59	- - 26.19 30	38.12 46	- 36.65 33
All Foremen 5-91 to 5-99	195	** 34.19 61	40.30 50	30.70 48	* 40.24 57	42.93 51
Tobacco Manufacturing Foremen 5-91.101	125	** 35.55 65	40.42 50	31.80 53	** 41.60 62	43.58 53

†All means in this table have been compared with the means of the corresponding scales of the base group. Differences significant at the 1% and 5% levels have been indicated as follows:

*Positive difference significant at 5% level.
**Positive difference significant at 1% level.
- -Negative difference significant at 5% level.
- -Negative difference significant at 1% level.

††The scores for Scales B and D have been corrected for age as called for in the second edition (September 1952) of the Adult profile.

Reprinted from Kuder Preference Record, examiner's manual, form A. © 1953, G. Frederic Kuder.

APPENDIX TABLE E-4

MEAN SCORES AND CORRESPONDING PERCENTILE RANKS OF WOMEN WHO LIKE THEIR WORK IN VARIOUS OCCUPATIONS†

(The first figure under each scale is the mean raw score; the second figure is the corresponding percentile, based on form A of the Kuder Preference Record)

Uses Occupational Code	OCCUPATION	Number of Cases	SCALES				
			A	B††	C	D††	E
0-11.20 to 0-11.50	College Professors	34	*33.94 / 65	*39.94 / 63	**39.56 / 68	**58.38 / 68	33.71 / 54
0-23	Librarians	20	30.20 / 54	35.00 / 46	35.35 / 52	57.45 / 63	33.80 / 54
0-26	Physicians and Surgeons	20	28.40 / 48	*41.25 / 67	*39.55 / 68	50.60 / 30	34.75 / 57
0-30.11	Grammar School Teachers	316	29.77 / 53	37.10 / 53	-- 33.48 / 44	**58.67 / 70	-- 29.07 / 39
0-31	All Secondary School Teachers and Principals	141	29.73 / 53	**39.29 / 61	35.28 / 52	**57.99 / 66 *	- 30.84 / 45
	High School Teachers of Commercial Subjects	36	31.36 / 57	38.25 / 58	36.53 / 56	56.72 / 60	33.00 / 52
	High School Teachers of Home Economics	36	29.36 / 52	**42.03 / 70	- 31.47 / 35	**61.42 / 83	-- 26.08 / 29

276

	N					
0-33 Trained Nurses	28	27.00 / 43	37.68 / 55	33.50 / 44	54.29 / 48	28.71 / 38
1-01 Bookkeepers and Cashiers, except Bank Cashiers	25	26.20 / 39	37.32 / 54	32.56 / 39	* 57.24 / 62	32.60 / 50
1-33.01 Secretaries	41	27.63 / 46	34.81 / 45	34.07 / 46	54.54 / 49	34.15 / 55
1-37 Stenographers and Typists	24	27.75 / 46	34.88 / 45	– – 31.92 / 37	55.79 / 55	27.13 / 33
Housewives	915	29.76 / 53	36.61 / 52	– – 33.13 / 42	** 56.48 / 58	30.23 / 43

†All means in this table have been compared with the means of the corresponding scales of the base group. Differences significant at the 1% and 5% levels have been indicated as follows:

*Positive difference significant at 5% level.
**Positive difference significant at 1% level.
– Negative difference significant at 5% level.
– – Negative difference significant at 1% level.

††The scores for Scales B and D have been corrected for age as called for in the second edition (September 1952) of the Adult profile.

Reprinted from Kuder Preference Record, examiner's manual, Form A. © 1953, G. Frederic Kuder.

APPENDIX TABLE E-5

COMPARISON OF MEAN SCORES OF OCCUPATIONAL GROUPS ACCORDING TO JOB SATISFACTION†

Uses Occupational Code	OCCUPATION (MEN)	Number of Cases	SCALES				
			A	B††	C	D††	E
0-01	Accountants and Auditors			**		**	
	Satisfied	97	30.07	38.01	32.03	42.59	45.47
	Dissatisfied	31	30.68	32.90	31.94	39.16	44.55
0-22	Lawyers and Judges						
	Satisfied	231	31.82	35.28	37.58	39.05	53.00
	Dissatisfied	52	32.03	33.75	36.75	38.56	50.13
0-31.20	Public School Superintendents		**				*
	Satisfied	215	34.84	40.17	38.51	44.18	50.00
	Dissatisfied	24	26.58	36.38	35.17	43.25	44.63
0-72	Retail Managers		**				
	Satisfied	84	35.48	37.91	31.74	39.58	44.70
	Dissatisfied	23	28.96	36.17	31.78	42.83	41.74
1-57	Insurance Salesmen				– –	– –	
	Satisfied	117	37.44	36.22	31.99	37.79	48.34
	Dissatisfied	20	37.40	32.45	39.05	42.30	47.10
5-79 to 5-83	Mechanics and Repairmen			*			–
	Satisfied	54	31.32	41.35	26.82	37.96	38.28
	Dissatisfied	22	33.27	37.09	30.14	40.32	42.73

Uses Occupational Code	OCCUPATION (WOMEN)	Number of Cases	SCALES					
			A	B††	C	D††	E	
0-30.11	Grammar School Teachers							
	Satisfied	316	29.77	37.10	33.48	58.67	– 29.07	
	Dissatisfied	23	28.39	34.35	33.04	56.52	32.65	
	Housewives			**		*		
	Satisfied	915	29.76	36.61	33.13	56.48	– 30.23	
	Dissatisfied	65	29.74	31.83	33.92	54.80	33.15	

†Means have been compared for satisfied and dissatisfied workers in each occupation. Significant differences are indicated as follows:

*Satisfied group significantly higher at 5% level.
**Satisfied group significantly higher at 1% level.
–Satisfied group significantly lower at 5% level.
- -Satisfied group significantly lower at 1% level.
††Scores for Scales B and D have been corrected for age as called for in the second edition (September, 1952) of the Adult profile.

Reprinted from Kuder Preference Record, examiner's manual, form A. © 1953, G. Frederic Kuder.

Appendix F

Bibliography of Publications Pertaining to Kuder Interest Inventories

Adams, F. J. A study of the stability of broad vocational interests at the high school level. Ph.D. dissertation, New York University, 1957.

Adjutant General's Office, Personnel Research and Procedures Branch, Personnel Research Section, Staff. The Kuder Preference scores of successful and unsuccessful enlisted men assigned to recruiting functions in the United States Army. *American Psychologist*, 1946, *1*, 249.

Adkins, D. C. The relation of primary mental abilities to preference scales and to vocational choice. *Psychometrika*, 1940, *5*, 316.

Adkins, D. C., and Kuder, G. F. The relation of primary mental abilities to activity preference. *Psychometrika*, 1940, *5*, 251-262.

Allen, C. L. The development of a battery of psychological tests for determining journalistic interests and aptitudes. Ph.D. dissertation, Northwestern University, 1948.

Allen, R. J. An analysis of the relationship between selected prognostic measures and achievement in the freshman program for secretarial majors at the Women's College of the University of North Carolina. Ph.D. dissertation, Pennsylvania State University, 1961.

Allis-Chalmers Manufacturing Co.: Scientific selection of engineering personnel. Milwaukee, Wis.: Employment Dept., Allis-Chalmers Mfg. Co.

Amar, W. F. An investigation of some factors relating to the identification of eighth grade children possessing musical potential. Ph.D. dissertation on file at Loyola University (Chicago), 1958.

American Nurses Association, Research Department. The Kuder Preference Record in the counseling of nurses. *American Journal of Nursing*, 1946, *46*, 312-316.

Anastasi, A. *Psychological testing*, 2d ed. New York: Macmillan, 1961, pp. 536-539.

Anastasi, A. *Psychological testing*, 3d ed. New York: Macmillan, 1968, p. 478.

Anderson, C. L. An analysis of the differences of the scores obtained by different cultural groups on the Kuder Preference Record. Master's thesis, University of Southern California, 1950.

Anderson, R. G. Do aptitudes support interests? *Personnel and Guidance Journal*, 1953, *32*, 14-17.

Anderson, T. E., Jr. The effect of reading skill on the comparability of the Kuder Preference Record and the Occupational Interest Survey. Master's thesis, University of Texas, 1968.

Anikeeff, A. M., and Bryan, J. L. Kuder interest pattern analysis of fire protection students and graduates. *Journal of Psychology*, 1958, *48*, 195-198.

Arbuckle, D. S. Client perception of counselor personality. *Journal of Counseling Psychology*, 1956, *3*, 93-96.

Arima, J. K. The validity of the Kuder Preference Record in predicting from profile peaks. Master's thesis on file at George Washington University, 1957.

Armstrong, M. E. A comparison of the interests and social adjustment of under-achievers, and normal achievers at the secondary school level. Ph.D. dissertation, The University of Connecticut, 1955.

Arnold, D. L. Student reaction to the Kuder. *Personnel and Guidance Journal*, 1958, *37*, 40-44.

Ash, P. Validity information exchange. *Personnel Psychology*, 1960, *13*, 454.

Atkinson, E., and Baron, S. Exploring vocational interests in the ninth year. *High Points*, 1955, *37*, 46-48.

Atkinson, G., and Lunneborg, C. E. Comparison of oblique and orthogonal simple structure solutions for personality and interest factors. *Multivariate Behavioral Research*, 1968, *3*, 221-35.

Atkinson, J. A. Factors related to the prediction of academic success for disabled veterans in a four year college engineering program. Ph.D. dissertation, University of Denver, 1962.

Ausubel, D. P., Schiff, H. M., and Zeleny, M. P. Real-life measures of level academic and vocational aspiration in adolescents: Relation to laboratory measures and to adjustment. *Child Development*, 1953, *24*, 155-168.

Baas, M. L. A study of interest patterns among professional psychologists. Master's thesis, Purdue University, 1949.

Baas, M. L. Kuder interest patterns of psychologists. *Journal of Applied Psychology*, 1950, *34*, 115-117.

Baer, B. S. Interest patterns for four occupations: Kuder Preference Record. Master's thesis, Utah State Agricultural College, 1953.

Baer, M. F. *Occupational information: The dynamics of its nature and use.* Chicago: Science Research Associates, 1964.

Baggaley, A. R. The relation between scores obtained by Harvard freshmen on the Kuder Preference Record and their fields of concentration. *Journal of Educational Psychology*, 1947, *38*, 421-427.

Baggaley, A. R. Development of a predictive academic interest inventory. *Journal of Counseling Psychology*, 1963, *10*, 41-46.

Bailey, H. C. The Kuder Preference Record as an instrument for diagnosing maladjustment in prospective members of the helping professions. Ph.D. dissertation, Florida State University, 1969.

Baker, B., and Peatman, J. C. Tests used in veterans administration advisement units. *American Psychologist*, 1947, *2*, 99-102.

Barnette, W. L., Jr. Occupational aptitude patterns of counseled veterans. Ph.D. dissertation, New York University, 1949, pp. 8, 385.

Barnette, W. L., Jr. Occupational aptitude pattern research. *Occupations*, 1950, *29*, 5-12.

Barnette, W. L., Jr. An occupational aptitude pattern for engineers. *Educational and Psychological Measurement*, 1951, *11*, 52-66.

Barnette, W. L., Jr. Occupational apptitude patterns of selected groups of counseled veterans. American Psychological Association, Psychological Monographs: General and Applied. Vol. 65. No. 5, Whole No. 322. Washington D.C.: The Association, Inc., 1951. pp. 5, 49.

Barrett, D. M. Prediction of achievement in typewriting and stenography in a liberal arts college. *Journal of Applied Psychology*, 1946, *30*, 624-630.

Barrett, R. E. The relation between strength of Kuder preferences and aptitude, temperament, and academic achievement. Ph.D. dissertation, University of Pittsburgh, 1952.

Barrett, R. S. The process of predicting job performance. *Personnel Psychology*, 1958, *11*, 39-57.

Barriliaux, L. E. High school science achievement as related to interest and I.Q. *Educational* and *Psychological Measurement*, 1961, *21*, 929-936.

Barry, C. M. Kuder Preference Record norms: Based on measurements made on high school seniors. *Occupations*, 1944, *22*, 487-488.

Barton, E. M. Development of Kuder Preference Record Occupational Form D, scoring key for secondary school counselors. Master's thesis, Iowa State University, 1958.

Bateman, R. M. The effect of work experience on high school students' vocational choice: As revealed by the Kuder Preference Record. *Occupations*, 1949, *27*, 453-456.

Bath, J. A. Differential interests of agricultural college students as measured by the Kuder Preference Record. *Proceedings of the Iowa Academy of Science*, 1950, *57*, 347-351.

Bauernfeind, R. H. The matter of 'ipsative scores.' *Personnel and Guidance Journal*, 1962, *41*, 210-217.

Bauernfeind, R. H. *Building a school testing program*. Boston: Houghton Mifflin, 1963, pp. 212-231.

Baumann, Sister M. J. F. A follow-up study of vocational interests of high school girl graduates. Master's thesis on file in the library of the Catholic University of America, Washington, D. C., 1950.

Bayley, N. Kuder masculinity-femininity scores in adolescent boys and girls related to their scores in somatic androgyny. *American Psychologist*, 1949, *4*, 251.

Bayley, N. Some psychological correlates of somatic androgyny. *Child Development*, 1951, *22*, 47-60.

Bayley, N., Findley, W. G., Gerberich, J. R., Justman, J., Mollenkopf, W. G., Sells, S. B., Stroud, J. J., Swineford, F., Symonds, P. M., and Wrightston, W. J. Educational measurements. *Review of Educational Research*, 1956, *26*, 268-291.

Beamer, G. C. The factors of interest in the counseling of adults. Ph.D. dissertation, University of Missouri, 1947. Abstract: *Microfilm Abstracts*, 1949, *9*, 158-160.

Beamer, G. C., Edmonson, L. D., and Strother, G. B. Improving the selection of Linotype trainees. *Journal of Applied Psychology*, 1948, *32*, 130-134.

Beamer, G. C., and Ledbetter, E. W. The relation between teacher attitudes and the social service interest. *Journal of Educational Research*, 1957, *50*, 655-666.

Beamer, G. C., Pender, F. R., and Parton, N. W. Selection of teachers of homemaking. *Journal of Home Economics*, 1953, *45*, 98-100.

Beaumont, J. B. Level of item specificity and the measurement of inventoried interests. Ph.D. dissertation, Columbia University, 1972.

Beaver, A. P. Kuder interest patterns of student nurses. *Journal of Applied Psychology*, 1953, *37*, 370-373.

Beaver, A. P. Psychometric data and survival in a college of nursing. *Psychological Reports*, 1956, *2*, 23-26.

Becker, J. A. An exploratory factor analytic study of interests, intelligence, and personality. *Psycholological Reports*, 1963, *13*, 847-851.

Becker, S. The relationship of discrepancy between expressed and inventoried interest scores to selected personality variables: A study of adolescents. Ph.D. dissertation, Loyola University (Chicago), 1973.

Belman, H. S., and Evans, R. N. Selection of students for a trade and industrial education curriculum. *Motives and aptitudes in education: Four studies*. Edited by H. H. Remmers. Purdue University, Division of Educational Reference, Studies in Higher Education, No. 74, Lafayette, Ind.: the Division, 1950, pp. 9-14.

Belman, H. S., and Evans, R. N. Selection of students for a trade and industrial education curriculum. *Journal of Educational Psychology*, 1951, *42*, 52-58.

Bendig, A. W. Validity of Kuder differences among honors majors. *Educational and Psychological Measurement*, 1957, *17*, 593-598.

Bendig, A. W. Development of the Psychological Activities Interest Record. *Educational and Psychological Measurement*, 1958, *18*, 159-166.

Bendig, A. W. Kuder differences between honors and pass majors in psychology. *Journal of Educational Research*, 1959, *52*, 199-202.

Bendig, A. W., and Hughes, J. B., III. Student attitude and achievement in a course in introductory statistics. *Journal of Educational Psychology*, 1954, *45*, 268-276.

Bendig, A. W., and Meyer, W. J. The factorial structure of the scales of the Primary Mental Abilities, Builford Zimmerman Temperament Survey, and Kuder Preference Record. *Journal of General Psychology*, 1963, *68*, 195-201.

Bennett, G. K., Seashore, H. G., and Wesman, A. G. *Counseling from profiles: A casebook for the Differential Aptitude tests*. New York: Psychological Corp., 1951.

Benton, A. L., and Kornhauser, S. I. A study of score faking on a medical interest test. *Journal of the Association of American Medical Colleges*, 1948, *23*, 57-60.

Berdie, R. F. Review of the Kuder Preference Record. In O. K. Buros (ed.), *The third mental measurements yearbook*. Highland Park, N. J.: Gryphon Gryphon Press, 1949, pp. 660-661.

Berdie, R. F. Scores on the Strong Vocational Interest Blank and the Kuder Preference Record in relation to self-ratings. *Journal of Applied Psychology*, 1950, *34*, 42-49.

Berdie, R. F., Layton, W. L., Swanson, E. O., and Hagenah, T. *Testing in guidance and counseling*. New York: McGraw-Hill, 1963.

Berg, I. A. A study of success and failure among student nurses. Abstract. *American Psychologist*, 1946, *1*, 249-250.

Berg, I. A. A study of success and failure among student nurses. *Journal of Applied Psychology*, 1947, *31*, 389-396.

Berhshire, J. R., Bugental, J. F. T., Cassens, F. P., and Edgerton, H. A. Test preferences in guidance centers. *Occupations*, 1948, *26*, 337-343.

Bernard, J. Selection of technical school students: An investigation of the relationship between certain personality characteristics, interests and abilities, and success in a radio and television curriculum. Ph.D. dissertation, New York University, 1954.

Bertrand, J. R. Relation between Kuder Preference Record scores and academic achievement of agricultural students. Unpublished manuscript on file at Agricultural and Mechanical College of Texas, College Station, Texas, 1954.

Bielander, A. Prévision du choix professionnel à partir des questionnaires de Kuder et de la batterie générale d'aptitudes (B.G.A.). Thèse (Fac. Lettres, Université de Neuchatel), Neuchatel, 1965.

Billing, P. S. Voluntary selection as corroborated by the Kuder Preference Record: To test the value of music as a universal outlet for extracurricular activity. Master's thesis, University of North Dakota, 1948.

Birge, W. R. Preferences and behavior ratings of dominance. *Educational and Psychological Measurement*, 1950, *10*, 392-394.

Blanchard, R. E. The development and validation of instruments for selecting farm operators for farm management services. Ph.D. dissertation, Purdue University, 1959.

Board of Examination Staff. *Report of examinations given by the board of examinations, 1939-1940.* Chicago: University of Chicago, 1941.

Bolanovich, D. J. Selection of female engineering trainees. *Journal of Educational Psychology*, 1944, 35, 545-553.

Balanovich, D. J., and Goodman, C. H. A study of the Kuder Preference Record. *Educational and Psychological Measurement*, 1944, *4*, 315-325.

Bone, J. H. A statistical analysis of interest patterns of high school students and their relationship to intelligence and achievement. Ph.D. dissertation, Pennsylvania State University, 1957.

Bonnardel, R., and Fichou, G. Recherche sur l'utilisation d'un inventaire d'intérêts professionnels pour l'orientation d'adolescents. (Studies on the use of a vocational interest inventory for guidance of adolescents.) *Travail Humain*, 1965, *38* (1-2), 57-79.

Bonnardel, R., and Lavoegie, M. S. Questionnaires d'intérêts et prévision du succès dans les études supérieures. (Questionnaires on interest and predictions of success in higher studies.) *Travail Humain*, 1966, *29* (3-4), 309-322.

Booth, M. D. A study of the relationship between certain personality factors and success in clinical training of occupational therapy students. *American Journal of Occupational Therapy*, 1957, *11*, 93-96.

Bordin, E. S. Relative correspondence of professed interests to Kuder and Strong interest test scores. Abstract. *American Psychologist*, 1947, *2*, 293.

Bordin, E. S. Review of the Kuder Preference Record — Vocational. In O. K. Buros (ed.), *The fourth mental measurements yearbook.* Highland Park, N. J.: Gryphon Press, 1953, pp. 737-738.

Bordin, E. S. Review of the Kuder Preference Record — Occupational, Form D. In O. K. Buros (ed.), *The fifth mental measurements yearbook.* Highland Park, N. J.: Gryphon Press, 1959, pp. 884-885.

Bordin, E. S., and Wilson, E. H. Change of interest as a function of shift in curricular orientation. *Educational and Psychological Measurement*, 1953, *13*, 297-307.

Borg, W. R. Does a perceptual factor exist in artistic ability? *Journal of Educational Research*, 1950, *44*, 47-53.

Borg, W. R. The interests of art students. *Educational and Psychological Measurement*, 1950, *10*, 100-106.

Bortree, D. W. An exploration of the potential usefulness of a vocational aptitude test in the selection of applicants. Research Grant, Kansas City College of Osteopathy and Surgery, 1968.

Bouton, A. G. The stability of Kuder vocational interest patterns during late adolescence and early adult life. Ph.D. dissertation, University of Pittsburgh, 1952.

Bowers, N. D., and Kelly, H. P. Vocational interests of naval flight instructors: I. Comparisons with naval aviation cadets. *USN School of Aviation Medical Research notes*. Proj. No. NM 001 108 107, Rep. No. 1, 1956.

Boyce, R. W. The construction and validity of an interest key for medical technologists. *American Journal of Medical Technology*, 1962, *28*, 349-351.

Bradfield, A. F. Predicting the success in training of graduate students in school administration. Ph.D. dissertation, Stanford University, 1950.

Bradley, A. D. Estimating success in technical and skilled trade courses using a multivariate statistical analysis. Ph.D. dissertation, on file at the University of Minnesota, 1958.

Brayfield, A. H. Clerical interest and clerical aptitude. *Personnel and Guidance Journal*, 1953, *31*, 304-306.

Brayfield, A. H., and Marsh, M. M. Aptitudes, interests, and personality characteristic of farmers. *Journal of Applied Psychology*, 1957, *41*, 98-103.

Brayfield, A. M. Review of the Kuder Preference Record. *Occupations*, 1942, *21*, 267-269.

Brewer, J. M. Classification of items in interest inventories. *Occupations*, 1943, *21*, 448-451.

Bridgeman, C. S., and Hollenbeck, G. P. Effect of simulated applicant status on Kuder Form D Occupational Interest scores. *Journal of Applied Psychology*, 1961, *45*, 237-239.

Brody, D. S. The utilization of an interest inventory in a PTA project for the purpose of fostering parent-child understanding. *School and Society*, 1950, *72*, 311-312.

Brody, D. S. Kuder interest patterns of professional forest service men. *Educational and Psychological Measurement*, 1957, *17*, 559-605.

Brogden, H. E., Baier, D. E., and Taylor, E. K. Experimental design: Utilization of an unreliable and a biased criterion. *Educational and Psychological Measurement*, 1953, *13*, 27-33.

Brooks, M. S., and Weynard, R. S. Interest preferences and their effect upon academic success. *Social Forces*, 1954, *32*, 281-285.

Brown, F. G. Test review of the Kuder Occupational Interest Survey, Form DD. *Measurement and Evaluation in Guidance*, 1971, *4*, 122-125.

Brown, M. N. Client evaluation of Kuder ratings. *Occupations*, 1950, *28*, 225-229.

Brown, M. N. Clinical status of veteran patients related to six interest variables. Ph.D. dissertation, University of Portland, 1951.

Brown, M. N. An interest inventory as a measure of personality. *Journal of Counseling Psychology*, 1954, *1*, 9-11.

Brown, M. N. Personnel managers mirrored. *Personnel Journal*, 1954, *33*, 90-91.

Brown, T. E. Factors relating to turnover among veterans administration nursing assistants. *Journal of Clinical and Experimental Psychopathology*, 1961, *22*, 226-234.

Brown, W. E. A study of the elements contributing to the successful selection of a job training vocational objective. Ph.D. dissertation, Pennsylvania State College, 1949. *(Abstracts of Doctoral Dissertations ... 1949, 1950*, pp. 318-324).

Bruce, M. M. A sales comprehension test. *Journal of Applied Psychology*, 1954, *38*, 302-304.

Bruce, M. M. Validity Information Exchange, no. 7-079: D. O. T. code 7-83058, electrical appliance serviceman. *Personnel Psychology*, 1954, 7, 425-426.

Bruce, M. M. Normative data information exchange, no. 10-42. *Personnel Psychology*, 1957, *10*, 534-535.

Bryan, J. G. A method for the exact determination of the characteristic equation and latest vectors of a matrix with applications to the discriminant function for more than two groups. Ph.D. dissertation on file at Harvard University Graduate School of Education, 1950.

Bryan, J. L. The Kuder Interest Test patterns of the student and the graduates of the fire protection school at Oklahoma A. & M. College. Ph.D. dissertation, Oklahoma Agricultural and Mechanical College, 1954.

Buckalew, R. J. An investigation of the interrelationships among measures of interests, intelligence, and personality for a sample of one hundred sixty-two eighth grade boys. Ph.D. dissertation, Temple University, 1962.

Budd, W. C. Prediction of interests between husband and wife. *Journal of Educational Sociology*, 1959, *33*, 37-39.

Buegel, H. F. Are students really interested in music? *School Activities*, 1951, *22*, 226.

Buegel, H. F., and Billing, P. S. Inventoried interests of participants in music groups. *Journal of Educational Research*, 1952, *46*, 141-146.

Buel, W. D., and Bachner, V. M. The assessment of creativity in a research setting. *Journal of Applied Psychology*, 1961, *45*, 353-358.

Burdette, W. E., Jr. Norms for the occupation of industrial arts teachers in conjunction with the Kuder Preference Record. Master's thesis, Kansas State Teachers College, 1948.

Bursch, C. W. II. The Kuder Preference Record in selecting vocational agriculture students. Abstract. *California Journal of Educational Research*, 1951, *2*, 184.

Bursch, C. W. II. Certain relationships between the Kuder Preference Record and the Minnesota Multiphasic Personality Inventory. *California Journal 51 Educational Research*, 1952, *3*, 224-227.

Bursch, C. W. II. Utility of the Kuder Preference Record in selection of students for vocational agriculture. Ph.D. dissertation, Stanford University, 1954.

Butler, F. J., Crinnion, J., and Martin, J. The Kuder Preference Record in adult vocational guidance. *Occupational Psychology*, 1972, *46*, 99-104.

Cain, E. T., II. Factors operative in curricular and/or occupational choice: A study of Super's theory. Ph.D. dissertation, University of Idaho, 1969.

Caine, T. M. Personality tests for nurses: An experiment. *Nursing Times*, Jl 24 1964, *60*, 973-974.

Calia, V. F. The use of discriminant analysis in the prediction of performance of junior college students in a program of general education at Boston University Junior College. Ph.D. dissertation, Boston University, 1959.

Calia, V. F. The use of discriminant analysis in the prediction of scholastic performance. Comments by David V. Tiedeman. *Personnel and Guidance Journal*, 1960, *39*, 184-192.

Callis, R., Engram, W. C., and McGowan, J. F. *Coding the Kuder Preference Record, Vocational (revised).* University of Missouri, Columbia: University Counseling Bureau, Research Report No. 9a, Sept. 1953. (Ed. review, 1962, by R. Callis, J. F. McGowan, and G. A. Rybolt).

Callis, R., Engram, W. C., and McGowan, J. F. Coding the Kuder Preference Record — Vocational. *Journal of Applied Psychology*, 1954, *38*, 359-363.

Campbell, D. P. Review of the Kuder Preference Record — Occupational, Form D. In O. K. Buros (ed.), *The sixth mental measurements yearbook.* Highland Park, N. J.: Gryphon Press, 1965, pp. 1284-1285.

Campbell, J. T., Otis, J. L., Liske, R. E., and Prien, E. P. Assessments of higher-level personnel: II. Validity of the over-all assessment process. *Personnel Psychology*, 1962, *15*, 63-74.

Campbell, R. E. Influence of the counselor's personality and background on his counseling style. Ph.D. dissertation, Ohio State University, 1961.

Campbell, R. E. Counselor personality and background and his interview subrole behavior. *Journal of Counseling Psychology*, 1962, *9*, 329-334.

Canfield, A. A. Administering Form BB of the Kuder Preference Record, half length. *Journal of Applied Psychology*, 1953, *37*, 197-200.

Cannon, W. M. A study of the responses of blind and sighted individuals to the Kuder Preference Record. Ph.D. dissertation, Duke University, 1959.

Capwell, D. F. *Psychological tests for retail store personnel.* Pittsburgh: Research Bureau for Retail Training, University of Pittsburgh, 1949, pp. 48.

Carek, R. Another look at the relationships between similar scales on the Strong Vocational Interest Blank and Kuder Occupational Interest Survey. *Journal of Counseling Psychology*, 1972, *19*, 218-223.

Carlson, S. L. Differences in aptitude, previous achievement, and nonintellectual traits (personality, values, interest, and attitude toward mathematics) of freshmen mathematics majors and transfers from the mathematics major at the University of Northern Colorado. Ed.D. dissertation, University of Northern Colorado, 1970.

Carroll, P., Jr. A summary of a paper "Ratings in Time Study," presented at the 4th American Time Study and Methods Conference April 21-22 of 1949. *Modern Management*, 1949, *9*, 15.

Carse, D. A study of the relationships between the Wechsler-Bellevue Intelligence Scale and the Kuder Preference Record — Personal. Master's thesis, North Texas State College, 1950.

Carter, G. C. Measurement of supervisory ability. *Journal of Applied Psychology*, 1952, *36*, 393-395.

Carter, G. C. Kuder Preference Record scores and success in engineering college. *Journal of Counseling Psychology*, 1954, *1*, 196.

Carter, H. D. Review of the Kuder Preference Record — Vocational. In O. K. Buros (ed.), *The fourth mental measurements yearbook.* Highland Park, N. J.: Gryphon Press, 1953, p. 738.

Carter, L., and Nixon, M. Ability, perceptual, personality, and interest factors associated with different criteria of leadership. *Journal of Psychology*, 1949, *27*, 377-388.

Case, H. W. The relationship of certain tests to grades achieved in an industrial class in aircraft design. *Educational and Psychological Measurement*, 1952, *12*, 90-95.

Casner, D. Certain factors associated with success and failure in personal adjustment counseling. Ph.D. dissertation, New York University, 1950.

Cass, J. C., and Tiedeman, D. V. Vocational development and the election of a high school curriculum. *Personnel and Guidance Journal*, 1960, *38*, 538-545.

Cassel, R. N. Comparing IBM card and hand scoring pad administration of the Kuder Vocational Preference Record. *California Journal of Educational Research*, 1963, *14*, 31-35.

Cãstano Lopez-Mesas, C. Kuder Preference Record: Form C, Vocational. *Revista de Psicologiá General y Aplicada*, 1972, *27*, 695-706.

Cãstano Lopez-Mesas, C., and Elizondo, J. M. Interpretation of the professional scales of the vocational themes of Garciá Yague. *Revista de Psicologiá General y Aplicada*, 1972, *27*, 417-420.

Castricone, N. R. A study of intrateacher group variations: The measured interests of teachers of the educably mentally handicapped. *Dissertation Abstracts*, 1968, *28* (10-A), 3879.

Cerf, A. Z. Kuder Preference Record, CE515A, *Printed classification tests*. Edited by J. P. Guilford with the assistance of John I. Lacey, Army Air Forces Aviation Psychology Program Research Reports, Report No. 5. Washington, D.C.: U.S. Government Printing Office, 1947.

Chambers, E. G. Review of the Kuder Preference Record. In O. K. Buros (ed.), *The third mental measurements yearbook*, Highland Park, N.J.: Gryphon Press, 1949, p. 661.

Champion, J. M. A method of predicting success of commerce students. Ph.D. dissertation, Purdue University, 1958.

Chaney, F. B. The life history antecedents of selected vocational interests. *Dissertation Abstracts*, 1963, *23* (8), 2974-2975.

Chapman, P. W. *Your personality and your job*. Chicago: Science Research Associates, 1949.

Chase, J. B., Jr. An analysis of the change of interest of one hundred and fifty secondary school pupils. Master's thesis, University of North Carolina, 1950.

Chatterjea, R. G., and Saha, G. B. Interest pattern of school teachers. *Journal of Psychological Researches*, 1962, *6*, 107-114.

Chatterjee, S., and Muderjee, M. Relation between Kuder Preference Record and a non-verbal interest inventory modelled after it to suit Indian conditions. *Journal of Psychological Researches*, 1962, *6*, 115-117.

Chen, M. K., Podshadley, D. W., and Schrock, J. G. A factorial study of some psychological, vocational interest, and mental ability variables as predictors of success in dental school. *Journal of Applied Psychology*, 1967, *51* (3), 236-241.

Christensen, C. M. Dimensions and correlates of texture preferences. *Journal of Consulting Psychology*, 1962, 26, 498-504.

Christensen, T. E. Some observations with respect to the Kuder Preference Record. *Journal of Educational Research*, 1946, *40*, 96-107.

Christensen, T. E. *Getting job experience.* Chicago: Science Research Associates, 1949.

Christiaens, X. Significance and value of the Kuder Interest Test for psychological testing in secondary schools. *Tijdschrift Studie-Beroepsorient,* 1957, *4,* 13-28.

Clemans, W. V. An analytical and empirical examination of some properties of ispsative measures. Ph.D. dissertation on file at the University of Washington (Seattle), 1956.

Clemans, W. V. An analytical and empirical examination of some properties of ipsative measures. *Psychometric Monographs,* 1968, p. 14.

Clemans, W. V. Interest measurement and the concept of ipsativity. *Measurement and Evaluation in Guidance,* 1968, *1,* 50-55.

Clendenen, D. M. Review of the Kuder Preference Record — Personal. In O. K. Buros (ed.), *The sixth mental measurements yearbook.* Highland Park, N. J.: Gryphon Press, 1965, pp. 275-277.

Coats, J. E., with the assistance of Garner, R. G. *A study of the nature of the chemical operator's occupation and the personal qualities that contribute to successful operator performance.* Midland, Mich.: Dow Chemical Co., 1961, pp. 4, 112.

Cockrum, L. V. Personality traits and interests of theological students. *Religious Education,* 1952, *47,* 28-32.

Cohen, L. M. The relationship between certain personality variables and prior occupational stability of prison inmates. Ph.D. dissertation, Temple University, 1959.

Cole, N. S. On measuring the vocational interests of women. *Journal of Counseling Psychology,* 1973, *20*(2), 105-112.

Cole, N. S., and Hanson, G. An analysis of the structure of vocational interests. *Journal of Counseling Psychology,* 1971, *18,* 478-486.

Cole, N. S., and Hanson, G. An analysis of the structure of vocational interests. *ACT Research Reports,* 1971, *40,* 17.

Comer, J. E., Jr. A study of the comparison of interests of social science majors with the interests of other adults as measured by the Kuder Preference Record. Master's thesis, Kansas State Teachers College, 1949.

Comrey, A. L., and High, W. S. Validity of some ability and interest scores. *Journal of Applied Psychology,* 1955, *39,* 247-248.

Conner, H. T. An investigation of certain factors for the selection and guidance of prospective students entering a school of public health. Ph.D. dissertation, University of North Carolina, 1954.

Cook, C. C. For the undecided — help in selecting a suitable career. *Duke University alumni register,* October, 1955, pp. 8-11.

Coomb, W. A. Word difficulty in the Kuder Preference Record. Master's thesis, Stanford University, 1946.

Cooper, M. N. To determine the nature and significance, if any, of certain differences in the social and personal adjustment of fifty-one successful and fifty-one non-successful college students at Texas Southern University. Ph.D. dissertation, York University, 1955.

Costello, C. G., and Anderson, M. E. The vocational and personal preferences of psychiatric and general nurses. *Nursing Research,* 1960, *9,* 155-156.

Cottingham, H. F. The value of the Kuder Preference Record in determining the vocational interests of high school sensiors. Unpublished master's thesis, State University of Iowa, 1940.

Cottle, W. C. A factorial study of selected instruments for measuring personality and interest. Abstract. *American Psychology*, 1948, *3*, 300.

Cottle, W. C. Relationships among selected personality and interest inventories. Abstract. *American Psychology*, 1949, *4*, 292-293.

Cottle, W. C. A factorial study of the Multiphasic, Strong, Kuder, and Bell inventories using a population of adult males. *Psychometrika*, 1950, *15*, 25-47.

Cottle, W. C. Relationships among selected personality and interest inventories. *Occupations*, 1959, *28*, 306-310.

Cottle, W. C., and Powell, J. O. Relationship of mean scores on the Strong, Kuder and Bell inventories with the MMPI M-F Scale as the criterion. *Transactions of the Kansas Academy of Science*, 1949, *52*, 396-398.

Coulson, R. W. Relationships among personality traits, ability and academic efficiency of college seniors. Ph.D. dissertation, State University of Iowa, 1958.

Coutts, R. LaR. Selected characteristics of counselor-candidates in relation to levels and types of competency in the counseling practicum. Ph.D. dissertation, Florida State University, 1962.

Crane, W. J. Screening devices for occupational therapy majors. *American Journal of Occupational Therapy*, 1962, *16*, 131-132.

Craven, E. C. Social concomitants of interest. Ph.D. dissertation, Columbia University, 1948.

Craven, E. C. *The use of interest inventories in counseling.* Chicago: Science Research Associates, 1961.

Crawford, A. B. Review of the Preference Record. In O. K. Buros, *The 1940 mental measurements yearbook.* Highland Park, N. J.: Gryphon Press, 1941, pp. 447-449.

Cronbach, L. J. Response sets and test validity, *Educational and Psychological Measurement*, 1946, *6*, 475-494.

Cronback, L. J. *Essentials of psychological testing, second edition.* New York: Harper & Row, 1960, p. 406.

Cronbach, L. J. *Essentials of psychological testing, third edition.* New York: Harper & Row, 1970, pp. 457-486.

Crosby, R. C. The measurement of interest and its utility in college personnel work. Unpublished Ph.D. dissertation, Cornell University, 1941. *(Abstracts of Theses . . . 1941, 1942, pp. 95-97).*

Corsby, R. C. Scholastic achievement and measured interests. *Journal of Applied Psychology*, 1943, *27*, 101-103.

Crosby, R. C., and Winsor, A. L. The validity of students' estimates of their interests. *Journal of Applied Psychology*, 1941, *25*, 408-414.

Cross, O. H. A study of faking on the Kuder Preference Record. Abstract. *American Psychology*, 1948, *3*, 293.

Cross, O. H. A study of faking on the Kuder Preference Record. *Educational and Psychological Measurement*, 1950, *10*, 271-277.

Cummings, I. M. The relation between interest and achievement: A comparison of scores of the Kuder Preference Record and those on co-operative achievement tests for college freshmen. Master's thesis, Southern Methodist University, 1946. *(Abstracts of Theses . . . 1046, 1947, pp. 66-67).*

Curran, J. P. A study of the effectiveness of the Kuder Preference Record — Vocational in a private secondary school for girls. Master's thesis, Catholic University of America, 1954.

Daley, J. M. Relationship of MMPI and Kuder Preference Record scores. Master's thesis, Catholic University of America, 1948.

Daley, J. M. A comparison of the relation of the Thurstone Interest Schedule to the Kuder Preference Record and to self-estimated interests. Master's thesis, Fordham University, 1951.

D'Arcy, P. F. Constancy of interest factor patterns within the specific vocation of foreign missioner. *Studies in Psychology and Psychiatry*, Vol. 9, No. 1. Washington: Catholic University of America Press, 1954, pp. 4, 54.

D'Arcy, P. F. Review of research on the vocational interests of priests, brothers and sisters. In *Screening candidates for the priesthood and religious life*. Chicago: Loyola University Press, 1962, pp. 149-200.

Darley, J. G. Evaluation of interest tests in O. J. Kaplan (ed.) *Encyclopedia of vocational guidance*, New York, Philosophical Library, 1948, 621-626.

Darley, J. G., and Marquis, D. G. Veteran guidance centers: A survey of their problems and activities. *Journal of Clinical Psychology*, 1946, *2*, 109-116.

Darnall, E. J., Jr. Falsification of interest patterns on the Kuder Preference Record. *Journal of Educational Psychology*, 1954, *45*, 240-243.

Daugherty, F. F. A psychometric analysis of the interests and abilities of a selected high school population. Ph.D. dissertation, Stanford University, 1951.

Dauwn, D. C. Vocational interests of highly creative computer personnel. *Personnel Journal*, 1967, *46*, 653-659.

David, C. Interpersonal measurement of two occupational interest groups. *Journal of Projective Techniques*, 1962, *26*(3), 276-282.

Davis, S. S. The relationship between school superintendents' ratings of elementary teachers and the Kuder Preference Record — Personal and other measured and rated teacher characteristics. Ph.D. dissertation, University of Colorado, 1954.

Day, M. E. Kuder Preference Record responses of a selected group of schizophrenics (counseling referrals) as a function of personality traits. Ph.D. dissertation, New York University, 1957.

Descombes, J.-P. *Manuel pour la version et adaptation française (abregéé) de l'inventaire de préférences professionel les du Professeur Kuder (Forme C)*. Institut de Psychologie, Université de Neuchatel, 1965.

Descombes, J.-P. *Intérêts et choix professionnels évaluées par l'inventaire de préférences professionnelle de Kuder*. Neuchâtel, Switzerland: Delachaux et Niestlé, 1971.

Descombes, J.-P. Les relations entre intérêts, aptitudes et notes scolaires, chez 129 gymnasiens lausannois. *Revue Suisse de Psychologie Pure et Appliquée*, 1975, *34*, 32-49.

Detchen, L. Factors affecting achievement in the social sciences: 1. Comprehensive examination, University of Chicago. Ph.D. dissertation, University of Chicago, 1944.

Detchen, L. The effect of a measure of interest factors on the prediction of performance in a college social sciences comprehensive examination. *Journal of Educational Psychology*, 1946, *37*, 45-52.

Diamond, E. E. Occupational level versus sex group as a system of classification. Abstract. *Proceedings, 76th Annual Convention of the American Psychological Association*, 1968, *3*, 199-200.

Diamond, E. E. Relationship between occupational level and masculine and feminine interests. Abstract. *Proceedings, 78th Annual Convention of the American Psychological Association*, 1970, 5, 177-178.

Diamond, S. The interpretation of interest profiles. *Journal of Applied Psychology*, 1948, 32, 512-520.

Diener, C. L. Similarities and differences between over-achieving and under-achieving students. *Personnel and Guidance Journal*, 1960, 38, 396-400.

DiMichael, S. G. The professed and measured interests of vocational rehabilitation counselors. *Educational and Psychological Measurement*, 1949, 9, 59-72.

DiMichael, S.˙ G. Work satisfaction and work efficiency of vocational rehabilitation counselors as related to measured interests. *Journal of Applied Psychology*, 1949, 33, 319-329.

DiMichael, S. G. Interest inventory results during the counseling interview. *Occupations*, 1951, 30, 93-97

DiMichael, S. G., and Dabelstein, D. H. Work satisfaction and work efficiency of vocational rehabilitation counselors as related to measured interests. Abstract. *American Psychologist*, 1947, 2, 342-343.

Dolliver, R. H. Review of the Kuder Occupational Interest Survey. In O. K. Buros (ed.), *The seventh mental measurements yearbook*. Highland Park, N. Y.: Gryphon Press, 1972, pp. 1427-1429.

Downie, N. M. The vocational interest patterns of students who stay in engineering compared with those who leave the engineering curriculum. Abstract. *Indiana Academy of Science Proceedings*, 1965, 66, 324.

Drasgow, J., and Carkhuff, R. R. Kuder neuropsychiatric keys before and after psychotherapy. *Journal of Counseling Psychology*, 1964, 11, (1), 67-71.

Dreese, M. *How to get the job*. Chicago: Science Research Associates, 1949.

Dressell, P. L., and Matteson, R. W. The relationship between experience and interest as measured by the Kuder Preference Record. *Educational and Psychological Measurement*, 1952, 12, 109-116.

Drew, A. S. The relationship of general reading ability and other factors to school and job performance of machinist apprentices. Ph.D. dissertation, University of Wisconsin, 1962.

Driscoll, J. The dimensions of satisfaction with the religious life among scholastics in a community of teaching brothers: A descriptive study. *Dissertation Abstracts*, 1966, 27(6-A), 1653.

Drum, D. J. A study of the relationships between level of development of educational interests and academic performance in first-year college students. Ph.D. dissertation, American University, 1969.

Dulsky, S. G., and Krout, M. H. Predicting promotion potential on the basis of psychological tests. *Personnel Psychology*, 1950, 3, 345-351.

Eaton, A. M., and Fiske, D. W. Item stability as related to implicit set and subject-item distance. *Journal of Consulting and Clinical Psychology*, 1971, 37(2), 259-266.

Eddings, E. L. A factor analytic study of interest patterns and their relationship to personality for two hundred high achieving high school seniors. *Dissertation Abstracts*, 1963, 23(9), 3464-3465.

Eimicke, V. W. Kuder Preference Record norms for sales trainees: With detailed description and additional psychological test results. *Occupations*, 1949, 38, 5-10.

Eimicke, V. W. A study of the effect of intensive sales training experience upon the measured abilities and personality characteristics of salesmen-candidates. Ph.D. dissertation, New York University, 1951. Abstract. *Microfilm Abstracts*, 11:951-2 No. 4. 1951.

Embree, R. B., Jr. Analysis of the scores made by students at various levels of counselor-training on measures of aptitude, preference, values, temperament, and adjustment. Abstract. *American Psychologist*, 1951, *6*, 377.

Embree, R. B., Jr. Method of interpretation and maturity as related to what conselees learn from test interpretations and how they feel about them. Abstract. *American Psychologist*, 1953, *8*, 346.

Evans, C. E. Interelations of evidences of vocational interest. Unpublished Ph.D. dissertation, Ohio State University, 1946. *(Abstracts of Dissertations . . .* Summer quarter 1945-1946, pp. 51-57.

Evans, M. C. Social adjustment and interest scores of introverts and extroverts. *Educational and Psychological Measurement*, 1947, *7*, 156-167.

Evans, M. C. Differentiation of home economics students according to major emphasis. *Occupations*, 1948, *27*, 120-125.

Ewens, W. P. Experience patterns as related to vocational preference. Ph.D. dissertation, Stanford University, 1949.

Ewens, W. P. Experience patterns as related to vocational preference. *Educational and Psychological Measurement*, 1956, *16*, 223-231.

Ewens, W. P. Relationship of interest to aptitude by profiles and by interest areas. *Personnel and Guidance Journal*, 1963, *42*, 359-363.

Faldet, B. W. Relationships between the measured interests of seventh grade students and their parents. Ed.D dissertation, Northern Illinois University, 1975.

Farber, R. H. Guidance implications of the freshman testing program at DePauw. University. Ph.D. dsssertation, Indiana University, 1951. *(Thesis Abstract Series . . .* 1951, 1952, pp. 37-42)

Farrow, E. G. The development of a masculinity-feminity scale for the Kuder Preference Record — Personal. Master's thesis, North Carolina State College of Agriculture and Engineering, 1953.

Feather, D. B. The relation of personality maladjustments of 503 University of Michigan students to their occupational interests. Ph.D. dissertation on file at the Universtiy of Michigan, 1949.

Feather, D. B. The relation of personality maladjustments of 503 University of Michigan students to their occupational interests. *Journal of Social Psychology*, 1950, *32*, 71-78.

Ferguson, L. W. *Personality measurement.* New York: McGraw-Hill, 1952, pp. 67-80.

Fjeld, H. A. A comparison of major groups of college women on the Kuder Preference Record — Personal. *Educational and psychological Measurement*, 1952, *12*, 664-668.

Fleming, W. G. The Kuder Preference Record, — Vocational as a predictor of post-high school educational and occupational choices. *Atkinson study of utilization of student resources, supplementary report No. 2.* Toronto, 1959 pp, 7, 49.

Fleming, W. G. The Kuder Preference Record — Vocational as a predictor of post-high school educational and occupational choices. Department of Educational Research, Ontario College of Education, University of Toronto, 1959.

Flowers, H. M. The relationship of parental identification to parental vocational interest similarity. Ph.D. dissertation, University of Kansas, 1971.

Flowers, J. F. Some aspects of the Kuder Preference Record — Personal as an instrument for prediction and guidance in Ontario secondary schools. Master's thesis, University of Toronto (Toronto, Ont., Canada), 1957.

Flowers, J. F. An evaluation of the Kuder Preference Record — Personal for use in Ontario. Atkinson *study of utilization of student resources, supplementary report No. 4.* Toronto, Canada: Department of Educational Research, Ontario College of Education, University of Toribtim 1961, pp. 8, 31.

Fogliatto, H. M. Factorial stability of two psychological tests: D.A.T. and Kuder. *Revista Inter-americana de Psicologia*, 1972, *6*(3-4), 213-223.

Fogliatto, H. M. Factorial stability of two psychological tests: D.A.T. and Kuder. *Revista de Psicologia General y Aplicada*, 1973, *28*(122), 353-360.

Foley, A. W. Adjustment through interest changes. *Journal of Counseling Psychology*, 1955, *2*, 66-67.

Foote, R. P. The prediction of success in automotive mechanics in a vocational-industrial curriculum on the secondary school level. Ph.D. dissertation, New York University, 1960.

Force, R. C. Development of a covert test for the detection of alcoholism by a keying of the Kuder Preference Record. *Quarterly Journal of Studies on Alcohol*, 1958, *19*, 72-78.

Force, R. C., and Thomas, P. Development of a covert test for the detection of alcohol addiction by a keying of the Kuder Preference Record. Abstract. *American Psychologist*, 1955, *10*, 449.

Ford, A. H. Prediction of academic success in three schools of nursing. *Journal of Applied Psychology*, 1950, *34*, 186-189.

Forer, B. R. Personality factors in occupational choice. *Educational and Psychological Measurement*, 1953, *13*, 361-366.

Forer, B. R. The stability of Kuder scores in a disabled population. *Educational and Psychological Measurement*, 1955, *15*, 166-169.

Forster, C. R. The relationship between test achievement and success in training of a selected group of tuberculosis patients. Ph.D. dissertation, New York University, 1955.

Fosselius, E. E. A study of the use of and the results of the Kuder Preference records in the Jefferson Junior High School, Elyria, Ohio. Unpublished master's thesis, Ohio State University, 1944, pp. 84.

Foster, R. Kuder-D Verfication Key sensitivity to various faking techniques. *Psychology*, 1965, *2*(2), 4-6.

Fowler, M. M. Interest measurement — questions and answers. *School Life*, 1945, *28*, 25-29.

Fowler, M. M. Review of the Kuder Preference Record — Vocational. In O. K. Burus (ed.), *The fourth mental measurements yearbook.* Highland Park, N. J.: Gryphon Press, 1953, pp. 738-742.

Fox, W. H. The stability of measured interests. *Journal of Educational Research*, 1947, *41*, 305-310.

Frandsen, A. N. Interests and general educational development. *Journal of Applied Psychology*, 1947, *31*, 57-66.

Frandsen, A. N. A note on Wiener's coding of Kuder Preference Record profiles. *Educational and Psychological Measurement*, 1952, *12*, 137-139.

Frandsen, A. N., and Sessions, A. D. Interests and school achievement. *Educational and Psychological Measurement*, 1953, *13*, 94-101.

Frankel, E. A comparative study of achieving and underachieving high school boys of high intellectual ability. Ph.D. dissertation, Yeshiva University, 1958.

Freehill, M. F. Student self-estimates as guidance in selecting courses. *College and University*, 1952, *27*, 233-242.

Freehill, M. F. Interest scores in selection of freshman courses. *College and University*, 1953, *28*, 197-203.

Freeman, F. S. *Theory and practice of psychological testing, third edition.* New York: Holt, Rinehart & Winston, 1962, pp. 581-584, 588-596.

French, J. L. Interests of the gifted. *Vocational Guidance Quarterly*, 1958, 7, 14-16.

Friesen, J. H. Vocal mutation in the adolescent male: Its chronology and a comparison with fluctuations in musical interest. D.M.A. dissertation, University of Oregon, 1972.

Froehlich, C. P. Letter regarding a comparison of scores on the Kuder Preference Record and the Job Qualification Inventory by Earl W. Seibert. *Journal of Educational Research*, 1946, *40*, 178-186. *Journal of Educational Research*, 1947, *40*, 477-479.

Froehlich, C. P. Review of Kuder Preference Record — Vocational. In O. K. Buros (ed.), *The fifth mental measurements yearbook.* Highland Park, N. J.: Gryphon Press, 1959, pp. 890-891.

Furst, E. J., and Fricke, B. G. Development and applications of structured tests of personality. *Review of Educational Research*, 1956, *26*, 26-55.

Gardner, R. W. Relationships between similar scales of the two major inventories. *Perceptual and Motor Skills*, 1973, *36*(2), 635-638.

Garrett, G. A. A study of the causes of unsatisfactory verification scores on the Kuder Preference Record Vocational. Master's thesis, University of Missouri, 1956.

Garrett, G. A. A comparison of the predictive power of the Kuder Preference Record and the Strong Vocational Interest Blank in a counseling setting. Ph.D. dissertation, University of Missouri, 1969.

Gash, I. A. The stability of measured interests as related to the clinical improvement of hospitalized psychiatric patients. *Dissertation Abstracts*, 1966, *27*(4-B), 1290.

Gehman, W. S. Validity generalization and cross-validation of the Kuder Electrical Engineering Scale for counseling college students. *Educational and Psychological Measurement*, 1959, *19*, 589-597.

Gehman, W. S., and Gehman, I. H. Stability of engineering interests over a period of four years. *Educational and Psychological Measurement*, 1968, *28*, 367-376.

Gehman, W. S., Kraybill, E. K., and Katzenmeyer, W. G. Application of new Kuder engineering scales for counseling university students. *Journal of Engineering Education*, 1959, *50*, 166-169.

Gehman, W. S., and Southern, J. A. The Kuder Electrical Engineering Scale for counseling college students. *Journal of Counseling Psychology*, 1956, *3*, 17-20.

Giblett, J. F. Differences among above average, average, and below average secondary school counselors. Ph.D. dissertation, University of Pennsylvania, 1960.

Gibson, R. L., and Higgins, R. E., eds. *Techniques of guidance, an approach to pupil analysis.* Chicago: Science Research Associates, 1966.

Gilbert, J. Vocational archetypes: A proposal for clinical integration of interests and values in vocational counseling and selection. *Psychological Reports,* 1963, *13,* 351-356.

Gitlin, S. A study of the interrelationships of parents' measured interest patterns and those of their children. Ph.D. dissertation, Temple University, 1958.

Givens, P. R. Kuder patterns of interest as related to achievement in college science courses. *Journal of Educational Research,* 1953, *46,* 627-630.

Glazer, S. H. Educational attainment and interest patterns. *Vocational Guidance Quarterly,* 1958, *6,* 183-186.

Glick, R. Practitioners and non-practitioners in a group of women physicians. *Dissertation Abstracts,* 1966, *26*(11), 6845.

Gobetz, W. Suggested personality implications of Kuder Preference Record (Vocational) scores. *Personnel and Guidance Journal,* 1964, *43,* 159-166.

Goche, L. N. Relationship of interest and temperament traits to attrition and survival of engineering students. Master's thesis, Iowa State College, 1954.

Golburgh, S. J. A study of the vocational interests of four types of psychotic subjects. Ph.D. dissertation, Boston University, 1960.

Goldstein, A. P. The fakability of the Kuder Preference Record and the Vocational Apperception Test. Master's thesis, City College of New York, 1956.

Goldstein, A. P. The fakability of the Kuder Preference Record and the Vocational Appreception Test. *Journal of Projective Techniques,* 1960, *24,* 133-136.

Gordon, H. C., and Herkness, W. W., Jr. Pupils appraise vocational interest blanks. *Occupations,* 1941, 20, 100-102.

Gordon, H. C., and Herkness, W. W., Jr. Do vocational interest questionnaires yield consistent results? *Occupations,* 1942, *20,* 424-429.

Gorman, J. R. A study of adjustment and interests for fourth year minor seminarians studying for the diocesan priesthood. Master's thesis, Loyola University (Chicago), 1961.

Goshorn, W. M. A study of the relationships between the Kuder Preference Record — Personal and certain sociometric ratings. Ph.D. dissertation, Indiana University, 1950. *(Thesis Abstract Series* . . . 1950, 1951, pp. 37-43).

Gowan, J. C. The interest patterns of student leaders. *Educational and Psychological Measurement,* 1954, *14,* 151-154.

Gowan, J. C. Achievement and personality test scores of gifted college students. *California Journal of Educational Research,* 1956, *7,* 105-109.

Gowan, J. C. Intelligence, interests, and reading ability in relation to scholastic achievement. *Psychological Newsletter,* 1957, *8,* 85-87.

Gowan, J. C. A summary of the intensive study of twenty highly selected elementary women teachers. *Journal of Experimental Education,* 1957, *26,* 115-124.

Gowan, J. C., and Seagoe, M. The relation between interest and aptitude tests in art and music. *California Journal of Educational Research,* 1957, *8,* 43-45.

Grant, D. L. Validity information exchange, no. 7-085: D.O.T. code 1-01.05, budget clerk. *Personnel Psychology*, 1954, *7*, 557-558.

Grant, D. L. Validity information exchange, no. 7-086: D.O.T. code 1-01.05, budget clerk. *Personnel Psychology*, 1954, *7*, 559-560.

Green, R. F. The validity of certain psychological tests in the selection and classification of juvenile police officers. Master's thesis, University of Southern California, 1949.

Green, R. F. Does a selection situation induce testees to bias their answers on interest and temperament tests? *Educational and Psychological Measurement*, 1951, *11*, 503-515.

Group, V. F. Characteristic differences between successful and unsuccessful candidates for apprentice carpentry training. Ed.D. dissertation on file at Rutgers University, 1951.

Guazzo, E. J., Jr. Predicting academic success of architecture students. Master's thesis, Alabama Polytechnic Institute, 1954.

Guba, E. G., and Getzels, J. W. *Printed classification tests*, A.A.F. Aviation Psycology Report, No. 5. Washington: Government Printing Office, 1947.

Guba, E. G., and Getzels, J. W. When not to factor analyze. *Psychological Bulletin*, 1952, *49*, 26-37.

Guba, E. G., and Getzels, J. W. Interest and value patterns of air force officers. *Educational and Psychological Measurement*, 1956, *16*, 465-470.

Guilford, J. P., Christensen, P. R., Bond, N. A., Jr., and Sutton, M. A. A factor analysis of human interests. *Psychological Monographs*, 1954, *68*, 1-38.

Gustad, J. W. Review of the Kuder Preference Record — Occupational, Form D. In O. K. Buros (ed.), *The Fifth Mental Measurements Yearbook*. Highland Park, N. J.: Gryphon Press, 1959, pp. 885-886.

Hackman, R. B. The problem of vocational choice in vocational guidance: An essay. *Counseling and guidance: A summary view*. Edited by J. F. Adams. New York: MacMillan, 1965.

Hahn, M. E. An investigation of measured aspects of social intelligence in a distributive occupation. Ph.D. dissertation, University of Minnesota, 1942.

Hahn, M. E. Notes on the Kuder Preference Record. *Occupations*, 1945, *23*, 467-470.

Hahn, M. E., and Williams, C. T. The measured interests of Marine Corps women reservists. *Journal of Applied Psychology*, 1945, *29*, 198-211.

Hakanson, I. S. A longitudinal validity study of the Kuder Vocational. Ed.D. dissertation, University of Oregon, 1970.

Hake, D. T., and Ruedisili, C. H. Predicting subject grades of liberal arts freshmen with the Kuder Preference Record. *Journal of Applied Psychology*, 1949, *33*, 553-558.

Hale, P. P. Tests employed by VA counselors for the guidance of P. L. 16 veterans rehabilitated as high school teachers. Master's thesis on file in the library of Duquesne University, 1950.

Hale, P. P. A comparison of Kuder teachers interest patterns with those of veteran teacher trainees. *Educational Aministration and Supervision*, 1952, *38*, 412-420.

Hale, P. P. Profiling the Kuder. *Vocational Guidance Quarterly*, 1958, *7*, 76.

Hale, P. P., and Leonard, R. J. The Kuder Preference Record and the professional curriculum. *Journal of Educational Research*, 1956, *50*, 71-74.

Hammill, D. An analysis of the interest patterns of high school seniors on Form CH of the Kuder Preference Record. Master's thesis, Fordham University, 1954.

Hanna, G. S. An attempt to validate an empirically-derived interest scale and standard Kuder scales for predicting success in high school geometry. *Educational and Psychological Measurement*, 1966, *26*(2), 445-448.

Hanna, J. V., and Barnette, W. L., Jr. Revised norms for the Kuder Preference Record for Men. *Occupations*, 1949, *38*, 168-170.

Harmon, L. R. Inter-relations of patterns on the Kuder Preference Record and the Minnesota Multiphasic Personality Inventory. Ph.D. dissertation, University of Minnesota, 1952.

Harrell, T. A., and Harrell, M. Army General Classification Test scores for civilian occupations. *Educational and Psychological Measurement*, 1945, *5*, 231-242.

Harrington, J. A. Multivariate test score patterns on the KPR-V, the KPR-P, and both combined for college women in four curriculum groups and college men in five curriculum groups. Ph.D. dissertation, Boston College, 1969.

Harrington, T. F., Jr., Lynch, M. D., and O'Shea, A. J. Factor analysis of twenty-seven similarly named scales of the Strong Vocational Interest Blank and the Kuder Occupational Interest Survey, Form DD. *Journal of Counseling Psychology*, 1971, *18*, 229-233.

Harrison, L. Application of certain Seashore measures of musical talent and the Kuder Preference Record to the building of a music program in Borger High School. Master's thesis, North Texas State College, 1949.

Harrow, M., and Schulberg, H. Case report: Implications from psychological testing for theoretical formulations of folie à deux, *Journal of Abnormal and Social Psychology*, 1963. *67*(2), 169-171.

Hartman, B. J. Effect of knowledge of personality test results on subsequent test performance. *Perceptual and Motor Skills*, 1968, *26*(1), 122-126.

Hascall, E. O., Jr. Predicting success in high school foreign language study. Ph.D. dissertation, University of Michigan, 1959.

Haselkorn, H. The vocational interests of a group of homosexuals. Ph.D. dissertation, New York University, 1953.

Haselkorn, H. The vocational interests of a group of male homosexuals. *Journal of Counseling Psychology*, 1956, *3*, 8-11.

Headlee, M. D. The Kuder Preference Record as a device for differentiating among majors in the division of home economics at Iowa State College. Master's thesis, Iowa State College, 1948.

Healy, I., and Borg, W. R. Personality characteristics of nursing school students and graduate nurses. *Journal of Applied Psychology*, 1951, *25*, 275-280.

Healy, I., and Borg, W. R. The vocational interests of nurses and nursing students. *Journal of Educational Research*, 1953, *46*, 347-352.

Henderson, E. C. The Kuder-Preference Record — Vocational in appraising the apparent suitability of vocational choices of high school students. Master's thesis, Utah State Agricultural College, 1956.

Henry, W. O. A study of two work tests in relation to the Kuder Preference Record. Master's thesis, University of Southern California, 1949.

Herzberg, F., and Bouton, A. A further study of the stability of the Kuder Preference Record. *Educational and Psychological Measurement*, 1954, *14*, 326-331.

Herzberg, F., Bouton, A., and Steiner, B. J. Students of the stability of the Kuder Preference Record. *Educational and Psychological Measurement,* 1954, *14,* 90-100.

Herzberg, F., and Russell, D. The effects of experience and change of job interest on the Kuder Preference Record. *Journal of Applied Psychology,* 1953, *37,* 478-481.

Heston, J. C. College freshman norms for the Kuder Preference Record. *Occupations,* 1947, *26,* 92-94.

Heston, J. C. A comparison of four masculinity-femininity scales. *Educational and Psychological Measurement,* 1948, *8,* 375-387.

Hill, G. E., and Hole, R. M. Comparison of the vocational interests of tenth grade students with their parents — judgments of these interests. *Educational and Psychological Measurement,* 1958, *18,* 173-187.

Hill, G. E., and Rogge, H. The relation of Kuder Preference Record scores to mental maturity scores in high school. *Journal of Educational Research,* 1958, *51,* 545-548.

Hillman, C. An empirical validation of a sales personnel selection program. Master's thesis, Vanderbilt University, 1951.

Hirt, M. Another look at the relationship between interests and aptitudes. *Vocational Guidance Quarterly,* 1959, 7, 171-173.

Hohenshil, T. H. A comparison of the inventoried interests of selected types of guidance specialists in Ohio. Ph.D. dissertation, Kent State University, 1971.

Hole, R. R. A comparison of students' vocational interests with parental judgments of students' interests. Unpublished master's thesis, Ohio University, 1956.

Holland, J. L, Krause, A. H., Nixon, M. E., and Trambath, M. F. The classification of occupations by means of Kuder interest profiles: 1, The development of interest groups. *Journal of Applied Psychology,* 1953, *37,* 263-269.

Hoover, K. H., and Micka, H. K. Student-parent interest comparisons in counseling high school students. *Personnel and Guidance Journal,* 1956, *34,* 292-294.

Hornaday, J. A. Measurement of interest in forestry. *Journal of Forestry,* 1959, *57,* 8-9.

Hornaday, J. A. Interest patterns of dietitians. *Journal of the American Dietetic Association,* 1963, *43,* 99-103.

Hornaday, J. A., and Aboud, J. Characteristics of successful entrepreneurs. *Personnel Psychology,* 1971, *24*(2), 141-153.

Hornaday, J. A., and Bunker, C. S. The nature of the entrepreneur. *Personnel Psychology,* 1971, *24*(2), 141-153.

Hornaday, J. A., and Kuder, G. F. A study of male occupational interest scales applied to women. *Educational and Psychological Measurement,* 1961, *21,* 859-864.

Horrocks, J. E. *Assessment of behavior.* Columbus, Ohio: Merrill, 1964, pp. 675-678.

Hosford, P. McI. Characteristics of science-talented and language-talented secondary school students. Ph.D. dissertation, University of Georgia, 1961.

Huffman, W. J. Personality variations among men preparing to teach physical education. Ph.D. dissertation, University of Illinois, 1951.

Humphreys, J. A. *Choosing your career.* Chicago: Science Research Associates, 1949.

Husek, T. R. Review of the Kuder General Interest Survey. *Journal of Educational Measurement,* 1965, *2,* 231–233.

Hyman, B. The relationship of social status and vocational interests. *Journal of Counseling Psychology,* 1956, *3,* 12–16.

Isaacson, L. E. Predictors of success for cooperative occupational educational classes in Kansas City, Missouri, high schools. Abstract. *American Psychology,* 1952, *7,* 379.

Iscoe, I., and Lucier, O. A comparison of the revised Allport-Vernon Scale of Values and the Kuder Preference Record. *Journal of Applied Psychology,* 1953, *37,* 195–196.

Ivey, A. E. Interests and work values. *Vocational Guidance Quarterly,* 1963, *11,* 121–124.

Ivey, A. E., and Peterson, M. B. Vocational preference patterns of communications graduates. *Educational and Psychological Measurement,* 1965, *25,* 849–856.

Jackson, J. A note on the crystallization of vocational interests. *Journal of Social Psychology,* 1947, *26,* 125–130.

Jacobs, R. Stability of interests at the secondary school level. *1949 achievement testing program in independent schools and supplementary studies.* Educational Records Bulletin, No. 52. New York: Educational Records Bureau, 1949, pp. 83–87.

Jacobs, R. A brief study of the relationship between scores on the Lee-Thorpe Occupational Interest Inventory and scores on the Kuder Preference Record. *1951 Achievement Testing Program in Independent Schools and Supplementary Studies.* Foreword by Ben D. Wood. Educational Records Bulletin No. 57. New York: Educational Records Bureau, 1951, pp. 79–85.

Jacobs, R., and Traxler, A. E. What manner of man is the average accountant? *Journal of Accountancy,* 1954, *97,* 465–469.

James, F. The stability of the civil, electrical, and mechanical engineering scales of the Kuder Preference Record Occupational, Form D, and some implications for counseling. Master's thesis, Duke University, 1959

Jensen, G. LeR. Relationship between school achievement and scholastic aptitude: Techniques for ascertaining this relationship, their application to data from a group of high school pupils and their use in school practice. Ph.D. dissertation, Stanford University, 1949. *(Abstracts of Dissertations . . . 1949–1950.* 1950, pp. 403–408)

Johnson, G. Meditations on an interest test. *Occupations,* 1952, *30,* 357–358.

Johnson, J. M. Student interests and values and curricular satisfaction in engineering. Master's thesis, Clark University, 1950. *(Abstracts of Dissertations and Theses . . . 1950,* pp. 136–138)

Johnson, R. W. Congruence of SVIB-W and KOIS interest profiles. *Journal of Counseling Psychology,* 1971, *18,* 450–455.

Kaufmann, J. D. Experience with Kuder Preference Record — Vocational: Class of 1964. Unpublished study, Warwick Valley High School, Warwick, N. Y., 1964.

Kegan, E. O. Interests of women lawyers shown on the Kuder Preference Record. *Personnel Psychology,* 1954, *7,* 499–507.

Kelley, E. P. An investigation into the value of selected tests and techniques for guidance of prospective teachers enrolled in community experiences course. Ph.D. dissertation, University of Houston, 1955.

Kelley, E. L., and Fiske, D. W. *The prediction of performance in clinical psychology.* Ann Arbor: University of Michigan, 1951.

Kelly, J. G. Feelings of dominance and judgments of humor as measured by a non-projective preference scale and a selected population of jokes. Master's thesis, Bowling Green State University, 1954.

Kelso, N. E. The relative correspondence of professed interest to the Kuder and Strong interest test scores. Master's thesis, State College of Washington, 1948.

Kendall, W. E., and Hahn, M. E. The use of tests in the selection of medical students by the College of Medicine of Syracuse University. Abstract. *American Psychology*, 1947, *2*, 297.

Kennedy, E. C. A comparison of the personality traits of successful and unsuccessful seminarians in a foreign mission seminary. Master's thesis, Catholic University of America, 1958.

Kenney, C. E. Differential vocational interest patterns of successful and unsuccessful foreign mission seminarians. Ph.D. dissertation, Loyola University (Chicago), 1959.

Kermeen, B. G. A factor analysis of the Differential Aptitude tests and a factor analysis of the Kuder Preference Record, Vocational. Master's thesis, University of California, 1951.

Kern, D. W. The prediction of academic success of freshmen in a community college. Ph.D. dissertation, New York University, 1953.

Kerns, R. DeN. The relation of interests as measured by the Kuder Preference Record to level of attainment in engineering school. Master's thesis, University of Pittsburgh, 1952.

Kimbell, F. T. The use of selected standardized tests as predictors of academic success at Oklahoma College for Women. Ph.D. dissertation, University of Oklahoma, 1960.

Kimber, J. A. M. Interests and personality traits of bible institute students. *Journal of Social Psychology*, 1947, *26*, 225-233.

King, P., and Norrell, G. A factorial study of the Kuder Preference Record — Occupational, Form D. *Educational and Psychological Measurement*, 1964. *24*, 57-63.

King, P., Norrell, G., and Erlandson, F. L. The prediction of academic success in a police administration curriculum. *Educational and Psychological Measurement*, 1959, *19*, 649-651.

King, P., Norrell, G., and Powers, G. P. Relationships between twin scales on the SVIB and the Kuder. *Journal of Counseling Psychology*, 1963, *10*, 395-401.

Kingston, A. J., George, C. E., and Ewens, W. P. Determining the relationship between individual interest profiles and occupational forms. *Journal of Educational Psychology*, 1956, *47*, 310-316.

Kirk, B. A. Review of the Kuder General Interest Survey. In O. K. Buros (ed.), *The seventh mental measurements yearbook.* Highland Park, N. H.: Gryphon Press, 1972, pp. 1421-1423.

Kline, M. V., and Cumings, R. Study of the learning characteristics of public health nurses in relation to mental health education and consultation: IV, Kuder Vocational Interest patterns. *Journal of Genetic Psychology*, 1956, *88*, 37-59.

Klugman, S. F. Spread of vocational interests and general adjustment status. *Journal of Applied Psychology*, 1950, *34*, 108-114.

Klugman, S. F. A study of the interest profile of a psychotic group and its bearing on interest-personality theory. Abstract. *American Psychology*, 1955, *10*, 366.

Klugman, S. F. A study of the interest profile of a psychotic group and its bearing on interest-personality theory. *Educational and Psychological Measurement*, 1957, *17*, 55-64.

Klugman, S. F. A profile coding system for the Kuder Preference Record — Vocational. *Educational and Psychological Measurement*, 1959, *19*, 569-576.

Klugman, S. F. Comparison of total interest profiles of a psychotic and a normal group. *Journal of Counseling Psychology*, 1960, *7*, 283-288.

Klugman, S. F. Intra-individual variability finding for a psychotic population on vocational interest inventories. *Journal of Counseling Psychology*, 1964, *2*, 191-193.

Klugman, S. F. Differential preference patterns between sexes for schizophrenic patients. *Journal of Clinical Psychology*, 1966, *22*, 170-172.

Kohn, N., Jr. An investigation and evaluation of the Kuder Preference, especially in comparison to the Strong Vocational Interest Blank. Ph.D. dissertation, Washington University, 1948.

Kohn, N., Jr. Kuder Preference Record Masculinity-Feminity Scale. *Journal of Social Psychology*, 1948, *27*, 127-128.

Kopp, T., and Tussing, L. The vocational choices of high school students as related to scores on vocational interest inventories. *Occupations*, 1947, *26*, 92-94.

Krause, A. H., and Baxter, J. L. A scale ranking method for profiling the Kuder. *Vocational Guidance Quarterly*, 1959, *8*, 19.

Kriedt, P. H., and Gadel, M. S. Use of the Kuder Preference Record in selecting clerical employees. Abstract. *American Psychology*, 1954, *9*, 409-410.

Krumm, R. L. Inter-relationships of measured interests and personality traits of introductory psychology instructors and their students as related to student achievement. Ph.D. dissertation, University of Pittsburgh, 1952.

Kuder, G. F. The stability of preference items. *Journal of Social Psychology*, 1939, *19*, 41-50.

Kuder, G. F. Note on classification of items in interest inventories. *Occupations*, 1944, *22*, 484-487.

Kuder, G. F. The use of preference measurement in vocational guidance. *Educational Record*, 1948, *29*, 65-76.

Kuder, G. F. Identifying the faker. *Personnel Psychology*, 1950, *3*, 155-167.

Kuder, G. F. Expected developments in interest and personality inventories. *Educational and Psychological Measurement*, 1954, *14*, 265-271.

Kuder, G. F. A comparative study of some methods of developing occupational keys. *Educational and Psychological Measurement*, 1957, *17*, 105-114.

Kuder, G. F. Kuder Preference Record — Occupational. Form D. High school, college, adult. 1 form. (20-30)min. IBM or hand scoring. Question booklet. *Journal, of Consulting Psychology*, 1957, *21*, 281-282.

Kuder, G. F. A rationale for evaluating interests. *Educational and Psychological Measurement*, 1963, *23*, 3-12.

Kuder, G. F. The Occupational Interest Survey. *Personnel and Guidance Journal*, 1966, *45*, 72-77.

Kuder, G. F. A note on the comparability of occupational scores from different interest inventories. *Measurement and Evaluation Guide*, 1969, *2*, 94-100.

Kuder, G. F. Some principles of interest measurement. *Educational and Psychological Measurement*, 1970, *30*, 205-226.

Kuder, G. F., and Crawford, L. E. *Kuder book list*. Chicago: Science Research Associates, 1951, pp. 8, (Instructor's guide, 1951, pp. 4)

Kuder, G. F., and Paulson, B. B. *Discovering your real interests: For use in grades 9-10*. Chicago: Science Research Associates, 1949, pp. 48.

Kuder, G. F., and Paulson, B. B. *Exploring children's interests*. Chicago: Science Research Associates, 1951, pp. 48.

Kuder, G. F., and Richardson, M. W. The theory of the estimation of test reliability. *Psychometrika*, 1937, *2*, 151-160.

Kullman, R. A comparison of mental patients and normal subjects in regard to stability of measured vocational interests. Master's thesis on file at the University of Cincinnati, 1928.

Kutner, M. The prognosis of the freshman achievement of chemistry and physics students on the basis of interest test items. Master's thesis, Pennsylvania State College, n.d.

Laird, J. T. A note on the scoring rationale of the Kuder Preference Record. *Canadian Journal of Psychology*, 1957, *11*, 133-135.

Lammi, E. H. An investigation of the relationship of interests in forestry and study habits and attitudes to grade-point average. M.S. thesis, North Carolina State University at Raleigh, 1966.

Lane, P. A. The relationship among some measures of preferred interest, vocational objectives and academic performance. Ph.D. dissertation, University of Connecticut, 1959.

Lange, H. M. An analysis of the Kuder Preference Record results at Hardin-Simmons University. Master's thesis, Hardin-Simmons University, 1956.

Lanna, M. G. Vocational interests in relation to some aspects of personality and adjustment. Ph.D. dissertation, Columbia University, 1962.

Lattin, G. W. Factors associated with success in hotel administration. *Occupations*, 1950, *24*, 36-39.

Launer, P. T. The relationship of given interest-patterns to certain aspects of personality. *Dissertation Abstracts*, 1963, *24*(6), 2564-2565.

Lauro, L. A note on machine scoring the Kuder Preference Record. *Journal of Applied Psychology*, 1948, *32*, 629-630.

Lawrence, R. M. An investigation of selected physical, psychological, and sociological factors associated with migraine and psychogenic headache. Ph.D. dissertation, New York University, 1950. Abstract. *Microfilm Abstracts*, 11:171-2 No. 1 '51.

Layton, W. L. Review of the Kuder Preference Record — Personal. In O.K. Buros (ed.), *The sixth mental measurements yearbook*, Highland Park, N.J.: Gryphon Press, 1965, pp. 277-278.

Leach, K. W. Intelligence levels and corresponding interest area choices of ninth grade pupils in thirteen Michigan schools. *Journal of Experimental Education*, 1954, *22*, 369-383.

LeBlanc, C. R. Vocational interests of ninth grade and twelfth grade students. *School Counselor*, 1960, *7*, 60-64.

Lee, M. C. Configural vs. linear prediction of collegiate academic performance. Ph.D. dissertation, University of Illinois, 1956.

Lee, P. J. The effectiveness of a test battery in predicting chemistry grades. Master's thesis, Alabama Polytechnic Institute, 1954.

Lefkowitz, D. M. Comparison of the Strong Vocational Interest Blank and the Kuder Occupational Interest Survey scoring procedures. *Journal of Counseling Psychology*, 1970, *17*, 357–363.

Lehman, R. T. Interpretation of the Kuder Preference Record for college students of home economics. *Educational Psychological Measurement*, 1944, *4*, 217–223.

Leonard, M. E. A clinical study of certain aspects of two standardized measures of interest. Master's thesis on file at Syracuse University, 1948.

Leshner, S. S. Interrelations between the vocational interest areas of the Gentry, Kuder and Thurstone Interest Inventories. Master's thesis, Temple University, 1942.

Lessing, E. E. Mother-daughter similarity on the Kuder Vocational Interest scales. *Educational and Psychological Meaaurement*, 1959, *19*, 395–400.

Levine, P. R., and Wallen, R. Adolescent vocational interests and later occupation. *Journal of Applied Psychology*, 1954, *38*, 428–431.

Levison, B. M. The vocational interests of Yeshiva College freshmen. *Journal of Genetic Psychology*, 1961, *99*, 235–244.

Lewis, E. C., and MacKinney, A. C. Counselor vs. statistical predictions of job satisfaction in engineering. *Journal of Counseling Psychology*, 1961, *8*, 224–230.

Lewis, J. A. Kuder Preference Record and MMPI scores for two occupational groups. *Journal of Consulting Psychology*, 1947, *11*, 194–201.

Lindeman, R. P. A study of selected non-intellectual variables among classes of students in a college of engineering. Ed.D. dissertation, Oklahoma State University, 1970.

Lindgren, H. C. A study of certain aspects of the Lee-Thorpe Occupational Interest Inventory. *Journal of Educational Psychology*, 1947, *38*, 353–362.

Lindsay, C. W. A study of the effects of three methods of teaching high school chemistry upon achievement in chemistry, critical thinking abilities and scientific interest. Ed.D. dissertation, Northeast Louisiana University, 1973.

Linn, M. R. Achievement, aptitude, interest, and personality variables as predictors of curriculum, graduation, and placement. Ed.D. dissertation, University of Pennsylvania, 1971.

Lipsett, L. Interpreting the Kuder Preference Record in terms of D.O.T., part IV. *Occupations*, 1947, *25*, 395–397.

Lipsett, L., and Wilson, J. W. Do suitable interests and mental ability lead to job satisfaction? *Educational and Psychological Measurement*, 1954, *14*, 373–380.

Livingston, C. D. The personality correlates of high and low identification with the father figure. Ph.D. dissertation, University of Houston, 1956.

Livingston, E. A comparison of the results of the Kuder Preference Record given to one hundred and four students as freshmen and again as juniors in the Helena High School. Master's thesis, Montana State University, 1953.

Loadman, W. E. A comparison of several methods of scoring the Kuder Occupational Interest Survey. Ph.D. dissertation, Michigan State University, 1971.

Lohnes, P. R. Review of the Kuder General Interest Survey. In O. K. Buros (ed.), *The seventh mental measurements yearbook.* Highland Park, N. J.: Gryphon Press, 1972, pp. 1423-1424.

Long, L., and Perry, J. D. Academic achievement in engineering related to selection procedures and interests. *Journal of Applied Psychology*, 1953, *37*, 468-471.

Longstaff, H. P. Fakability of the Strong Interest Blank and the Kuder Preference Record. *Journal of Applied Psychology*, 1948, *32*, 360-369.

Lorge, I., and Blau, R. D. Broad occupational grouping by intelligence levels. *Occupations*, 1942, *20*, 419-423.

Lowrie, K. H. Factors which relate to the extra-curricular performance of college women. Unpublished Ph.D. dissertation, University of Iowa, 1942.

Lucio, W. H., and Risch, F. Relationships among tests of intelligence, vocational interest and aptitude. *California Journal of Educational Research*, 1957, *8*, 198-203.

Luton, J. N. A study of the use of standardized tests in the selection of potential educational administrators. Ph.D. dissertation, University of Tennessee, 1955.

McCall, J. N. Review of the Kuder General Interest Survey. In O. K. Buros (ed.), *The seventh mental measurements yearbook.* Highland Park, N. J.: Gryphon Press, 1972, p. 1425.

McCall, J. N., and Moore, G. D. Do interest inventories measure estimated abilities? *Personnel and Guidance Journal*, 1965, *43*, 1034-1037.

McCarthy, J. J. Validity information exchange, no. 7-007, D.O.T. code 5-02.621, foreman II. *Personnel Psychology*, 1954, 7, 420-421.

McCarthy, J. J. Normative data information exchange, no. 10-37. *Personnel Psychology*, 1957, *10*, 527-528.

McCarthy, J. J., Westberg, W. C., and Fitzpatrick, E. D. Validity information exchange, no. 7-091, D.O.T. code 5-92.621, foreman II. *Personnel Psychology*, 1954, 7, 568-569.

McCarthy, T. N. The relationship of vocational interests to personality traits. Master's thesis, Catholic University of America, 1952.

McCoy, R. A. Stability and change of measured vocational interests of high school students. Ph.D. dissertation, University of Missouri, 1954.

McCully, C. H. The validity of the Kuder Preference Record. Ph.D. dissertation, George Washington University, 1954.

McCully, C. H. A longitudinal study of the validity of the Kuder Preference Record. Abstract. *American Psychologist*, 1955, *10*, 374.

McDonagh, A. J. A study of adjustments and interests of first-year college seminarians for the diocesan priesthood. M.A. thesis, Loyola University (Chicago), 1961.

McGuire, F. L. (USN Medical Neuropsychiatric Research Unit, San Diego) The Kuder Preference Record — Personal as a measure of personal adjustment. *Journal of Clinical Psychology*, 1961, *17*, 41-42.

McMillen, D. M. A study of the effectiveness of the Kuder Preference Record — Vocational in discriminating among Purdue engineering graduates. Ph.D. dissertation, Purdue University, 1961.

MacPhail, A. H. That changing Kuder. *Occupations*, 1951, *30*, 202-203.

McRae, G. G. The relationship of job satisfaction and earlier measured interests. Ph.D. dissertation, University of Florida, 1959.

Madaus, G. F. Multivariate test score patterns for high school boys in nine occupational groups. Unpublished Ph.D. dissertation, Boston College, 1964.

Madaus, G. F., and O'Hara, R. P. Vocational interest patterns of high school boys: A multivariate approach. *Journal of Counseling Psychology*, 1967, *14*, 106-112.

Magill, J. W. A validation of the Kuder Preference Record against functional criteria of campus activity. Ph.D. dissertation, University of Pittsburgh, 1952.

Magill, J. W. Interest profiles of college activity groups: Kuder Preference Record validation. *Journal of Applied Psychology*, 1955, *39*, 53-56.

Mahoney, S. C., and Auston, C. A. The empathy test and self-awareness of Kuder interest pattern. *Psychological Reports*, 1958, *4*, 422.

Maier, G. E. The contribution of interest test scores to differential academic prediction. Ph.D. dissertation, University of Washington, 1957.

Malcolm, D. D. The relative usefulness of several extensively used vocational interest inventories in counseling at various academic levels. Ph.D. dissertation, Northwestern University, 1948. (*Summaries of Doctoral Dissertations* . . . June-September 1948. 1949, pp. 245-250).

Malcolm, D. D. Which interest inventory should I use? *Journal of Educational Research*, 1950, *44*, 91-98.

Mallinson, G. G., and Crumrine, W. M. An investigation of the stability of interests of high school students. *Journal of Educational Research*, 1952, *45*, 369-383.

Mann, H., Jr. A study of selected academic and interest variables in relation to achievement in a college of engineering. Ed.D. dissertation, Oklahoma State University, 1971.

Manzano, I. B. The relation of personality adjustment to occupational interests. Ph.D. dissertation, University of Southern California, 1951.

Margolis, V. H. Kuder-Strong discrepancy in relation to conflict and congruence of vocational preference. *Dissertation Abstracts*, 1967, *28*(4-B), 1685-1686.

Marsden, R. D. Topological representation and vector analysis of interest patterns. *Dissertation Abstracts*, 1968, *28*(10-A), 4004-4005.

Mathewson, R. H., and Herbert, R. *Kuder Preference Record profiles for 48 occupational fields in 16 major groups*. Cambridge, Mass.: The Guidance Center, 1949.

Mayeske, G. W. Prediction of forester retention and advancement from the Kuder Preference Record. USDA PRS 63-3. (Office of Personnel, USDA, Washington, D.C.).

Mayeske, G. W. The validity of Kuder Preference Record scores in predicting forester turnover and advancement. *Personnel Psychology*, 1964, *17*, 207-210.

Meek, C. R. The effect of knowledge of aptitude upon interest scores. Ph.D. dissertation, George Peabody College for Teachers, 1954.

Melbika, L. K. Intra-individual variability in relation to achievement, interest, and personality. Ph.D. dissertation, Stanford University, 1952.

Meyers, E. S. The statistical analysis of the Kuder Preference Record. Unpublished master's thesis, University of Denver, 1945.

Miles, R. W. A proposed short form of the Kuder Preference Record. *Journal of Applied Psychology*, 1948, *32*, 282-285.

Miller, A. D. The role of Kuder interests in prediction of course marks of freshman engineering students. Master's thesis, Iowa State College, 1948.

Miller, W. G., and Hannum, T. E. Characteristics of homosexually involved incarcerated females. Abstract. *Journal of Consulting Psychology*, 1963, *27*, 277.

Miner, J. B. The Kuder Preference Record in management appraisal. *Personnel Psychology*, 1960, *13*, 187-196.

Mink, O. G. A study of certain cognitive and conative factors affecting academic progress in chemical and metallurgical engineering at Cornell University. Ph.D. dissertation, Cornell University, 1961.

Moffett, C. R. Operational characteristics of beginning master's students in educational administration and supervision. Ph.D. dissertation, University of Tennessee, 1954.

Monroe, M. B. The Kuder Preference Record as a measure of interest in certain areas of the liberal arts curriculum at the University of North Carolina. Master's thesis, University of North Carolina, 1947, (Research in progress, October, 1945-December, 1948, 1949, p. 309.)

Mooney, R. F. A multiple discriminant analysis of the interest patterns of high school girls. Ph.D. dissertation, Boston College, 1968.

Mooney, R. F. Categorizing high school girls into occupational preference groups on the basis of discriminant-function analysis of interests. *Measurement and Evaluation in Guidance*, 1969, *2*, 178-190.

Moore, C. W. Some relationships between standarized test scores and academic performance in the college of business administration of the University of Houston. Ph.D. dissertation, University of Houston, 1958.

Moorman, J. D. A study of the meaning of high and low social service and persuasive scores on the Kuder Preference Record as measured by the semantic differential. Ph.D. dissertation, University of Kansas, 1963.

Morey, E. A. Vocational interests and personality characteristics of women teachers. *Australian Journal of Psychology*, 1949, 1, 26-37.

Morris, J. L., and Parkinson, M. Vocational interests of data processing personnel. *Australian Psychologist*, 1971, *6*(1), 19-25.

Morrison, J. W., Jr. An investigation of relationships between the experiences of high school students and changes in their vocational interest profiles. Ph.D. dissertation, The University of Connecticut, 1971.

Mosel, J. N., and Roberts, J. B. The comparability of measures and profile similarity: An empirical study. *Journal of Consulting Psychology*, 1954, *18*, 61-66.

Moser, W. E. The influence of certain cultural factors upon the selection of vocational preferences by high school students. *Journal of Educational Research*, 1952, *45*, 523-526.

Mosier, M. F., and Kuder, G. F. Personal perference differences among occupational groups. *Journal of Applied Psychology*, 1949, *33*, 231-239.

Motto, J. J. Interest scores in predicting success in vocational school programs. *Personnel and Guidance Journal*, 1959, *37*, 674-676.

Mowbray, J. K., and Taylor, R. G. Validity of interest inventories for the prediction of success in a school of nursing. *Nursing Research*, 1967, *16*, 78-81.

Mugaas, H. D., and Hester, R. The development of an equation for identifying the interests of carpenters. *Educational and Psychological Measurement*, 1952, *12*, 408-414.

Munson, H. R. Comparison of interest and attitude patterns of three selected groups of teacher candidates. Ph.D. dissertation, State College of Washington, 1959.

Murray, L. E., and Bruce, M. M. Kuder Preference Record — Personal, Form AH. *Personnel Psychology*, 1957, *10*, 94-96.

Nafziger, D. H., and Helms, S. T. Cluster analysis of the SVIB, MVII, and Kuder OIS as tests of an occupational classification. *Center for social organization of schools report, Johns Hopkins University*, 1972, *138*, 47.

Namani, A.-K. Factors associated with high and low correlations between individuals' scores on two interest inventories. Ph.D. dissertation, Cornell University, 1958.

Napier, C. S. Reliability of an orally presented interest measure. Ed.D. dissertation, Temple University, 1970.

Nash, Allan N. Vocational interests of effective managers: A review of the literature. *Personnel Psychology*, 1965, *18*, 21-37.

Neumann, T. M. A study of the relation of occupational interests to certain aspects of personality. Master's thesis, Illinois State Normal University, 1950.

Newkirk, G. F. Occupational patterns in the Kuder Preference Record. Master's thesis on file at George Washington University, 1948.

Newman, J. The Kuder Preference Record and personal adjustment: A study of tuberculous patients. *Educational and Psychological Measurement*, 1955, *15*, 274-280.

North, R. D., Jr. An analysis of the personality dimensions of introversion-extroversion. *Journal of Personality*, 1949, *17*, 352-367.

North, R. D., Jr. An analysis of the personality dimensions of introverion-extroversion. Ph.D. dissertation, Columbia University, 1950.

North, R. D., Jr. Tests for the accounting profession. *Educational and Psychological Measurement*, 1958, *18*, 691-713.

Novak, B. J., and Scheuhing, M. A. Predicting success in high school industrial courses. *Industrial Arts and Vocational Education*, 1951, *40*, 391-394.

Novak, D. F. A comparison of delinquent and non-delinquent vocational interests. *Exceptional Children*, 1961, *28*, 63-66.

Nugent, F. A. The relationship of discrepancies between interest and aptitude scores to other selected personality variables. *Personnel and Guidance Journal*, 1961, *39*, 388-395.

Nugent, F. A. Relationship of Kuder Preference Record verification scores to adjustment: Implications for vocational development theory. *Journal of Applied Psychology*, 1968, *52*, 429-431.

Nunnally, J. C. *Tests and measurements*. New York: McGraw-Hill, 1959.

Nunnally, J. C. *Educational measurement and evaluation*. New York: McGraw-Hill, 1964.

Nunnery, M. Y. How useful are standardized psychological tests in the selection of school administrators? *Educational Administration and Supervision*, 1959, *45*, 349-356.

Oakes, F., Jr. The contribution of certain variables to the academic achievement of gifted seventh grade students in an accelerated general science curriculum. Ph.D. dissertation, New York University, 1959.

Occupational briefs on America's major fields. 2 vols. Chicago: Science Research Associates, 1948.

Occupational monographs. American Job Series. Chicago: Science Research Associates, 1941.

O'Hara, R. P. Acceptance of vocational interest areas by high school students. *Vocational Guidance Quarterly*, 1962, *10*, 101-105.

O'Hara, R. P. Vocational self concepts of boys choosing science and non-science careers. *Educational and Psychological Measurement*, 1967, *27*, 139-149.

Olejnik, S., and Porter, A. C. An empirical investigation comparing the effectiveness of four scoring strategies on the Kuder Occupational Interest Survey Form DD. *Educational and Psychological Measurement*, 1975, *35*, 37-46.

O'Loughlin, D. R. Helping students understand the Kuder. *School Counselor*, 1971, *9*, 60-61.

Onarheim, J. Scientific selection of sales engineers. *Personnel*, 1947, *24*, 24-34.

O'Shea, A. J., and Harrington, T. F., Jr. Using the Strong Vocational Interest Blank and Kuder Occupational Interest Survey, Form DD, with the same clients. *Journal of Counseling Psychology*, 1971, *18*, 44-50.

O'Shea, A. J., and Harrington, T. F., Jr. Strong Vocational Interest Blank and Kuder Occupational Interest Survey differences reexamined in terms of Holland's vocational theory. *Journal of Counseling Psychology*, 1972, *19*(5), 455-460.

O'Shea, A. J., Lynch, M. D., and Harrington, T. F., Jr. A reply to Kuder's criticism of SVIB-KOIS comparative studies. *Measurement and Evaluation in Guidance*, 1972, *5*(1), 306-309.

Ostlund, L. A. Kuder interest patterns of outstanding science teachers. *Peabody Journal of Education*, 1958, *39*, 101-108.

Overall, J. E. A masculinity-femininity scale for the Kuder Preference Record. *Journal of General Psychology*, 1963, *69*, 209-216.

Overstreet, P. L. A comparison of expressed and measured vocational interests. Ph.D. dissertation, George Washington University, n.d.

Parkash, J., and Namdeo, G. Vocational interests and personality types. *Manas*, 1967, *14*, 61-68.

Parker, J. W., Jr. Psychological and personal history data related to accident records of commercial truck drivers. *Journal of Applied Psychology*, 1953, *37*, 317-320.

Paterson, D. G. Vocational interest inventories in selection. *Occupations*, 1946, *25*, 152-153.

Paterson, D. G., et al. *Minnesota Occupational Rating Scales*. Chicago: Science Research Associates, 1941.

Patterson, C. H. Test and background factors related to drop-outs in an industrial institute. Ph.D. dissertation, University of Minnesota, 1955.

Patterson, C. H. A Kuder pattern for bakers and baking students. *Personnel and Guidance Journal*, 1956, *25*, 110-111.

Patterson, C. H. Kuder patterns of industrial institute students. *Personnel Psychology*, 1959, *12*, 561-571.

Pemberton, C. L. Personality inventory data related to ACE subscores. *Journal of Consulting Psychology*, 1951, *15*, 160-162.

Perrine, M. W. The selection of drafting trainees. *Journal of Applied Psychology*, 1955, *39*, 56-61.

Perry, J. D., and Shuttleworth, F. K. Kuder profiles of college freshmen by degree objectives. *Journal of Educational Research*, 1948, *41*, 363-365.

Perry, M. L. The relationship of selected variables to the success of camp counselors. Ph.D. dissertation, University of Southern California, 1963.

Pervin, D. W. The interests of graduate students in psychology as measured by the Kuder Preference Record. Master's thesis, University of Pittsburgh, 1949.

Peters, E. F. Vocational interests as measured by the Strong and Kuder inventories. *School and Society*, 1942, *55*, 453-455.

Peterson, M. E. An evaluation of relationships between test data and success as a residence hall counselor. Ph.D. dissertation, University of Kansas, 1959.

Petro, P. K. Student aptitudes and abilities correlated with achievement in first semester high school bookkeeping. Master's thesis, Iowa State Teachers College, 1957.

Phillips, W. S., and Osborne, R. T. A note on the relationship of the Kuder Preference Record scales to college marks, scholastic aptitude and other variables. *Educational and Psychological Measurement*, 1949, *9*, 331-337.

Pierce-Jones, J. The readability of certain standard tests. *California Journal of Educational Research*, 1954, *5*, 80-82.

Pierce-Jones, J. Review of the Kuder Preference Record — Vocational. In O. K. Buros (ed.), *The fifth mental measurements yearbook.* Highland Park, N. J.: Gryphon Press, 1959, pp. 891-892.

Pierce-Jones, J. Socio-economic status and adolescents' interests. *Psychological Reports*, 1959, *5*, 683.

Pierce-Jones, J. Vocational interest correlates of socio-economic status in adolescence. *Educational and Psychological Measurement*, 1959, *19*, 65-71.

Pierce-Jones, J. Social mobility orientations and interests of adolescents. *Journal of Counseling Psychology*, 1961, *8*, 75-78.

Pierce-Jones, J., and Carter, H. D. Vocational interest measurement using a photographic inventory. *Educational and Psychological Measurement*, 1954, *14*, 671-679.

Piotrowski, A. A. Difference between cases giving valid and invalid personality inventory responses. *Annals of the New York Academy of Science*, 1946, *46*, 633-640.

Plata, M. A comparative study of the occupational aspirations and interests of high school age emotionally disturbed, vocational-technical and regular academic students. Ph.D. dissertation, University of Kansas, 1971.

Plotkin, A. L. The effect of occupational information classes upon the vocational interest patterns of below average, adolescent males. Ph.D. dissertation, Catholic University of America, 1966.

Plummer, R. H. Characteristics and needs of selected ninth grade pupils as a basis for curricular changes to meet life adjustment needs. Ph.D. dissertation, Indiana University, 1951. (*Thesis Abstract Series . . .* 1951, 1952, pp. 113-119).

Pollock. D. M. Testing programs for girls at Stephens College. *Vocational Guidance Quarterly*, 1953, *1*, 41-43.

Pool, D. A., and Brown, R. A. Kuder-Strong discrepancies and personality adjustment. *Journal of Counseling Psychology*, 1964, *11*, 63-71.

Porter, Andrew C. A chi-square approach to discrimination among occupations, using an interest inventory. M.S. thesis, University of Wisconsin, 1965.

Quimbly, N. F. The vocational interests of blind high school students. *Outlook for Blind*, 1944, *38*, 127-129.

Racky, D. J. Predictions of ninth grade woodshop performance from aptitude and interest measures. *Educational and Psychological Measurement*, 1959, *19*, 629-636.

Radcliffe, J. A. Some properties of ipsative score matrices and their relevance for some current interest tests. *Australian Journal of Psychology*, 1963, *15*, 1-11.

Radom, M. Picking better foremen. *Factory Management and Maintenance (factory)*, 1950, *108*, 119-122.

Redlener, J. A comparative study of the efficiency of the Kuder Preference Record and the Strong Vocational Interest Blank in the prediction of job satisfaction. Master's thesis, University of Southern California, 1948.

Reed, W. W., Lewis, E. C., and Wolins, L. Differential interest patterns of engineering graduates. *Personnel and Guidance Journal*, 1960, *38*, 571-573.

Reid, J. W. Stability of measured Kuder interests in young adults. Abstract. *American Psychology*, 1951, *6*, 378.

Reid, J. W. Stability of measured Kuder interests in young adults. *Journal of Educational Research*, 1951, *45*, 307-312.

Reid, J. W. An error noted. *Personnel and Guidance Journal*, 1960, *39*, 147.

Reid, J. W., Johnson, A. P., Entwisle, F. N., and Angers, W. P. A four-year study of the characteristics of engineering students. *Personnel and Guidance Journal*, 1962, *41*, 38-43.

Remmers, H. H., and Gage, N. L. Student personnel studies of The Pharmaceutical Survey. *Pharmaceutical Survey*, Monograph No. 3. Washington, D.C.: American Council on Education, 1949.

Renke, W. W. Discrimination of the Kuder Preference Record. Ph.D. dissertation, University of North Dakota, 1952.

Replogle, J. R. The relation of teacher-pupil profile pattern similarities on measures of interest and personality to grades and perceived compatibility. Ph.D. dissertation, Lehigh University, 1968.

Rezler, A. G. Characteristics of high school girls choosing traditional or pioneer vocations. *Personnel and Guidance Journal*, 1967, *45*, 659-665.

Rezler, A. G. the joint use of the Kuder Preference Record and the Holland Vocational Preference Inventory in the vocational assessment of high school girls. *Psychology in the Schools*, 1967, *4*, 82-84.

Richard J. T. Study of the relationship of certain background factors and the choice of police work as a career. Ph.D. dissertation, Temple University, 1968.

Richardson, M. W.. The combination of measures. Supplementary study D in *The prediction of personal adjustment*. New York: Social Science Research Council, 1941, pp. 377-401.

Risher, C. C. Some characteristics which differentiate between academically successful and unsuccessful college business students. Ph.D. dissertation, University of Missouri, 1958.

Ritchie, C. McC.. Vocational interests as a factor in the academic achievement of male students in a teacher education institution. Ph. D. dissertation, Rutgers — The State University, 1968.

Robb, G. P. Relationships between interests and student teaching achievement. Ph.D. dissertation, Indiana University, 1953.

Robbins, A. An experimental study of the relationship between needs as manifested on the Thermatic Apperception Test and Kuder Preference Record scales of adolescent boys. Ph.D. dissertation, Columbia University, 1953.

Robbins, J. E., and King, D. C. Validity information exchange, no. 14-02: D.O.T. code 0-97.61, manager, sales. *Personnel Psychology*, 1961, *14*, 217-219.

Roberts, S. O., and Gunter, L. M. An evaluation of the Kuder interest patterns of negro nurses. Abstract. *American Psychology*, 1954, *9*, 456.

Roberts, W. H. Test scores and merit ratings of graduate engineers. Abstract. *American Psychology*, 1946, *1*, 284.

Robinson, H. R. A comparison of American Indian and white student occupational interests with respect to family background factors. Ph.D. dissertation, The University of Nebraska — Lincoln, 1973.

Roeber, E. C. A comparison of seven interest inventories with respect to word usage. *Journal of Educational Research*, 1948, *42*, 8-17.

Roeber, E. C. The relationship between parts of the Kuder Preference Record and parts of the Lee-Thorpe Occupational Interest Inventory. *Journal of Educational Research*, 1949, *42*, 598-608.

Rogge, H. J. A statistical study of certain personality factors among pupils in a selected high school. Master's thesis, Ohio University, 1952.

Rohrs, D. K. Predicting academic success in a liberal arts college music education program. Ph.D. dissertation, State University of Iowa, 1962.

Rollins, R. W. A revision of the Kuder Preference Record for the sixth grade. Unpublished master's thesis, Syracuse Uuniversity, 1945.

Romney, A. K. The Kuder Literary Scale as related to achievement in college English. *Journal of Applied Psychology*, 1950, *34*, 40-41.

Rose, W. A comparison of relative interest in occupational groupings and activity interests as measured by the Kuder Preference Record. *Occupations*, 1948, *26*, 302-307.

Rosenberg, N. Stability and maturation of Kuder interest patterns during high school. *Educational and Psychological Measurement*, 1953, *13*, 449-458.

Rosenberg, N., and Izard, C. E. Vocational interests of naval aviation cadets. *Journal of Applied Psychology*, 1954, *38*, 354-358.

Rosenberg, P. The predictive value of the Kuder Preference Record. Master's thesis, Western Reserve University, 1952.

Ross, G. R. Changes in interests between 1947 and 1950 of 388 Texas A. and M. college students as measured by the Kuder Preference Record. Master's thesis, Agricultural and Mechanical College of Texas, 1950.

Rupiper, O. J. Psychometric evaluation of experienced teachers. *Journal of Educational Research*, 1962, *55*, 368-371.

Russell, D. The effect of experience and change of occupational choice on tehe Kuder Preference Record. Master's thesis, University of Pittsburgh, 1952.

Russell, D., and Herzberg, F. Kuder Occupational Interest patterns in vocational counseling. Abstract. *American Psychology*, 1952, 7, 383.

Ryan, D. W., and Gaier, E. L. Interest inventories and the development framework. *Personnel and Guidance Journal*, 1967, *46*, 37-41.

Samuelson, C. O. Interest scores in predicting success of trade school students. *Personnel and Guidance Journal*, 1958, *36*, 538-541.

Samuelson, C. O., and Pearson, D. T. Interest scores in identifying the potential trade school dropout. *Journal of Applied Psychology*, 1956, *40*, 386-388.

Sartian, A. Q. Relation between scores on certain standard tests and supervisory success in an aircraft factory. *Journal of Applied Psychology*, 1946, *30*, 328-332;

Savastano, H. Motivacao e satisfacao profesional de educadores sanitarios. Una contribucao a Kuder Preference Record e a Questionario de Allport. (Motivation and professional satisfaction of health educators. A contribution to the Kuder Preference Record and Allport Study of Values.) *Revista de Psicologia Normal e Patologica*, 1962, *8*, 58-90.

Savastano, H. Interests of a group of dental medicine students through the Kuder Preference Record: Some reasons for choosing their profession. *Revista de Psicologia Normal e Patologica*, 1966, *11*, 67-89.

Scheuning, M. A. An analysis of the predictive efficiency of certain test scores and grades in the selection of high school students for the industrial auto and electric shop courses. Master's thesis, Temple University, 1948.

Schloerb, L. *School subjects and jobs.* Chicago: Science Research Associates, 1950.

Schnebly, L. M. A comparison of the scores made by teachers on the Kuder Preference Record and the California Test of Personality. Master's thesis, Montana State University, 1951.

Schneider, D. L. Perceptions of family atmosphere and the vocational interests of physically handicapped adolescents: An application of Anne Roe's theory. Ph.D. dissertation, New York University, 1968.

Scholl, C. E., Jr. The development and evaluation of methods for isolating factors that differentiate between successful and unsuccessful executive trainees in a large, multibranch bank. Ph.D. dissertation, University of Michigan, 1957.

Schroeder, P. Relationship of Kuder's conflict avoidance and dominance to academic accomplishment. *Journal of Counseling Psychology*, 1965, *12*(4), 395-399.

Schuh, A. J. The predictability of employee tenure: A review of the literature. *Personnel Psychology*, 1967, *20*, 133-152.

Schutz, R. E., and Baker, R. L. A comparison of the factor structure of the Kuder Occupational, Form D for males and females. *Educational and Psychological Measurement*, 1962, *22*, 485-492.

Schutz, R. E., and Baker, R. L. A factor analysis of the Kuder Preference Record — Occupational, Form D. *Educational and Psychological Measurement*, 1962, *22*, 97-104.

Seibert, E. W. A comparison of scores on the Kuder Preference Record and the Job Qualification Inventory. *Journal of Educational Research*, 1946, *40*, 178-186.

Shaffer, L. F. Review of the Kuder Preference Record — Personal. *Journal of Consulting Psychology*, 1949, *13*, 67.

Shaffer, R. H. Kuder interest patterns of university business school seniors. *Journal of Applied Psychology*, 1949, *33*, 489-493.

Shaffer, R. H. The measured interest of business school seniors. *Occupations*, 1949, *27*, 462-465.

Shaffer, R. H., and Kuder, G. F. Kuder interest patterns of medical, law, and business school alumni. *Journal of Applied Psychology*, 1953, *37*, 367-369.

Shann, M. H. Multiple discriminant prediction of occupational choice of vocational high school boys based on inventoried and self-rated interest patterns. Ph.D. dissertation, Boston College, 1969.

Shaw, C. E. An investigation of the validity of the Kuder Preference Record — Vocational for educational guidance. Ph.D. dissertation, Purdue University, 1954.

Sherman, E. C. Relationship of Kuder scores to differential college achievement. Master's thesis, Iowa State College, 1951.

Shierson, H. E. Pointing up the occupational interviews: Occupational dictionary and scores on interest inventory utilized. *Occupations*, 1945, *23*, 207–209.

Shinn, ·E. O. Interest and intelligence as related to achievement in tenth grade. *California Journal of Educational Research*, 1956, 7, 217–220.

Shoemaker, W. L. Rejection of measured vocational interest areas by high school students. Ph.D. dissertation, University of Missouri, 1955.

Shoemaker, W. L. Rejection of vocational interest areas by high school students. *Vocational Guidance Quarterly*, 1959–1960, *8*, 72–74.

Silver, R. J., and Casey, E. W. Stability of the Kuder Vocational Preference Record in psychiatric patients. *Educational and Psychological Measurement*, 1961, *21*, 879–882.

Silverman, P. Characteristics of a negro college environment and its relationship to student value systems. Ed.D. dissertation, North Texas State University, 1964.

Silvey, H. M. *Change in status of Iowa State Teachers College students as revealed by repeating placement tests.* Research Report No. 58, Bureau of Research, Iowa State Teachers College, 1949.

Silvey, H. M. Changes in test scores after two years in college. *Educational and Psychological Measurement*, 1951, *11*, 494–502.

Simmons, L. C. Personal and financial determinants of civil rights strategies. Ph.D. dissertation, Case Western Reserve University, 1968.

Singh, N. P. A Hindi adaptation of Kuder Record — Vocational Form CH. *Manas*, 1967, *14*, 61–68.

Singh, N. P. Stability of interest patterns. *Indian Psychological Review*, 1969, *6*(1), 14–15.

Sininger, R. A. Development and evaluation of visual aids for interpreting the Differential Aptitude Test and Kuder Preference Record. Master's thesis, University of Texas, 1957.

Sinnett, E. R. Some determinants of agreement between measured and expressed interests. *Educational and Psychological Measurement*, 1956, *16*, 110–118.

Slaymaker, R. R. Admission test procedure. *Journal of English Education*, 1947, *37*, 402–413.

Smith, D. D. Abilities and interests: 1, A factorial study. *Canadian Journal of Psychology*, 1958, *12*, 191–201.

Smith, D. D. Abilities and interests: 2, Validation of factors. *Canadian Journal of Psychology*, 1958, *12*, 253–258.

Smith, D. D. Traits and college achievement. *Canadian Journal of Psychology*, 1959, *13*, 93–101.

Smith D. E. A preliminary study of adjustment to life in the north. *Canadian Journal of Psychology*, 1949, *3*, 89–97.

Speer, G. S. The vocational interests of engineering and non-engineering students. Abstract. *American Psychology*, 1947, *2*, 341–342.

Speer, G. S. The interest and personality patterns of fire protection engineers. Abstract. *American Psychology*, 1948, *3*, 364.

Speer, G. S. The Kuder interest test patterns of fire protection engineers. *Journal of Applied Psychology*, 1948, *32*, 521-526.

Speer, G. S. Measuring the social orientation of freshman engineers. *Journal of English Education*, 1948, *39*, 86-89.

Speer, G. S. The vocational interests of engineering students and non-engineering students. *Journal of Psychology*, 1948, *25*, 357-363.

Spivey, G. M. The relationship between temperament and achievement of a selected group of John Muir College students. Ph.D. dissertation, University of Southern California, 1950. (*Abstracts of Dissertations . . .* 1950, 1951, pp. 298-300)

Springbob, H. K. Relationship of interests as measured by the Kuder Preference Record to personality as measured by the California Psychological Inventory Scales. *Personnel and Guidance Journal*, 1963, *41*, 624-628.

Springbob, H. K., and Jackson, C. W. Measured abilities and inventoried interests of ninth grade boys. *Vocational Guidance Quarterly*, 1962, *11*, 37-40.

Stahmann, R. F. Review of the Kuder General Interest Survey, Form E. *Journal of Counseling Psychology*, 1971, *18*, 190-192.

Stahmann, R. F. Test review of the Kuder Occupational Interest Survey, Form DD. *Journal of Counseling Psychology*, 1971, *18*, 191-192.

Stahmann, R. F. Test review of the Kuder Preference Record — Occupational Form D. *Journal of Counseling Psychology*, 1971, *18*, 188-190.

Stahmann, R. F., and Matheson, G. F. The Kuder OIS as a measure of vocational maturity. *Educational and Psychological Measurement*, 1973, *33*(2), 477-479.

Stanley, J. C., and Waldrof, R. S. Inter-correlations of Study of Values and Kuder Preference Record scores. *Educational and Psychological Measurement*, 1952, *12*, 707-719.

Stauffacher, J. C., and Anderson, C. L. The performance of schizophrenics on the Kuder Preference Record. *Educational and Psychological Measurement*, 1959, *19*, 253-257.

Steffire, B. The reading difficulty of interest inventories. *Occupations*, 1947, *26*, 95-96.

Steinberg, A. The relation of vocational preference to emotional adjustment. *Educational and Psychological Measurement*, 1952, *12*, 96-104.

Stephens, P. A. The effect of a simulation gaming technique and supplementary activities of modification of occupational interests toward congruence with aptitudes of ninth grade students. Ph.D. dissertation, University of Southern California, 1973.

Sternberg, C. Differences in measured interest, values, and personality among college students majoring in nine subject areas. *Abstracts of American Psychology*, 1953, *8*, 442-443.

Sternberg, C. The relation of interests, values and personality to the major field of study in college. Ph.D. dissertation, New York University, 1953.

Sternberg, C. Personality trait patterns of college students majoring in different fields. *Psychological Monographs*, 1955, *69*, 1-21.

Sternberg, C. Interests and tendencies toward maladjustment in a normal population. *Personnel and Guidance Journal*, 1956, *35*, 94-99.

Sterne, D. M. The Kuder Occupational Interest Survey with hospitalized VA counselees. *Newsletter for Research in Psychology*, 1972, *14*(1), 5-7.

Stinson, M. C. A study of the results of a Kuder test battery for use in vocational guidance. Master's thesis, Indiana State Teachers College, 1950. Abstract. *Teachers College Journal*, 1950, *22*, 16.

Stinson, P. J. A method for counseling engineering students. *Personnel and Guidance Journal*, 1958, *37*, 294-295.

Stone, S. The contribution of intelligence, interests, temperament and certain personality variables to academic achievement in a physical science and mathematics curriculum. Ph.D. dissertation, New York University, 1957.

Stoops, J. A. Stability of the measured interests of high school pupils between grades nine and eleven. *Educational Outlook*, 1953, *27*, 116-118.

Stowe, E. W. The relation of the Kuder Vocational Preference Record to Ammons' Apperception Test. Master's thesis, Illinois State Normal University, 1955.

Strong, E. K., Jr. The role of interests in guidance. *Occupations*, 1949, *27*, 517-522.

Super, D. E. The Kuder Preference Record in vocational diagnosis. *Journal of Conculting Psychology*, 1947, *11*, 184-193.

Super, D. E. Vocational interests and vocational choice: Present knowledge and future research in their relationships. *Educational and Psychological Measurement*, 1947, 7, 375-383.

Super, D. E. Review of the Kuder Preference Record. In O.K. Buros (ed.), *The third mental measurements yearbook*. Highland Park, N.J.: Gryphon Press, 1949, p. 661.

Super, D. E., and Crites, J. O. *Appraising vocational fitness by means of psychological tests*, New York: Harper & Row, 1962, pp. 461-501.

Super, D. E., and Dunlap, J. W. Sect. 16, Interest in work and play, *Handbook of Applied Psychology*, Vol. I. Edited by Douglas H. Fryer and Edwin R. Henry, New York: Rinehart and Co., 1950, pp. 100-108.

Sutter, C. R. A comparative study of the interest and personality patterns of major seminarians. Ph.D. dissertation, Fordham University, 1961.

Sweeney, F. J. Intelligence, vocational interests and reading speed of senior boys in Catholic high schools of Los Angeles. *California Journal of Educational Research*, 1954, *5*, 159-165.

Tavris, E. C. D2 as a profile similarity measure of Kuder scales. Ph.D. dissertation, Illinois Institute of Technology, 1959.

Taylor, P. L. A study of the relationship between intelligence as measured by SRA Primary Mental Abilities tests and validity scores on the Kuder Vocational Preference Record. Master's thesis, Texas Southern University, 1956.

Terwillinger, J. S. Dimensions of occupational preference. *Educational and Psychological Measurement*, 1963, *23*, 525-542.

Tharpe, F. D. Usefulness of the Kuder Preference Record for predicting shop achievement of senior high school students in industrial arts. Master's thesis, Iowa State College, 1956.

Thayer, R. A. Occupational interests and socio-economic position of high school boys. Ph.D. dissertation, St. Louis University, 1966.

Thomas, P. L. The development of a covert test for the detection of alcoholism by a keying of the Kuder Preference Record. Master's thesis, West Texas State College, 1958.

Thompson, C. E. Personality and interest factors in dental school success. *Educational and Psychological Measurement*, 1944, *4*, 299-306.

Thompson, C. E. Selecting executives by psychological tests, *Educational and Psychological Measurement*, 1947, 7, 773-778.

Thorndike, R. L., and Hagen, E. *Measurement and evaluation in psychology and education*, (2nd. ed.) New York: John Wiley & Sons, 1961, 327-8, 527-8, 586-7.

Thrash, P. A. Women student leaders at Northwestern University: Their characteristics, self-concepts, and attitudes toward the university. Ph.D. dissertation, Northwestern University, 1959.

Tiedeman, D. V., and Bryan, J. G. Prediction of college field of concentration. *Harvard Educational Review*, *1954*, 24, 122-139.

Tiffin, J., and Phelan, R. F. Use of the Kuder Preference Record to predict turnover in an industrial plant. *Personnel Psychology*, 1953, *6*, 195-204.

Tillinghast, B. S., Jr., Shapiro, R. M., and Carrett, P. Experimental use of the Kuder General Interest Survey, Form E, with sixth grade pupils. *Measurement and Evaluation in Guidance*, 1969, *2*, 174-177.

Topetzes, N. J. A program for the selection of trainees in physical medicine. *Journal of Experimental Education*, 1957, *25*, 263-311.

Townsend, A. Academic aptitude and interest ratings for independent-school pupils. *1945 fall testing program in independent schools and supplementary studies*. Educational Record Bulletin, No. 44. New York: Educational Records Bureau, 1946, pp. 51-57.

Traxler, A. E. Review of the Preference Record. In O. K. Buros (ed.), *The 1940 mental measurements yearbook*. Highland Park, N. J.: Gryphon Press, 1941, pp. 449-451.

Traxler, A. E. A note on the reliability of the revised Kuder Preference Record. *Journal of Applied Psychology*, 1943, 27, 510-511.

Traxler, A. E. Some results of the Kuder Preference Record in independent schools. *1945 fall testing program in independent schools and supplementary studies*. Educational Records Bulletin, No. 44. New York: Educational Records Bureau, 1946, pp. 37-50.

Traxler, A. E. The stability of profiles on the Kuder Preference Records — Vocational and Personal for different groups of public accountants. *Yearbook National Council of Measurement Used in Education*, 1954, *11*, 9-14.

Traxler, A. E., and McCall, W. C. Some data on the Kuder Preference Record. *Educational and Psychological Measurement*, 1941, 1, 253-268.

Triggs, F. O. A study of the relation of Kuder Preference Record scores to various other measures. *Educational and Psychological Measurement*, 1943, *3*, 341-354.

Triggs, F. O. A further comparison of interest measurement by the Kuder Preference Record and the Strong Vocational Interest Blank for Men. *Journal of Educational Research*, 1944, *37*, 538-544.

Triggs, F. O. A further comparison of interest measurement by the Kuder Preference Record and the Strong Vocational Interest Blank for Women. *Journal of Educational Research*, 1944, *38*, 193-200.

Triggs, F. O. Kuder Preference Record in the counseling of nurses. *American Journal of Nursing*, 1946, *46*, 312-316.

Triggs, F. O. The measured interests of nurses. *Journal of Educational Research*, 1947, *41*, 25-34.

Triggs, F. O. A study of the relationship of measured interests to measured mechanical aptitude, personality, and vocabulary. Abstract. *American Psychology*, 1947, *2*, 296-297.

Triggs, F. O. The measured interests of nurses: A second report. *Journal of Educational Research*, 1948, *42*, 113–121.

Triggs, F. O. Kuder Preference Record, In *Contributions to medical psychology: Theory and psychodiagnostic methods*. Vol. II. Edited by Arthur Weider. New York: Ronald Press, 1953, pp. 782–788.

Troxel, L. L. A study of three vocational interest measures: Preference Record, Academic Interest Inventory, and Work Interest Analysis. Master's thesis, University of Kentucky, 1949.

Truesdell, A. B. Accuracy of clinical judgments of attrition and survival of students in engineering training. *Proceedings of the Iowa Academy of Science*, 1954, *61*, 442–445.

Tuckman, J. High school student norms — Revised Kuder Preference Record. *Occupations*, 1944, *23*, 26–32.

Turner, A. B. The predictive significance in home economics of tests of abilities, interests, adjustments, and study habits. Master's thesis on file in the library of Utah State Agricultural College, 1941.

Tutton, M. E. Stability of adolescent vocational interest. *Vocational Guidance Quarterly*, 1955, *3*, 78–80.

Tyler, F. T. The Kuder Preference Record in a student veteran counseling programme. *Canadian Journal of Psychology*, 1947, *1*, 44–48.

Uecker, A. E. A comparative study of the vocational interests, aspirations, and achievements of selected groups of veteran psychiatric patients. Ph.D. dissertation, University of Minnesota, 1952.

Urschalitz, M. O. Measurement of general interests and interests relevant to vocation aim among religious women. Master's thesis, Fordham University, 1956.

U. S. Employment Service. Division of Standards and Research, Job Analysis and Information Section. *United States employment service manual, part III, use of employment service tools*. Washington: Government Printing Office, 1943.

Vaughan, G. E., Jr. Interest and personality patterns of experienced teachers. Master's thesis, North Texas State College, 1950.

Vaughan, L. E. Relationship of values to leadership, scholarship, and vocational choice. Ph.D. dissertation, University of Nebraska, 1959.

Veterans Administration Guidance Center. R. H. Mathewson, director, Graduate School of Education, Harvard University. *Distribution of test scores among veteran counselees*. Cambridge, Mass., 1948.

Viswanathan, K. Interest measurement with particular reference to the Kuder Preference Record and its use in the selection of student teachers. Master's thesis, McGill University, 1965.

Voas, R. B. Vocational interests of Naval aviation cadets: Final results. *Journal of Applied Psychology*, 1959, *43*, 70–73.

Vopatek, S. H. Normative data information exchange, no. 32. *Personnel Psychology*, 1956, *9*, 544.

Wagman, M. Persistence in ability-achievement discrepancies and Kuder scores, *Personnel and Guidance Journal*, 1964, *43*, 383–389.

Wagner, E. E. Predicting success for young executives from objective test scores and personal data. Ph.D. dissertation, Temple University, 1959.

Wagner, E. E. Differences between old and young executives on objective psychological test variables. *Journal of Gerontology*, 1960, *15*, 296–299.

Wald, R. M. A psycho-educational study of top-level business and industrial executives. *Dissertation Abstracts*, 1953, *13*, 1096–1097.

Walker, R. O. A study of vocational interest responses leading to the development and evaluation of an industrial interest inventory for use in general industrial plant employment practice. Ph.D. dissertation, Pennsylvania St State College, 1950. (*Abstracts of Doctoral Dissertations* . . . 1950, 1951, pp. 30-36.)

Walker, R. W. Development of a vocational agriculture interest inventory for guidance of eighth grade students. Ph.D. dissertation, Pennsylvania State University, 1962.

Walsh, W. B. Review of the Kuder Occupational Interest Survey. In O. K. Buros (ed.), *The seventh mental measurements yearbook.* Highland Park, N. J.: Gryphon Press, 1972, 1429-1431.

Warburton, F. W., Butcher, H. J., and Forrest, G. M. Predicting student performance in a university department of education. *British Journal of Educational Psychology*, 1963, *33*, 68-79.

Ward, G. R. Interest patterns of the Kuder Preference Record — Occupational Form D. Master's thesis, Utah State University, 1961.

Ward, G. R. A profile analysis of the Kuder Preference Record — Occupational. Form D. *California Journal of Educational Research*, 1968, *19*, 232-240.

Ward, P. L. A study of the relationship of evaluative attitudes to scholastic ability and academic achievement. Ph.D. dissertation, The Ohio State University, 1959.

Watkins, R. W. Classification of medical school students by the Kuder Preference Record using the discriminant function and group profiles. Master's thesis, University of Pittsburgh, 1950.

Wauck, L. An investigation of the usefulness of psychological tests in the selection of candidates for the diocesan priesthood. Ph.D. dissertation, Loyola University (Chicago), 1956.

Way, H. H. The relationship between forced choice scores and differentiated response scores on the Kuder Preference Record — Vocational. Ph.D. dissertation, Indiana University, 1953.

Webster, E. C., Winn, A., and Oliver, J. A. Selection tests for engineers: Some preliminary findings. *Personnel Psychology*, 1951, *4*, 339-362.

Welna, C. T. A study of reasons for success or failure in college mathematics courses. Ph.D. dissertation, University of Connecticut, 1960.

Wesley, S. M., Corey, D. G., and Stewart, B. M. The intra-individual relationships between interest and ability. *Journal of Applied Psychology*, 1950, *34*, 193-197.

Wesley, S. M., Stewart, B., and Corey, D. A study of the intra-individual relationships between interest and ability. Abstract. *American Psychologist*, 1947, *2*, 411.

Westberg, W. C., Fitzpatrick, E. D., and McCarty, J. H. Validity information exchange, no. 7-7073: D.O.T. code 1-37:32, typist. *Personnel Psychology*, 1954, *7*, 411-412.

Westberg, W. C., Fitzpatrick, E. D., and McCarty, J. H. Validity information exchange, no. 7-087: D.O.T. code 1-37:32, typist, *Personnel Psychology*, 1954, *7*, 561-562.

Westmoreland, LaN. An analysis of certain educational implications of Kuder interest scores among high school pupils. Unpublished master's thesis, University of Georgia, 1944, pp. 48.

Wetherell, M. G. Interest patterns of students of physical education and of physical therapy as revealed by the Kuder Preference Record. Master's thesis on file in the College of Liberal Arts and in the Library of the School of Education, Boston University, 1949.

Weynand, R. S. A study of the relationship between interest preferences and academic success for 622 A. and M. College students. Master's thesis, Agricultural and Mechanical College of Texas, 1950.

White, H. G. Typing performance as related to mental abilities and interests: A preliminary study. *Journal of Educational Research*, 1963, *56*, 535-539.

White, R. M. The predictive relationship of selected variables to the vocational interest stability of high school students. Ph.D. dissertation, University of Minnesota, 1958.

Wiener, D. N. Empirical occupational groupings of Kuder Preference Record profiles. *Educational and Psychological Measurement*, 1951, *11*, 273-279.

Wiggins, R. E. A report on the use of the Kuder Preference Record. *Pittsburgh Schools*, 1946, *21*, 1-3.

Wilson, E. H. Stability of interest patterns as reflected in the Kuder Preference Record. Master's thesis, State College of Washington, 1948.

Wilson, E. H., and Bordin, E. S. Instability of interest patterns as a function of shift in curricular orientation. Abstract. *American Psychology*, 1948, *3*, 351.

Wilson, R. N. A comparison of similar scales on the Strong Vocational Interest Blank and the Kuder Occupational Interest Survey, Form DD. Master's thesis, Kansas State University, 1967.

Wilson, R. N., and Kaiser, H. E. A comparison of similar scales on the SVIB and the Kuder, Form DD. *Journal of Counseling Psychology*, 1968, *15*, 468-470.

Winn, J. C. Kuder profiles of college freshmen by their expressed fields of concentration. Master's thesis, University of Pittsburgh, 1949.

Wisdom, J. R. A study of the interest patterns of premedical students as revealed by the Kuder Preference Record and the Strong Vocational Interest Inventory. Master's thesis, North Texas State College, 1950.

Witherspoon, R. P. A comparison of the temperament trait, interest, achievement, and Scholastic Aptitude Test Score patterns of college seniors majoring in different fields at the Arkansas State Teachers College. Ph.D. dissertation, University of Arkansas, 1961.

Wittenborn, J. R., Triggs, F. O., and Feder, D. D. A comparison of interest measurement by the Kuder Preference Record and the Strong Vocational Interest blanks for men and women. *Educational and Psychological Measurement*, 1943, *3*, 239-257.

Wolff, W. M., and North, A. T. Selection of municipal firemen. *Journal of Applied Psychology*, 1951, *35*, 2509.

Wolins, L., MacKinney, A. C., and Stephans, P. Factor analyses of high school science achievement measures. *Journal of Educational Research*, 1961, *54*, 173-177.

Womer, F. B., and Furst, E. J. Interest profiles of student nurses. *Nursing Research*, 1955, *3*, 125-126.

Woods, W. A. The role of language handicap in the development of artistic interest. *Journal of Consulting Psychology*, 1948, *12*, 240-245.

Woodward, C. L. A critical analysis of certain interest tests. *Yearbook, national council on measurements used in education*, 1952, *9*, 101-108.

Woody, C. *Guidance implications from measurements of achievements, aptitudes and interests.* University of Michigan, School of Education, Bureau of Educational Reference and Research, Bulletin No. 156, 1944.

Worthy, J. C. *What employers want.* Chicago: Science Research Associates, 1950.

Wright, E. W. A comparison of individual and multiple counseling for test interpretation interviews. *Journal of Counseling Psychology*, 1963, *10*, 126-133.

Wright, J. C., and Scarborough, B. B. Relationship of the interests of college freshmen to their interests as sophomores and as seniors. *Educational and Psychological Measurement*, 1958, *18*, 153-158.

Wright, R. L. Comparison of mental ability and interest preferences of a group of high school students as measured by the Terman-McNemar Test of Mental Ability and the Kuder Preference Record. Master's thesis, Southwest State Teachers College, 1954.

Wysock, R. A. An analysis of the relationships of selected occupational interests, aptitudes, and grade point averages of industrial arts education students in the state of California. Ed.D. dissertation, Utah State University, 1972.

Yum, K. S. Student preferences in divisional studies and their preferential activities. *Journal of Psychology*, 1942, *13*, 193-200.

Zenti, R. N. A comparison of the results obtained by the Mitchell and Kuder interest measures when administered to male freshmen at the University of Michigan. Ph.D. dissertation, University of Michigan, 1956.

Zimmerer, A. M. A study of selected variables for predicting success in a college of engineering. Ph.D. dissertation, University of Houston, 1963.

Zuckerman, J. V. Interest item response arrangement as it affects discrimination between professional groups. *Journal of Applied Psychology*, 1952, *36*, 79-85.

Zwilling. V. T. The prediction of grades in freshman English from a battery of tests of mental ability, interests and aptitudes administered to students entering a liberal arts college. Ph.D. dissertation, Fordham University, 1949. (*Dissertations . . .*, 1949, pp. 62-65).

Zytowski, D. G. Characteristics of male university students with weak occupational similarity on the Strong Vocational Interest Blank. *Journal of Counseling Psychology*, 1965, *12*, 182-185.

Zytowski, D. G. Relationships of equivalent scales on three interest inventories. *Personnel and Guidance Journal*, 1968, 47, 44-49.

Zytowski, D. G. A test of criterion group sampling error in two comparable interest inventories. *Measurement and Evaluation in Guidance*, 1969, 2, 37-40.

Zytowski, D. G. A concurrent test of accuracy-of-classification for the Strong Vocational Interest Blank and Kuder Occupational Interest Survey. *Journal of Vocational Behavior*, 1972, 2, 245-250.

Zytowski, D. G. Equivalence of the Kuder Occupational Interest Survey and the Strong Vocational Interest Blank revisited. *Journal of Applied Psychology*, 1972, 56, 184-185.

Zytowski, D. G. The Kuder Occupational Interest Survey. In *Contemporary approaches to interest measurement.* Minneapolis: University of Minnesota Press, 1973, pp. 116-125.

Zytowski, D. G. Predictive validity of the Kuder Preference Record, Form B, over a 25-year span. *Measurement and Evaluation in Guidance*, 1974, 7(2), 122–129.

Zytowski, D. G. Factor analysis of the Kuder Occupational Interest Survey. *(Measurement and Evaluation in Guidance*. (In press.)

Zytowski, D. G. Predictive validity of the Kuder Occupational Interest Survey: A 12 to 19 year follow-up. *Journal of Counseling Psychology*. (In press.)

Index

adult men factor, 188
adult women factor, 188
age and interests, 163
agriculture-law-political science
   factor, 192, 204
artistic factor, 199-204

Balchin, N., vii, viii
behavioral sciences factor, 194
Berdie, R. F., 4
best impression index, 141-144
B. I. index (fig. 12), 142-143
"best impression" vs. sincere
   groups:
   correlations (table 35), 136
   score distances (table 36), 137
bibliography of publications pertaining to Kuder interest
   inventories (appendix F),
   278-320
Blau, P. M., 170
Bond, N. A. 173, 202, 203, 204,
   205, 206
Bordin, E. S., 19
Bradburn, N. M., vii
Brayfield, A. H., 152, 153

Campbell, D. P., 34, 145, 153
Cardinet, J., 170
career matching, 163
Carroll, J. D., 155
centour scores, relation to lambda
   scores, 72-74
Chaplin, C., vii
Christensen, P. R., 173, 202, 203,
   204, 205, 206
Clark, K. E., 4, 10, 154
Clemans, W. V., 41, 48, 158-160,
   178
context and item form, 17
Coombs, C. H., 170

correlation:
   biserial, 29
   point biserial, 29
Cowdery, K. M., 12
Craven, E. C., 2
Crawford, C. B., 171
criterion, the, 28
criterion in occupational counseling, the, 8
criterion vector method of test
   construction, the (appendix A),
   211
Cronbach, L. J., 3, 18
Crumrine, W. M., 3

Dabelstein, D. H., 153
Darley, J. G., 2
difference scores (figs. 5, 6, 7, 8,
   9, 11), 45-48
difference scores F–Mo and M–W,
   130-133
difference scores M–MBI, 139, 140
difference scores, W–WBI, 140, 141
differentiation between groups, 49
DiMichael, S. D., 153
dissatisfied vs. satisfied workers:
   correlation between response
   proportions (table 43), 150
   score distance (table 43), 150
dissatisfied workers, percentage in
   groups (tables 41, 42), 147-
   148
Dolliver, R. H., 18
domains of interests, comparability of, 16
Duncan, O. D., 170

engineering factor, 199
errors of classification (table 3),
   65

factor analysis of response proportions, 178-201
factor loadings, factor analysis VI
(appendix D), 242-256
factors:
factor analysis I (table 44), 179
factor analyses II, III, and IV
(table 45), 180-181
factor analysis V (table 46), 182
factor analysis VI (table 48), 185
factors in study by Guilford,
Christensen, Bond, and Sutton
(table 49), 202
feminine scores and masculine
scores, 126-129
femininity-masculinity factor, 187
Ferguson, G. A., 171
Findley, W. G., 29
food-nutrition factor, 197
forced-choice questions, stability
of, 17
Freyd, M., 12
Friedlander, F., 156

Gendre, F., 170
Ghiselli, E. E., 165
Gilbert, J., 4
Guilford, J. P., 170, 172, 173,
174, 178, 201, 202, 203, 204,
205, 206

Hagen, E., 4
Hagenah, T., 2
Hahn, M. E., 152
Hailey, A., vii
Harris, C. W., 171
Harris, M. L., 171
Hartshorne, H., 141
Herzberg, F., 151-153
hierarchical rotation (appendix C),
239-240
homogeneities:
of "best-impression" groups
(table 34), 134
of 217 groups (table 1), 36-41
homogeneity:
of interests, 164
measurement of, 35-41
and specialization, 165
variations in effect of, 31-35

Hornaday, J. A., xii, 22
Horrick, N. O., vii
Horst, P., 155

influencing people-social approval
factor, 190, 204
intercorrelations:
of difference scores, 71
of proportions from 217 groups
(appendix B), 214
17 areas (table 4), 68-69

Jackson, D. N., 18
Jacobs, R., 153
job families, reporting scores for,
25-26
job satisfaction, 145-146
journalism factor, 200, 205

Katzenmeyer, W., 178
Kelley, T. L., 210
Kreidt, P. H., 34
Kuder, G. F., 3, 13, 17, 22, 70,
153
Kuder-Richardson formulas, 15

lambda coefficient, 41-42
lambda scores, 41-71
relation to centours, 72-74
Langmuir, C. R., 72
Lefkowitz, D. M., 64, 66
library science factor, 200
Lipsett, L., 152, 156
Lorge, I., 18

M scores, 130, 161
Mallinson, G. G., 3
Marsh, M. M., 153
masculine and feminine scores of
social case worker (table 30),
127
masculine scores and feminine
scores, 126-129
matching:
career, 163-167
person to person, 163-167
Mathews, C. O., 18
May, M. A., 131
McCully, C. H., 4
McRae, G. G., 151, 155-156

mean score distances (*see* score
distances)
medical professions factor, 196
Messick, S., 18
Minnesota Vocational Interest
Inventory, 34
Moore, B. V., 12
Morris, R. G., 19
Murphy, R. J., 19

North, R. D., 153
Nunnally, J. C., Jr., 2

occupational dissatisfaction factor,
191
occupational titles in interest inventories, 19-21
Olejnik, S., 49
Overall, J. E., 171
overlapping, 28
overlapping within 37 groups
(table 2), 51

percentile ranks, occupational
groups, 258-277
physical education and therapy
factor, 197, 204
Porter, A. C., 49
principles of interest measurement,
7-27
profiles of occupational groups
(appendix E), 258-277

Ream, M. J., 12
reliability:
and age, 25
within the person, 23-24
response bias, 18
Rulon, P. J., 72
Russell, D., 153

sales factor, 194, 204
satisfaction in work, 145-156
Satter, G. A., 170
science-mathematics factor, 195,
203
score distances between groups:
satisfied and dissatisfied workers
(table 43), 150

the sexes in same occupation or
major (table 31), 128
score distances mean, from other
groups:
architects (table 5), 78-79
art majors (table 25), 116-117
auto mechanics (table 14), 94-95
business and marketing majors
(table 15), 96-97
carpenters (table 6), 80-81
chemists (table 17), 100-101
county agricultural agents (table
13), 92-93
dieticians (table 21), 108-109
English majors (table 19), 104-
105
interior decorators, female
(table 12), 90-91
interior decorators, male (table
11), 88-89
librarians (table 27), 120-121
mathematicians (table 18), 102-
103
mechanical engineer majors
(table 26), 118-119
ministers (table 24), 114-115
motel managers, female (table
10), 86-87
motel managers, male (table 9),
84-85
music majors (table 29), 124-
125
newspaper editors (table 28),
122-123
physical education majors
(table 22), 110-111
physicians (table 20), 106-107
psychiatric social workers (table
23), 112-113
psychologists, counseling (table
16), 98-99
score distances:
within female occupational
groups (table 8), 83
within male occupational groups
(table 7), 82
score level, 156-157
sex bias, 210
sex differences, 126

Sheppard, H. L., i
skilled trades factor, 193, 203
social welfare factor, 198, 203
stability of answers, 23
standard error of a score, 24
Steinmetz, H. L., 22
Strong, E. K., Jr., xii, 12, 20, 22,
    154, 170, 176
Strong Vocational Interest Blank, 4
    48, 66, 67, 173
Sutton, M. A., 173, 202, 203, 204,
    205, 206

Tatsuoka, M. M., 72
Terkel, S., vii
Thorndike, E. L., 154
Thorndike, R. L., 4
Thurstone, L. L., 13, 170
Tiedeman, D. V., 72
Tilton, J. W., 50
Traxler, A. E., 153
Tucker, L. R., 155
Tutton, M. E., 3
typical response factor, 186

validity, 11
vocabulary level in interest inven-
    tories, 15

Wherry, R. J., 178, 239-240
Wherry-Wherry hierarchical rotation
    methoc, 178, 183, 239-240
White, R. M., 3
Williams, C. T., 152
Wilson, J. W., 152, 156
Wright, B. D., 15

Zytowski, D. G., 48, 66, 67, 190,
    204, 207